HarlemBeat 9

by Yuriko Nishiyama

Los Angeles — Tokyo

Translator – Yuki Ichimura
Retouch Artists – Ryan Caraan and Roselyn Santos
Production Specialist – Colin Mahan
Graphic Assistant – Akemi Imafuku
Graphic Designer – Anna Kernbaum
Associate Editor – Stephanie Donnelly
Editor – Robert Coyner

Senior Editor – Jake Forbes
Art Director – Matt Alford
Production Manager – Joaquin E Reyes
VP of Production – Ron Klamert
Publisher – Stuart Levy

Email: editor@press.TOKYOPOP.com
Come visit us at www.TOKYOPOP.com

A **TOKYOPOP**® book

TOKYOPOP® is an imprint of Mixx Entertainment, Inc.
5900 Wilshire Blvd., Ste. 2000, Los Angeles, CA 90036

ISBN: 1-931514-01-1

First TOKYOPOP® printing: February 2002

10 9 8 7 6 5 4 3 2
Printed in the USA

CONTENTS

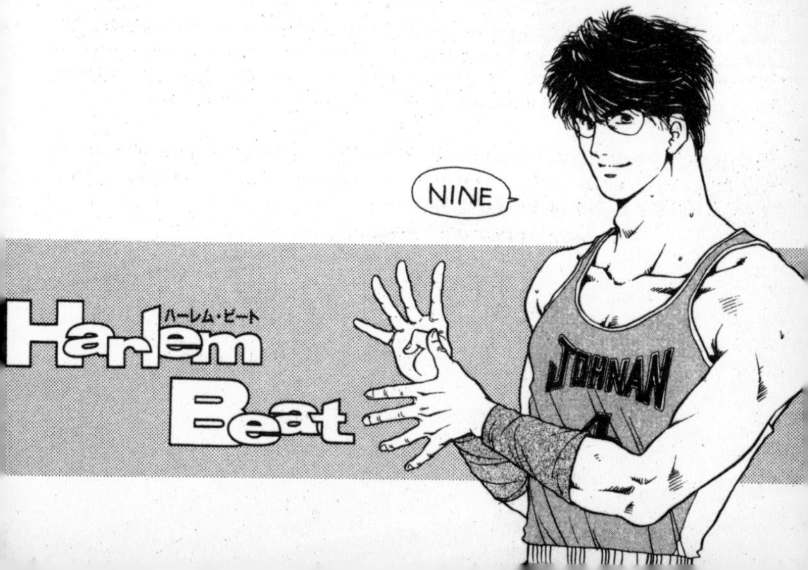

NINE
Harlem Beat
ハーレム・ビート
JOHNAN

The story so far:

In the last volume of the Harlem Beat, Johnan High began their meeting with the tournament favorites Hara. With Hara's MVP, Kuwata, set on burying Shurman and Johnan, the man and the team that upset Hara in last year's Semis, the cocky Junior figured to bury Johnan early in the game. But his team couldn't anticipate the late season additions of Nate and Sawamura to the roster. Unscouted, and undefended, the freshmen led Johnan to a 15-point lead by the end of the first half. Ready to dominate the game, they and Hara now prepare for one of the most important halves of their lives.

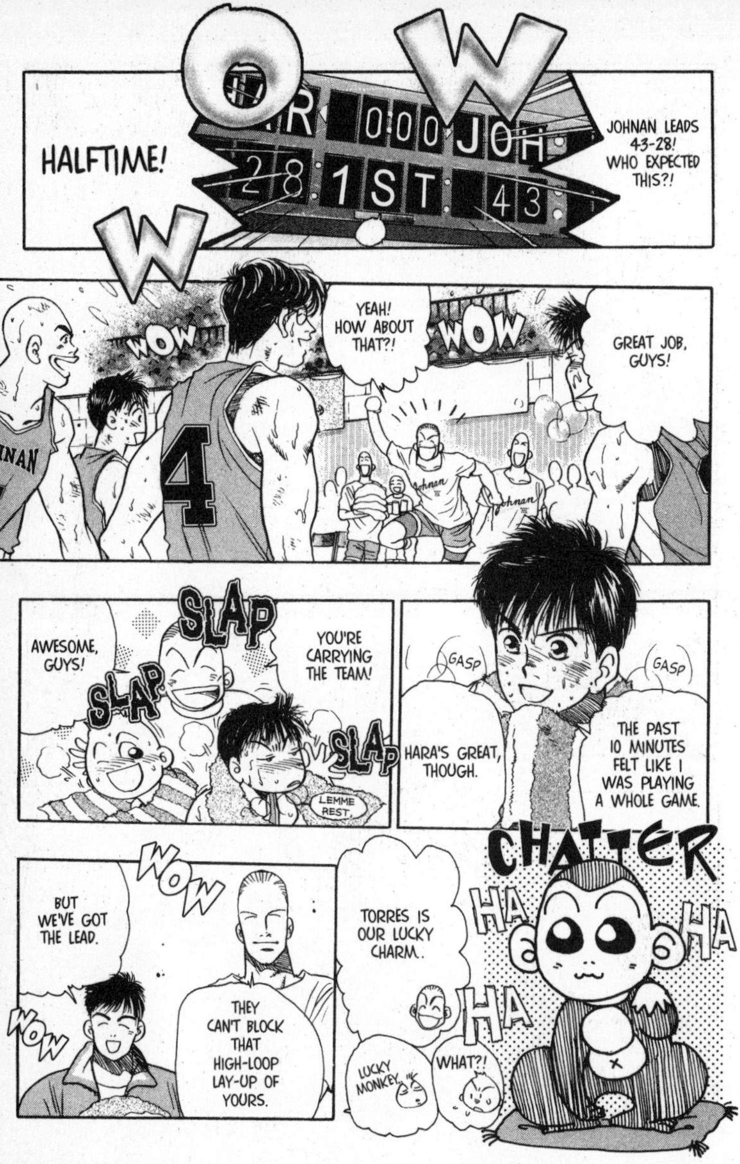
WOW
HALFTIME!
R 0:00 JOH
28 1ST 43
JOHNAN LEADS 43-28! WHO EXPECTED THIS?!
WOW
YEAH! HOW ABOUT THAT?!
WOW
GREAT JOB, GUYS!
JOHNAN
Johnan
Johnan
AWESOME, GUYS!
SLAP
YOU'RE CARRYING THE TEAM!
SLAP
SLAP
LEMME REST.
GASP
GASP
HARA'S GREAT, THOUGH.
THE PAST 10 MINUTES FELT LIKE I WAS PLAYING A WHOLE GAME.
BUT WE'VE GOT THE LEAD.
WOW
WOW
THEY CAN'T BLOCK THAT HIGH-LOOP LAY-UP OF YOURS.
TORRES IS OUR LUCKY CHARM.
CHATTER
HA HA HA
LUCKY MONKEY.
WHAT?!

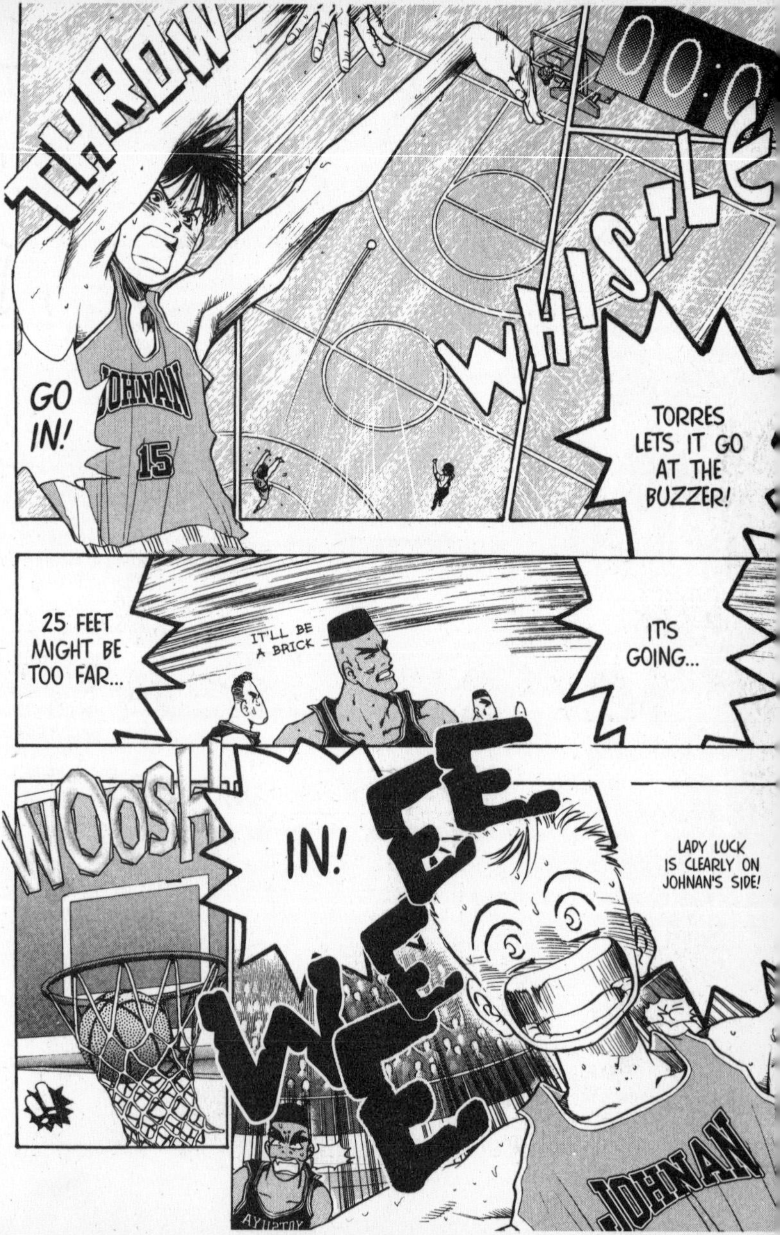
WHISTLE
TORRES LETS IT GO AT THE BUZZER!
THROW
GO IN!
IT'S GOING...
IT'LL BE A BRICK
25 FEET MIGHT BE TOO FAR...
LADY LUCK IS CLEARLY ON JOHNAN'S SIDE!
WEEEE
IN!
WOOSH!

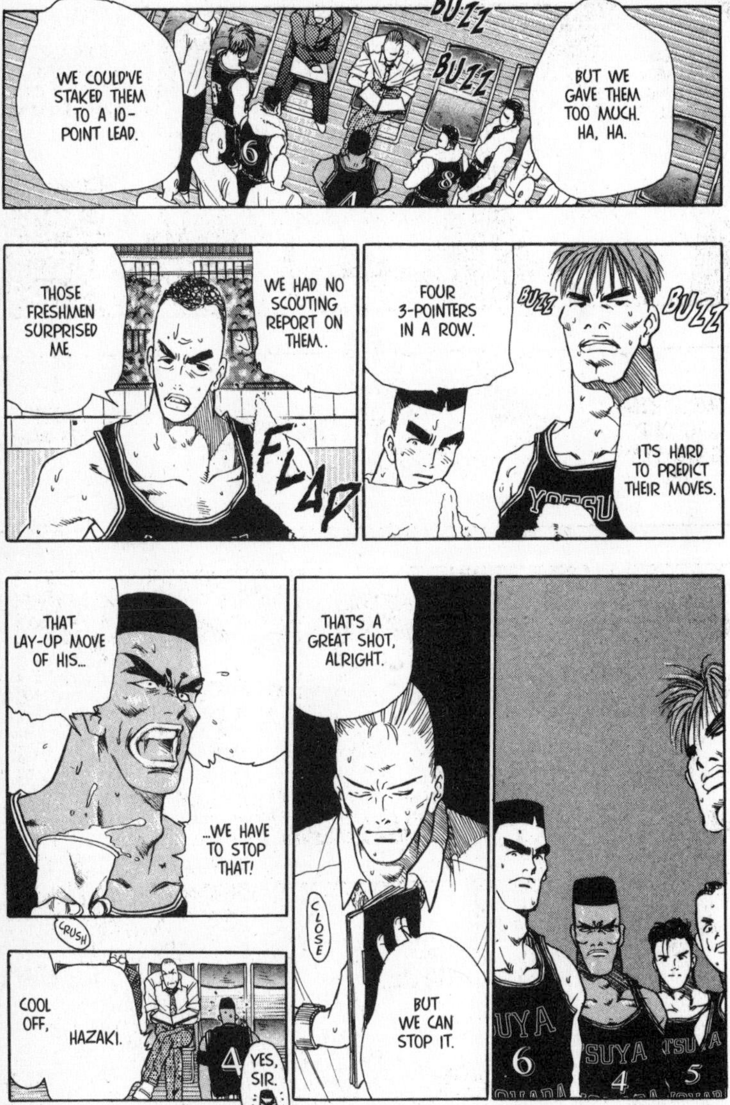
WE COULD'VE STAKED THEM TO A 10-POINT LEAD.
BUZZ
BUZZ
BUT WE GAVE THEM TOO MUCH. HA, HA.
THOSE FRESHMEN SURPRISED ME.
WE HAD NO SCOUTING REPORT ON THEM..
FLAP
FOUR 3-POINTERS IN A ROW.
BUZZ
BUZZ
IT'S HARD TO PREDICT THEIR MOVES.
THAT LAY-UP MOVE OF HIS...
...WE HAVE TO STOP THAT!
CRUSH
COOL OFF,
HAZAKI.
YES, SIR.
THAT'S A GREAT SHOT, ALRIGHT.
CLOSE
BUT WE CAN STOP IT.

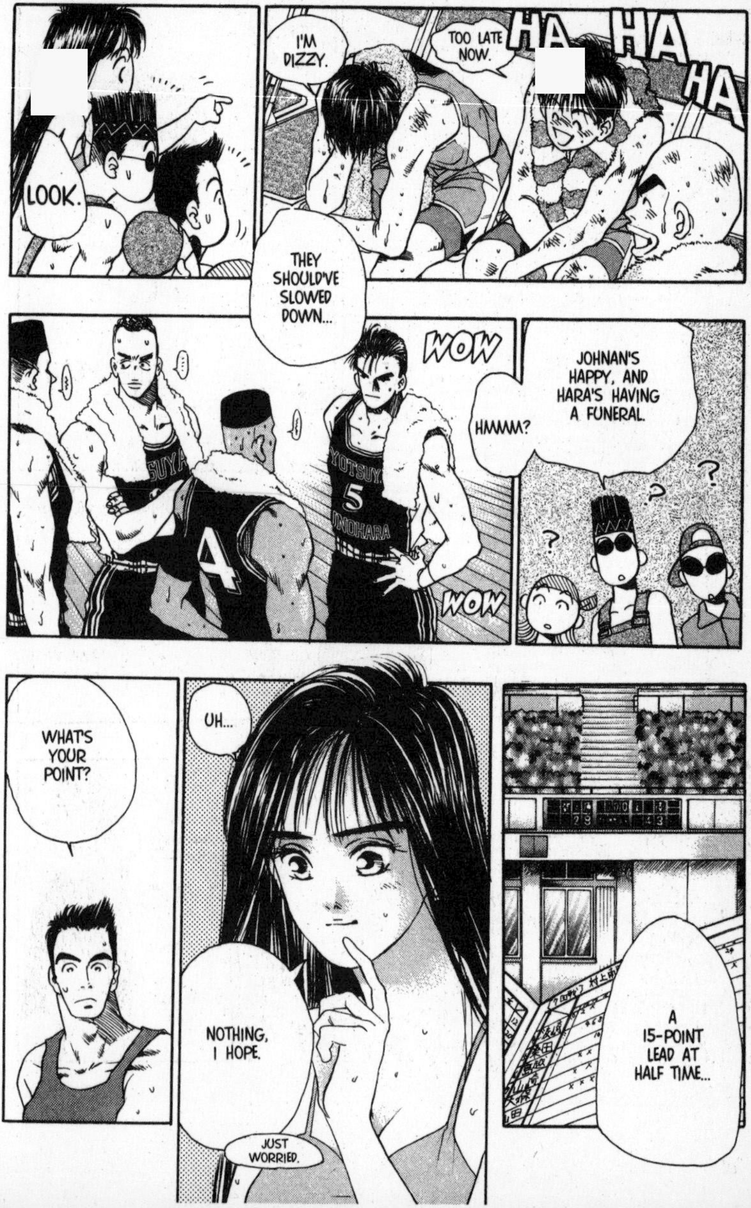
HA HA HA
TOO LATE NOW.
I'M DIZZY.
LOOK.
JOHNAN'S HAPPY, AND HARA'S HAVING A FUNERAL.
HMMM?
WOW
WOW
THEY SHOULD'VE SLOWED DOWN...
A 15-POINT LEAD AT HALF TIME...
UH...
NOTHING, I HOPE.
JUST WORRIED.
WHAT'S YOUR POINT?

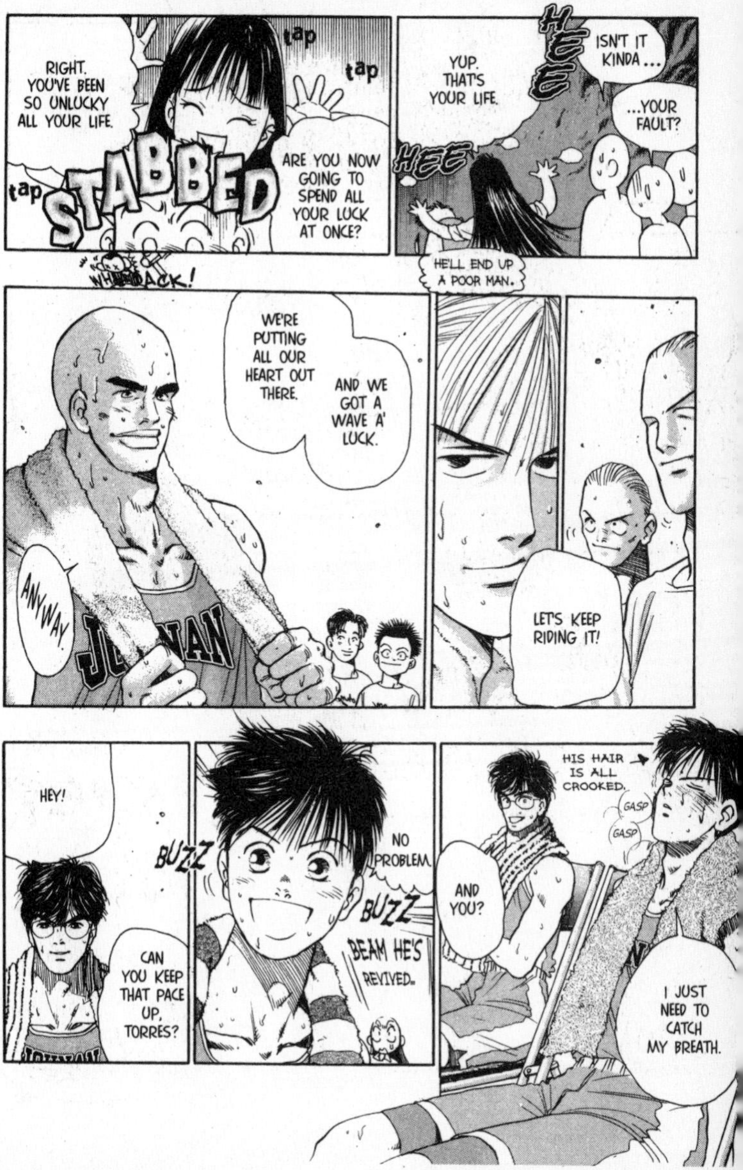

RIGHT. YOU'VE BEEN SO UNLUCKY ALL YOUR LIFE.
tap
tap
tap
STABBED
ARE YOU NOW GOING TO SPEND ALL YOUR LUCK AT ONCE?
HEE
ISN'T IT KINDA ...
...YOUR FAULT?
YUP. THAT'S YOUR LIFE.
HEE
HE'LL END UP A POOR MAN.
ANYWAY.
WE'RE PUTTING ALL OUR HEART OUT THERE.
AND WE GOT A WAVE 'A' LUCK.
LET'S KEEP RIDING IT!
HEY!
CAN YOU KEEP THAT PACE UP, TORRES?
BUZZ
NO PROBLEM.
BUZZ
BEAM HE'S REVIVED.
HIS HAIR IS ALL CROOKED.
GASP
GASP
AND YOU?
I JUST NEED TO CATCH MY BREATH.

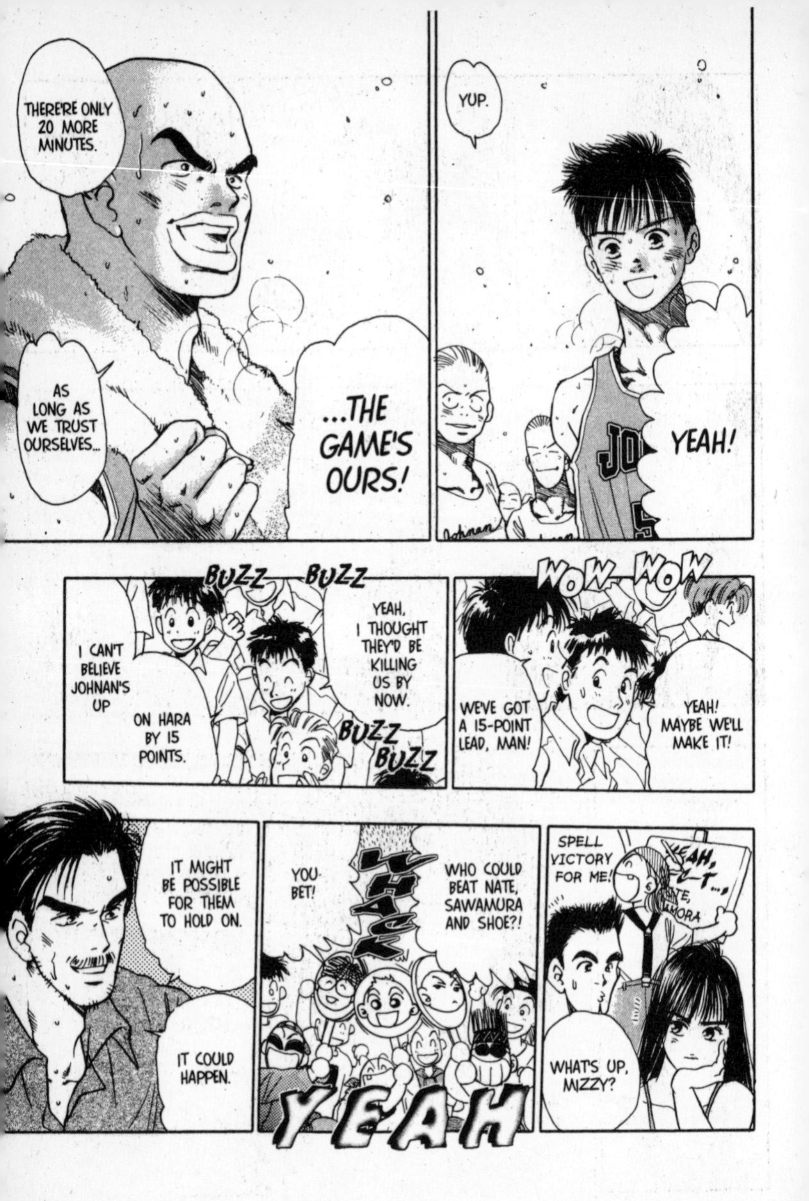

THERE'RE ONLY 20 MORE MINUTES.
AS LONG AS WE TRUST OURSELVES...
...THE GAME'S OURS!
YUP.
YEAH!
BUZZ BUZZ
I CAN'T BELIEVE JOHNAN'S UP
ON HARA BY 15 POINTS.
YEAH, I THOUGHT THEY'D BE KILLING US BY NOW.
BUZZ BUZZ
WOW WOW
WE'VE GOT A 15-POINT LEAD, MAN!
YEAH! MAYBE WE'LL MAKE IT!
IT MIGHT BE POSSIBLE FOR THEM TO HOLD ON.
IT COULD HAPPEN.
YOU BET!
WHO COULD BEAT NATE, SAWAMURA AND SHOE?!
YEAH
SPELL VICTORY FOR ME!
WHAT'S UP, MIZZY?

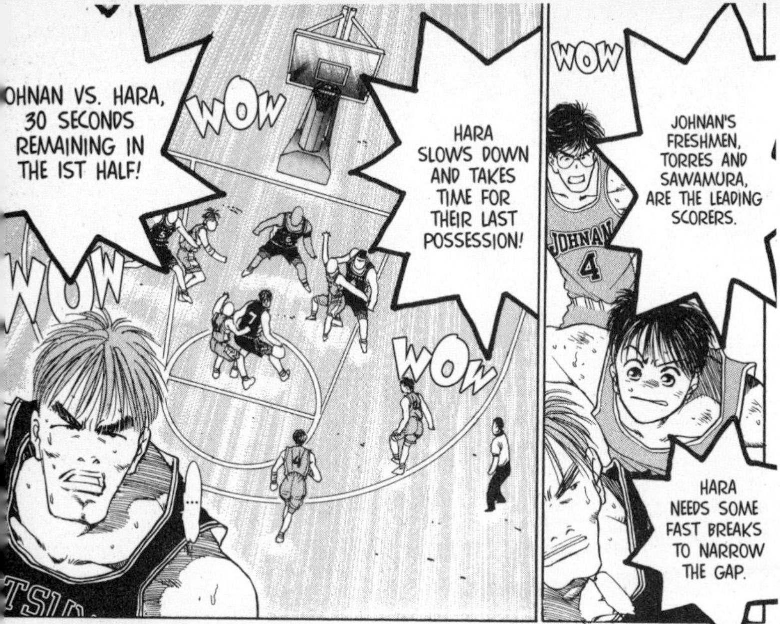
WOW
JOHNAN'S FRESHMEN, TORRES AND SAWAMURA, ARE THE LEADING SCORERS.
HARA NEEDS SOME FAST BREAKS TO NARROW THE GAP.
HARA SLOWS DOWN AND TAKES TIME FOR THEIR LAST POSSESSION!
WOW
OHNAN VS. HARA, 30 SECONDS REMAINING IN THE 1ST HALF!
WOW
WOW
...

Harlem Beat

■Street 69 Be Frightened

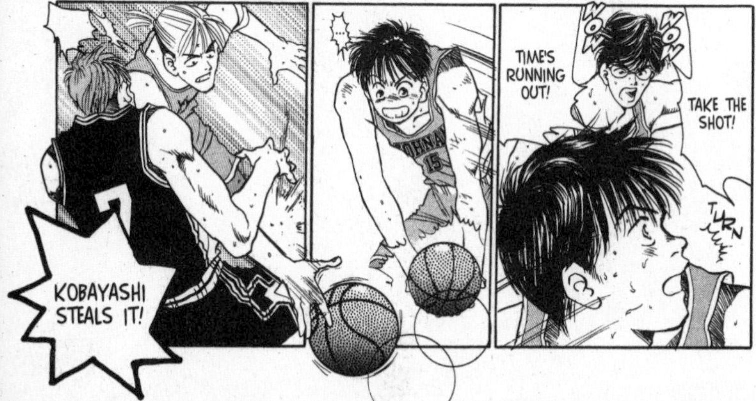
WOW
WOW
TAKE THE SHOT!
TIME'S RUNNING OUT!
TURN
...
KOBAYASHI STEALS IT!

Hi, everyone! We're your Johnan players!

BACK WHEN WE FIRST STARTED THIS COMIC, WE NEVER EXPECTED THAT THE SCHOOL TEAM WOULD GET POPULATED SO QUICKLY WITH ALL THESE NEW PLAYERS. AT ANY RATE, HERE THEY ARE TO HELP YOU KEEP TRACK. THEY APPRECIATE YOUR SUPPORT.

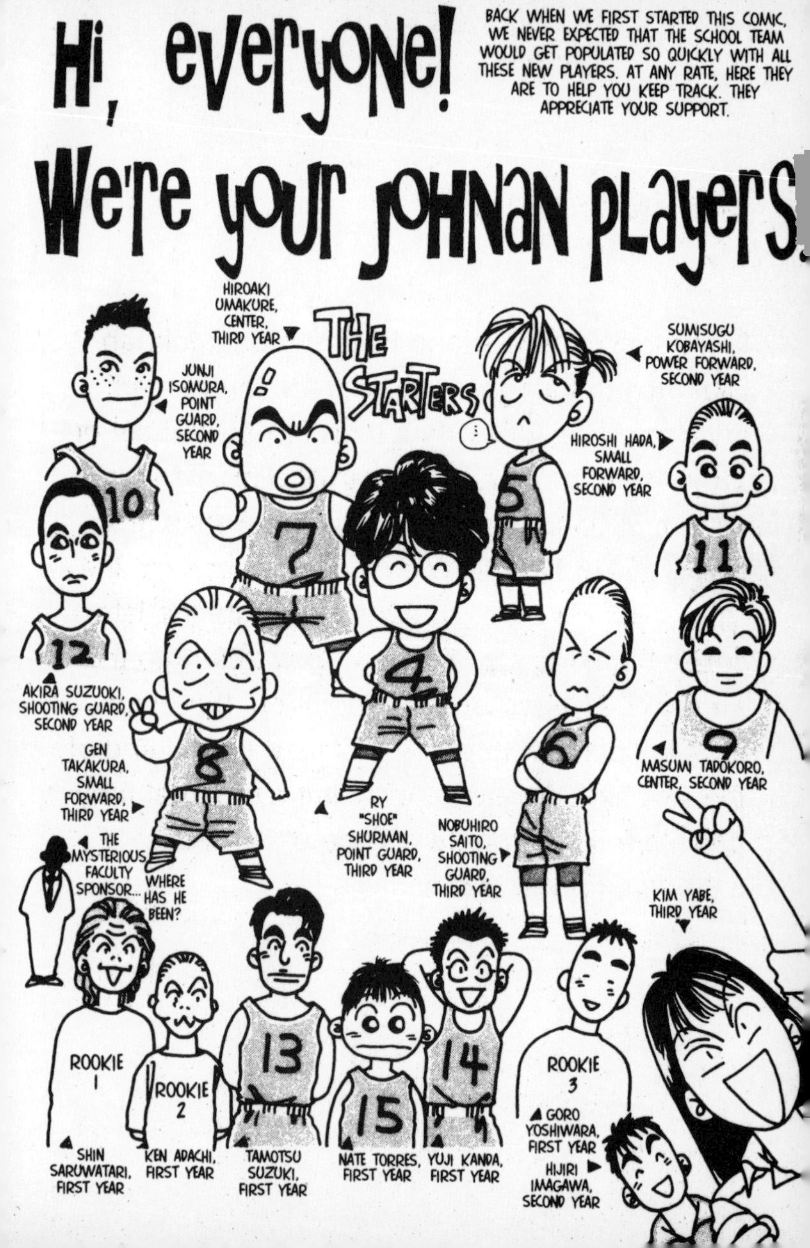
THE STARTERS
HIROAKI UMAKURE, CENTER, THIRD YEAR
JUNJI ISOMURA, POINT GUARD, SECOND YEAR
SUMISUGU KOBAYASHI, POWER FORWARD, SECOND YEAR
HIROSHI HADA, SMALL FORWARD, SECOND YEAR
AKIRA SUZUOKI, SHOOTING GUARD, SECOND YEAR
GEN TAKAKURA, SMALL FORWARD, THIRD YEAR
RY "SHOE" SHURMAN, POINT GUARD, THIRD YEAR
NOBUHIRO SAITO, SHOOTING GUARD, THIRD YEAR
MASUMI TADOKORO, CENTER, SECOND YEAR
THE MYSTERIOUS FACULTY SPONSOR... WHERE HAS HE BEEN?
KIM YABE, THIRD YEAR
ROOKIE 1
ROOKIE 2
ROOKIE 3
GORO YOSHIWARA, FIRST YEAR
HIJIRI IMAGAWA, SECOND YEAR
SHIN SARUWATARI, FIRST YEAR
KEN ADACHI, FIRST YEAR
TAMOTSU SUZUKI, FIRST YEAR
NATE TORRES, FIRST YEAR
YUJI KANDA, FIRST YEAR

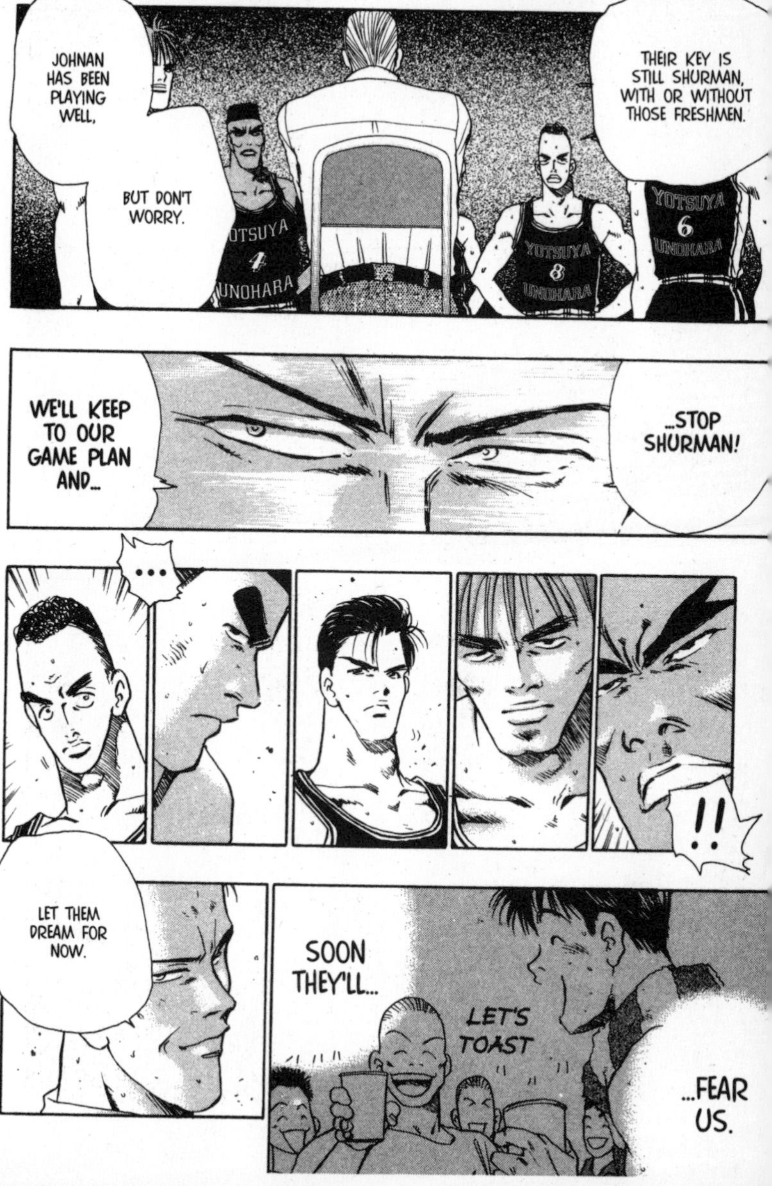
JOHNAN HAS BEEN PLAYING WELL,
BUT DON'T WORRY.
THEIR KEY IS STILL SHURMAN, WITH OR WITHOUT THOSE FRESHMEN.
YOTSUYA 4 UNOHARA
YOTSUYA 8 UNOHARA
YOTSUYA 6 UNOHARA
WE'LL KEEP TO OUR GAME PLAN AND...
...STOP SHURMAN!
...
!!
LET THEM DREAM FOR NOW.
SOON THEY'LL...
LET'S TOAST
...FEAR US.

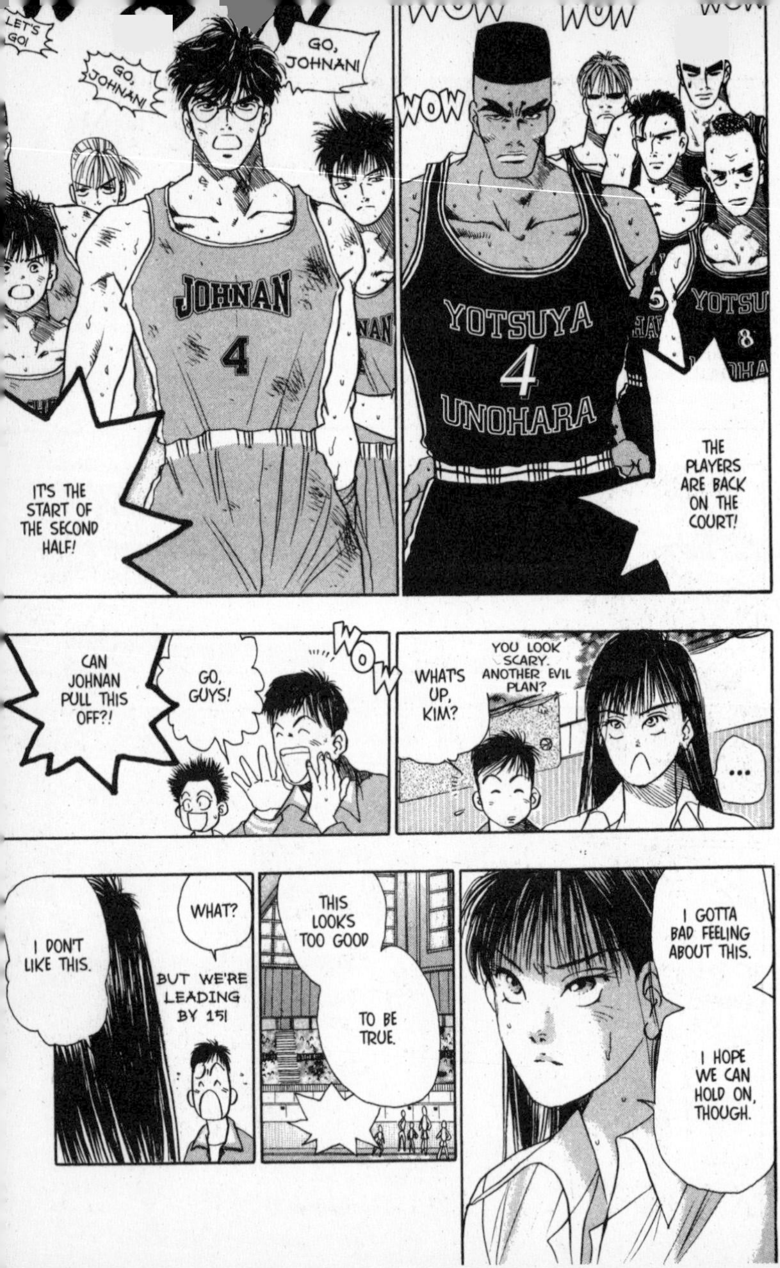
LET'S GO!
GO, JOHNAN!
GO, JOHNAN!
IT'S THE START OF THE SECOND HALF!
WOW WOW WOW
WOW
THE PLAYERS ARE BACK ON THE COURT!
CAN JOHNAN PULL THIS OFF?!
GO, GUYS!
WOW
WHAT'S UP, KIM?
YOU LOOK SCARY. ANOTHER EVIL PLAN?
...
I DON'T LIKE THIS.
WHAT?
BUT WE'RE LEADING BY 15!
THIS LOOKS TOO GOOD
TO BE TRUE.
I GOTTA BAD FEELING ABOUT THIS.
I HOPE WE CAN HOLD ON, THOUGH.

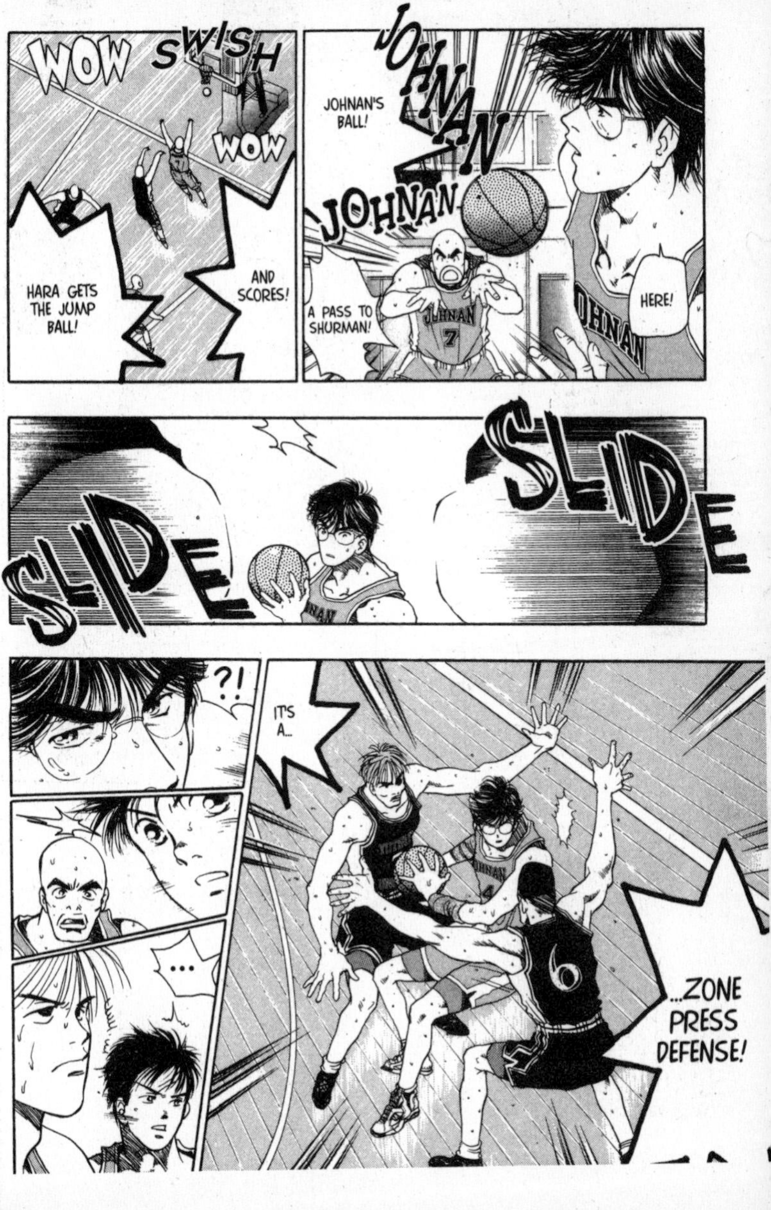
WOW
SWISH
HARA GETS THE JUMP BALL!
AND SCORES!
WOW
JOHNAN
JOHNAN'S BALL!
JOHNAN
A PASS TO SHURMAN!
HERE!
SLIDE
SLIDE
?!
...
IT'S A...
...ZONE PRESS DEFENSE!

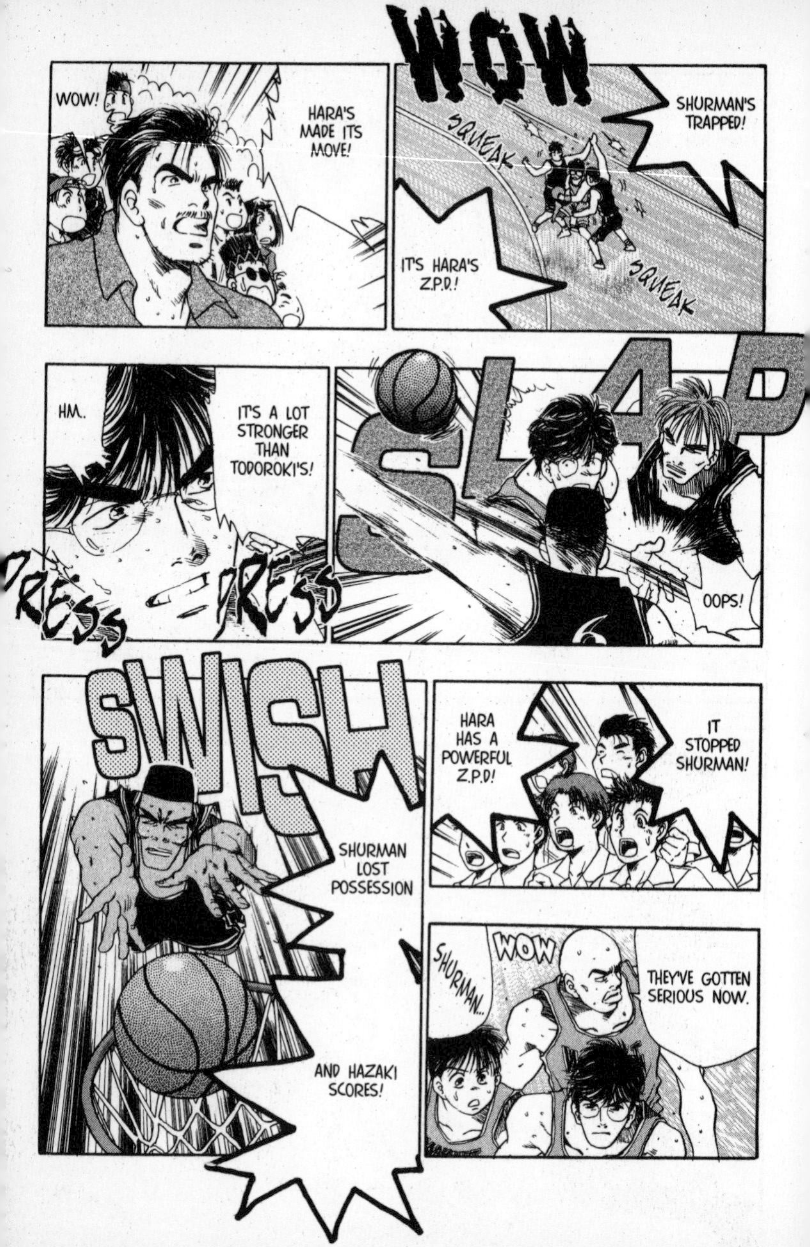
WOW!
HARA'S MADE ITS MOVE!
WOW
SQUEAK
SHURMAN'S TRAPPED!
IT'S HARA'S Z.P.D.!
SQUEAK
HM.
IT'S A LOT STRONGER THAN TODOROKI'S!
PRESS
PRESS
SLAP
OOPS!
SWISH
SHURMAN LOST POSSESSION
AND HAZAKI SCORES!
HARA HAS A POWERFUL Z.P.D.!
IT STOPPED SHURMAN!
WOW
SHURMAN...
THEY'VE GOTTEN SERIOUS NOW.

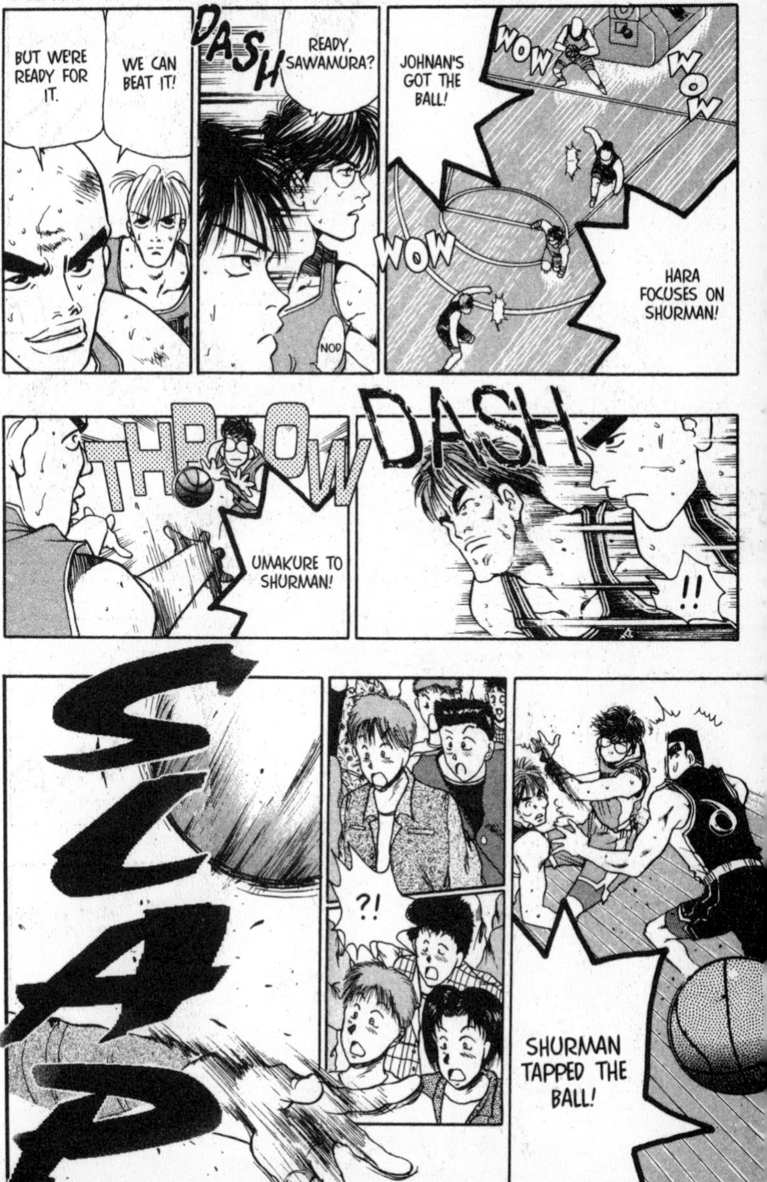
WOW
WOW
JOHNAN'S GOT THE BALL!
WOW
HARA FOCUSES ON SHURMAN!
DASH
READY, SAWAMURA?
NOD
WE CAN BEAT IT!
BUT WE'RE READY FOR IT.
DASH
!!
THROW
UMAKURE TO SHURMAN!
SHURMAN TAPPED THE BALL!
?!
SNAP

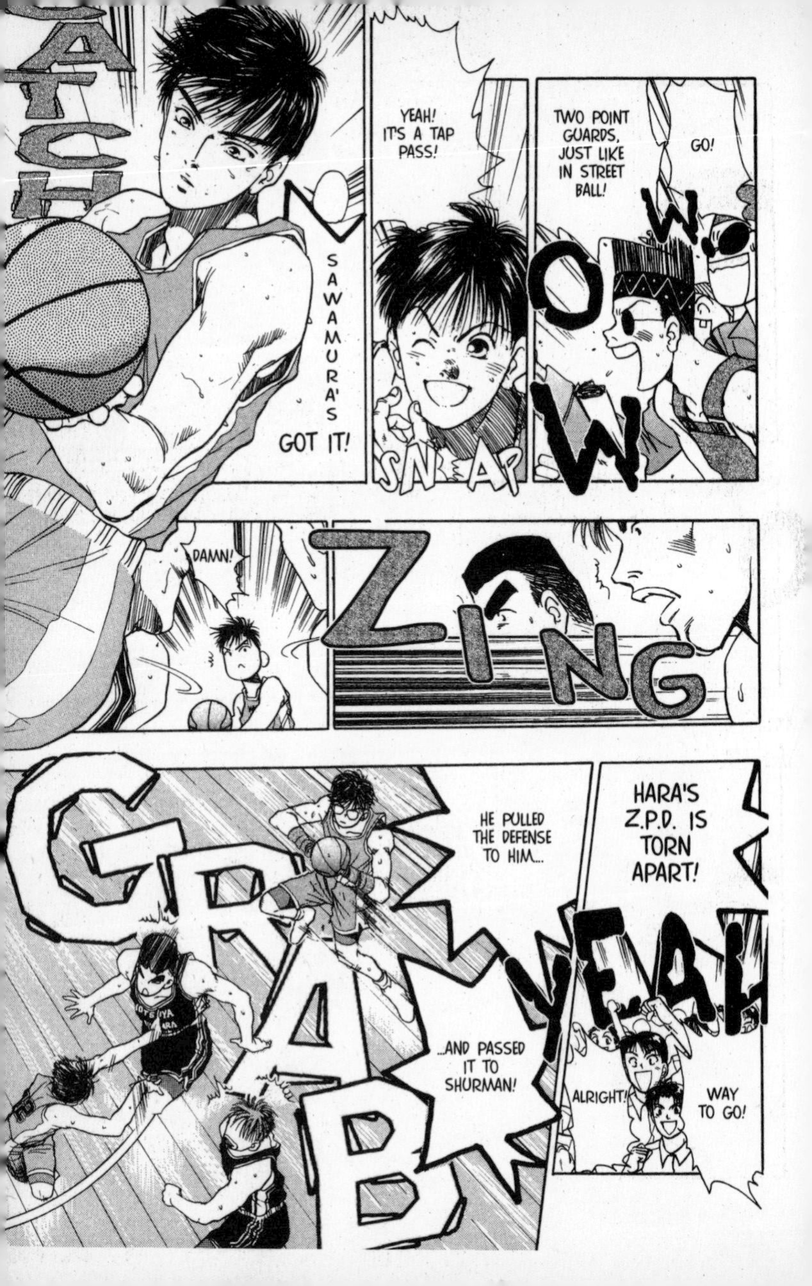
TWO POINT GUARDS, JUST LIKE IN STREET BALL!
GO!
WOW
YEAH! IT'S A TAP PASS!
SNAP
ATCH
SAWAMURA'S GOT IT!
ZING
DAMN!
HARA'S Z.P.D. IS TORN APART!
YEAH
ALRIGHT!
WAY TO GO!
HE PULLED THE DEFENSE TO HIM...
GRAB
...AND PASSED IT TO SHURMAN!

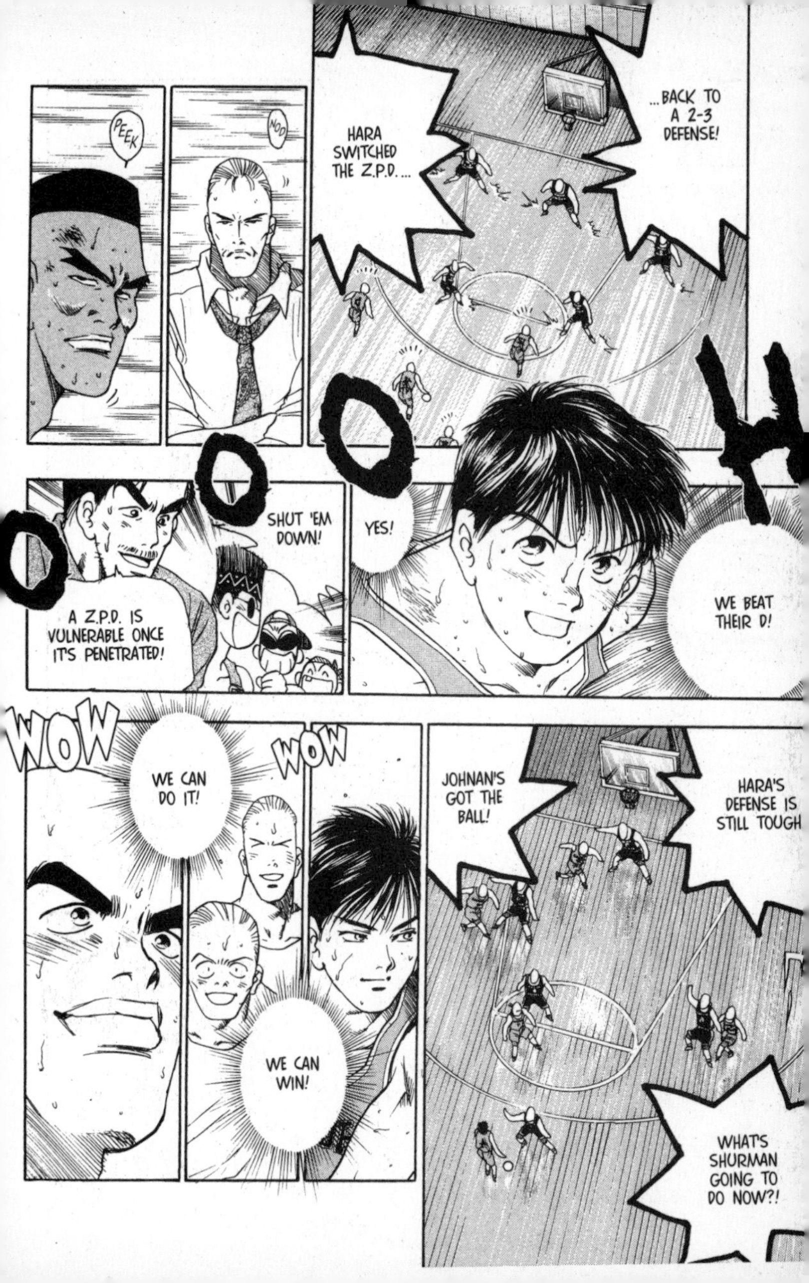
HARA SWITCHED THE Z.P.D. ...
...BACK TO A 2-3 DEFENSE!
NOD
PEEK
OOOOH
WE BEAT THEIR D!
YES!
SHUT 'EM DOWN!
A Z.P.D. IS VULNERABLE ONCE IT'S PENETRATED!
HARA'S DEFENSE IS STILL TOUGH
JOHNAN'S GOT THE BALL!
WHAT'S SHURMAN GOING TO DO NOW?!
WOW
WE CAN WIN!
WOW
WE CAN DO IT!

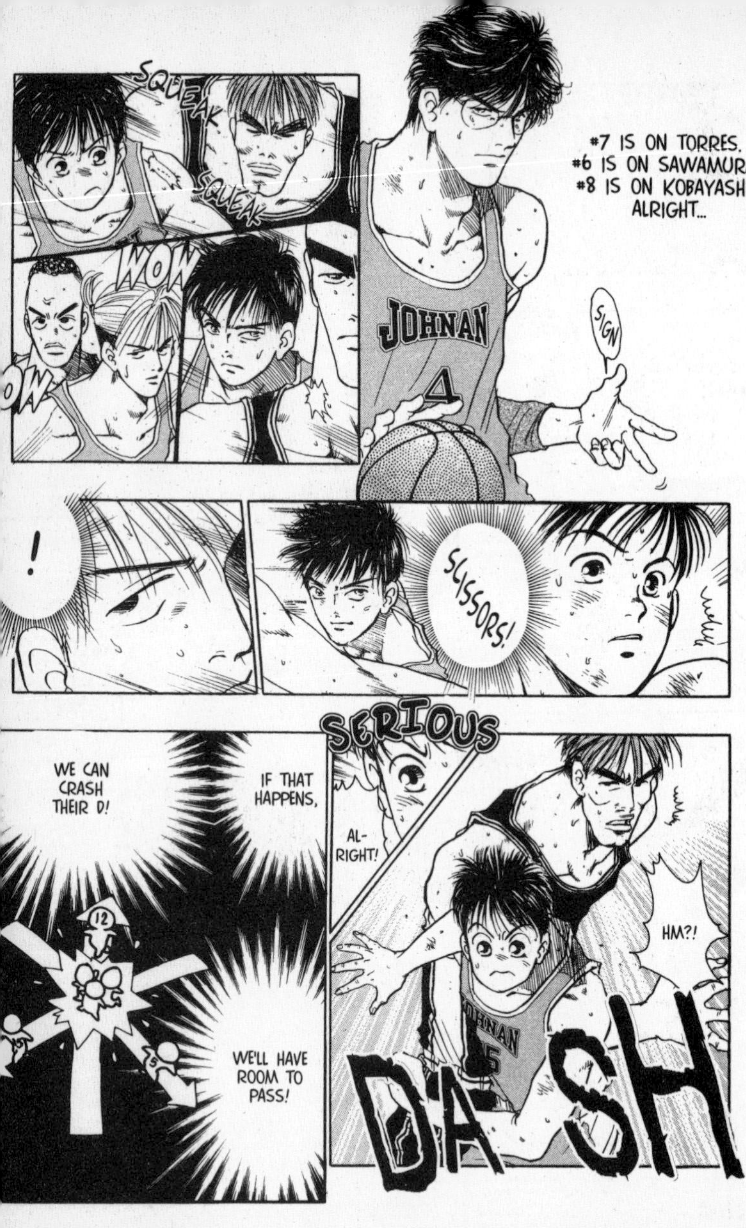
#7 IS ON TORRES.
#6 IS ON SAWAMURA.
#8 IS ON KOBAYASHI.
ALRIGHT...
SIGN
JOHNAN
SQUEAK
SQUEAK
WOW
WOW
SCISSORS!
!
SERIOUS
HM?!
DASH
AL-
RIGHT!
IF THAT
HAPPENS,
WE CAN
CRASH
THEIR D!
WE'LL HAVE
ROOM TO
PASS!

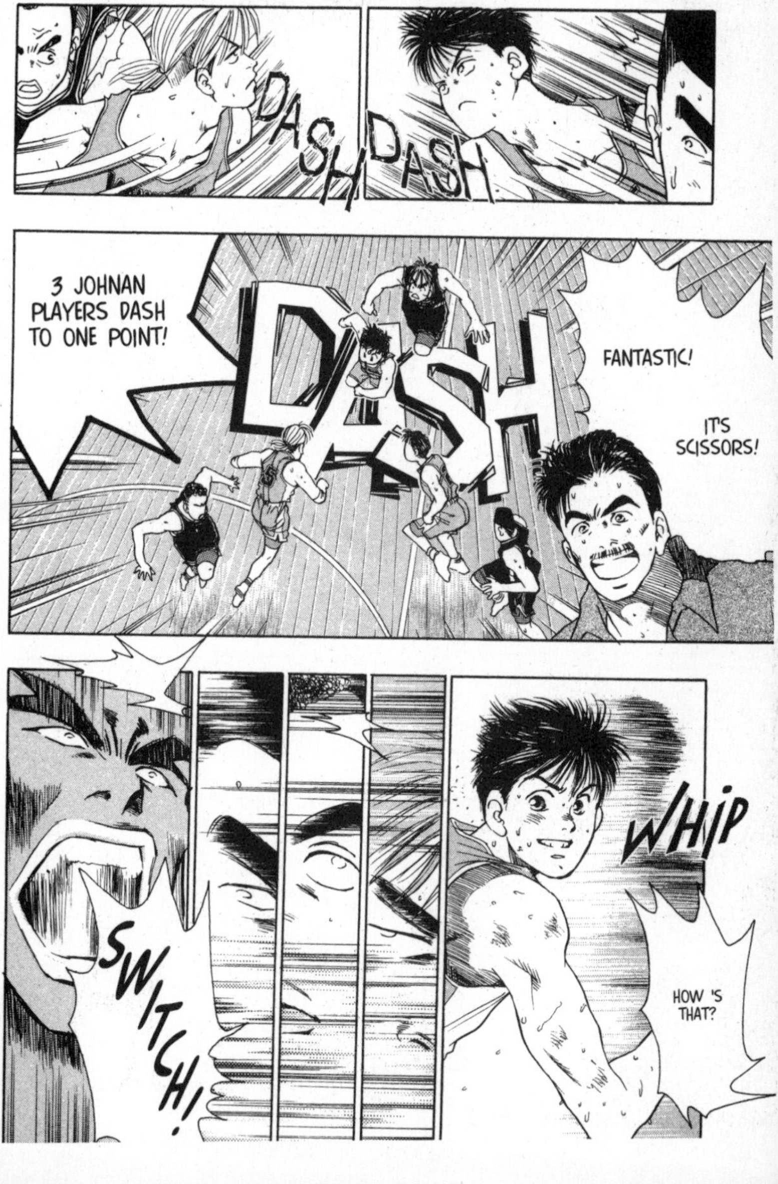
DASH
DASH
FANTASTIC!
IT'S SCISSORS!
3 JOHNAN PLAYERS DASH TO ONE POINT!
DASH
WHIP
HOW 'S THAT?
SWITCH!

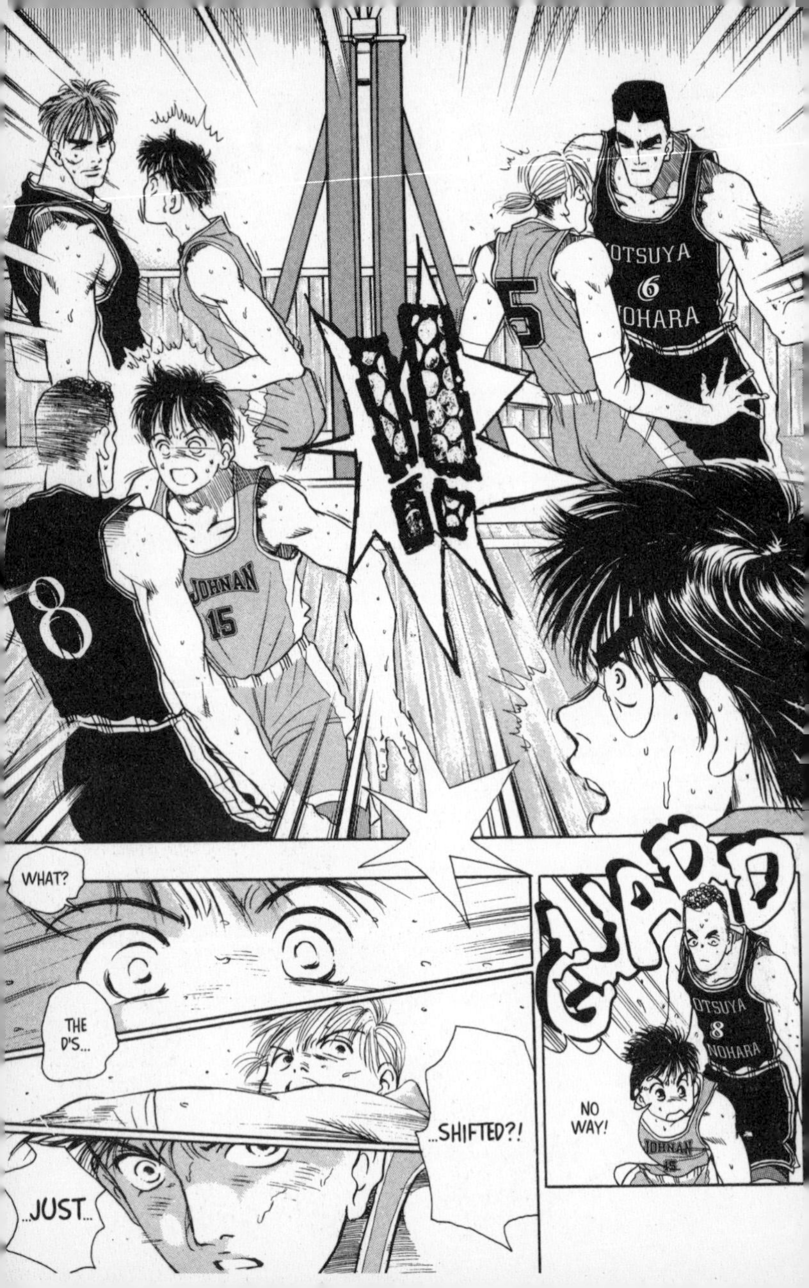
GUARD
NO WAY!
WHAT?
THE D'S...
...SHIFTED?!
...JUST...

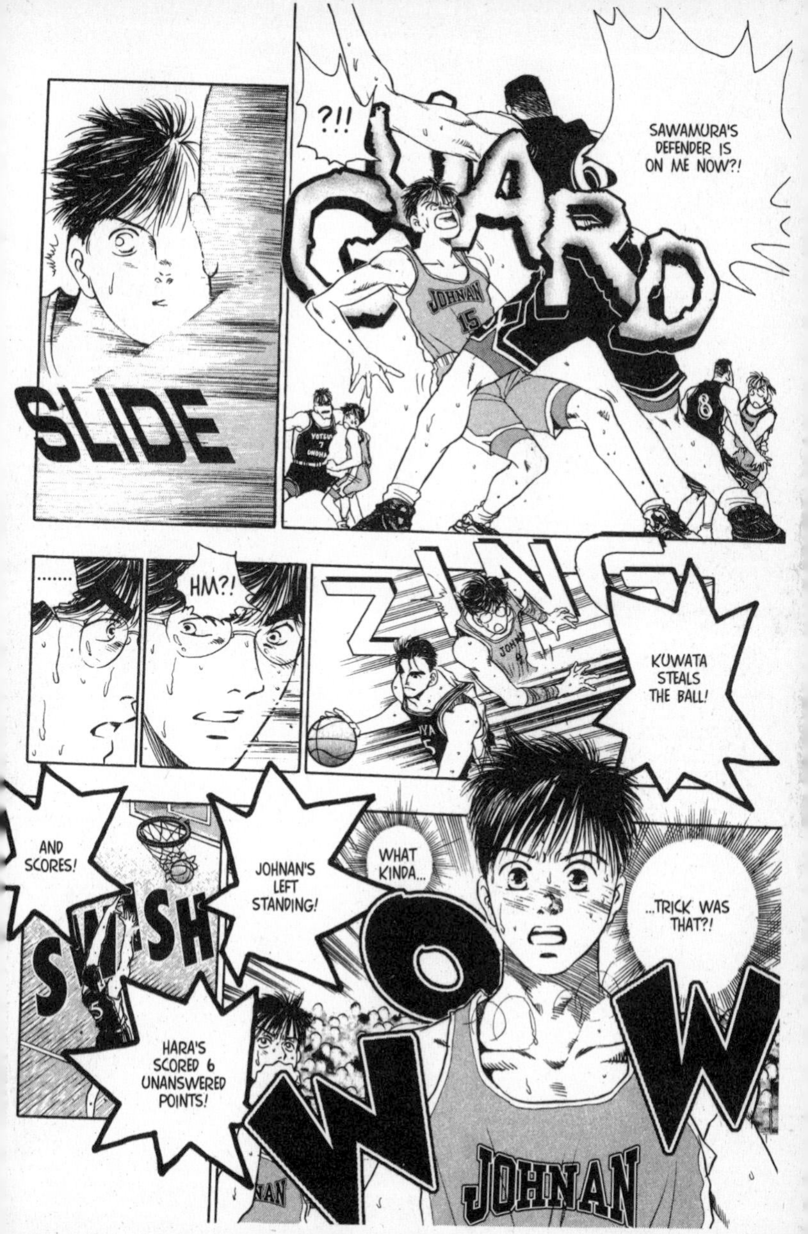
SLIDE
?!!
GUARD
SAWAMURA'S DEFENDER IS ON ME NOW?!
......
HM?!
ZING
KUWATA STEALS THE BALL!
AND SCORES!
SWISH
JOHNAN'S LEFT STANDING!
HARA'S SCORED 6 UNANSWERED POINTS!
WHAT KINDA...
...TRICK WAS THAT?!
WOW

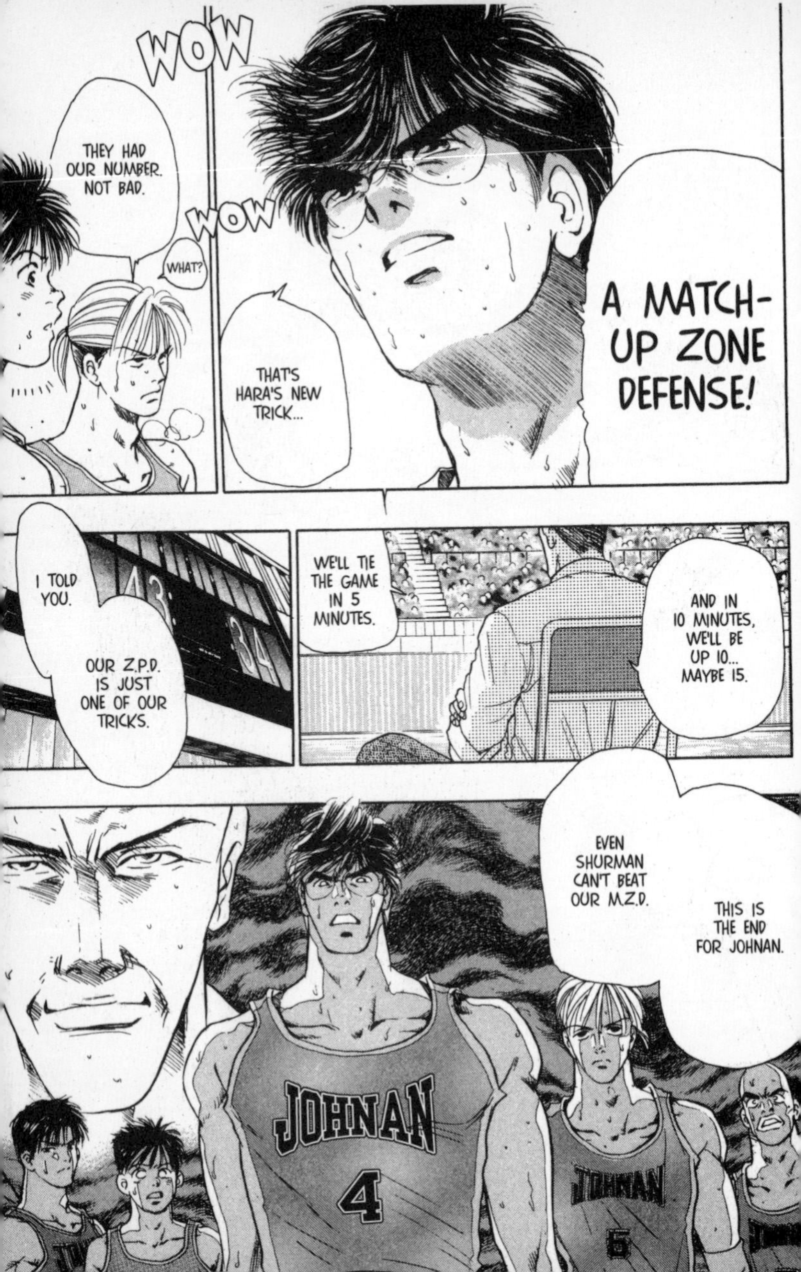
WOW
THEY HAD OUR NUMBER. NOT BAD.
WOW
WHAT?
THAT'S HARA'S NEW TRICK...
A MATCH-UP ZONE DEFENSE!
I TOLD YOU.
OUR Z.P.D. IS JUST ONE OF OUR TRICKS.
WE'LL TIE THE GAME IN 5 MINUTES.
AND IN 10 MINUTES, WE'LL BE UP 10... MAYBE 15.
EVEN SHURMAN CAN'T BEAT OUR M.Z.D.
THIS IS THE END FOR JOHNAN.
JOHNAN
4
JOHNAN
5

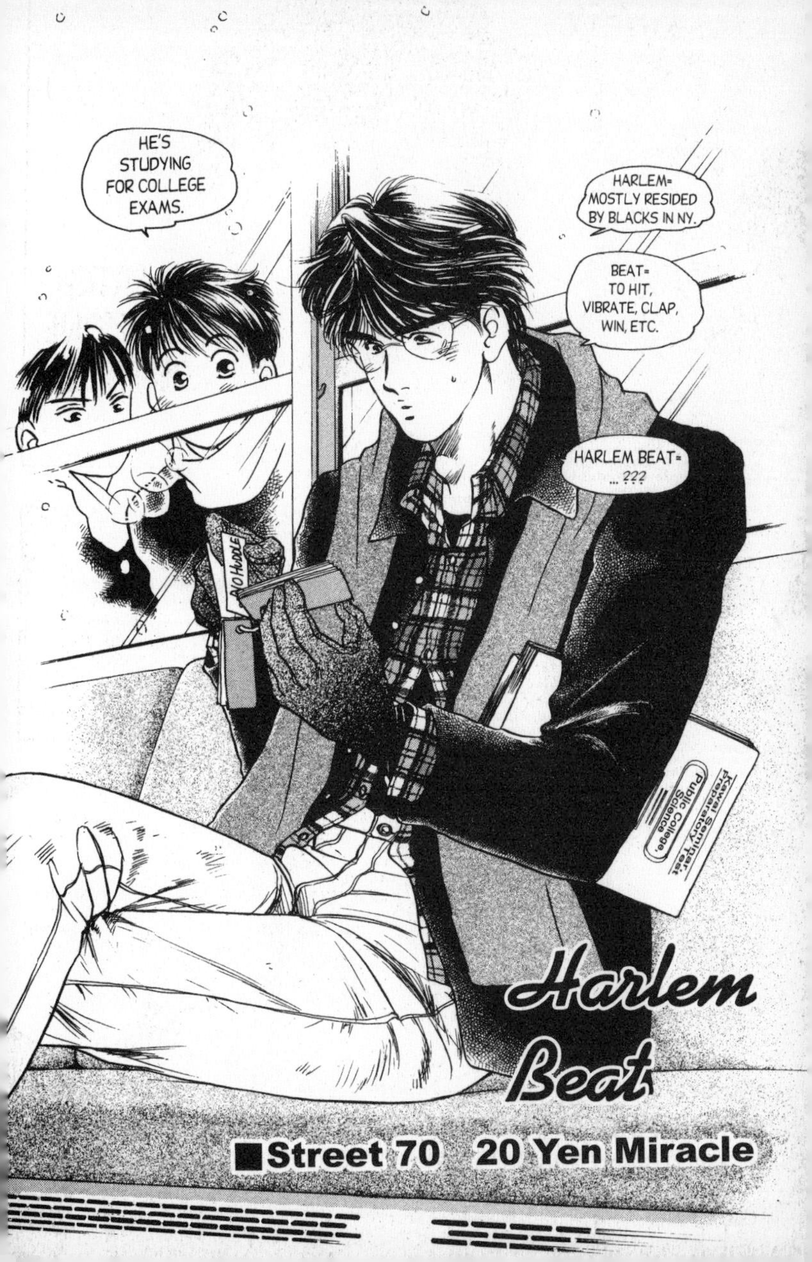
HARLEM= MOSTLY RESIDED BY BLACKS IN NY.
BEAT= TO HIT, VIBRATE, CLAP, WIN, ETC.
HARLEM BEAT= ...???
HE'S STUDYING FOR COLLEGE EXAMS.
Kawai Seminar Preparatory Test Public College Science
Harlem Beat
■Street 70 20 Yen Miracle

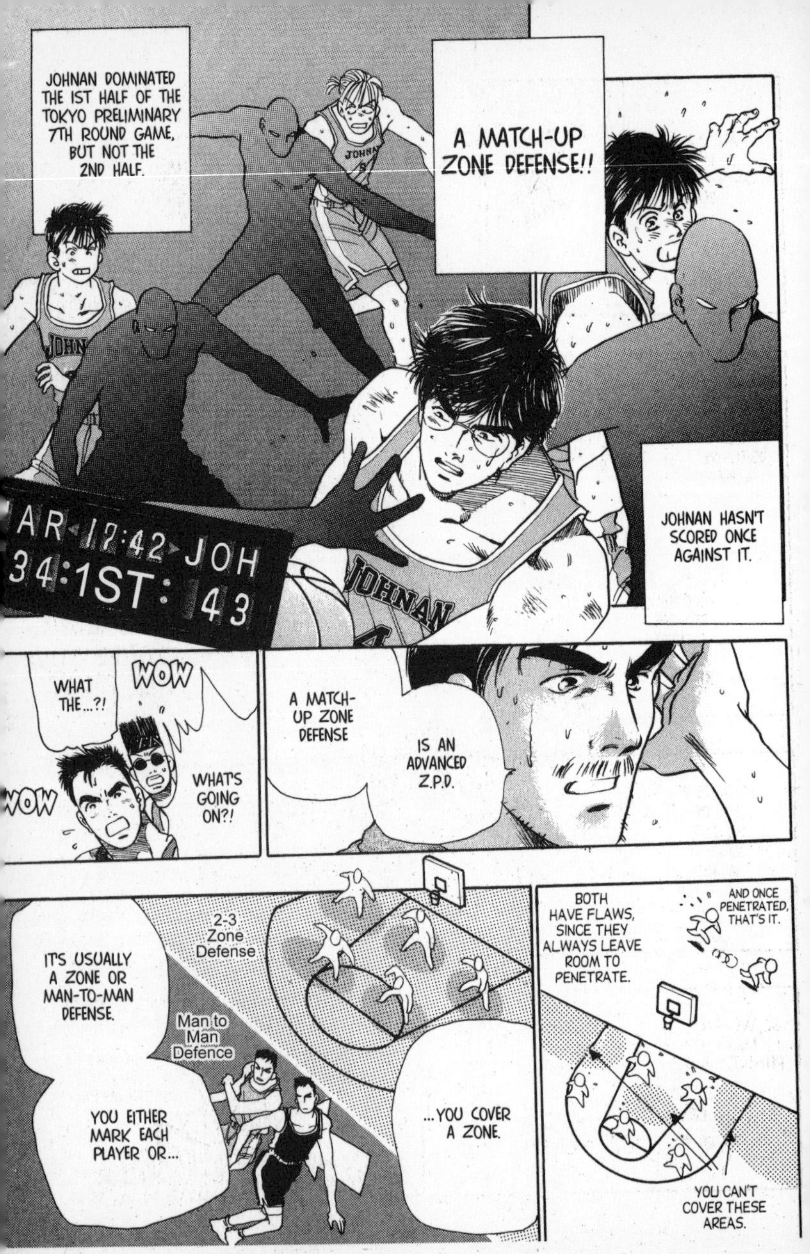
JOHNAN DOMINATED THE 1ST HALF OF THE TOKYO PRELIMINARY 7TH ROUND GAME, BUT NOT THE 2ND HALF.
A MATCH-UP ZONE DEFENSE!!
AR 17:42 JOH
34 1ST 43
JOHNAN HASN'T SCORED ONCE AGAINST IT.
WHAT THE...?!
WOW
WOW
WHAT'S GOING ON?!
A MATCH-UP ZONE DEFENSE
IS AN ADVANCED Z.P.D.
IT'S USUALLY A ZONE OR MAN-TO-MAN DEFENSE.
2-3 Zone Defense
Man to Man Defence
YOU EITHER MARK EACH PLAYER OR...
...YOU COVER A ZONE.
BOTH HAVE FLAWS, SINCE THEY ALWAYS LEAVE ROOM TO PENETRATE.
AND ONCE PENETRATED, THAT'S IT.
YOU CAN'T COVER THESE AREAS.

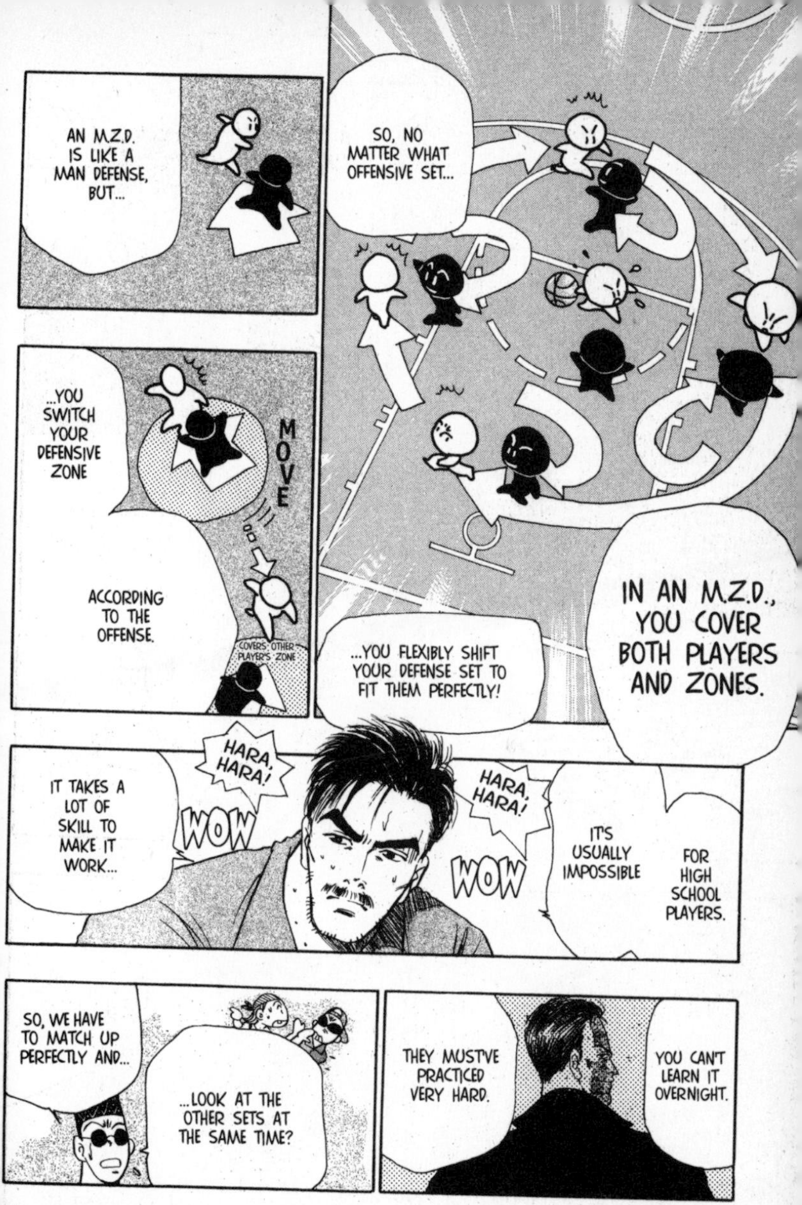
AN M.Z.D. IS LIKE A MAN DEFENSE, BUT...
...YOU SWITCH YOUR DEFENSIVE ZONE
MOVE
ACCORDING TO THE OFFENSE.
COVERS OTHER PLAYER'S ZONE
SO, NO MATTER WHAT OFFENSIVE SET...
...YOU FLEXIBLY SHIFT YOUR DEFENSE SET TO FIT THEM PERFECTLY!
IN AN M.Z.D., YOU COVER BOTH PLAYERS AND ZONES.
IT TAKES A LOT OF SKILL TO MAKE IT WORK...
HARA, HARA!
WOW
HARA, HARA!
WOW
IT'S USUALLY IMPOSSIBLE
FOR HIGH SCHOOL PLAYERS.
SO, WE HAVE TO MATCH UP PERFECTLY AND...
...LOOK AT THE OTHER SETS AT THE SAME TIME?
THEY MUST'VE PRACTICED VERY HARD.
YOU CAN'T LEARN IT OVERNIGHT.

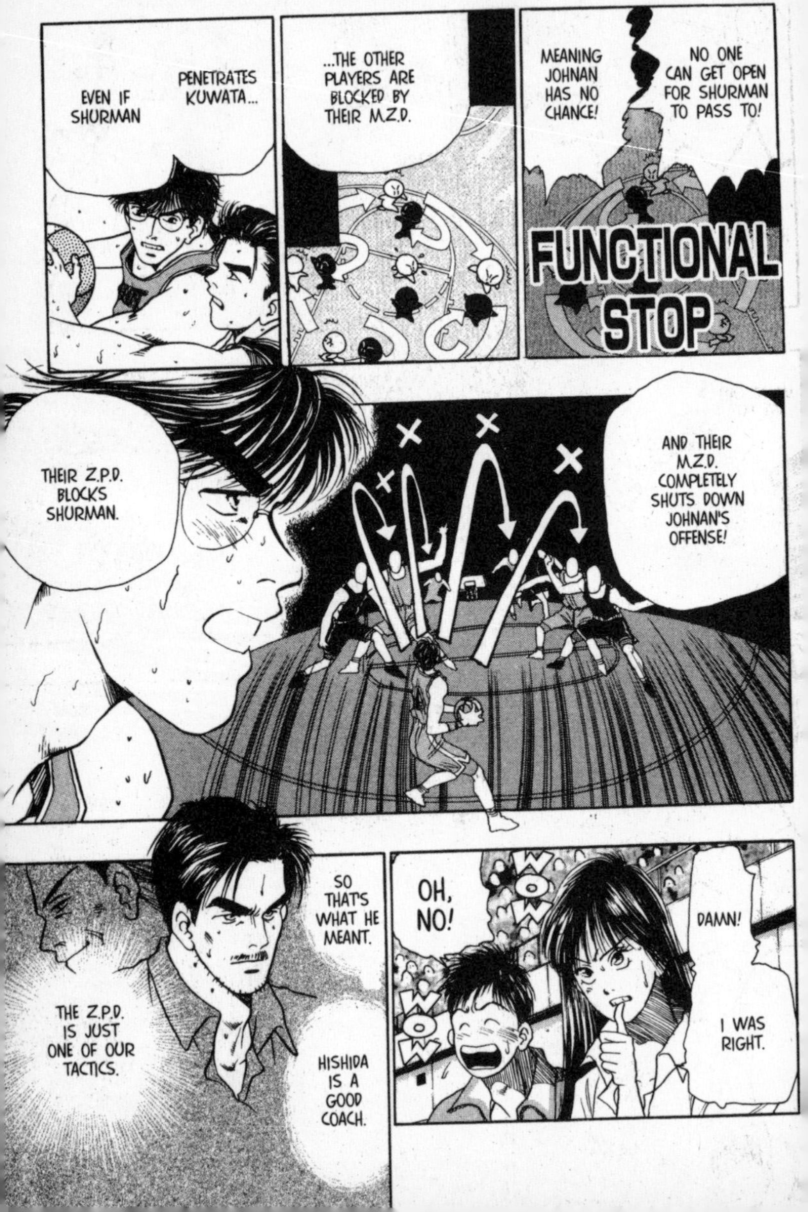
EVEN IF SHURMAN
PENETRATES KUWATA...
...THE OTHER PLAYERS ARE BLOCKED BY THEIR M.Z.D.
MEANING JOHNAN HAS NO CHANCE!
NO ONE CAN GET OPEN FOR SHURMAN TO PASS TO!
FUNCTIONAL STOP
THEIR Z.P.D. BLOCKS SHURMAN.
AND THEIR M.Z.D. COMPLETELY SHUTS DOWN JOHNAN'S OFFENSE!
THE Z.P.D. IS JUST ONE OF OUR TACTICS.
SO THAT'S WHAT HE MEANT.
HISHIDA IS A GOOD COACH.
OH, NO!
WOW
WOW
DAMN!
I WAS RIGHT.

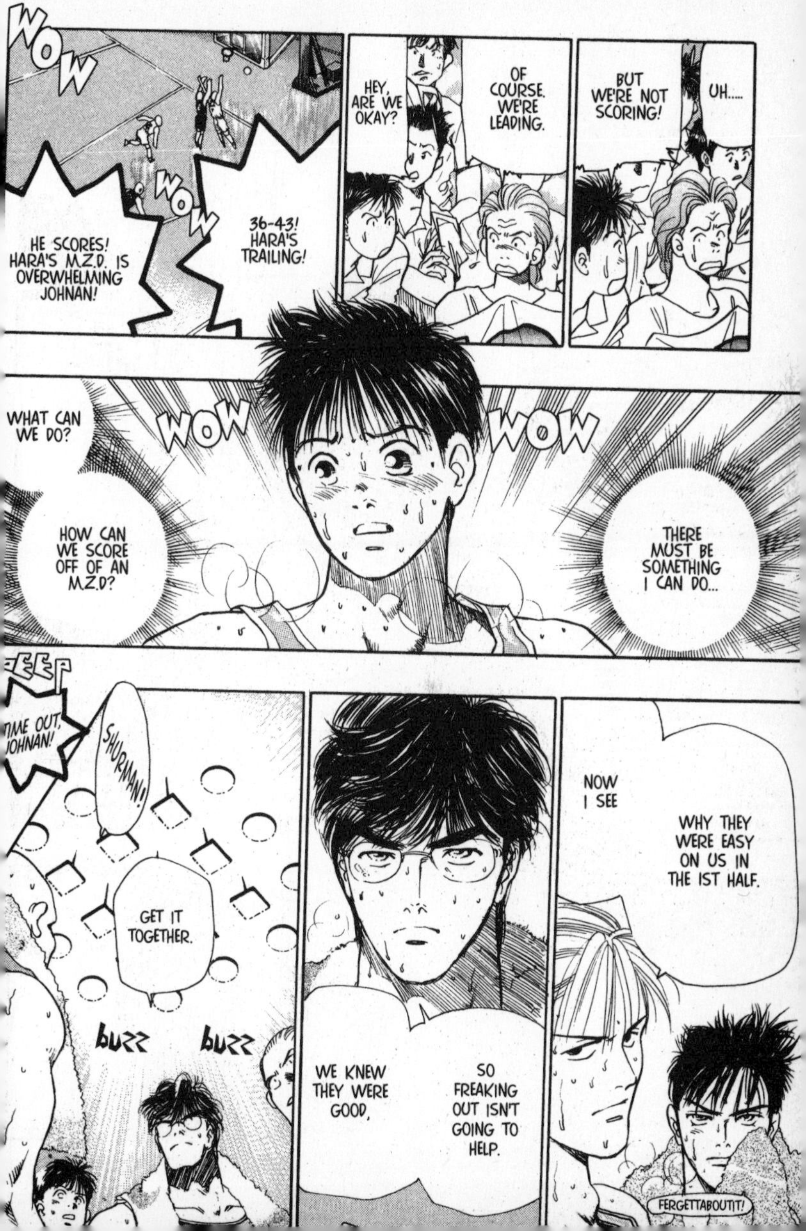
WOW
WOW
HE SCORES! HARA'S M.Z.D. IS OVERWHELMING JOHNAN!
36-43! HARA'S TRAILING!
HEY, ARE WE OKAY?
OF COURSE. WE'RE LEADING.
BUT WE'RE NOT SCORING!
UH....
WHAT CAN WE DO?
WOW
WOW
HOW CAN WE SCORE OFF OF AN M.Z.D?
THERE MUST BE SOMETHING I CAN DO...
TIME OUT, JOHNAN!
SHURMAN!
GET IT TOGETHER.
buzz
buzz
WE KNEW THEY WERE GOOD,
SO FREAKING OUT ISN'T GOING TO HELP.
NOW I SEE
WHY THEY WERE EASY ON US IN THE 1ST HALF.
FERGETTABOUTIT!

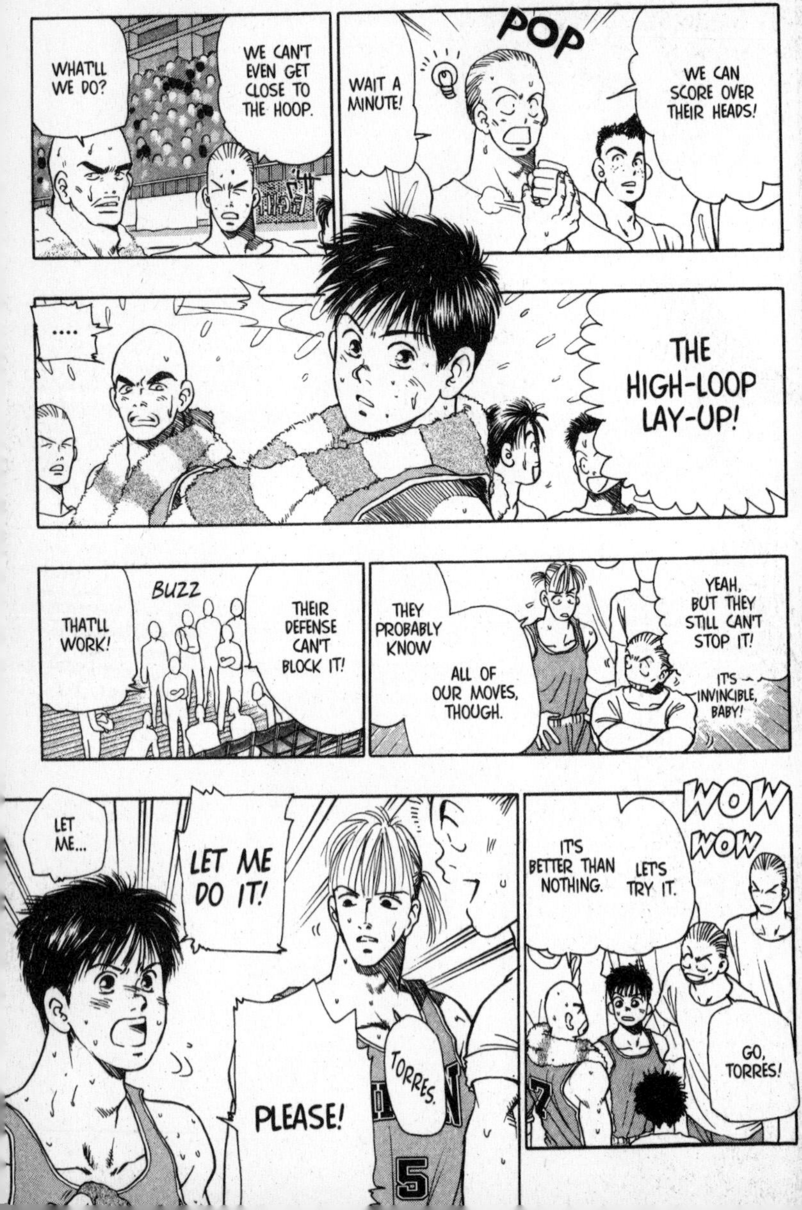
WHAT'LL WE DO?
WE CAN'T EVEN GET CLOSE TO THE HOOP.
WAIT A MINUTE!
POP
WE CAN SCORE OVER THEIR HEADS!
....
THE HIGH-LOOP LAY-UP!
THAT'LL WORK!
BUZZ
THEIR DEFENSE CAN'T BLOCK IT!
THEY PROBABLY KNOW
ALL OF OUR MOVES, THOUGH.
YEAH, BUT THEY STILL CAN'T STOP IT!
IT'S INVINCIBLE, BABY!
LET ME...
LET ME DO IT!
TORRES.
PLEASE!
WOW
WOW
IT'S BETTER THAN NOTHING.
LET'S TRY IT.
GO, TORRES!

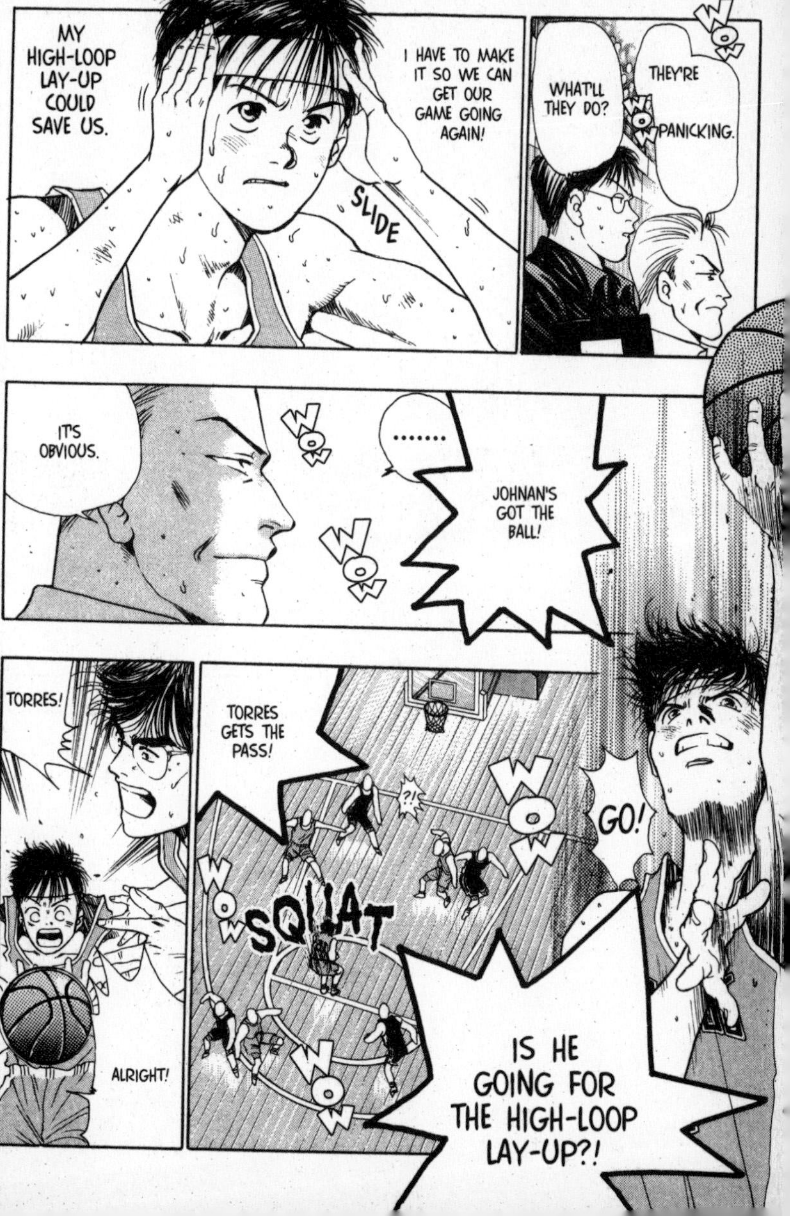
MY HIGH-LOOP LAY-UP COULD SAVE US.
I HAVE TO MAKE IT SO WE CAN GET OUR GAME GOING AGAIN!
SLIDE
WHAT'LL THEY DO?
WOW
THEY'RE PANICKING.
WOW
IT'S OBVIOUS.
WOW
....
WOW
JOHNAN'S GOT THE BALL!
TORRES!
ALRIGHT!
TORRES GETS THE PASS!
?!
WOW
SQUAT
WOW
WOW
GO!
IS HE GOING FOR THE HIGH-LOOP LAY-UP?!

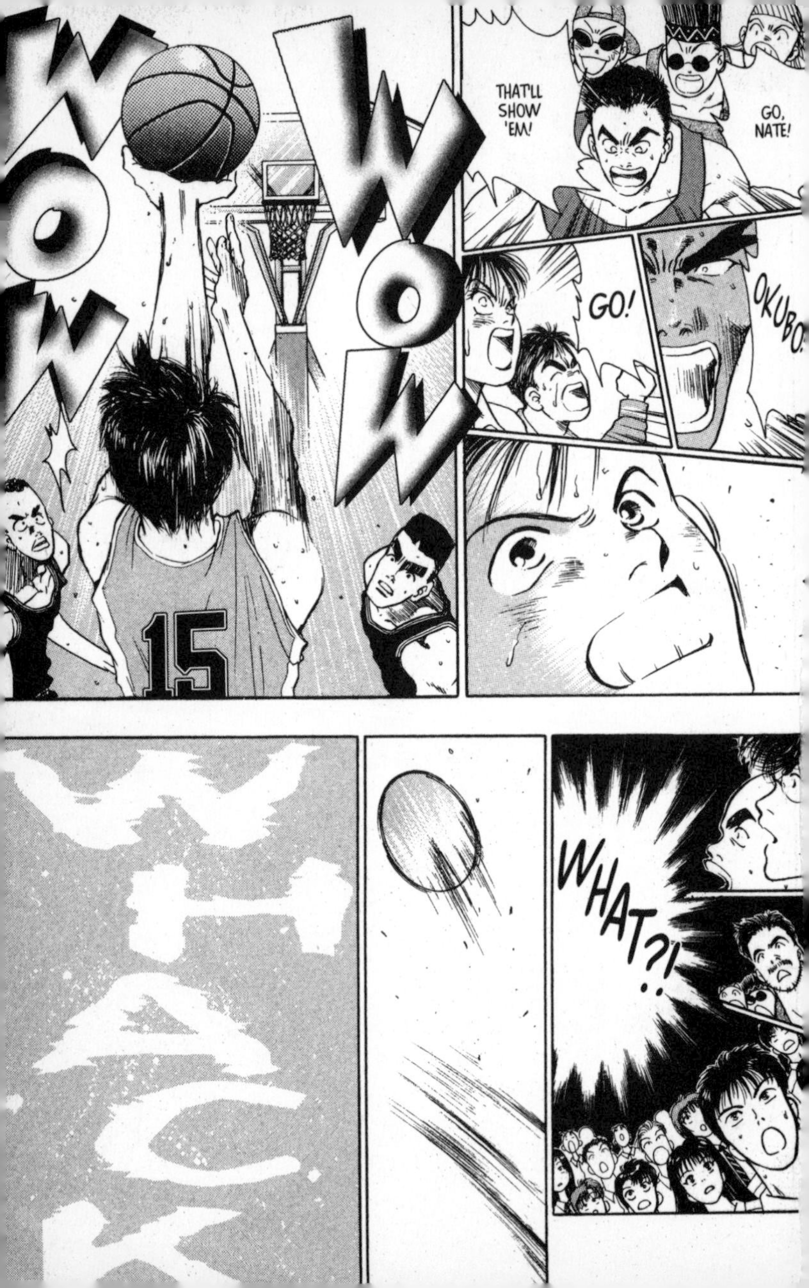
GO, NATE!
THAT'LL SHOW 'EM!
OKUBO!
GO!
WOW
WOW
WHAT?!

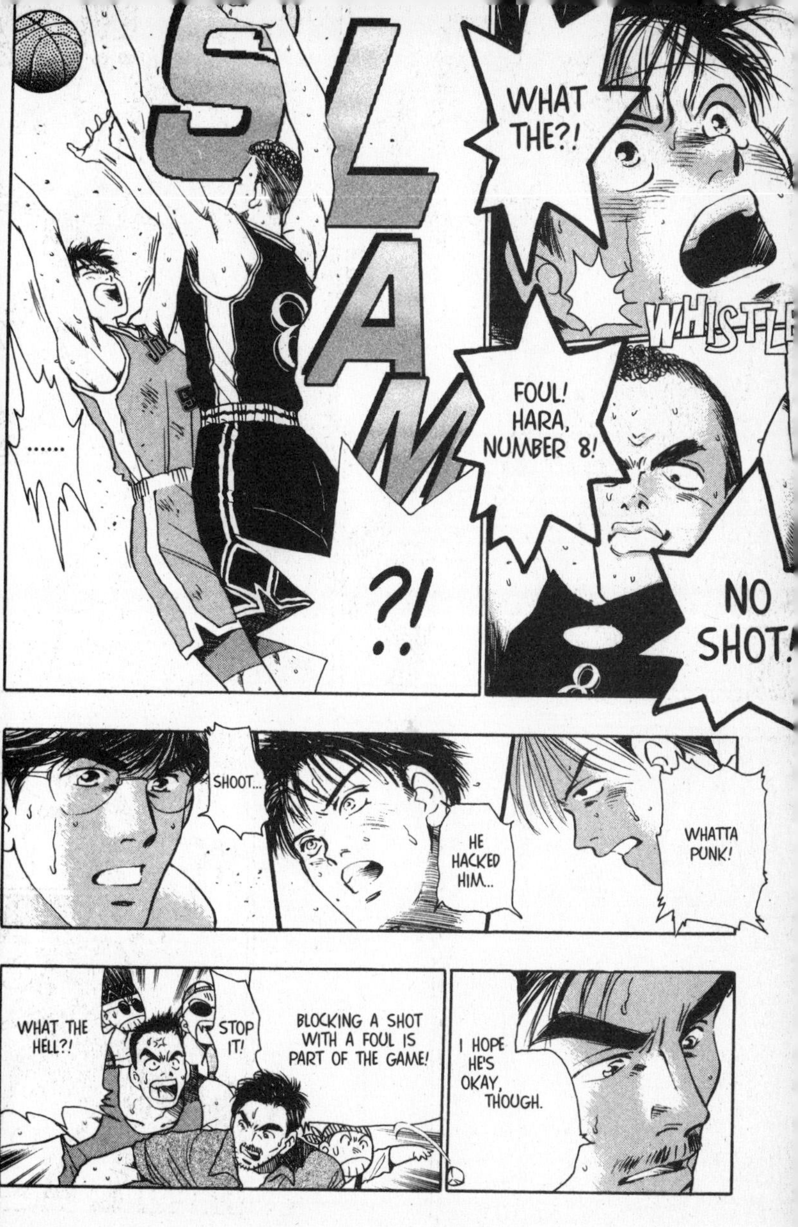
SLAM
......
?!
WHAT THE?!
WHISTLE
FOUL! HARA, NUMBER 8!
NO SHOT!
SHOOT...
HE HACKED HIM...
WHATTA PUNK!
WHAT THE HELL?!
STOP IT!
BLOCKING A SHOT WITH A FOUL IS PART OF THE GAME!
I HOPE HE'S OKAY, THOUGH.

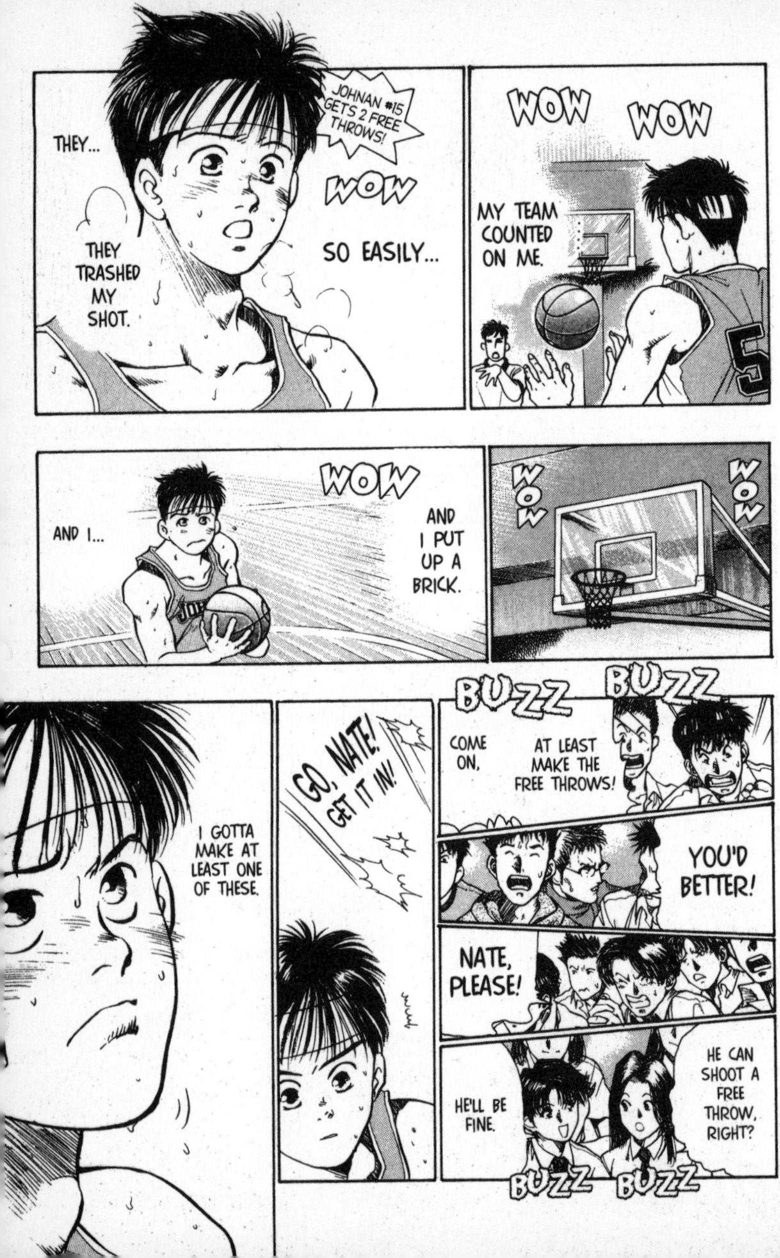
THEY...
JOHNAN #15 GETS 2 FREE THROWS!
WOW
THEY TRASHED MY SHOT.
SO EASILY...
WOW
WOW
MY TEAM COUNTED ON ME.
AND I...
WOW
AND I PUT UP A BRICK.
WOW
WOW
I GOTTA MAKE AT LEAST ONE OF THESE.
GO, NATE! GET IT IN!
BUZZ
BUZZ
COME ON,
AT LEAST MAKE THE FREE THROWS!
YOU'D BETTER!
NATE, PLEASE!
HE'LL BE FINE.
HE CAN SHOOT A FREE THROW, RIGHT?
BUZZ
BUZZ

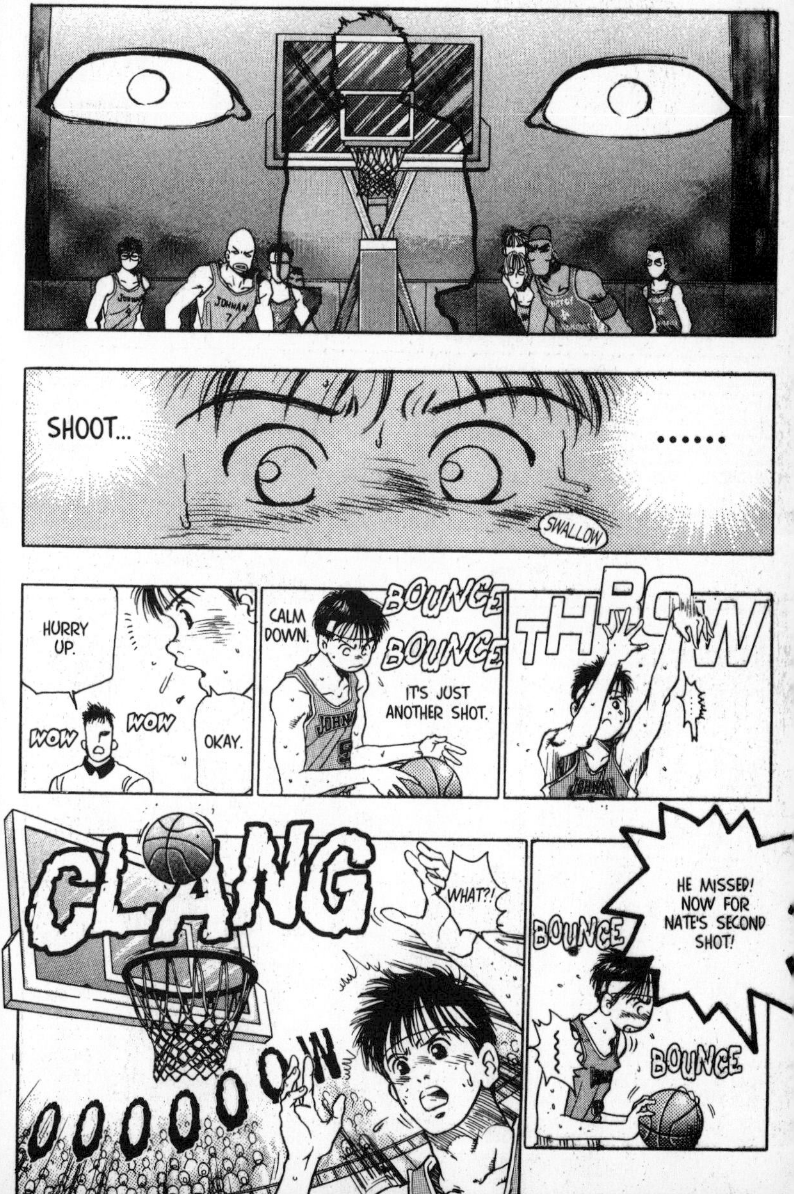
SHOOT...
SWALLOW
......
HURRY UP.
WOW
WOW
OKAY.
CALM DOWN.
BOUNCE
BOUNCE
IT'S JUST ANOTHER SHOT.
THROW
CLANG
WHAT?!
OOOOOOOW
BOUNCE
HE MISSED! NOW FOR NATE'S SECOND SHOT!
BOUNCE

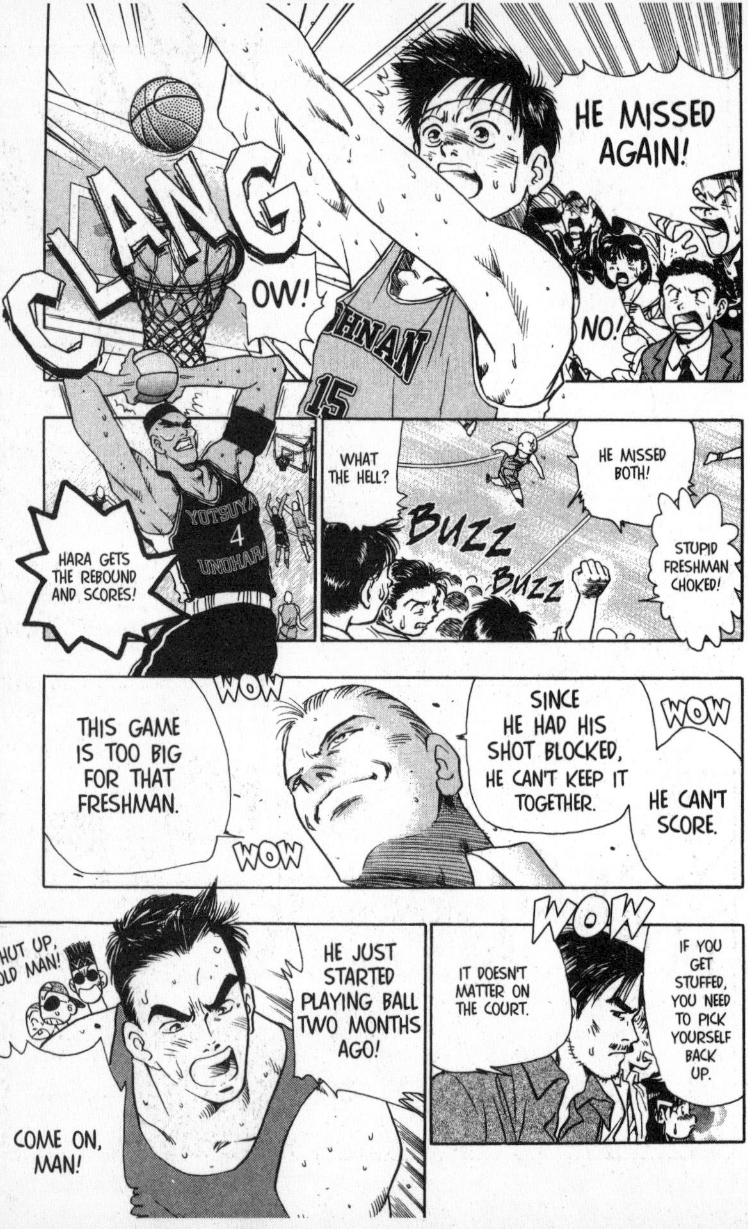
CLANG
OW!
HE MISSED AGAIN!
NO!
HARA GETS THE REBOUND AND SCORES!
WHAT THE HELL?
BUZZ
BUZZ
HE MISSED BOTH!
STUPID FRESHMAN CHOKED!
WOW
THIS GAME IS TOO BIG FOR THAT FRESHMAN.
WOW
SINCE HE HAD HIS SHOT BLOCKED, HE CAN'T KEEP IT TOGETHER.
WOW
HE CAN'T SCORE.
SHUT UP, OLD MAN!
HE JUST STARTED PLAYING BALL TWO MONTHS AGO!
COME ON, MAN!
WOW
IT DOESN'T MATTER ON THE COURT.
IF YOU GET STUFFED, YOU NEED TO PICK YOURSELF BACK UP.

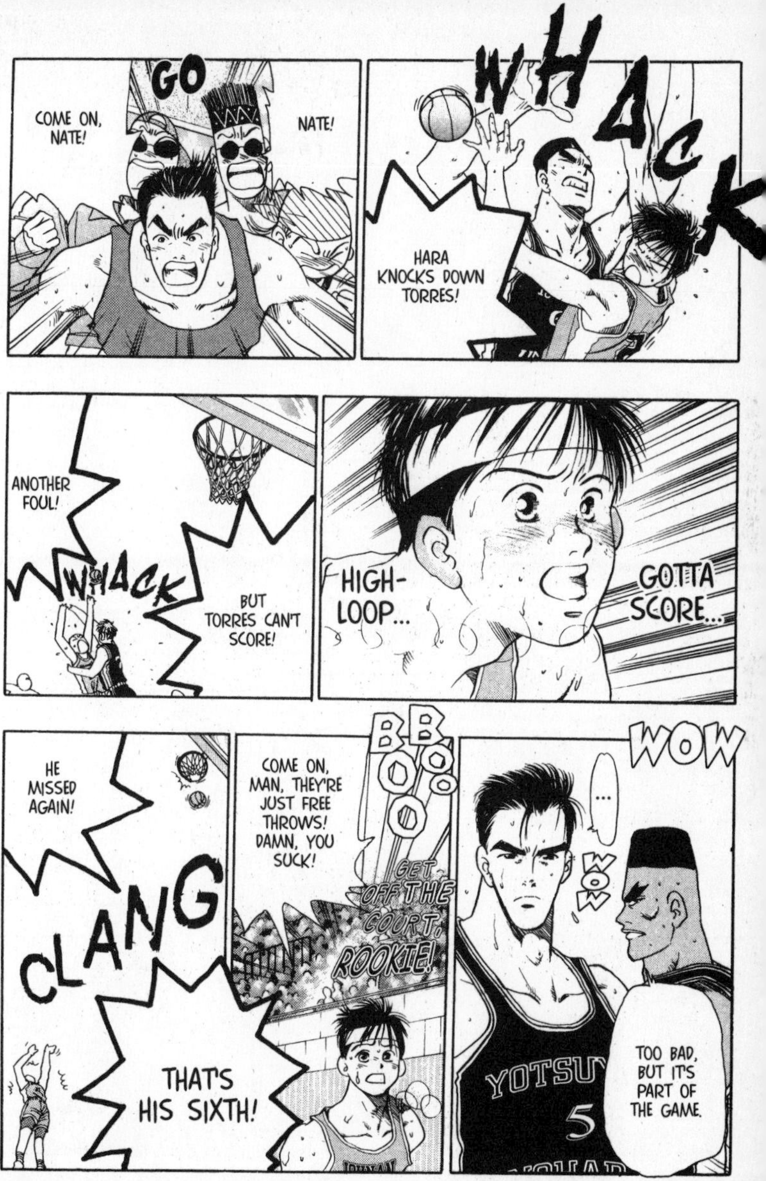
GO
COME ON, NATE!
NATE!
WHACK
HARA KNOCKS DOWN TORRES!
ANOTHER FOUL!
WHACK
BUT TORRES CAN'T SCORE!
HIGH-LOOP...
GOTTA SCORE...
HE MISSED AGAIN!
CLANG
THAT'S HIS SIXTH!
BBOOOOO
COME ON, MAN, THEY'RE JUST FREE THROWS! DAMN, YOU SUCK!
GET OFF THE COURT, ROOKIE!
WOW
...
WOW
TOO BAD, BUT IT'S PART OF THE GAME.
YOTSUYA
5

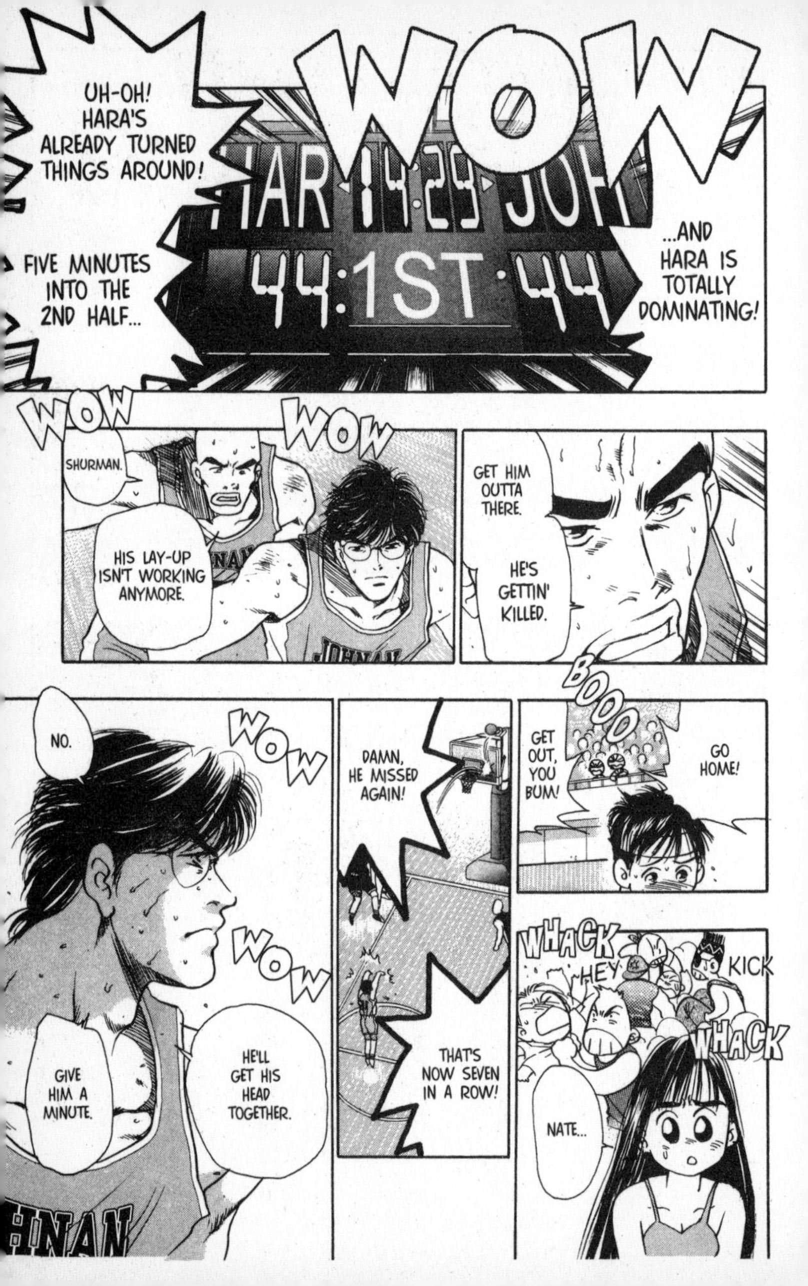
WOW
UH-OH! HARA'S ALREADY TURNED THINGS AROUND!
HAR 14:29 JOH
44 1ST 44
FIVE MINUTES INTO THE 2ND HALF...
...AND HARA IS TOTALLY DOMINATING!
WOW
WOW
SHURMAN.
HIS LAY-UP ISN'T WORKING ANYMORE.
GET HIM OUTTA THERE.
HE'S GETTIN' KILLED.
BOOO
NO.
WOW
WOW
GIVE HIM A MINUTE.
HE'LL GET HIS HEAD TOGETHER.
DAMN, HE MISSED AGAIN!
THAT'S NOW SEVEN IN A ROW!
GET OUT, YOU BUM!
GO HOME!
WHACK
HEY
KICK
WHACK
NATE...

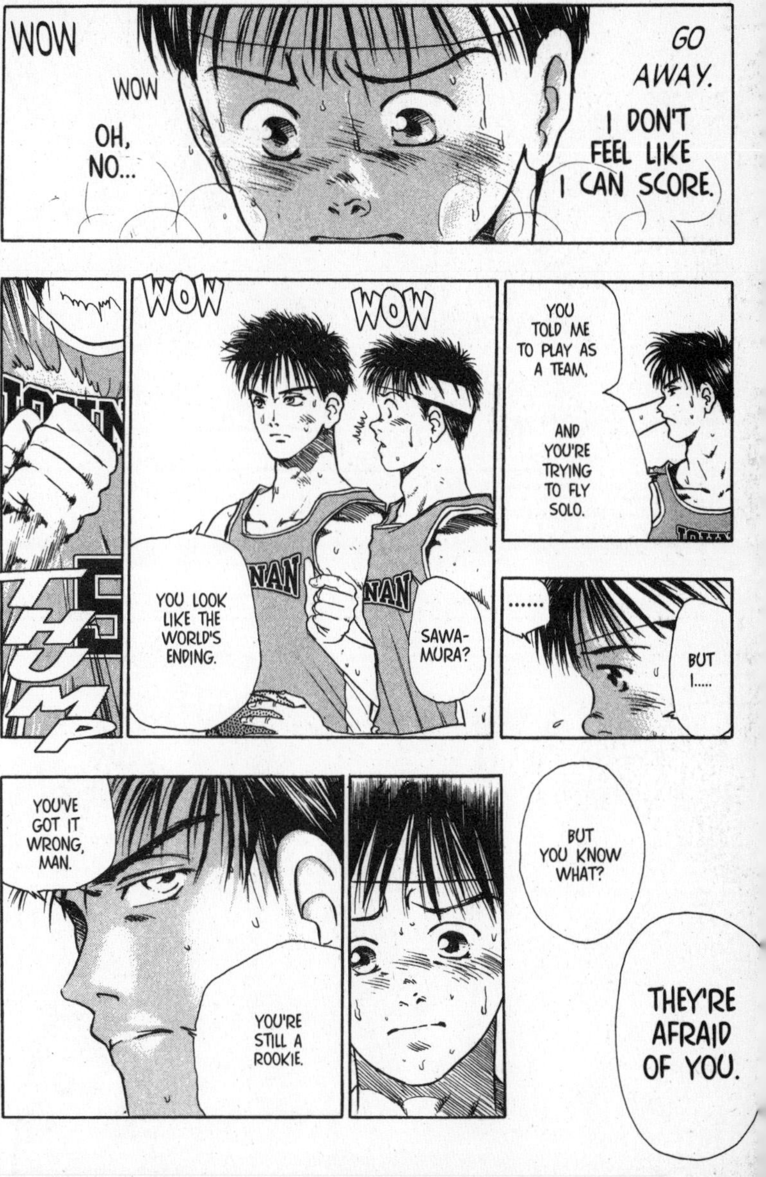
WOW
WOW
OH, NO...
GO AWAY.
I DON'T FEEL LIKE I CAN SCORE.
THUMP
WOW
WOW
YOU LOOK LIKE THE WORLD'S ENDING.
SAWA-MURA?
YOU TOLD ME TO PLAY AS A TEAM,
AND YOU'RE TRYING TO FLY SOLO.
......
BUT I.....
YOU'VE GOT IT WRONG, MAN.
YOU'RE STILL A ROOKIE.
BUT YOU KNOW WHAT?
THEY'RE AFRAID OF YOU.

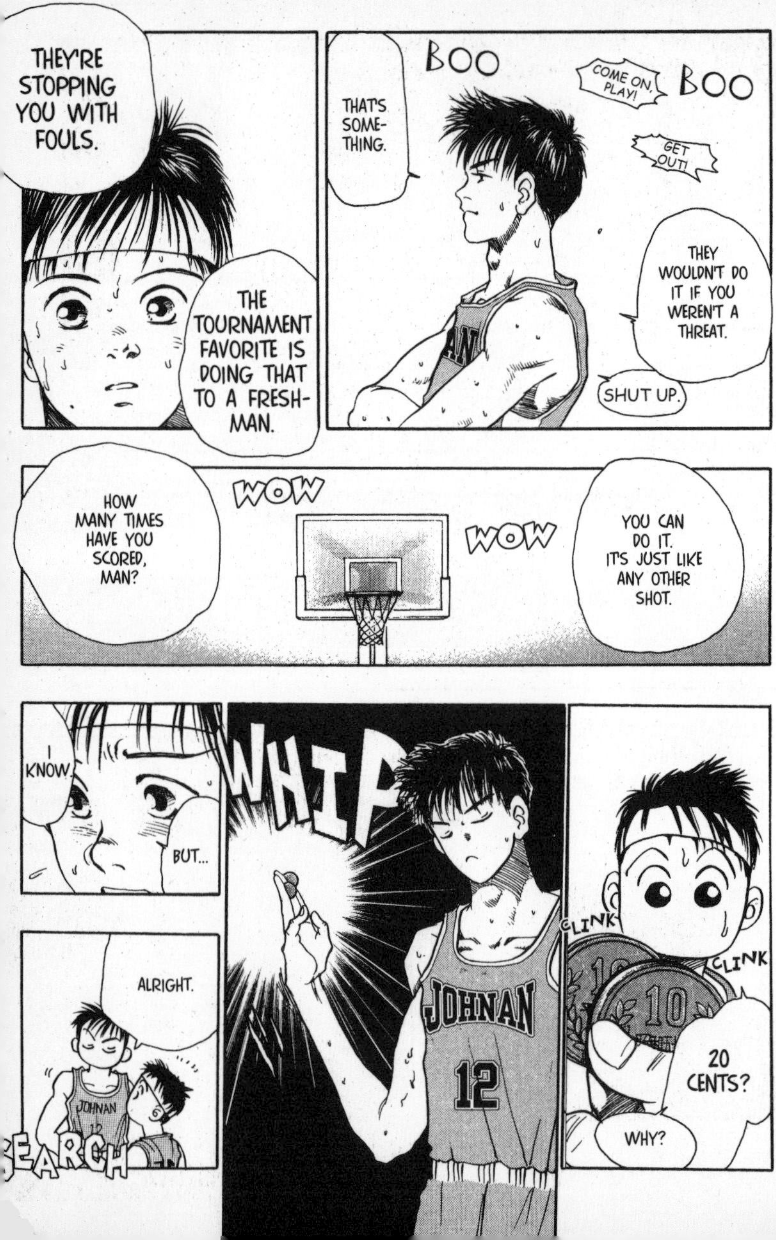
THEY'RE STOPPING YOU WITH FOULS.
THE TOURNAMENT FAVORITE IS DOING THAT TO A FRESH-MAN.
BOO
COME ON, PLAY!
BOO
GET OUT!
THAT'S SOME-THING.
THEY WOULDN'T DO IT IF YOU WEREN'T A THREAT.
SHUT UP.
HOW MANY TIMES HAVE YOU SCORED, MAN?
WOW
WOW
YOU CAN DO IT. IT'S JUST LIKE ANY OTHER SHOT.
I KNOW.
BUT...
ALRIGHT.
SEARCH
WHIP
JOHNAN
12
CLINK
CLINK
20 CENTS?
WHY?

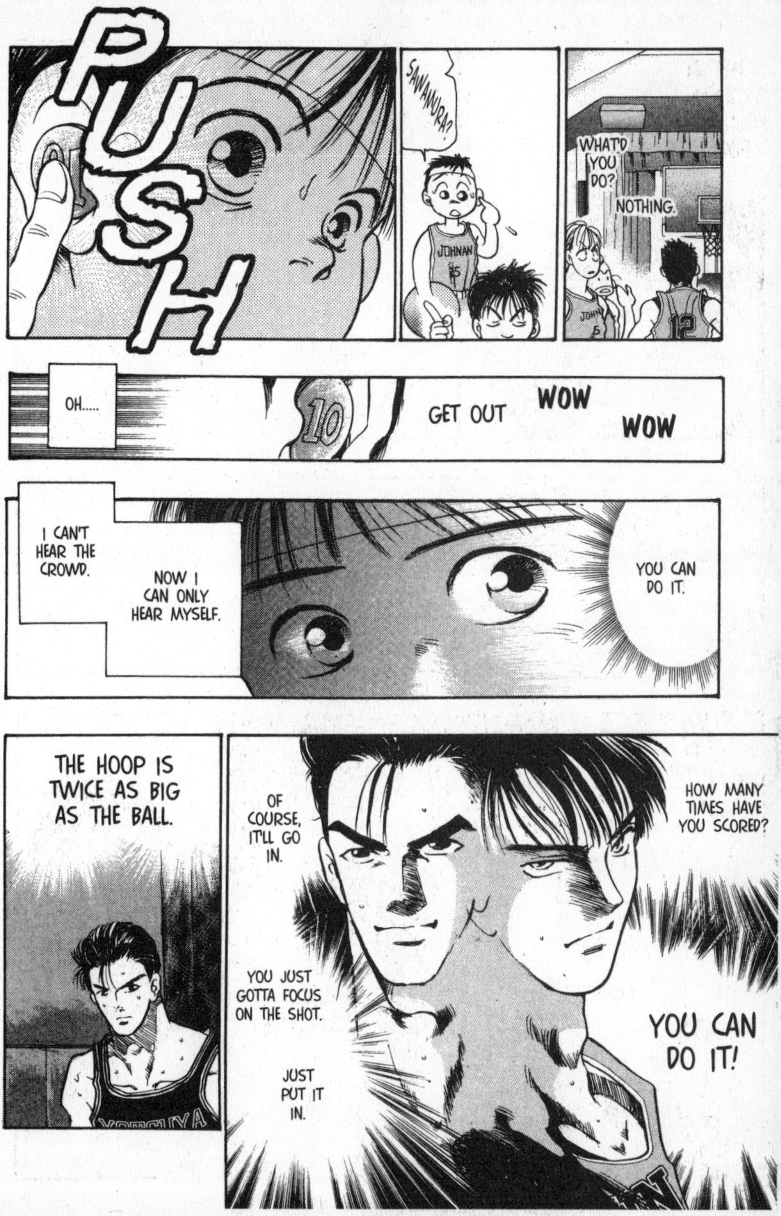
PUSH
SAWAMURA?
WHAT'D YOU DO?
NOTHING.
OH.....
GET OUT
WOW
WOW
I CAN'T HEAR THE CROWD.
NOW I CAN ONLY HEAR MYSELF.
YOU CAN DO IT.
THE HOOP IS TWICE AS BIG AS THE BALL.
OF COURSE, IT'LL GO IN.
HOW MANY TIMES HAVE YOU SCORED?
YOU JUST GOTTA FOCUS ON THE SHOT.
JUST PUT IT IN.
YOU CAN DO IT!

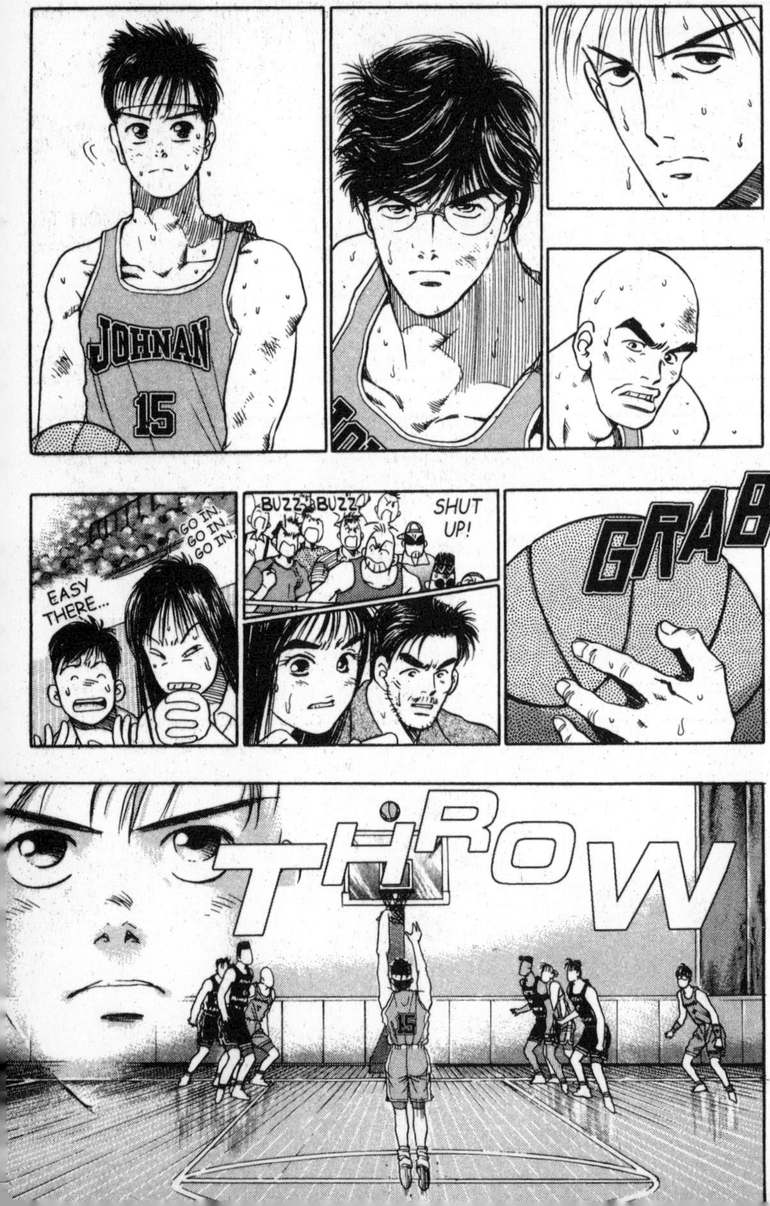
JOHNAN
15
GRAB
SHUT UP!
BUZZ BUZZ
GO IN. GO IN. GO IN.
EASY THERE...
THROW

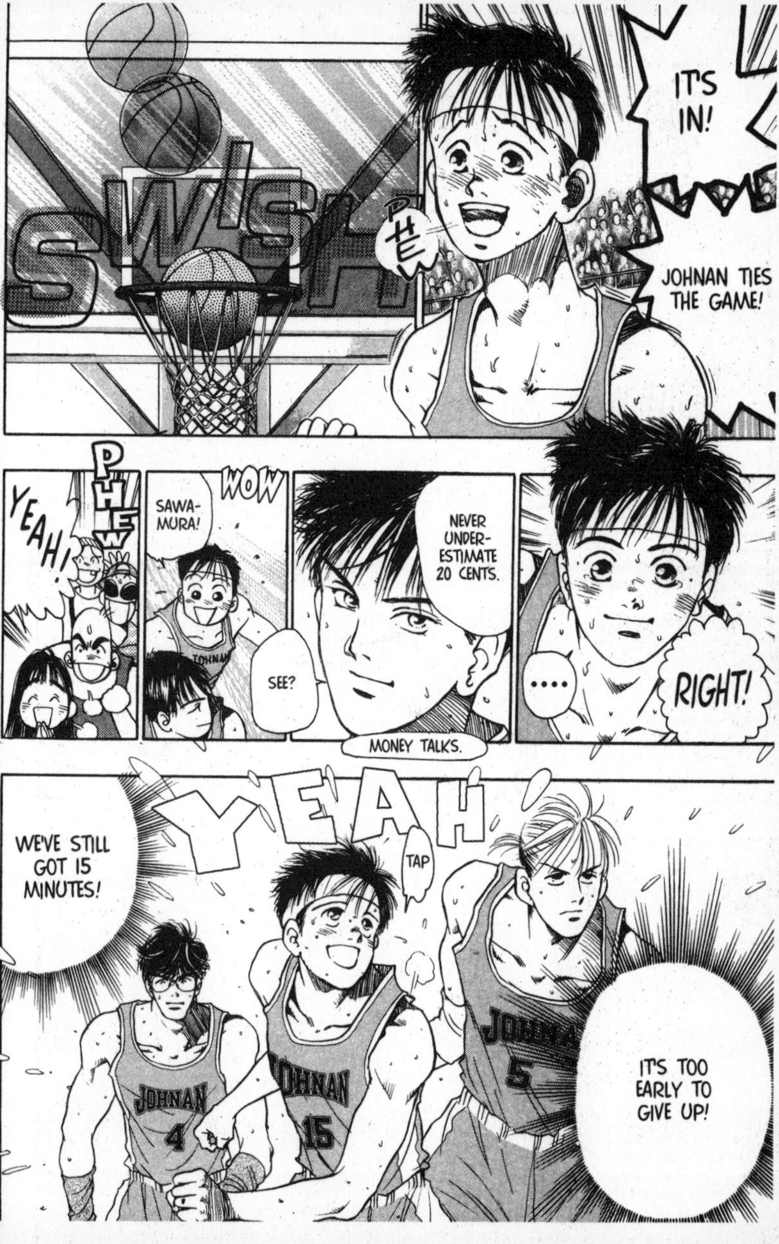
IT'S IN!
JOHNAN TIES THE GAME!
PHEW
SWISH
RIGHT!
....
NEVER UNDER-ESTIMATE 20 CENTS.
SEE?
MONEY TALKS.
WOW
SAWA-MURA!
PHEW
YEAH!
YEAH
TAP
WE'VE STILL GOT 15 MINUTES!
IT'S TOO EARLY TO GIVE UP!

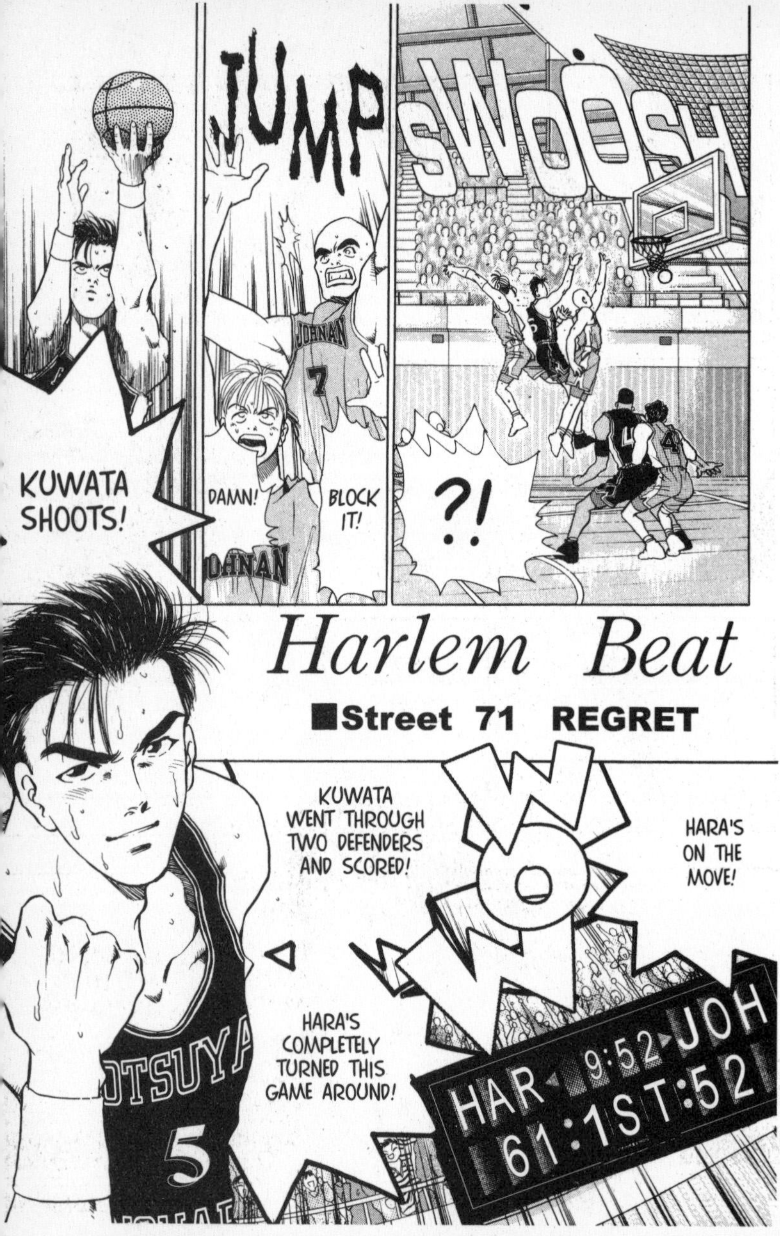
KUWATA SHOOTS!
JUMP
DAMN!
BLOCK IT!
SWOOSH
?!
Harlem Beat
■Street 71 REGRET
WOW
KUWATA WENT THROUGH TWO DEFENDERS AND SCORED!
HARA'S ON THE MOVE!
HARA'S COMPLETELY TURNED THIS GAME AROUND!
HAR 9:52 JOH
61 1ST 52

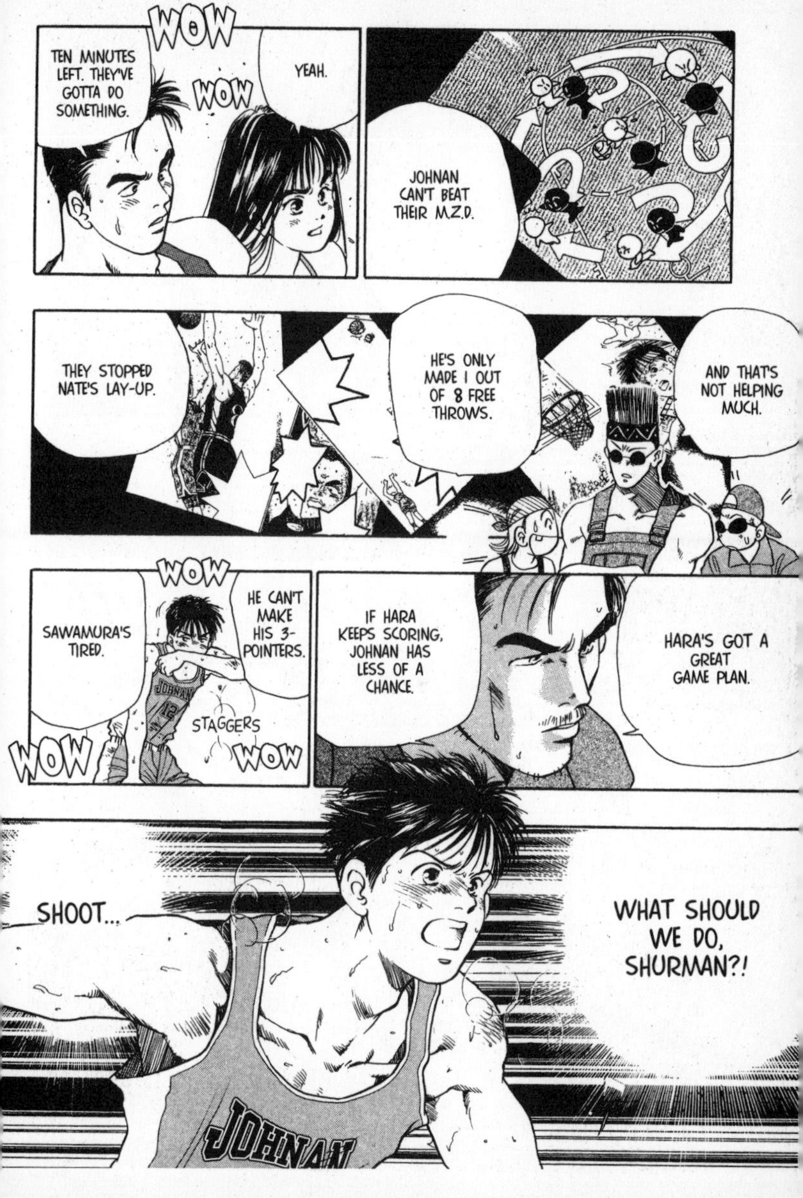
WOW
TEN MINUTES LEFT. THEY'VE GOTTA DO SOMETHING.
WOW
YEAH.
JOHNAN CAN'T BEAT THEIR M.Z.D.
THEY STOPPED NATE'S LAY-UP.
HE'S ONLY MADE 1 OUT OF 8 FREE THROWS.
AND THAT'S NOT HELPING MUCH.
WOW
SAWAMURA'S TIRED.
HE CAN'T MAKE HIS 3-POINTERS.
STAGGERS
WOW
WOW
IF HARA KEEPS SCORING, JOHNAN HAS LESS OF A CHANCE.
HARA'S GOT A GREAT GAME PLAN.
SHOOT...
WHAT SHOULD WE DO, SHURMAN?!

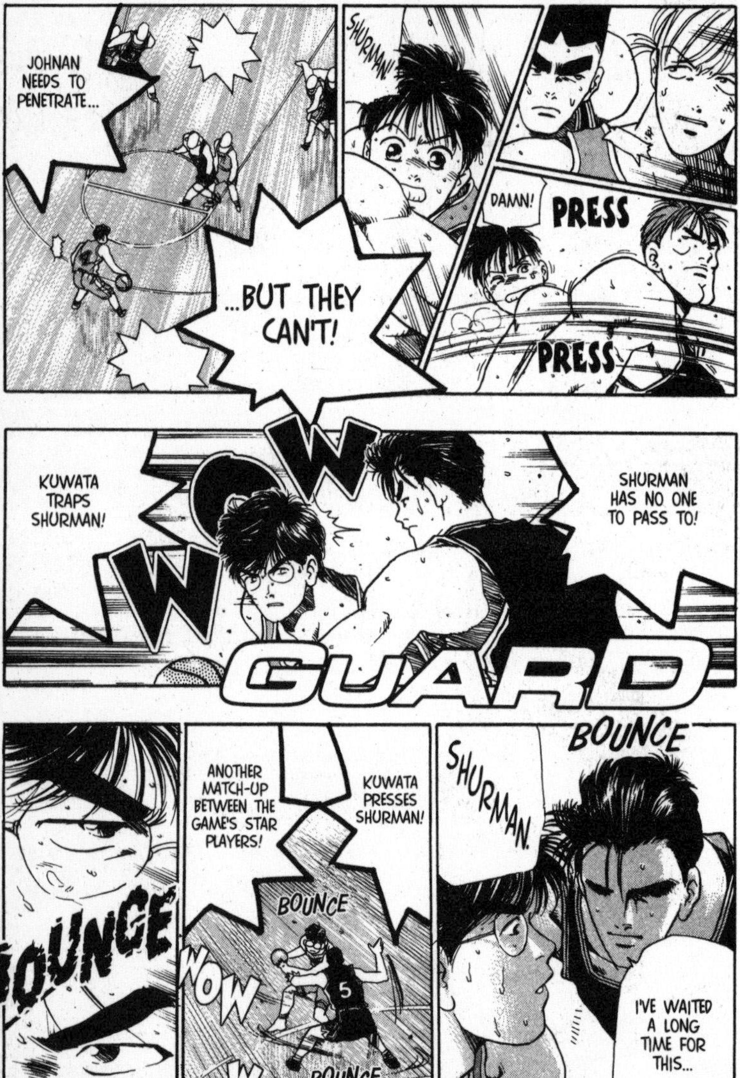
JOHNAN NEEDS TO PENETRATE...
...BUT THEY CAN'T!
SHURMAN!
DAMN!
PRESS
PRESS
WOW
KUWATA TRAPS SHURMAN!
SHURMAN HAS NO ONE TO PASS TO!
GUARD
BOUNCE
ANOTHER MATCH-UP BETWEEN THE GAME'S STAR PLAYERS!
KUWATA PRESSES SHURMAN!
BOUNCE
WOW
WOW
BOUNCE
BOUNCE
SHURMAN.
I'VE WAITED A LONG TIME FOR THIS...
BOUNCE

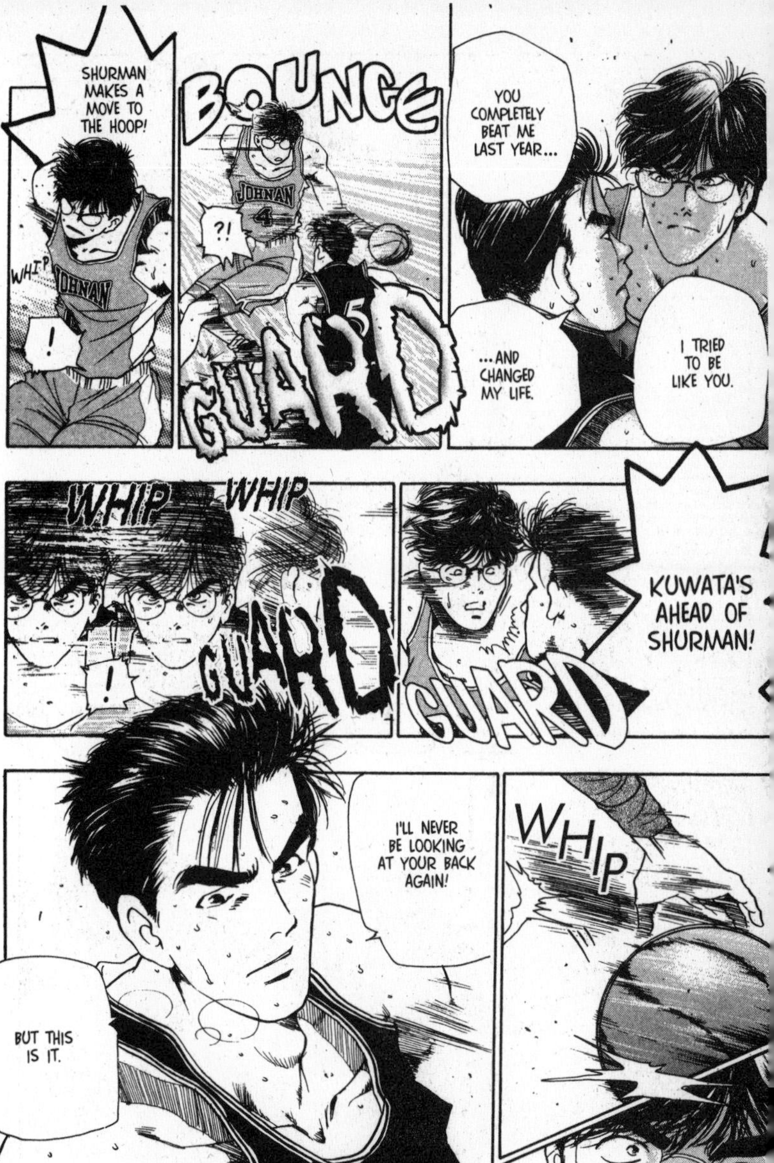
SHURMAN MAKES A MOVE TO THE HOOP!
WHIP
!
BOUNCE
?!
GUARD
YOU COMPLETELY BEAT ME LAST YEAR...
...AND CHANGED MY LIFE.
I TRIED TO BE LIKE YOU.
WHIP
WHIP
!
GUARD
GUARD
KUWATA'S AHEAD OF SHURMAN!
I'LL NEVER BE LOOKING AT YOUR BACK AGAIN!
BUT THIS IS IT.
WHIP

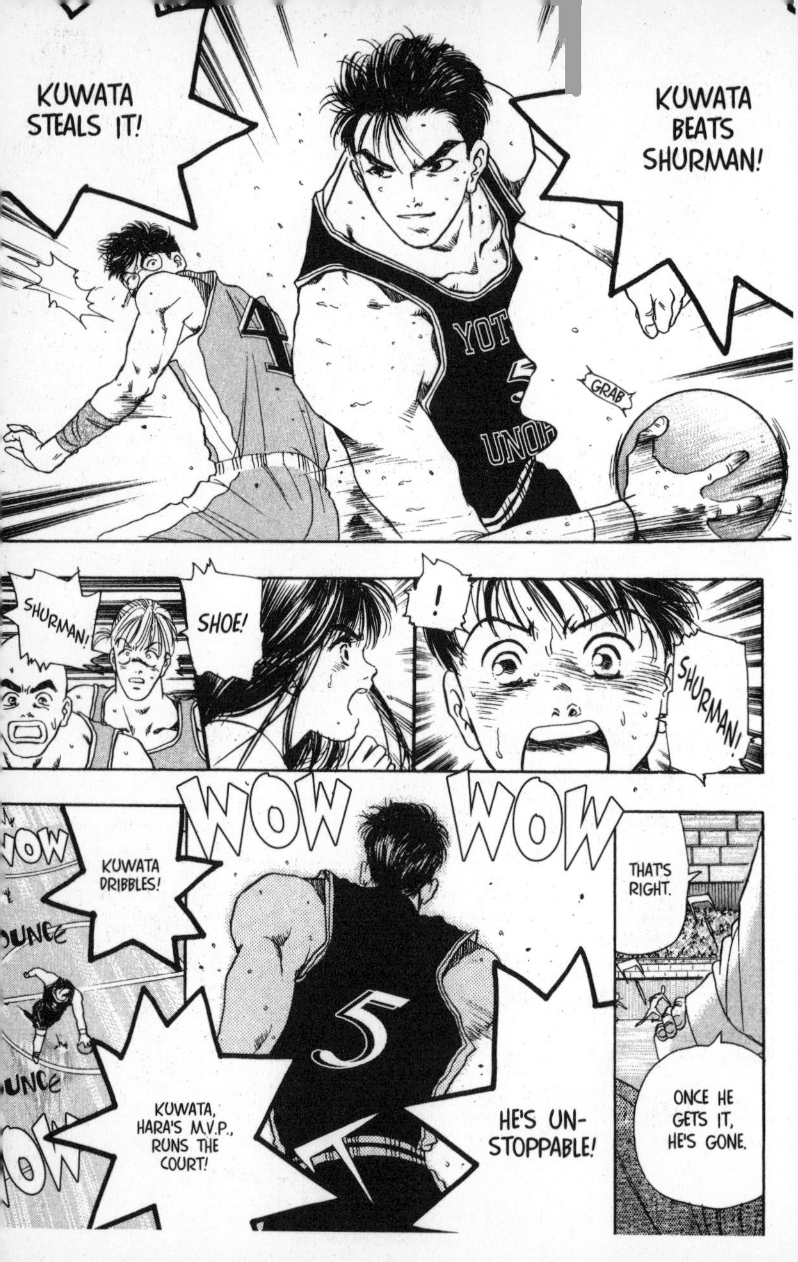
KUWATA STEALS IT!
KUWATA BEATS SHURMAN!
GRAB
SHURMAN!
SHOE!
!
SHURMAN!
WOW WOW
WOW
KUWATA DRIBBLES!
BOUNCE
BOUNCE
KUWATA, HARA'S M.V.P., RUNS THE COURT!
HE'S UN-STOPPABLE!
THAT'S RIGHT.
ONCE HE GETS IT, HE'S GONE.

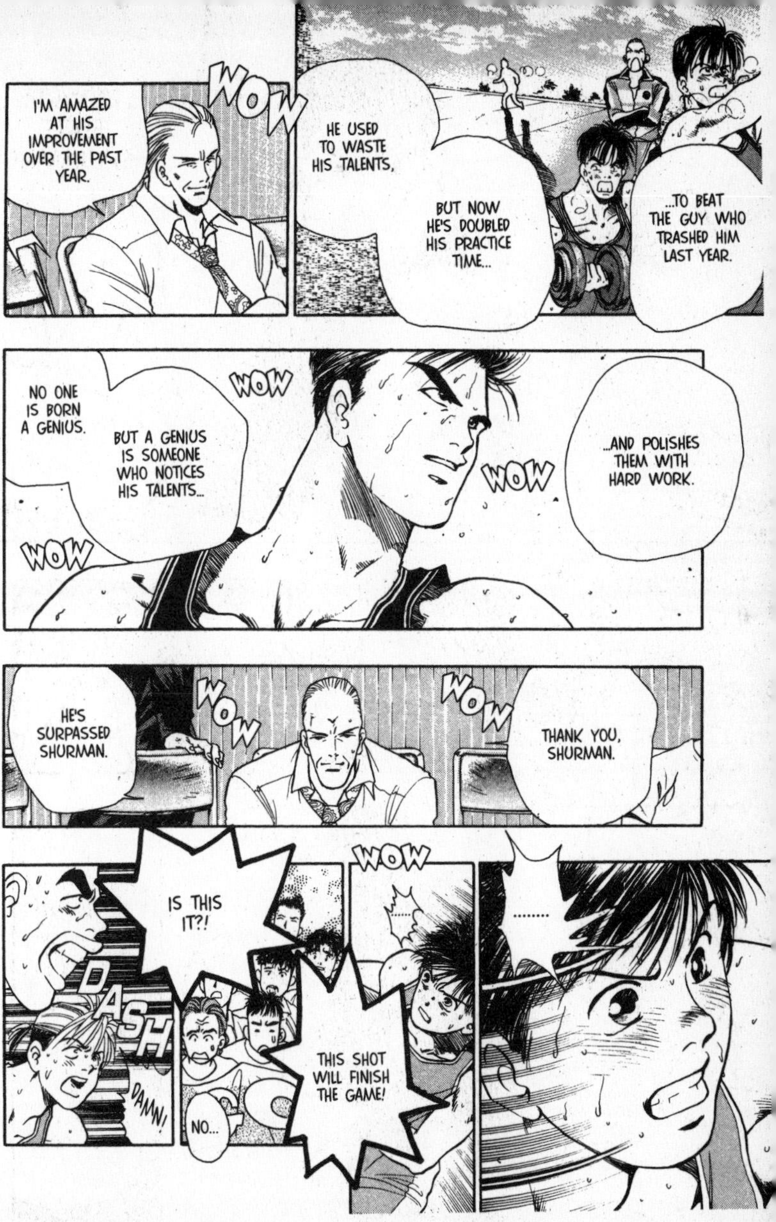
WOW
I'M AMAZED AT HIS IMPROVEMENT OVER THE PAST YEAR.
HE USED TO WASTE HIS TALENTS,
BUT NOW HE'S DOUBLED HIS PRACTICE TIME...
...TO BEAT THE GUY WHO TRASHED HIM LAST YEAR.
NO ONE IS BORN A GENIUS.
BUT A GENIUS IS SOMEONE WHO NOTICES HIS TALENTS...
WOW
WOW
WOW
...AND POLISHES THEM WITH HARD WORK.
HE'S SURPASSED SHURMAN.
WOW
WOW
THANK YOU, SHURMAN.
IS THIS IT?!
DASH
DAMN!
NO...
THIS SHOT WILL FINISH THE GAME!
WOW
......
....

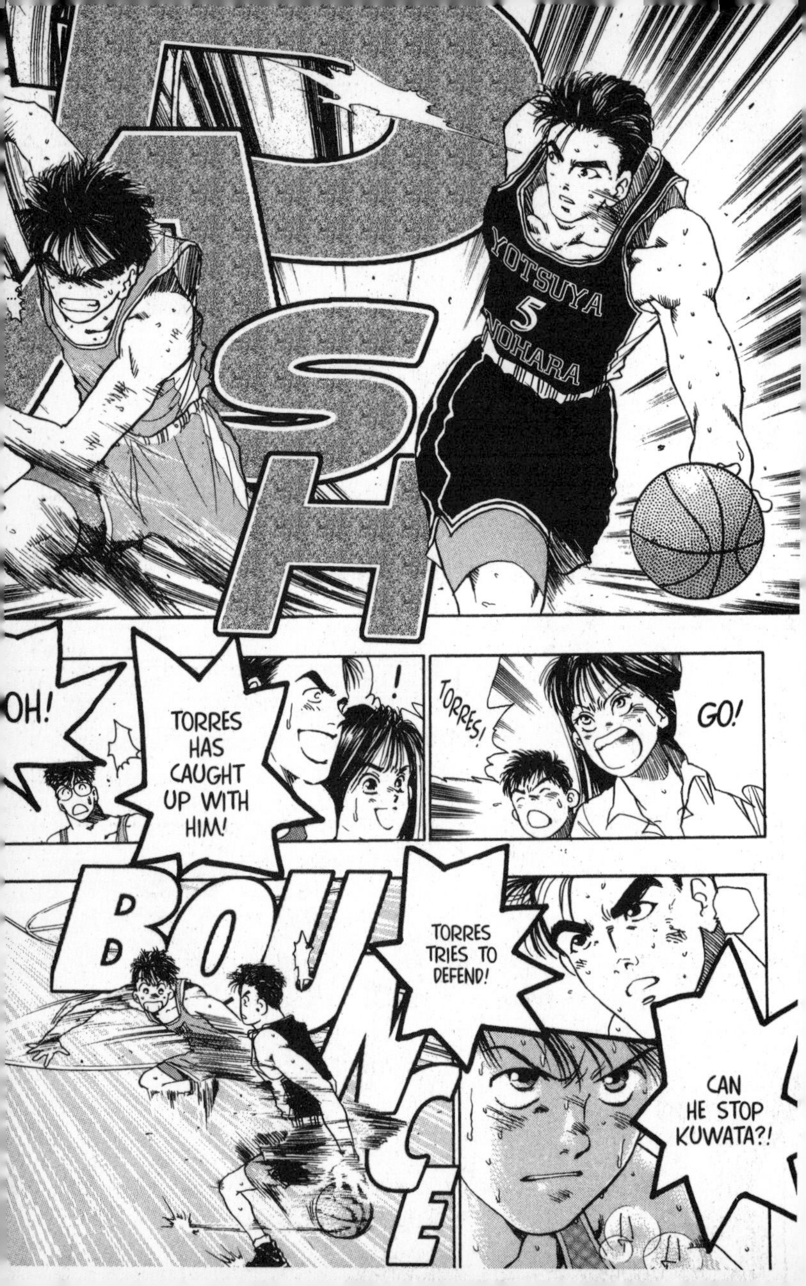
DASH
YOTSUYA 5 NOHARA
OH!
TORRES HAS CAUGHT UP WITH HIM!
!
TORRES!
GO!
BOUNCE
TORRES TRIES TO DEFEND!
CAN HE STOP KUWATA?!

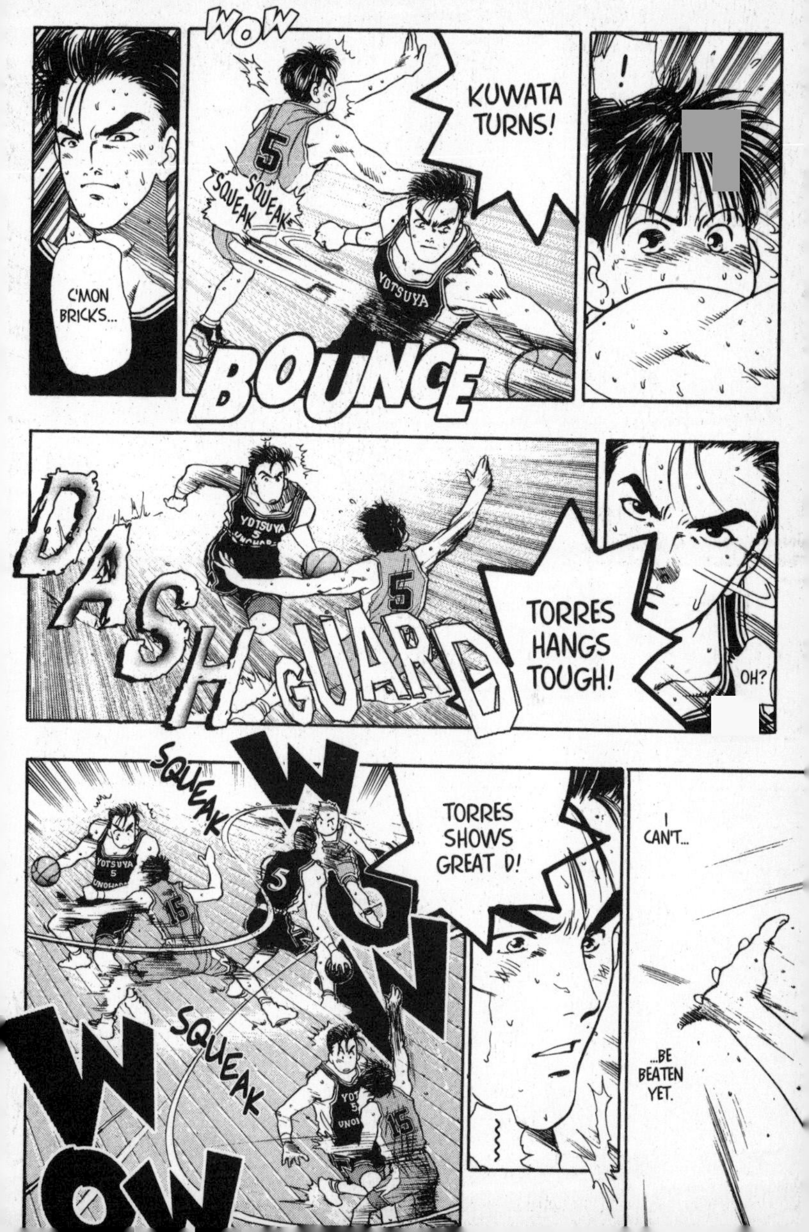
!
WOW
KUWATA TURNS!
SQUEAK
SQUEAK
BOUNCE
C'MON BRICKS...
OH?
TORRES HANGS TOUGH!
DASH
GUARD
I CAN'T...
...BE BEATEN YET.
TORRES SHOWS GREAT D!
WOW
SQUEAK
SQUEAK
WOW

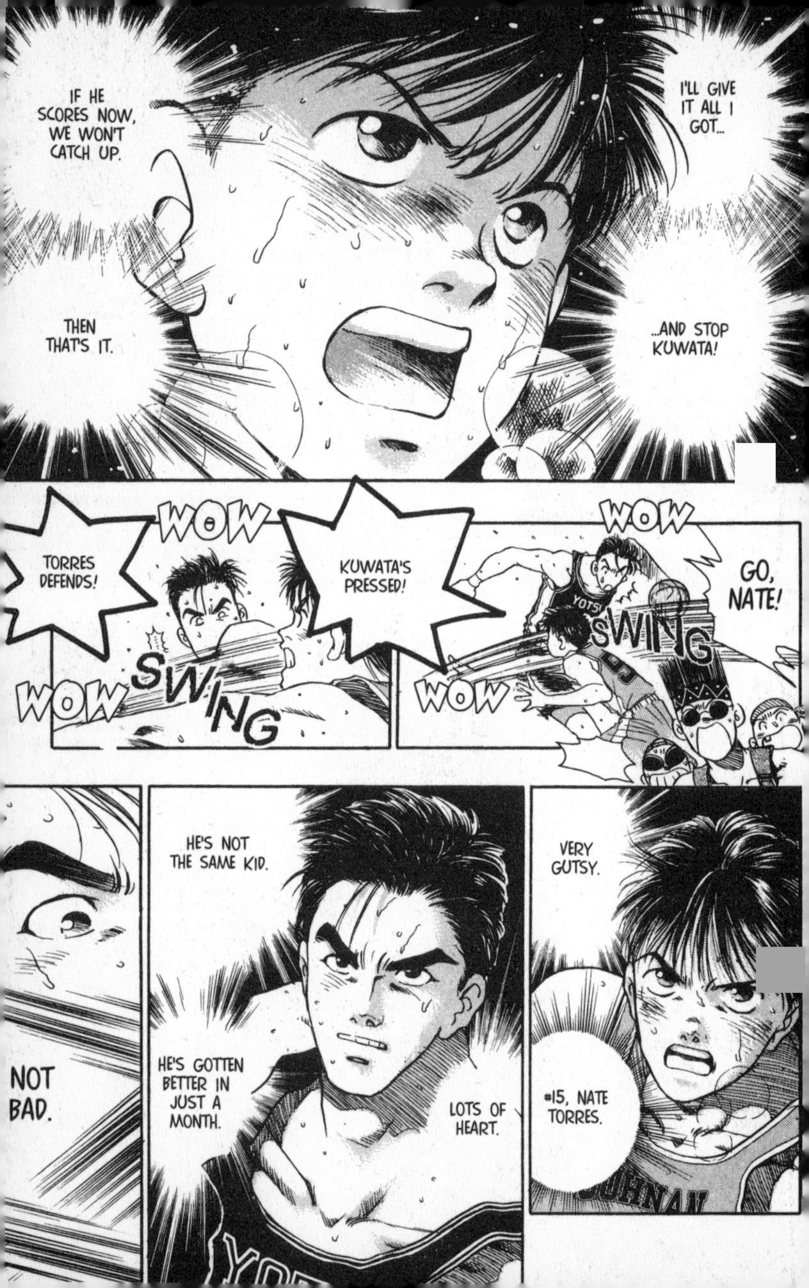
I'LL GIVE IT ALL I GOT...
...AND STOP KUWATA!
IF HE SCORES NOW, WE WON'T CATCH UP.
THEN THAT'S IT.
WOW
GO, NATE!
SWING
WOW
KUWATA'S PRESSED!
WOW
TORRES DEFENDS!
SWING
WOW
VERY GUTSY.
#15, NATE TORRES.
HE'S NOT THE SAME KID.
HE'S GOTTEN BETTER IN JUST A MONTH.
LOTS OF HEART.
NOT BAD.

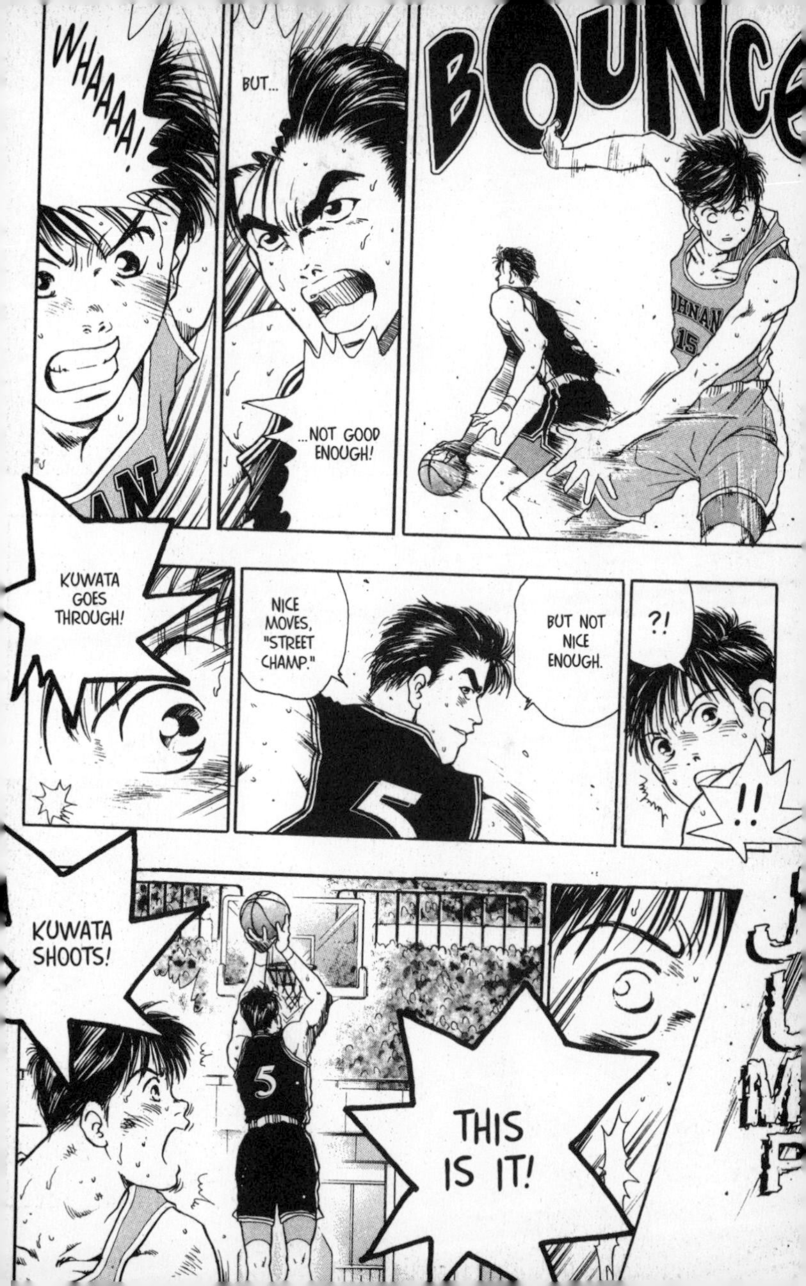
WHAAAAA!
BUT...
...NOT GOOD ENOUGH!
BOUNCE
KUWATA GOES THROUGH!
NICE MOVES, "STREET CHAMP."
BUT NOT NICE ENOUGH.
?!
!!
KUWATA SHOOTS!
THIS IS IT!

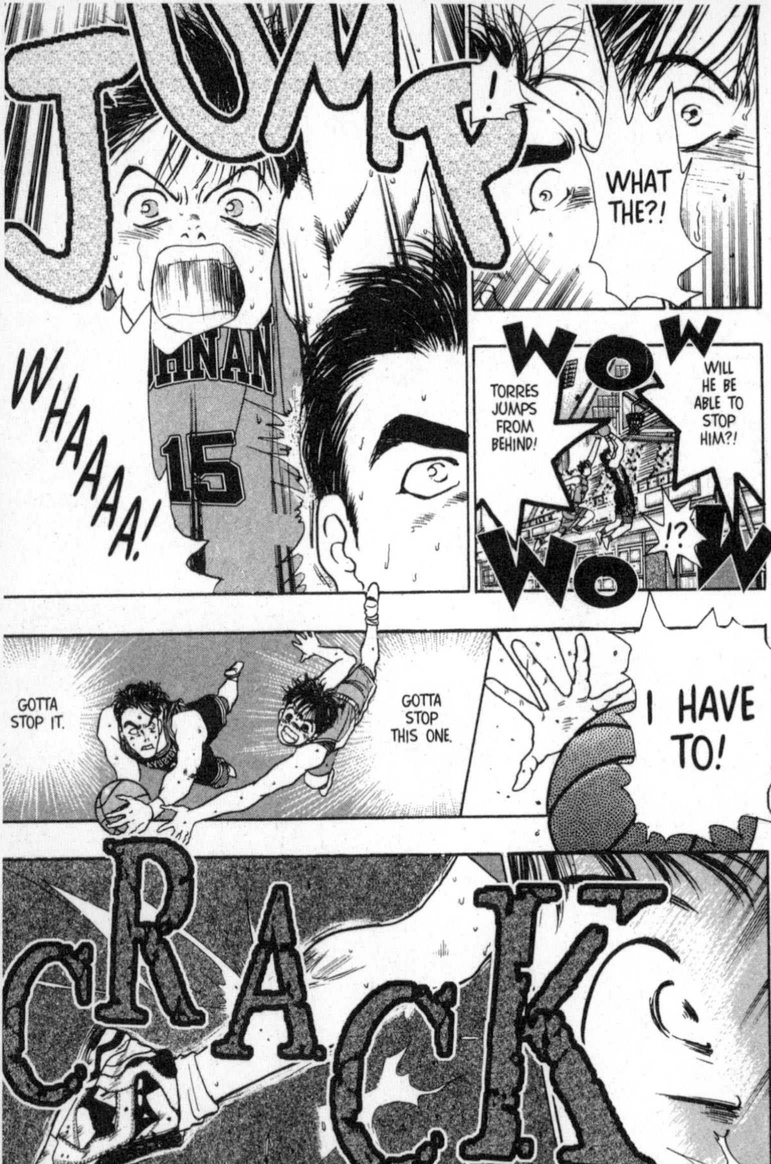
WHAT THE?!
JUMP
!
WHAAAAA!
WOW WOW
WILL HE BE ABLE TO STOP HIM?!
TORRES JUMPS FROM BEHIND!
!?
I HAVE TO!
GOTTA STOP THIS ONE.
GOTTA STOP IT.
CRACK

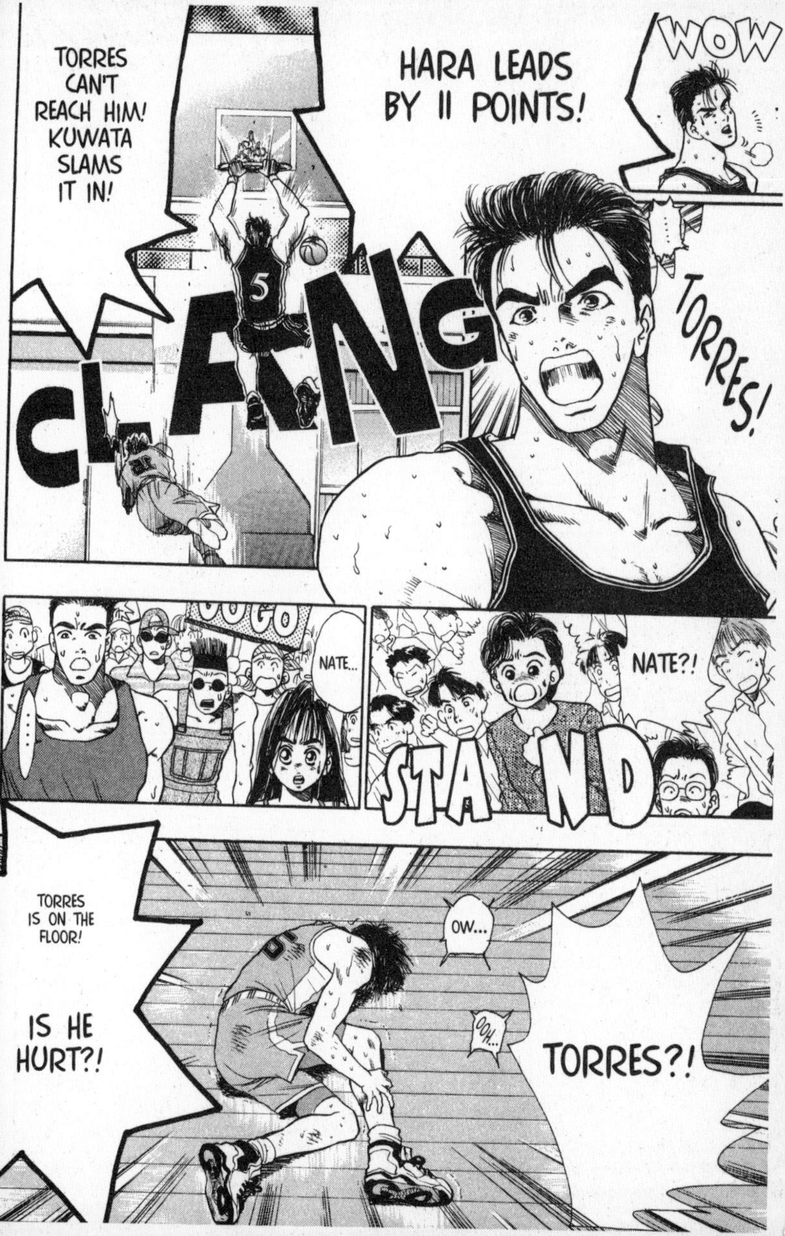
TORRES CAN'T REACH HIM! KUWATA SLAMS IT IN!
CLANG
HARA LEADS BY 11 POINTS!
WOW
...
TORRES!
NATE...
NATE?!
STAND
TORRES IS ON THE FLOOR!
IS HE HURT?!
OW...
OOH...
TORRES?!

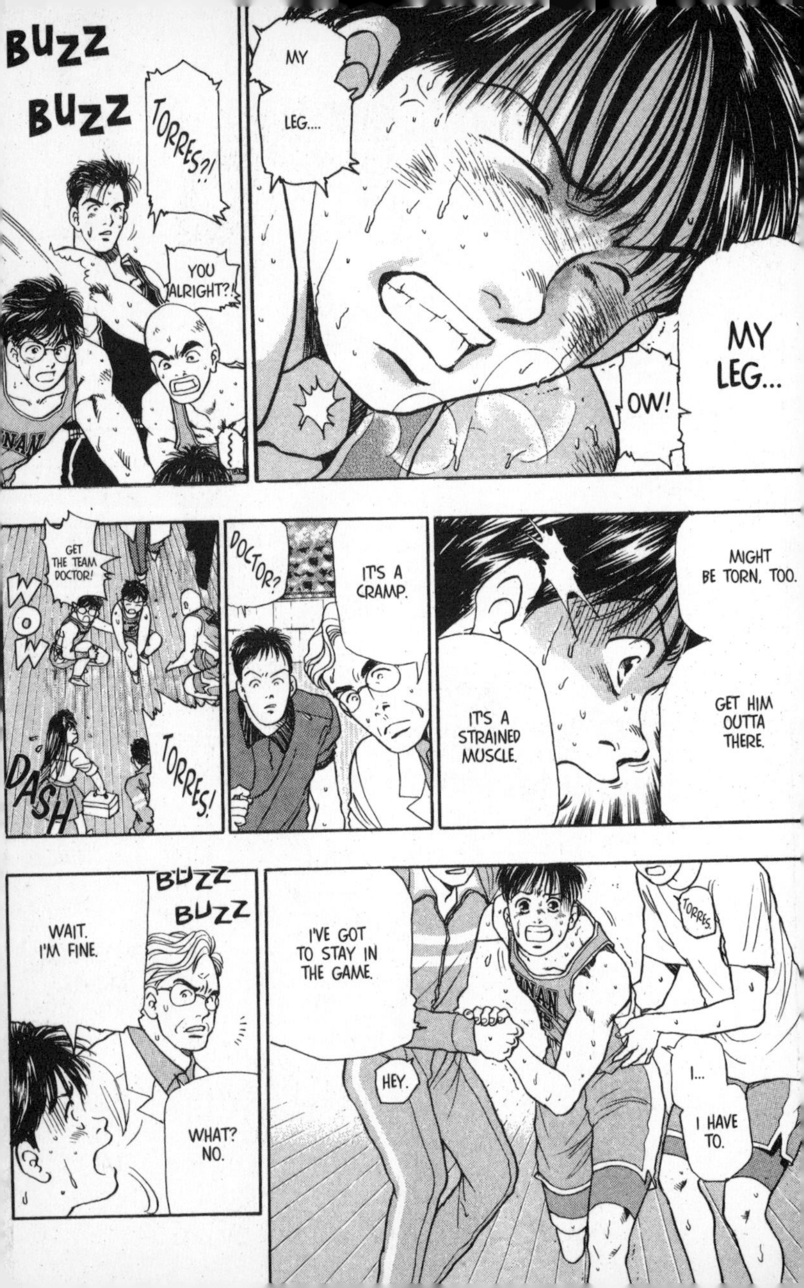
BUZZ
BUZZ
TORRES?!
YOU ALRIGHT?!
MY LEG....
OW!
MY LEG...
GET THE TEAM DOCTOR!
WOW
DASH
TORRES!
DOCTOR?
IT'S A CRAMP.
MIGHT BE TORN, TOO.
IT'S A STRAINED MUSCLE.
GET HIM OUTTA THERE.
BUZZ
BUZZ
WAIT. I'M FINE.
WHAT? NO.
I'VE GOT TO STAY IN THE GAME.
TORRES.
HEY.
I...
I HAVE TO.

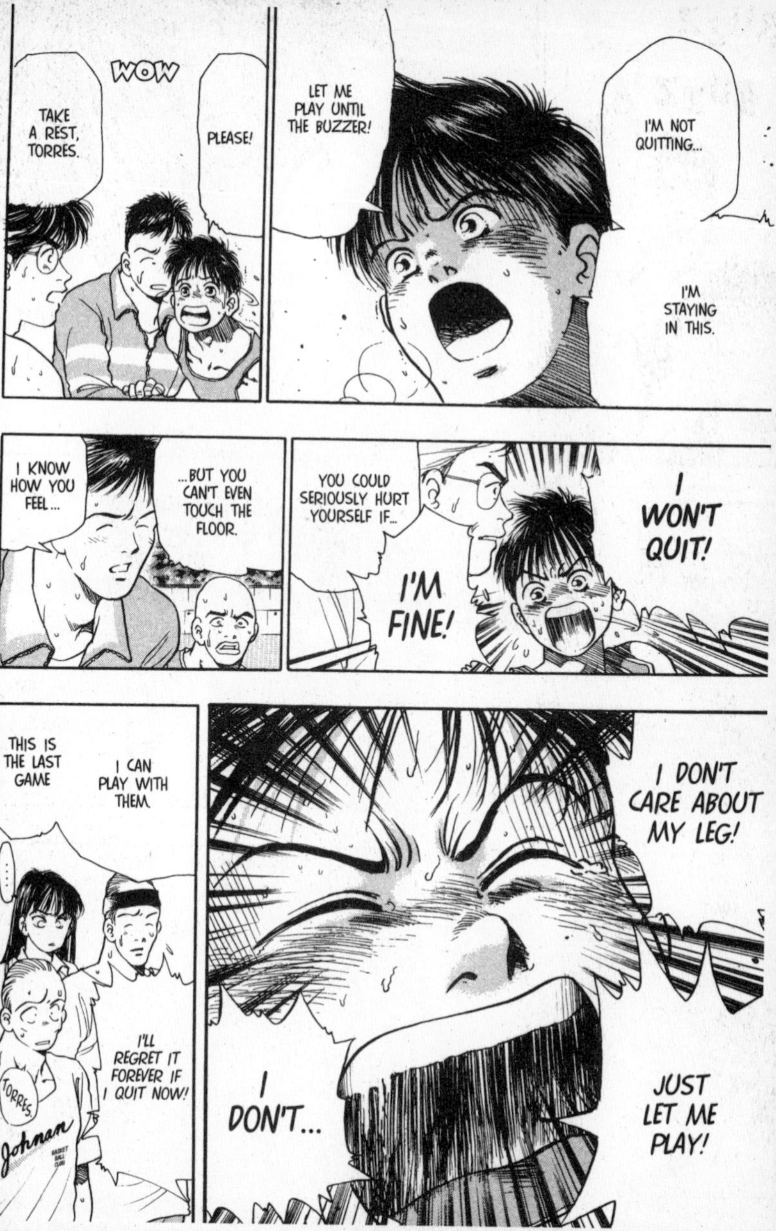
TAKE A REST, TORRES.
WOW
PLEASE!
LET ME PLAY UNTIL THE BUZZER!
I'M NOT QUITTING...
I'M STAYING IN THIS.
I KNOW HOW YOU FEEL...
...BUT YOU CAN'T EVEN TOUCH THE FLOOR.
YOU COULD SERIOUSLY HURT YOURSELF IF...
I'M FINE!
I WON'T QUIT!
THIS IS THE LAST GAME
I CAN PLAY WITH THEM.
...
I'LL REGRET IT FOREVER IF I QUIT NOW!
TORRES.
Johnan
I DON'T CARE ABOUT MY LEG!
I DON'T...
JUST LET ME PLAY!

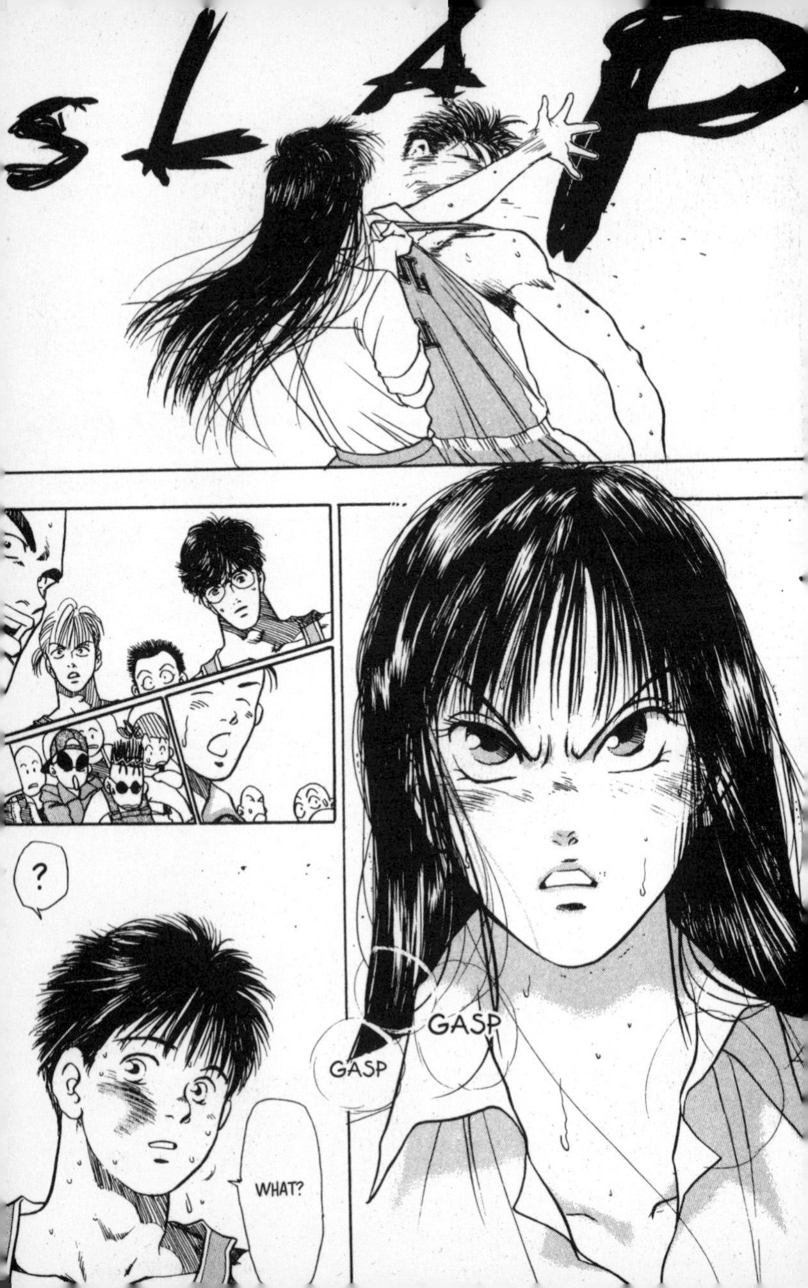
SLAP
GASP
GASP
?
WHAT?

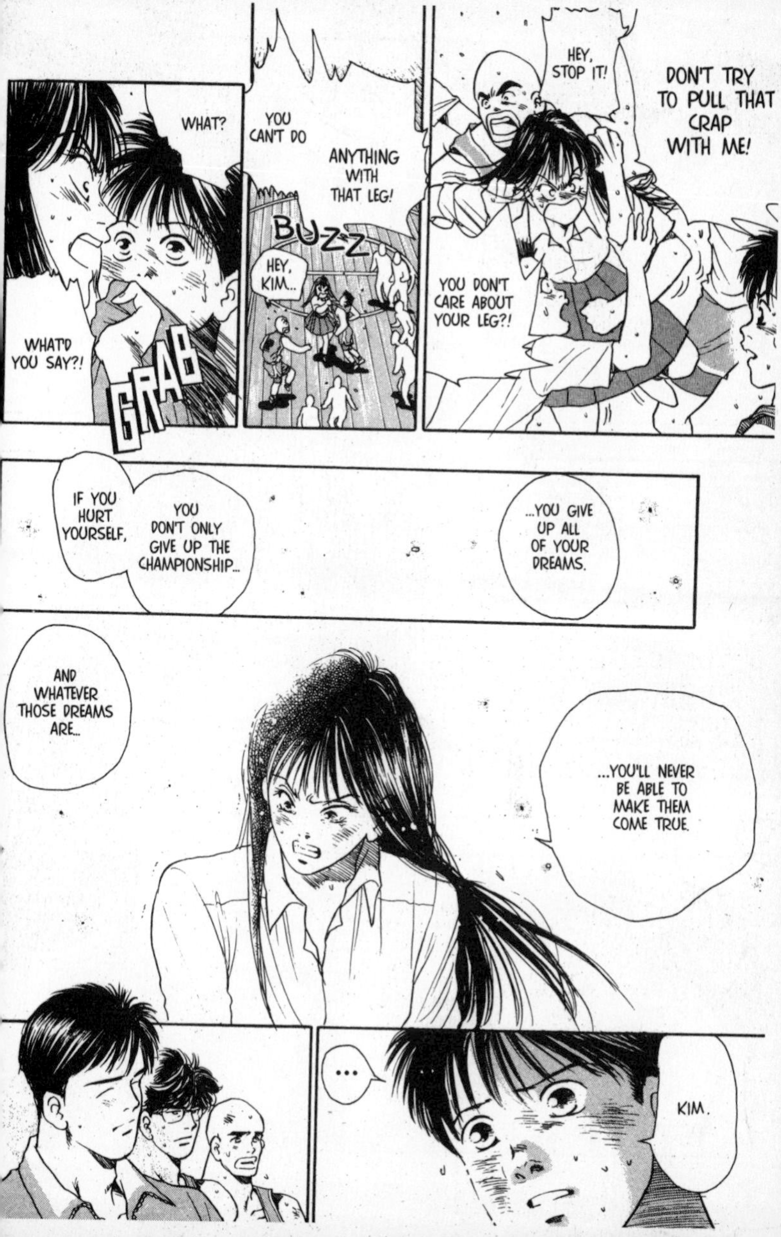
WHAT?
WHAT'D YOU SAY?!
GRAB
YOU CAN'T DO
ANYTHING WITH THAT LEG!
BUZZ
HEY, KIM...
HEY, STOP IT!
DON'T TRY TO PULL THAT CRAP WITH ME!
YOU DON'T CARE ABOUT YOUR LEG?!
IF YOU HURT YOURSELF,
YOU DON'T ONLY GIVE UP THE CHAMPIONSHIP...
...YOU GIVE UP ALL OF YOUR DREAMS.
AND WHATEVER THOSE DREAMS ARE...
...YOU'LL NEVER BE ABLE TO MAKE THEM COME TRUE.
...
KIM.

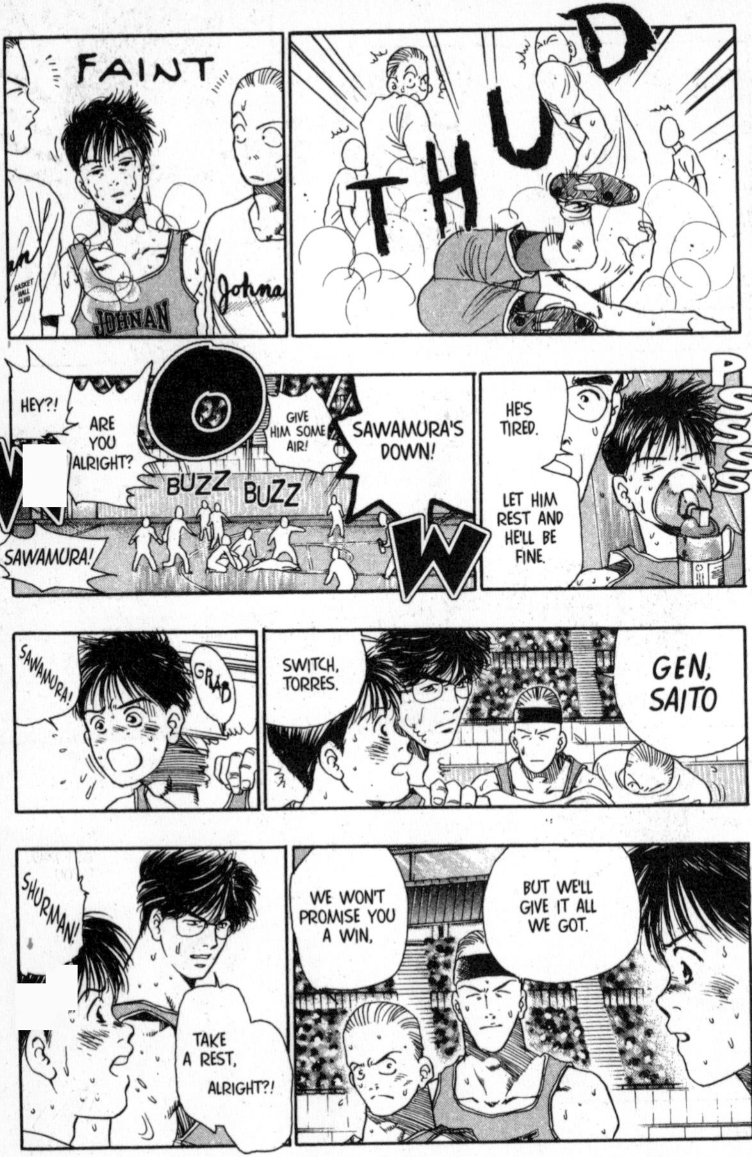
FAINT
THUD
HEY?!
ARE YOU ALRIGHT?
SAWAMURA!
WOW
BUZZ BUZZ
GIVE HIM SOME AIR!
SAWAMURA'S DOWN!
HE'S TIRED.
LET HIM REST AND HE'LL BE FINE.
PSSSS
SAWAMURA!
GRAB
SWITCH, TORRES.
GEN, SAITO
SHURMAN!
TAKE A REST, ALRIGHT?!
WE WON'T PROMISE YOU A WIN,
BUT WE'LL GIVE IT ALL WE GOT.

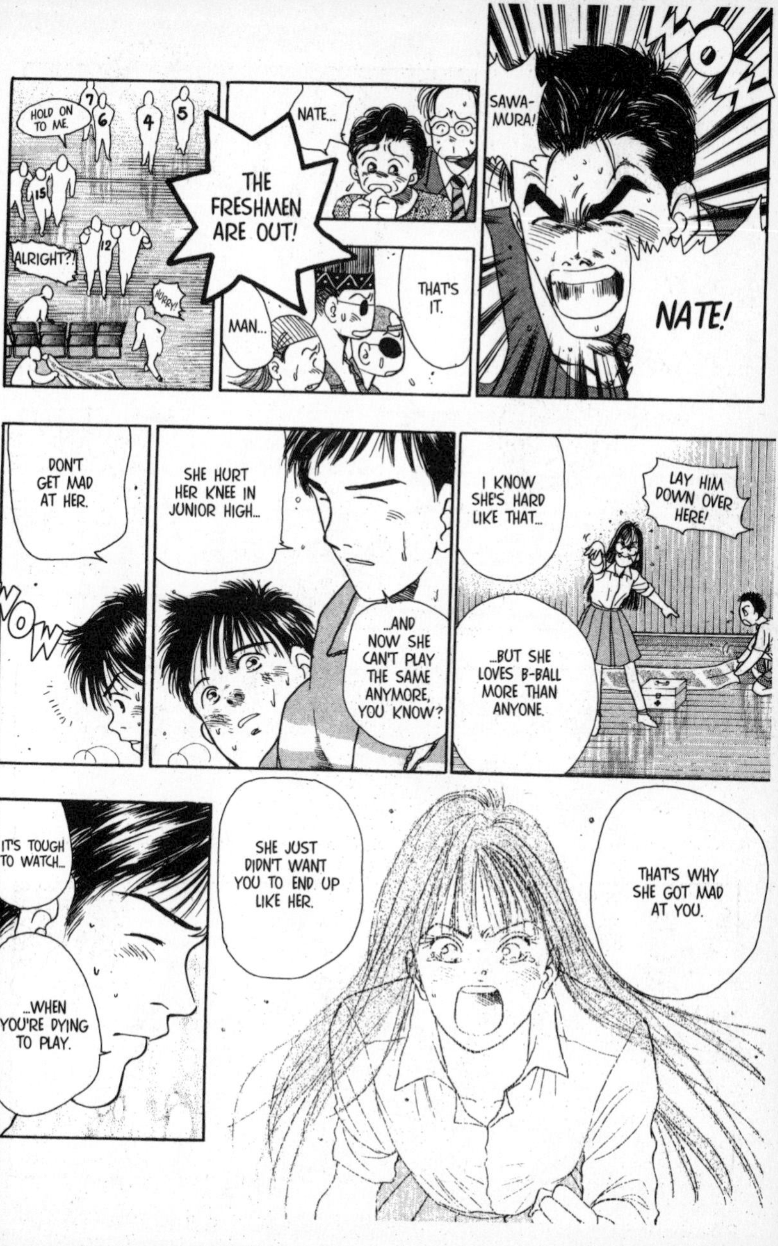
WOW
SAWA-MURA!
NATE!
NATE...
THE FRESHMEN ARE OUT!
THAT'S IT.
MAN...
HOLD ON TO ME.
ALRIGHT?!
HURRY!
LAY HIM DOWN OVER HERE!
I KNOW SHE'S HARD LIKE THAT...
...BUT SHE LOVES B-BALL MORE THAN ANYONE.
SHE HURT HER KNEE IN JUNIOR HIGH...
...AND NOW SHE CAN'T PLAY THE SAME ANYMORE, YOU KNOW?
DON'T GET MAD AT HER.
WOW
THAT'S WHY SHE GOT MAD AT YOU.
SHE JUST DIDN'T WANT YOU TO END UP LIKE HER.
IT'S TOUGH TO WATCH...
...WHEN YOU'RE DYING TO PLAY.

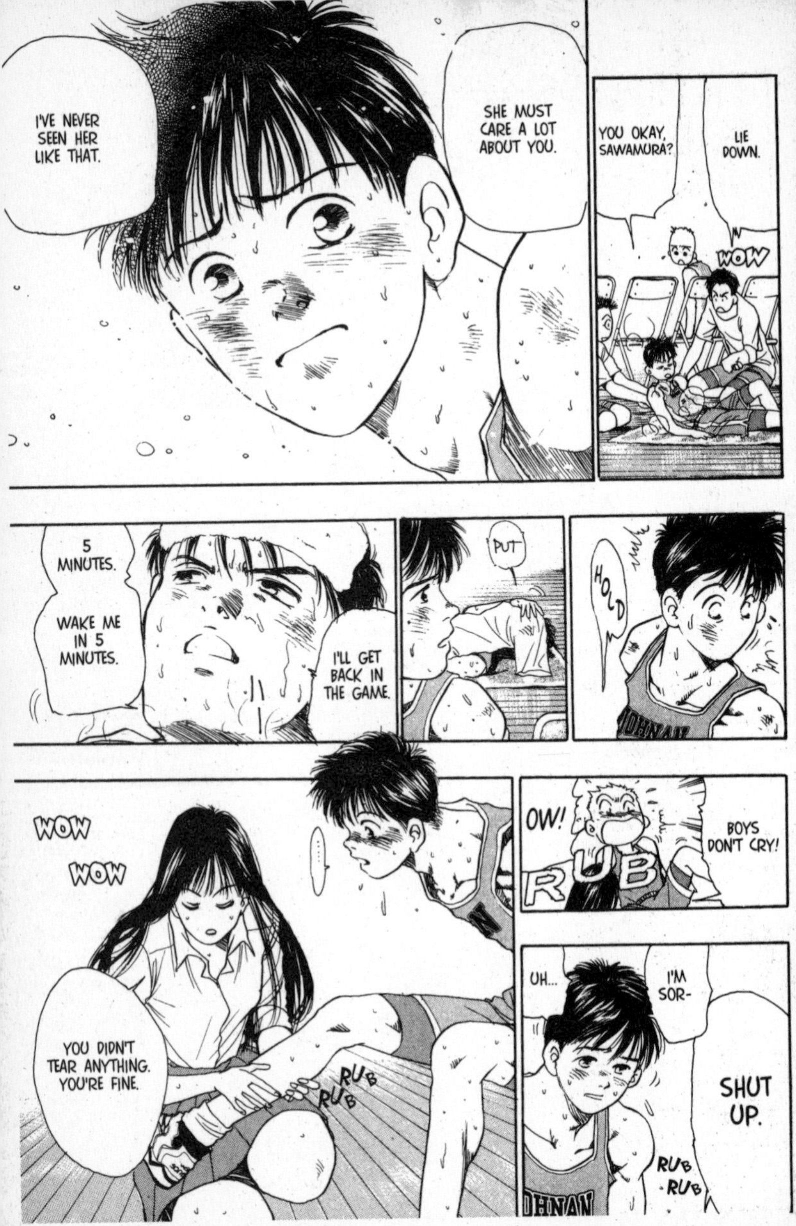
I'VE NEVER SEEN HER LIKE THAT.
SHE MUST CARE A LOT ABOUT YOU.
YOU OKAY, SAWAMURA?
LIE DOWN.
WOW
5 MINUTES.
WAKE ME IN 5 MINUTES.
I'LL GET BACK IN THE GAME.
PUT
HOLD
WOW
WOW
...
YOU DIDN'T TEAR ANYTHING. YOU'RE FINE.
RUB RUB
OW!
BOYS DON'T CRY!
RUB
UH...
I'M SOR-
SHUT UP.
RUB RUB

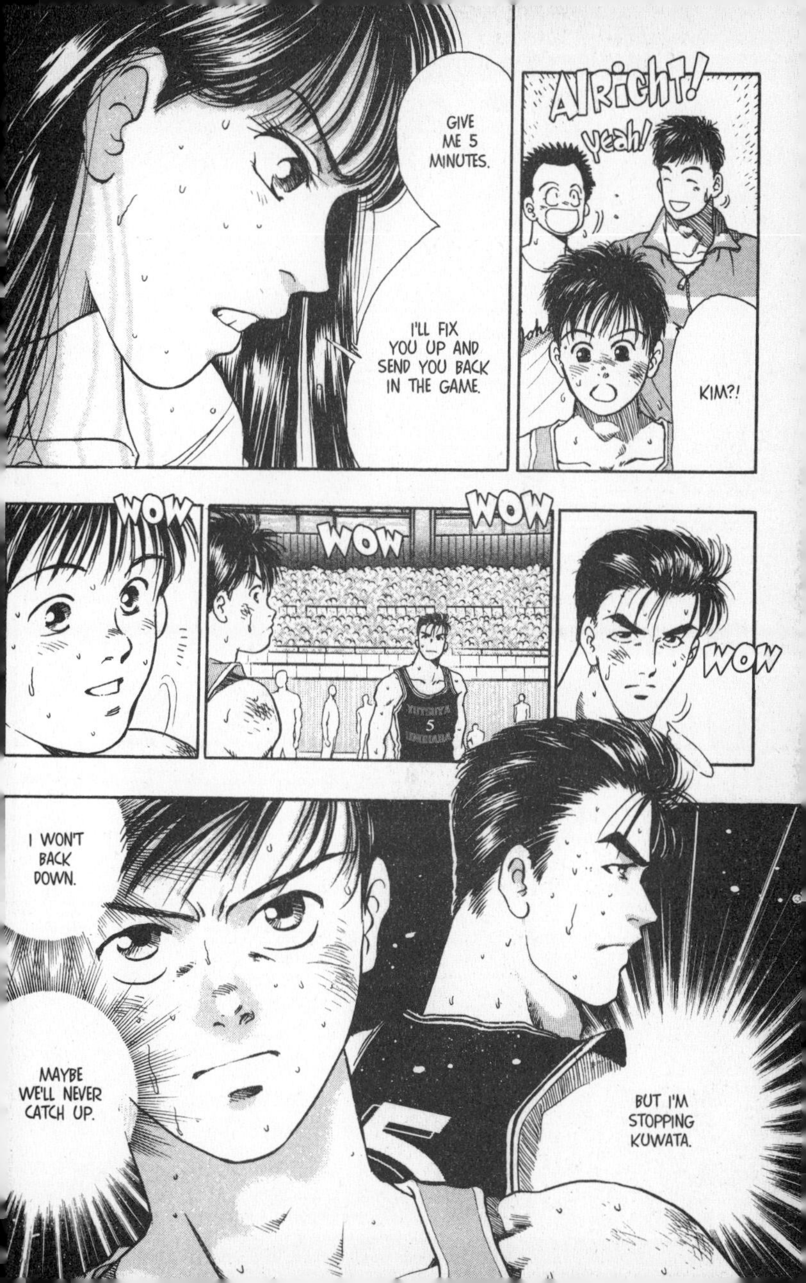
GIVE ME 5 MINUTES.
I'LL FIX YOU UP AND SEND YOU BACK IN THE GAME.
AlRIGHT!
yeah!
KIM?!
WOW
WOW
WOW
WOW
I WON'T BACK DOWN.
MAYBE WE'LL NEVER CATCH UP.
BUT I'M STOPPING KUWATA.

HB Character Profile

PROFILE

BACK WITH GRE DEMAND

NAME	RY SHURMAN	YASUHIKO KUWATA	NAOSUGU KOBAYASHI	KIM YABE
BIRTHDAY & BLOOD TYPE	11/20 O	8/1 B	1/21 O	12/20 B
HEIGHT	6'2"	6'1"	6'1"	5'6"
WEIGHT	180lb	171lb	165lb	I'M NOT TELLING!
SHOES	NEW BALANCE BB800	BACK-JAM MID CONVERSE	AXL DANCER PRO MIZUNO	
FAVORITE DRINK	COFFEE RATHER THAN TEA, COCOA	LOVE GULPING MILK	WATER, GREEN TEA, SAKE	
FAVORITE BOOK	ON INDIVIDUALISM BY SOSEKI NATSUME	LOSERS BY KOTARO SAWAKI ONIDAIRA HANKACHO BY SHOTARO IKENAMI	~~JUST~~ ~~SAY~~ MAGAZINE	SUCK UP MAGAZINE
BELIEVE IN SPIRITS	MAYBE THEY EXIST, BUT I HAVE TO SEE'EM.	I WANT TO SEE "KITARO" OR "Q-CHAN." HA, HA, HA.	THEY'RE IN MY STORAGE.	I'M THE DEVIL, HUMPH!
WHO'S YOUR TYPE?	KIND GIRLS, MAYBE.	GIRLS WHO FIX ME MY LUNCH WITH SOME FRIED EGGS.	LET'S NOT DO THIS AGAIN.	FORGET IT AND GET TO WORK!

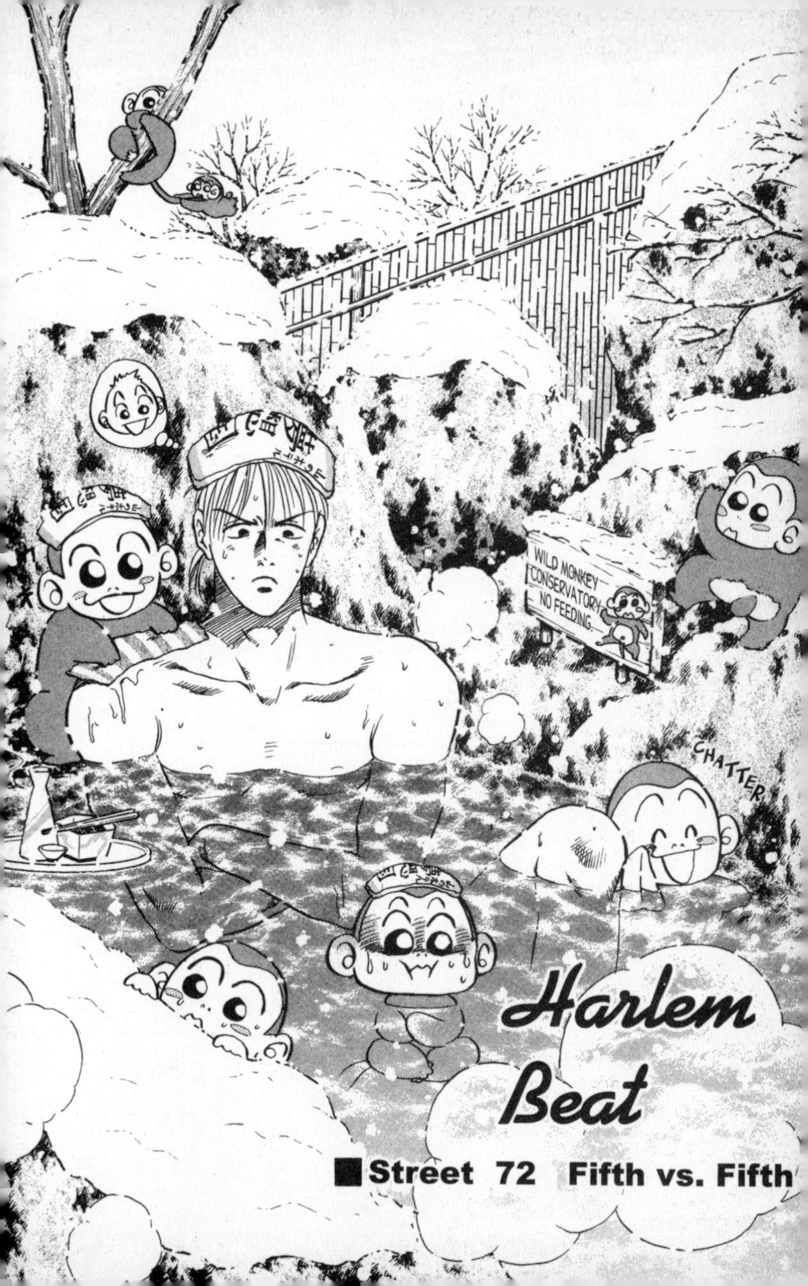
WILD MONKEY CONSERVATORY NO FEEDING.
CHATTER
Harlem Beat
■Street 72 Fifth vs. Fifth

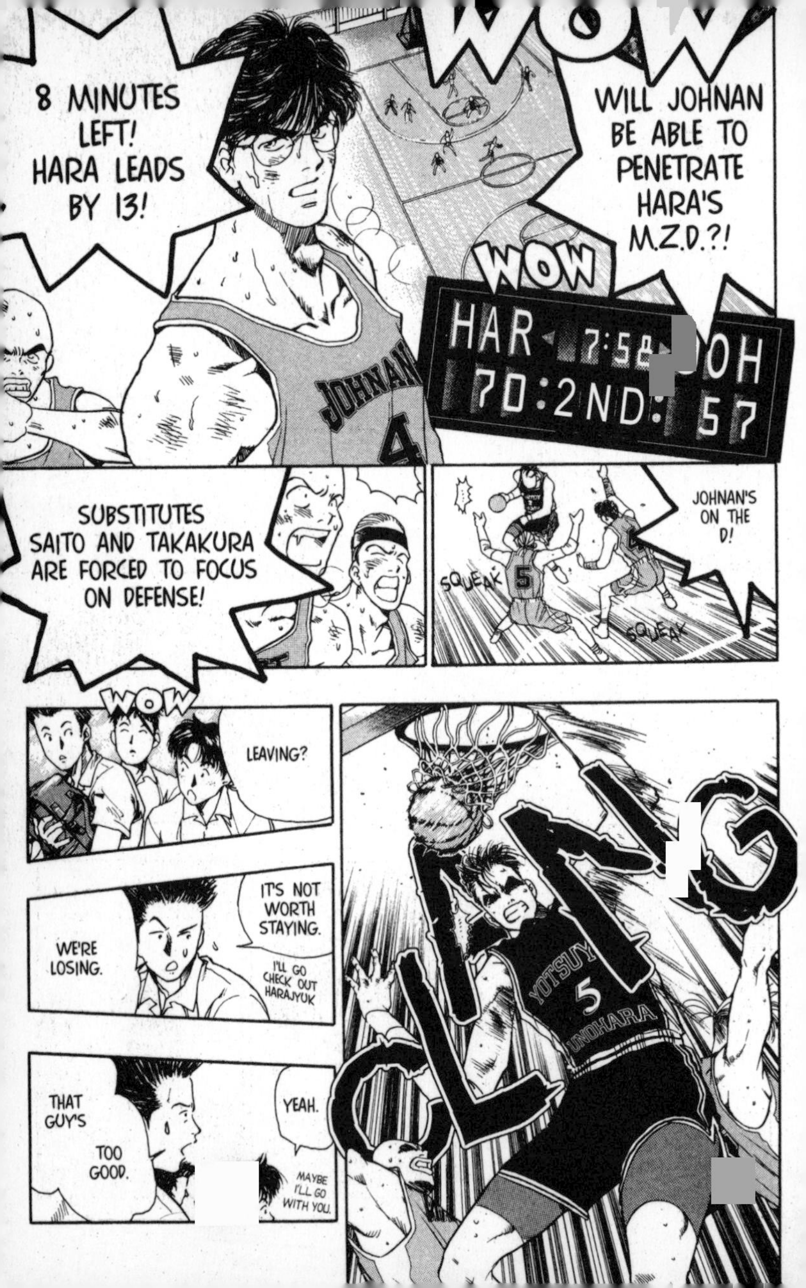
WOW
8 MINUTES LEFT! HARA LEADS BY 13!
WILL JOHNAN BE ABLE TO PENETRATE HARA'S M.Z.D.?!
WOW
HAR 7:58 OH
70 2ND 57
SUBSTITUTES SAITO AND TAKAKURA ARE FORCED TO FOCUS ON DEFENSE!
JOHNAN'S ON THE D!
SQUEAK
SQUEAK
WOW
LEAVING?
WE'RE LOSING.
IT'S NOT WORTH STAYING.
I'LL GO CHECK OUT HARAJYUK
THAT GUY'S TOO GOOD.
YEAH.
MAYBE I'LL GO WITH YOU.

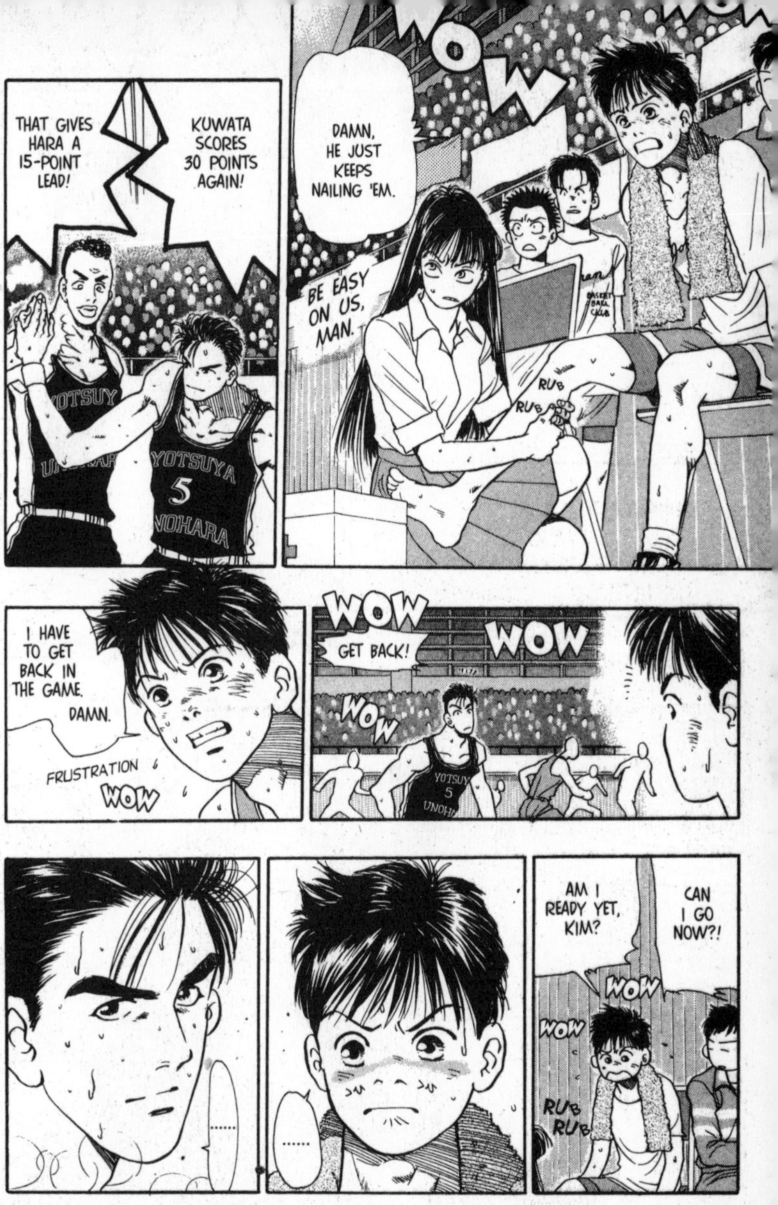
KUWATA SCORES 30 POINTS AGAIN!
THAT GIVES HARA A 15-POINT LEAD!
WOW
DAMN, HE JUST KEEPS NAILING 'EM.
BE EASY ON US, MAN.
RUB RUB
I HAVE TO GET BACK IN THE GAME.
DAMN.
FRUSTRATION
WOW
WOW
GET BACK!
WOW
WOW
......
......
AM I READY YET, KIM?
CAN I GO NOW?!
WOW
WOW
RUB RUB

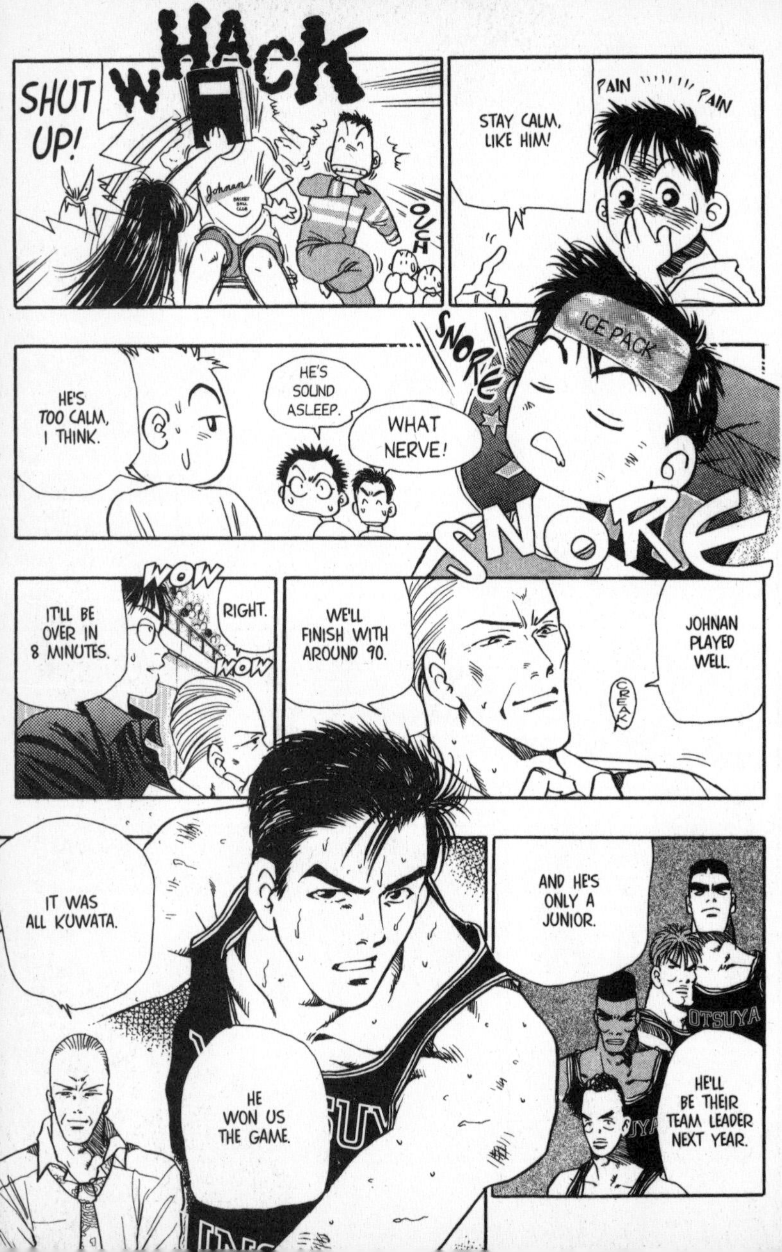
WHACK
SHUT UP!
OUCH
PAIN PAIN
STAY CALM, LIKE HIM!
ICE PACK
SNORE
HE'S TOO CALM, I THINK.
HE'S SOUND ASLEEP.
WHAT NERVE!
SNORE
WOW
IT'LL BE OVER IN 8 MINUTES.
RIGHT.
WOW
WE'LL FINISH WITH AROUND 90.
CREAK
JOHNAN PLAYED WELL.
IT WAS ALL KUWATA.
HE WON US THE GAME.
AND HE'S ONLY A JUNIOR.
HE'LL BE THEIR TEAM LEADER NEXT YEAR.

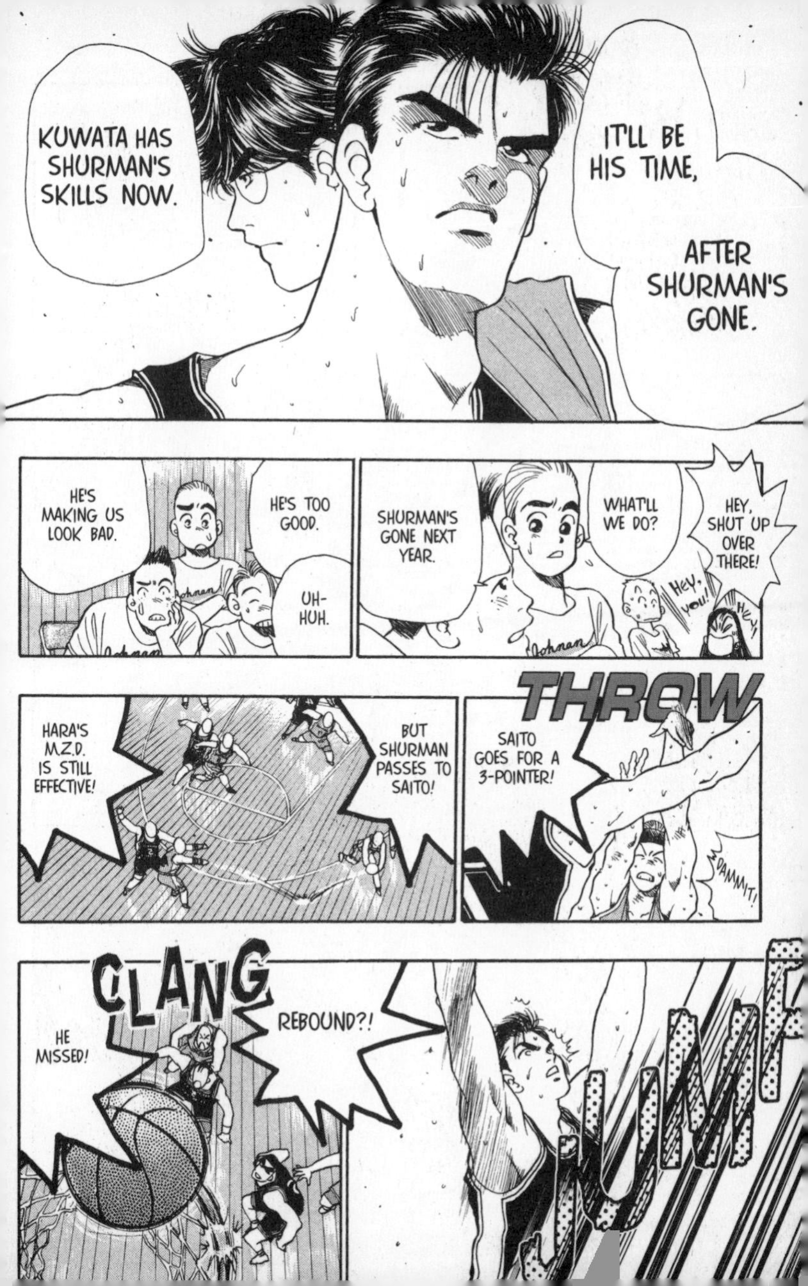
KUWATA HAS SHURMAN'S SKILLS NOW.
IT'LL BE HIS TIME,
AFTER SHURMAN'S GONE.
HE'S MAKING US LOOK BAD.
HE'S TOO GOOD.
UH-HUH.
SHURMAN'S GONE NEXT YEAR.
WHAT'LL WE DO?
HEY, SHUT UP OVER THERE!
HEY, YOU!
HEY!
HARA'S M.Z.D. IS STILL EFFECTIVE!
BUT SHURMAN PASSES TO SAITO!
THROW
SAITO GOES FOR A 3-POINTER!
DAMMIT!
CLANG
HE MISSED!
REBOUND?!

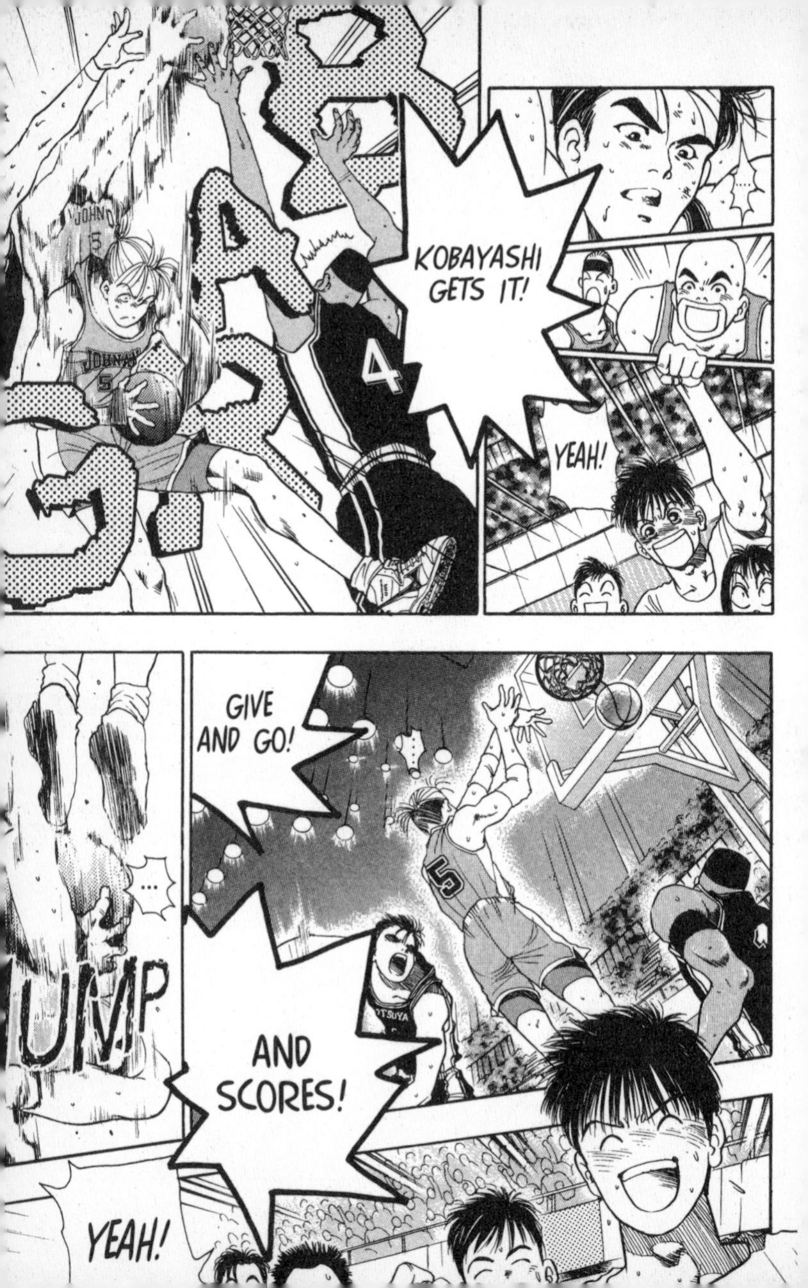
...
KOBAYASHI GETS IT!
YEAH!
GIVE AND GO!
AND SCORES!
YEAH!
...
UMP

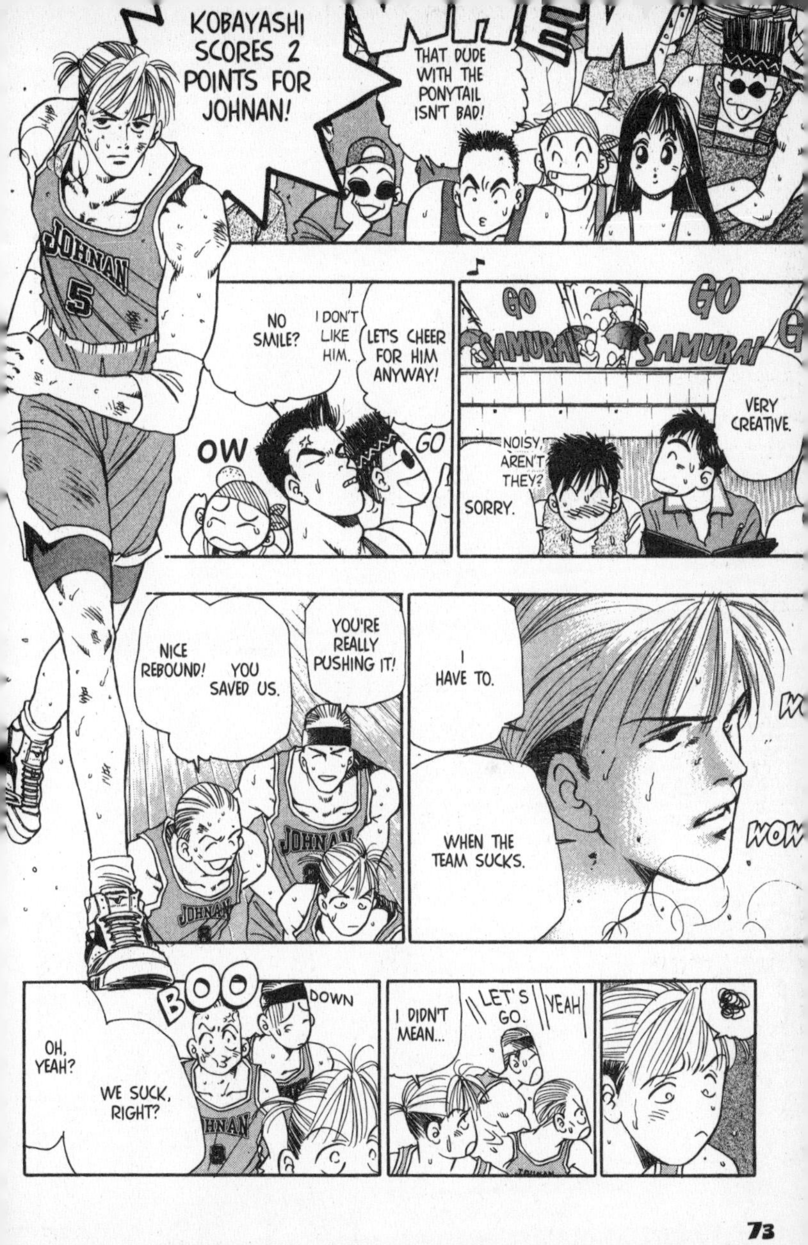
KOBAYASHI SCORES 2 POINTS FOR JOHNAN!
WHEW
THAT DUDE WITH THE PONYTAIL ISN'T BAD!
JOHNAN 5
NO SMILE?
I DON'T LIKE HIM.
LET'S CHEER FOR HIM ANYWAY!
OW
GO
GO SAMURAI
GO SAMURAI
NOISY, AREN'T THEY?
SORRY.
VERY CREATIVE.
NICE REBOUND!
YOU SAVED US.
YOU'RE REALLY PUSHING IT!
I HAVE TO.
WHEN THE TEAM SUCKS.
WOW
BOO
DOWN
OH, YEAH?
WE SUCK, RIGHT?
I DIDN'T MEAN...
LET'S GO.
YEAH

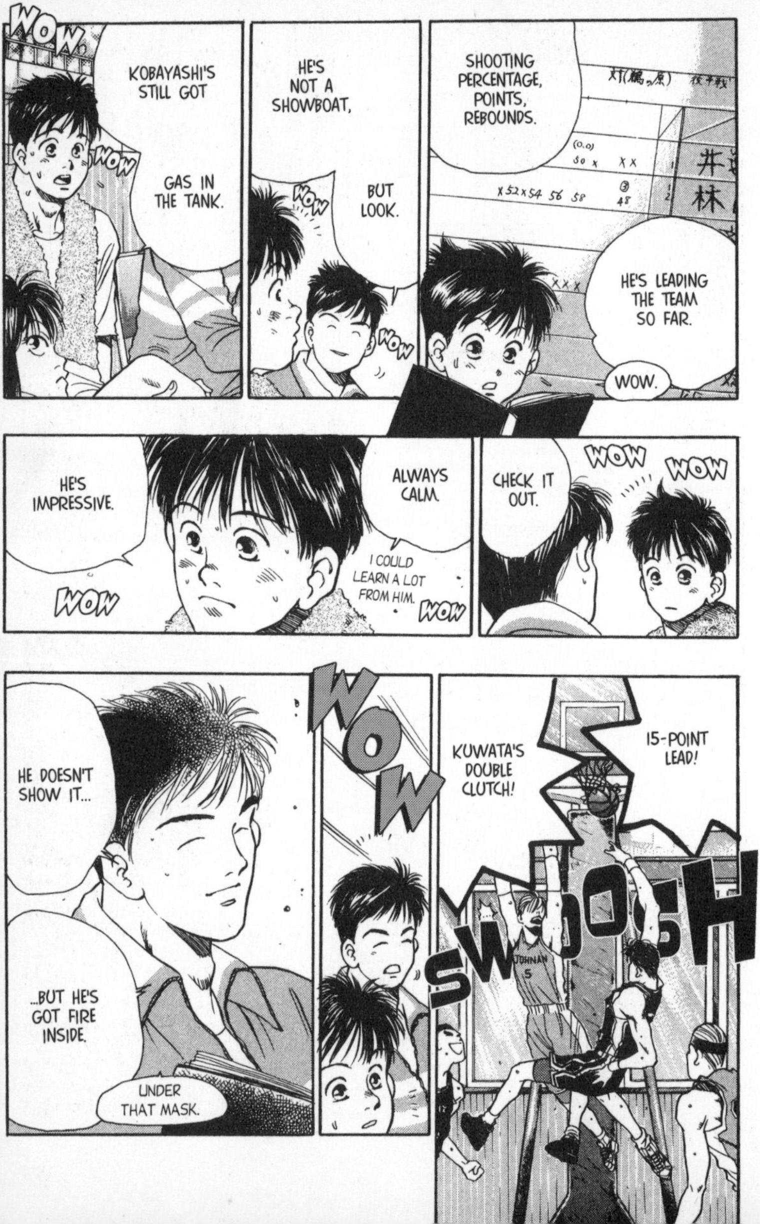
WOW
KOBAYASHI'S STILL GOT
GAS IN THE TANK.
WOW
HE'S NOT A SHOWBOAT,
BUT LOOK.
WOW
WOW
SHOOTING PERCENTAGE, POINTS, REBOUNDS.
HE'S LEADING THE TEAM SO FAR.
WOW.
HE'S IMPRESSIVE.
WOW
ALWAYS CALM.
I COULD LEARN A LOT FROM HIM.
WOW
CHECK IT OUT.
WOW
WOW
HE DOESN'T SHOW IT...
...BUT HE'S GOT FIRE INSIDE.
UNDER THAT MASK.
WOW
KUWATA'S DOUBLE CLUTCH!
15-POINT LEAD!
SWOOSH

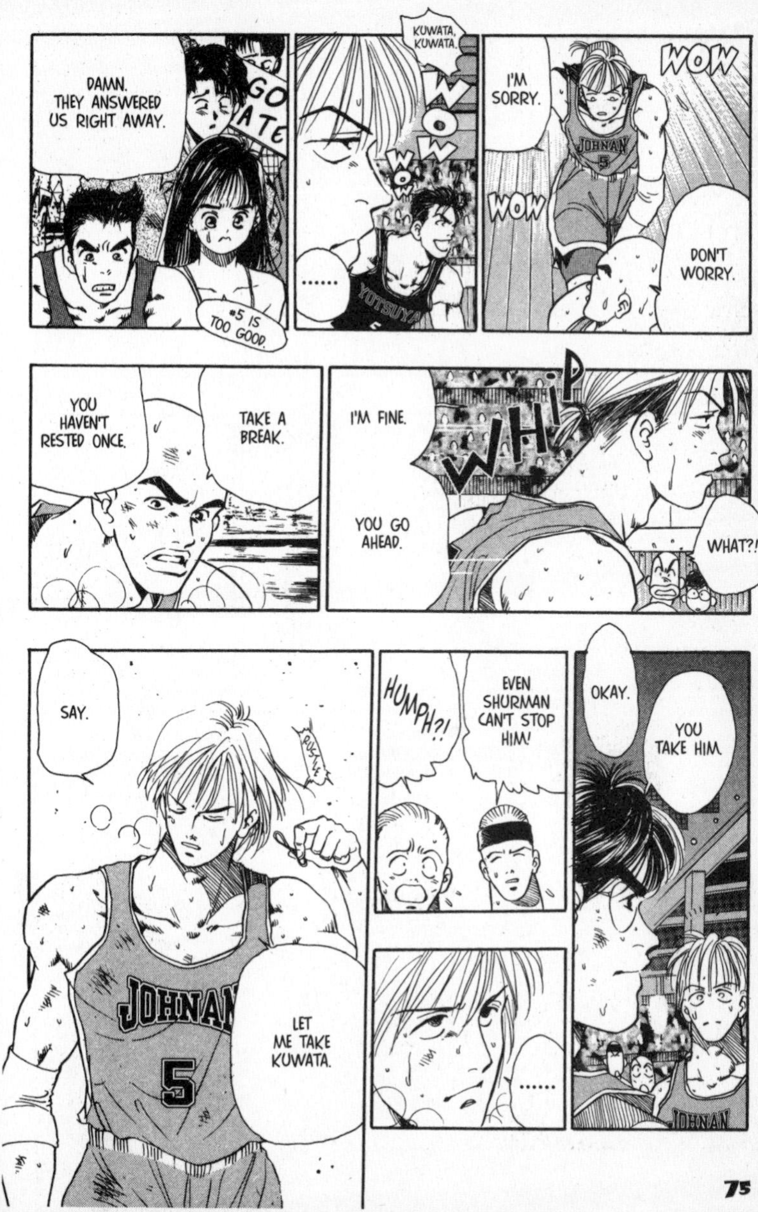
WOW
I'M SORRY.
WOW
DON'T WORRY.
KUWATA, KUWATA.
WOW
WOW
......
DAMN. THEY ANSWERED US RIGHT AWAY.
#5 IS TOO GOOD.
WHIP
I'M FINE.
YOU GO AHEAD.
WHAT?!
TAKE A BREAK.
YOU HAVEN'T RESTED ONCE.
OKAY.
YOU TAKE HIM.
EVEN SHURMAN CAN'T STOP HIM!
HUMPH?!
......
SAY.
RUSTLE
LET ME TAKE KUWATA.

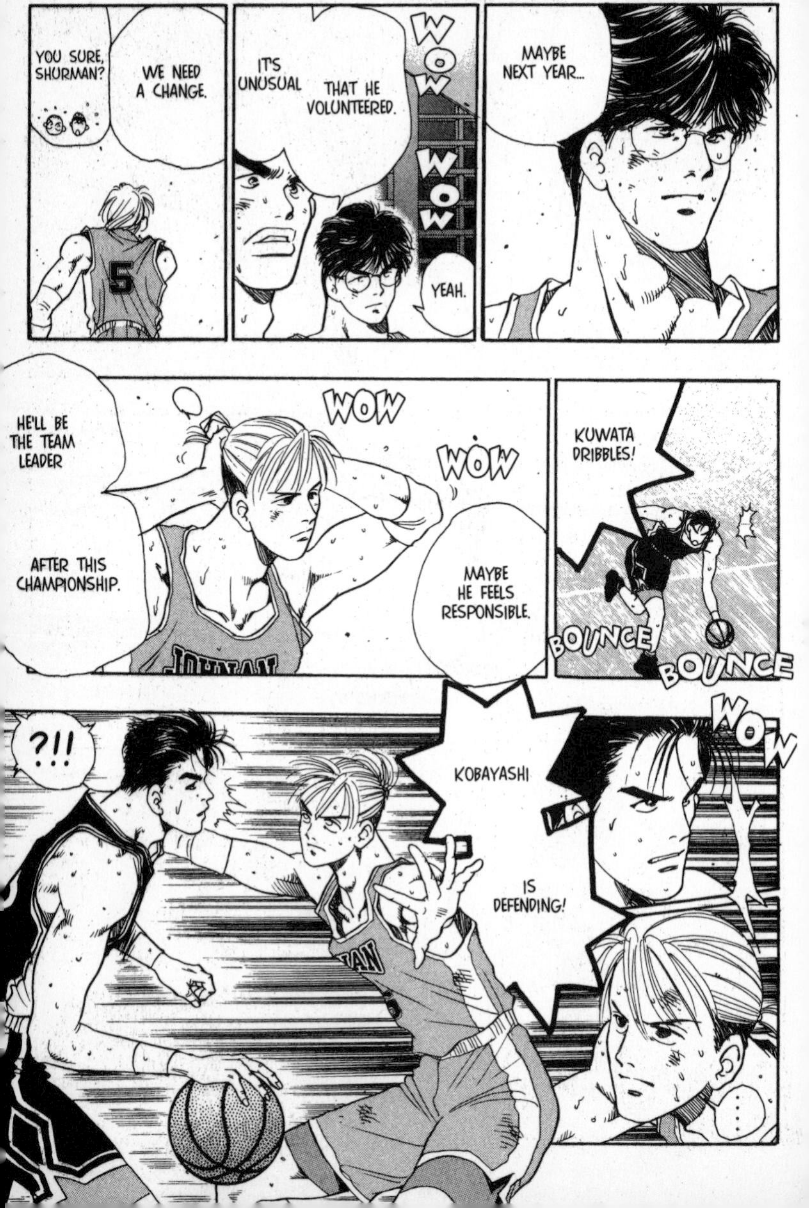
YOU SURE, SHURMAN?
WE NEED A CHANGE.
IT'S UNUSUAL
THAT HE VOLUNTEERED.
WOW WOW
WOW WOW
YEAH.
MAYBE NEXT YEAR...
HE'LL BE THE TEAM LEADER
AFTER THIS CHAMPIONSHIP.
WOW
WOW
MAYBE HE FEELS RESPONSIBLE.
KUWATA DRIBBLES!
BOUNCE
BOUNCE
?!!
KOBAYASHI
IS DEFENDING!
WOW

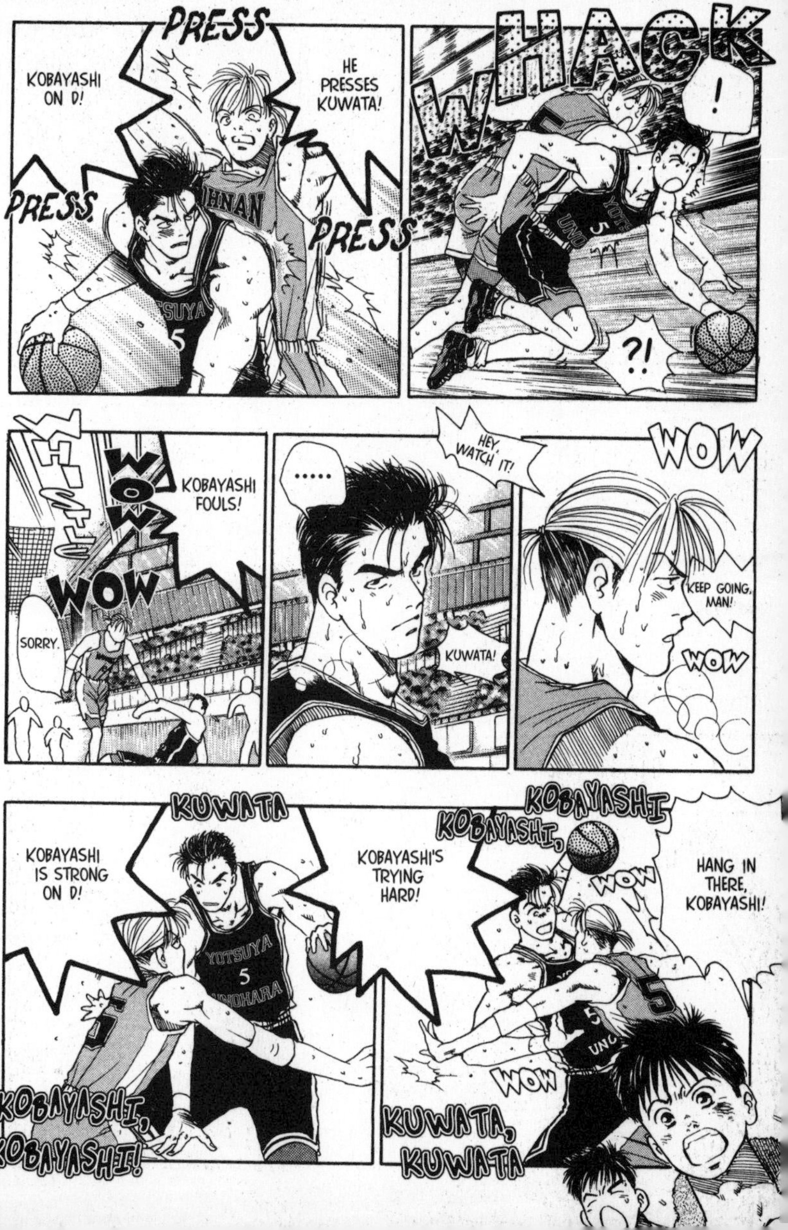
PRESS
KOBAYASHI ON D!
HE PRESSES KUWATA!
PRESS
PRESS
WHACK
!
?!
WHISTLE
WOW
WOW
WOW
KOBAYASHI FOULS!
SORRY.
......
KUWATA!
HEY, WATCH IT!
WOW
KEEP GOING, MAN!
WOW
KUWATA
KOBAYASHI IS STRONG ON D!
KOBAYASHI'S TRYING HARD!
KOBAYASHI, KOBAYASHI!
KOBAYASHI, KOBAYASHI
WOW
HANG IN THERE, KOBAYASHI!
WOW
KUWATA, KUWATA

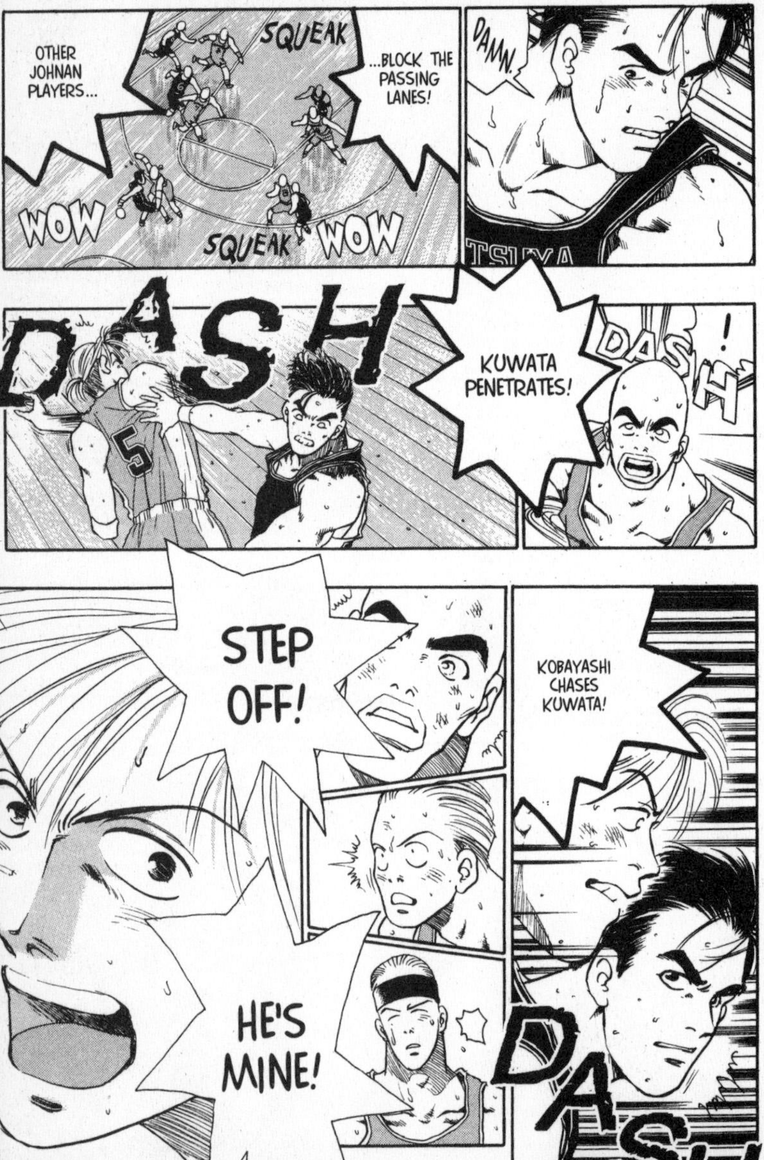
DAMN.
OTHER JOHNAN PLAYERS...
...BLOCK THE PASSING LANES!
SQUEAK
WOW
SQUEAK
WOW
DASH!
KUWATA PENETRATES!
DASH
KOBAYASHI CHASES KUWATA!
DASH
STEP OFF!
HE'S MINE!

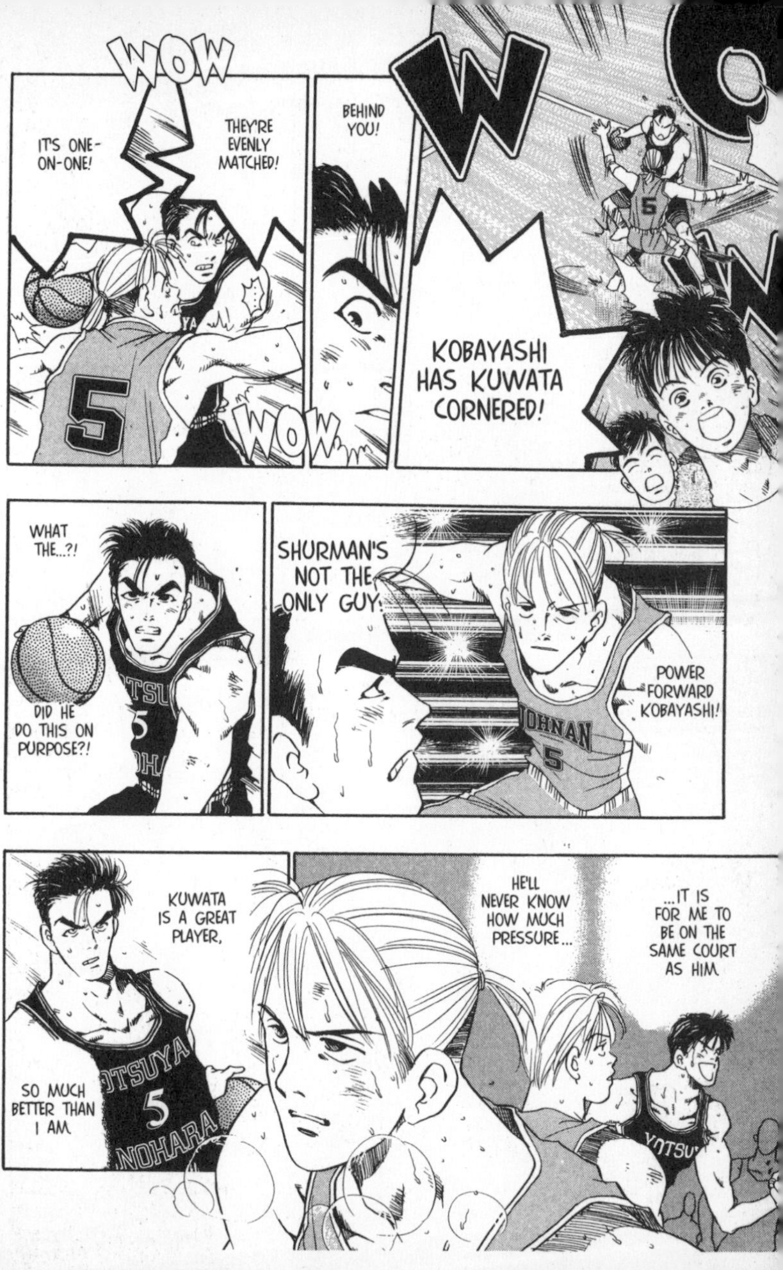
WOW
IT'S ONE-ON-ONE!
THEY'RE EVENLY MATCHED!
WOW
BEHIND YOU!
WOW
KOBAYASHI HAS KUWATA CORNERED!
WHAT THE...?!
DID HE DO THIS ON PURPOSE?!
SHURMAN'S NOT THE ONLY GUY!
POWER FORWARD KOBAYASHI!
KUWATA IS A GREAT PLAYER,
SO MUCH BETTER THAN I AM.
HE'LL NEVER KNOW HOW MUCH PRESSURE...
...IT IS FOR ME TO BE ON THE SAME COURT AS HIM.

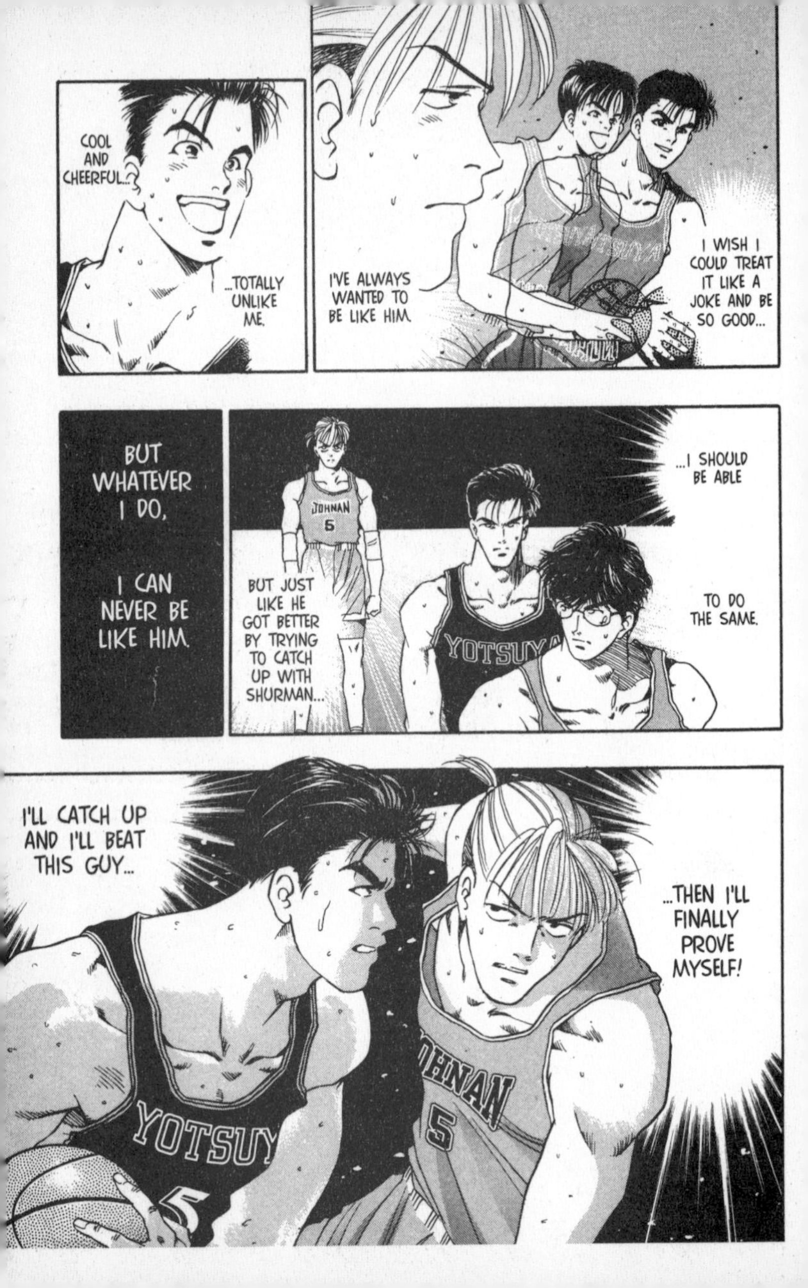
COOL AND CHEERFUL...
...TOTALLY UNLIKE ME.
I'VE ALWAYS WANTED TO BE LIKE HIM.
I WISH I COULD TREAT IT LIKE A JOKE AND BE SO GOOD...
BUT WHATEVER I DO,
I CAN NEVER BE LIKE HIM.
BUT JUST LIKE HE GOT BETTER BY TRYING TO CATCH UP WITH SHURMAN...
...I SHOULD BE ABLE
TO DO THE SAME.
I'LL CATCH UP AND I'LL BEAT THIS GUY...
...THEN I'LL FINALLY PROVE MYSELF!

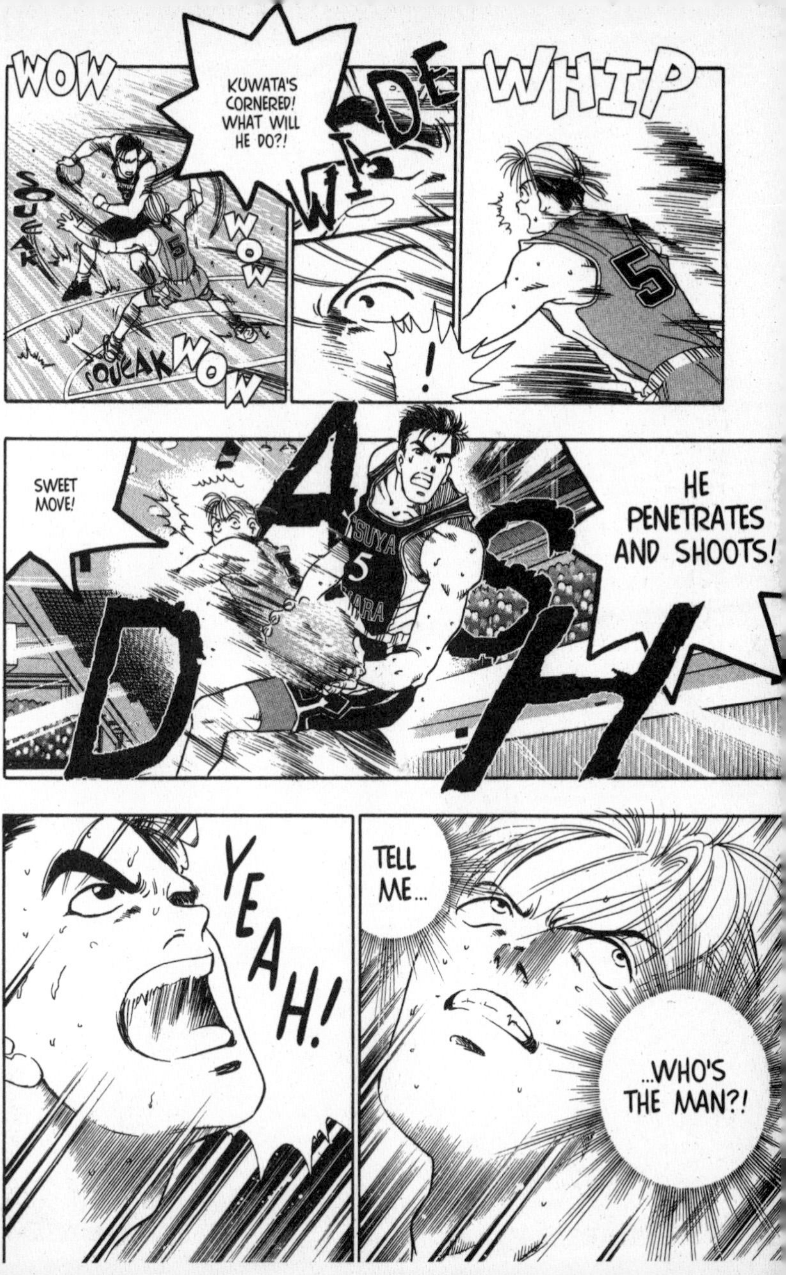
WOW
KUWATA'S CORNERED! WHAT WILL HE DO?!
SQUEAK
WOW
SQUEAK
WOW
WHIP
!
SWEET MOVE!
DASH
HE PENETRATES AND SHOOTS!
YEAH!
TELL ME...
...WHO'S THE MAN?!

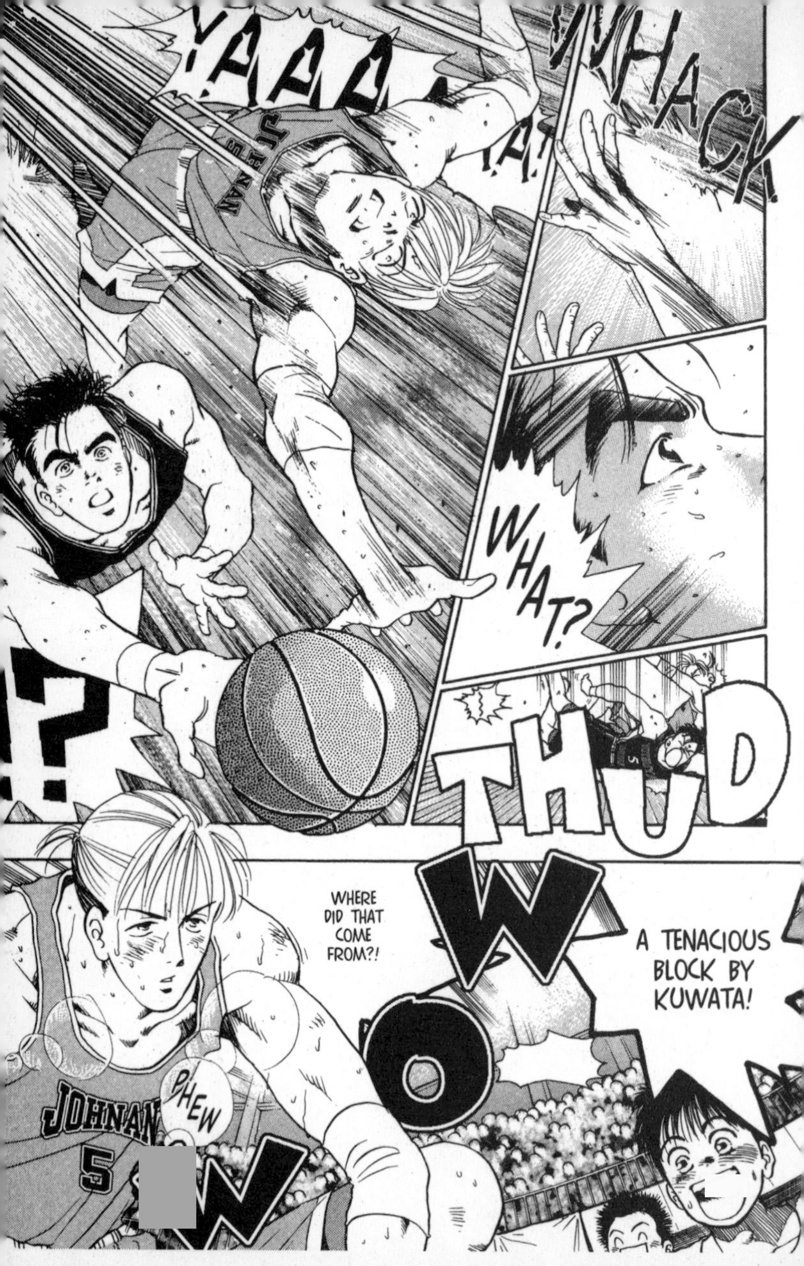

WHACK
WHAT?!
THUD
YAAAAA!
!?
A TENACIOUS BLOCK BY KUWATA!
WHERE DID THAT COME FROM?!
WOW
PHEW

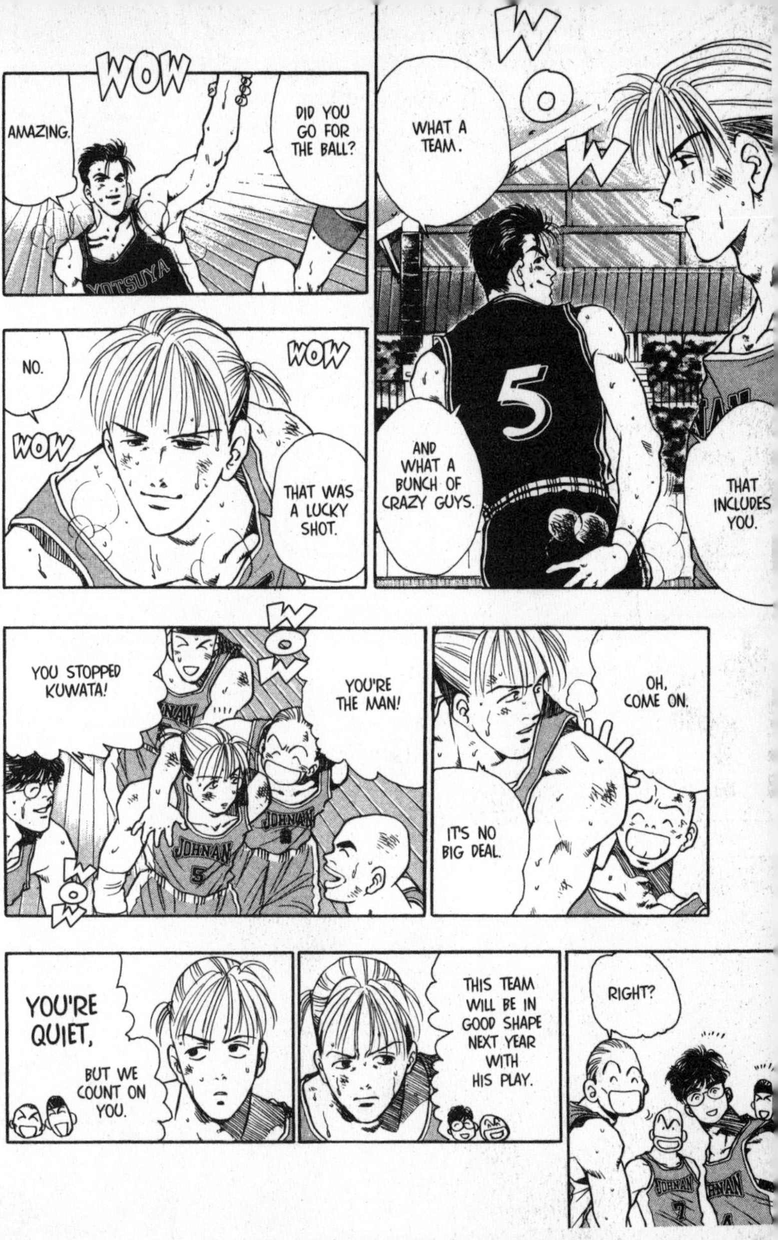
WOW
AMAZING.
DID YOU GO FOR THE BALL?
YOTSUYA
NO.
WOW
WOW
THAT WAS A LUCKY SHOT.
W O W
WHAT A TEAM.
5
AND WHAT A BUNCH OF CRAZY GUYS.
THAT INCLUDES YOU.
W O W
YOU STOPPED KUWATA!
YOU'RE THE MAN!
JOHNAN
W O W
OH, COME ON.
IT'S NO BIG DEAL.
YOU'RE QUIET,
BUT WE COUNT ON YOU.
THIS TEAM WILL BE IN GOOD SHAPE NEXT YEAR WITH HIS PLAY.
RIGHT?

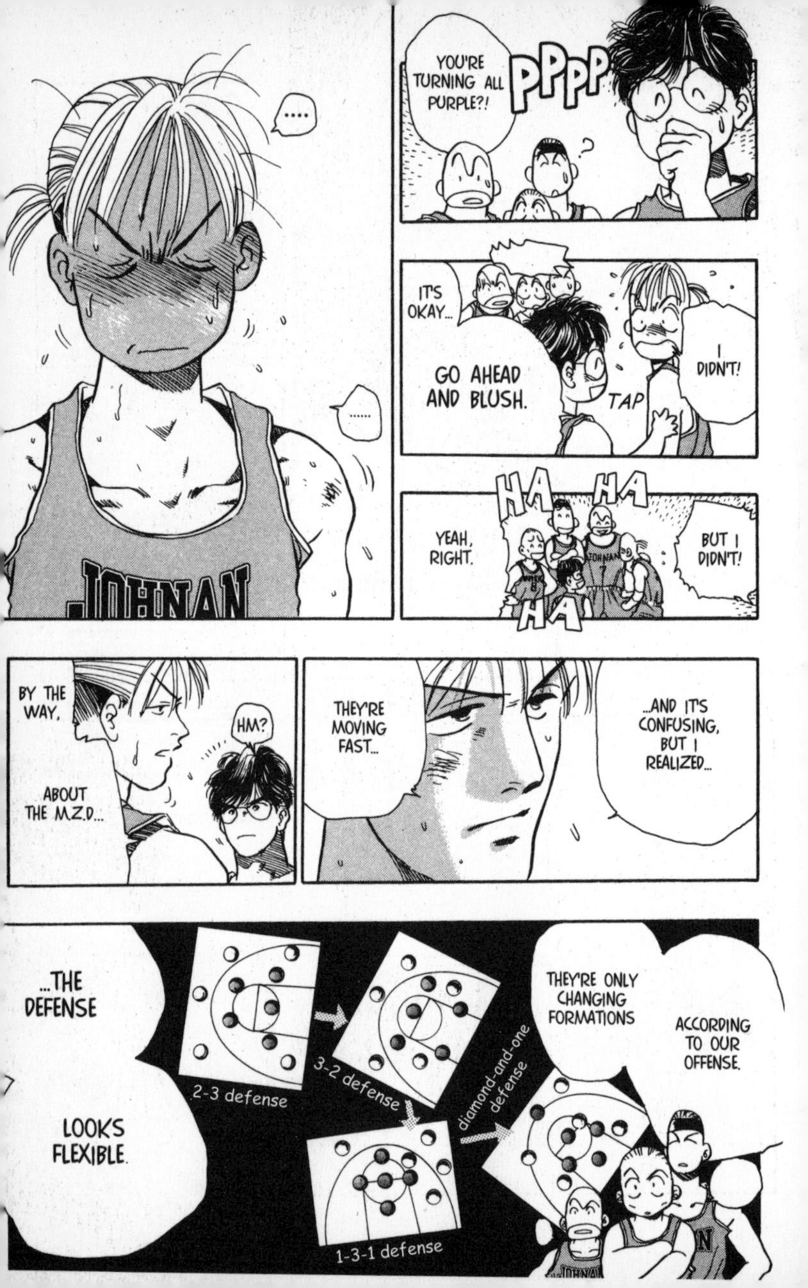
.....
......
YOU'RE TURNING ALL PURPLE?!
PPPP
?
IT'S OKAY...
GO AHEAD AND BLUSH.
TAP
I DIDN'T!
HA HA
HA
YEAH, RIGHT.
BUT I DIDN'T!
JOHNAN
BY THE WAY,
ABOUT THE M.Z.D...
HM?
THEY'RE MOVING FAST...
...AND IT'S CONFUSING, BUT I REALIZED...
...THE DEFENSE
LOOKS FLEXIBLE.
2-3 defense
3-2 defense
1-3-1 defense
diamond-and-one defense
THEY'RE ONLY CHANGING FORMATIONS
ACCORDING TO OUR OFFENSE.

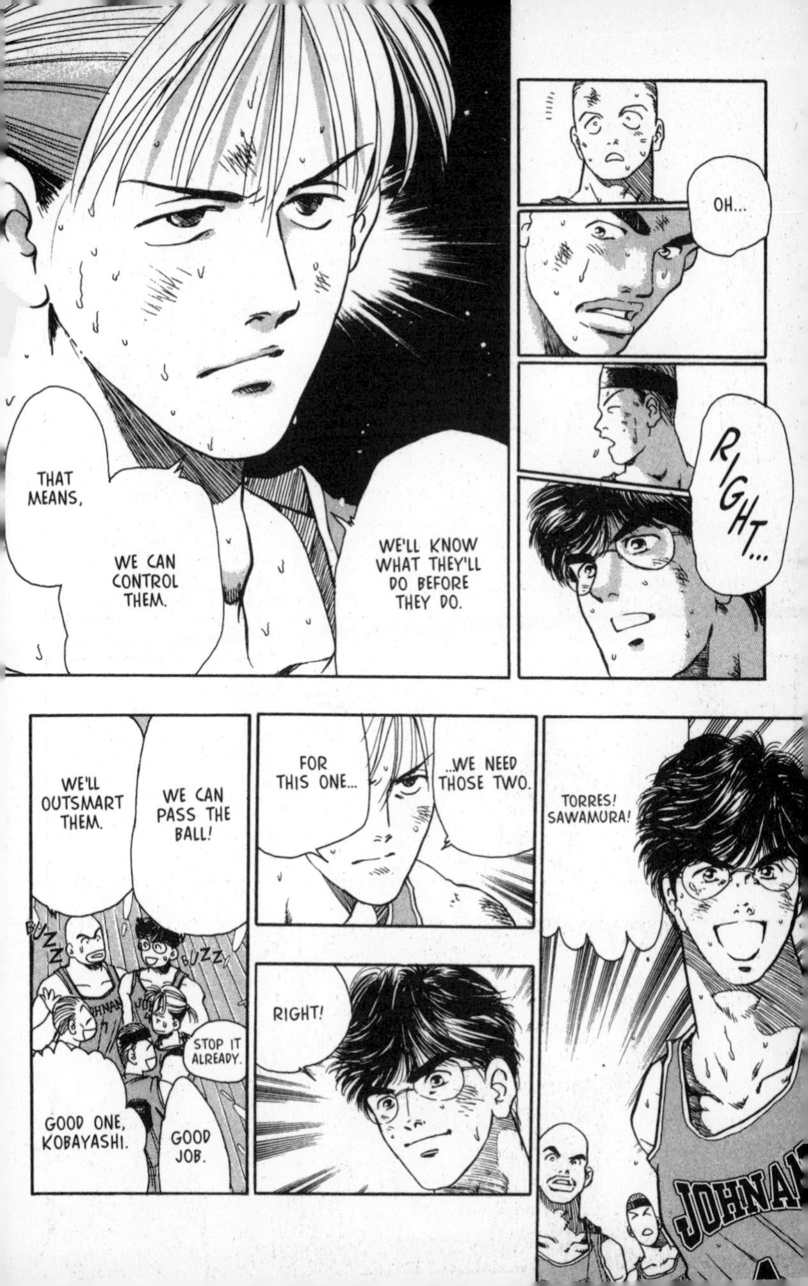
OH...
RIGHT...
THAT MEANS,
WE'LL KNOW WHAT THEY'LL DO BEFORE THEY DO.
WE CAN CONTROL THEM.
TORRES! SAWAMURA!
FOR THIS ONE...
...WE NEED THOSE TWO.
RIGHT!
WE CAN PASS THE BALL!
WE'LL OUTSMART THEM.
BUZZ
BUZZ
STOP IT ALREADY.
GOOD JOB.
GOOD ONE, KOBAYASHI.

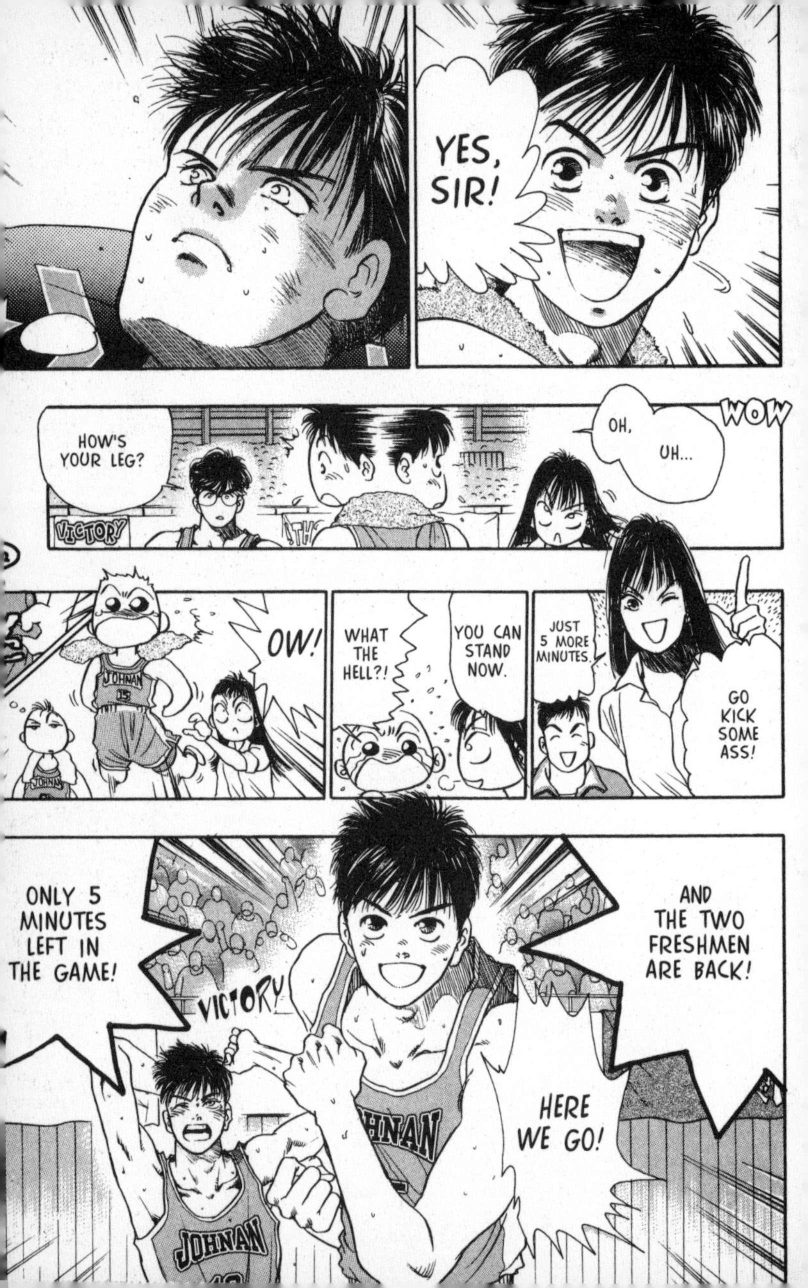
YES, SIR!
HOW'S YOUR LEG?
OH, UH...
WOW
VICTORY
OW!
WHAT THE HELL?!
YOU CAN STAND NOW.
JUST 5 MORE MINUTES.
GO KICK SOME ASS!
ONLY 5 MINUTES LEFT IN THE GAME!
AND THE TWO FRESHMEN ARE BACK!
VICTORY
HERE WE GO!

■Street 73 Pass and Run

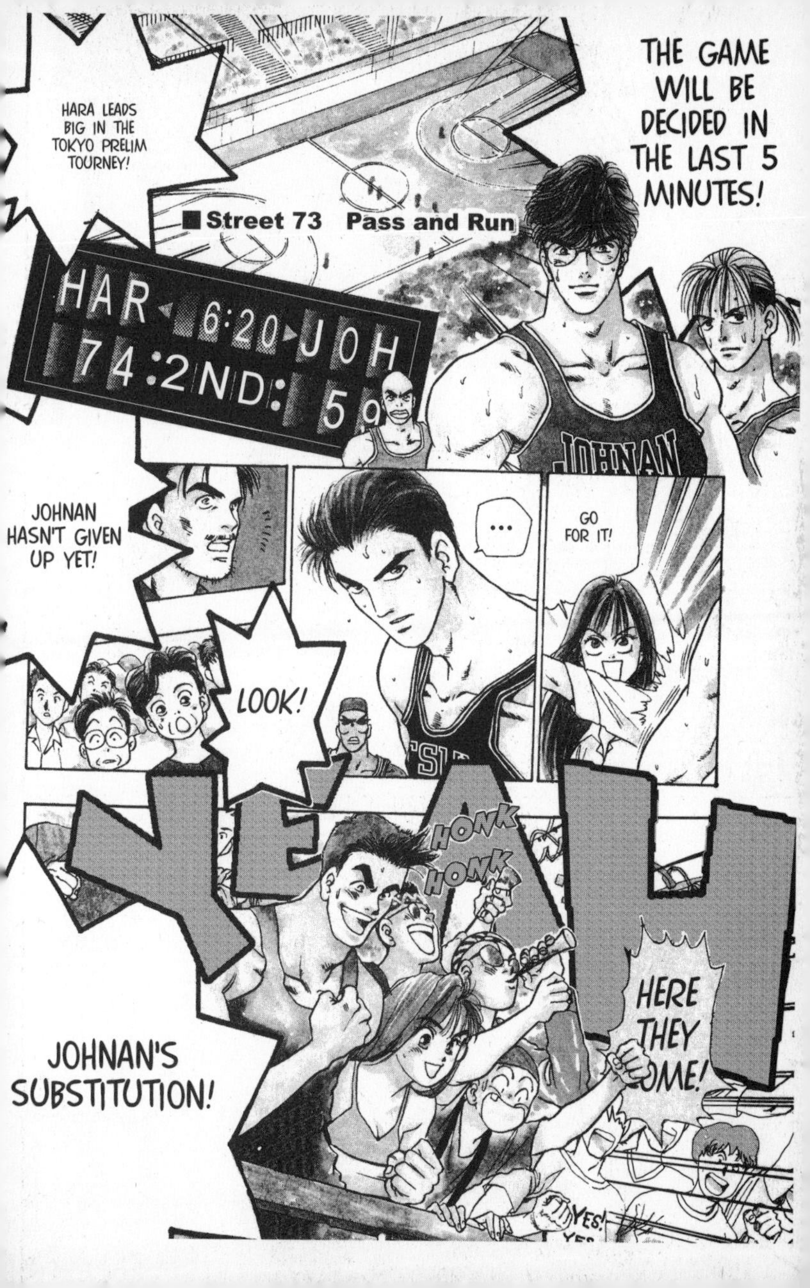
THE GAME WILL BE DECIDED IN THE LAST 5 MINUTES!
HARA LEADS BIG IN THE TOKYO PRELIM TOURNEY!
HAR 6:20 JOH
74 2ND 59
GO FOR IT!
...
JOHNAN HASN'T GIVEN UP YET!
LOOK!
YEAH
HONK
HONK
HERE THEY OME!
JOHNAN'S SUBSTITUTION!
YES!

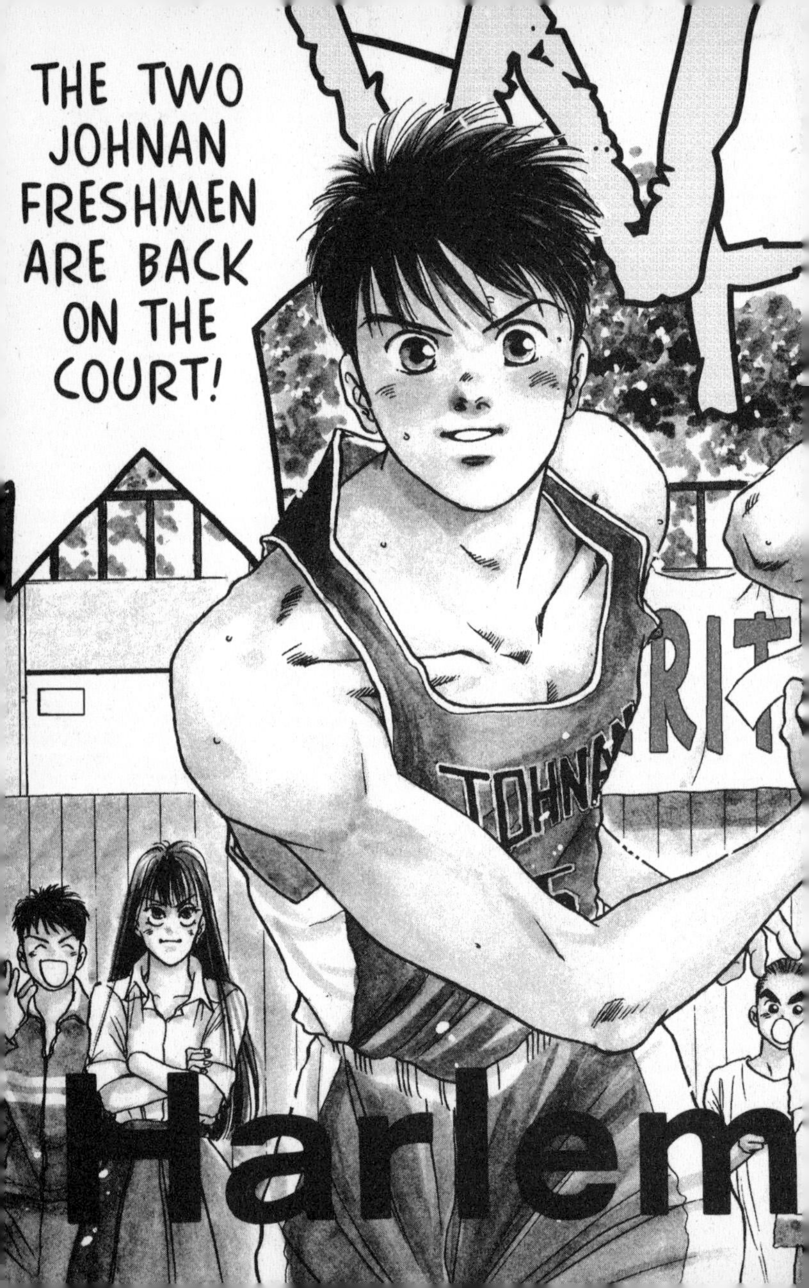
THE TWO JOHNAN FRESHMEN ARE BACK ON THE COURT!
JOHNAN
Harlem

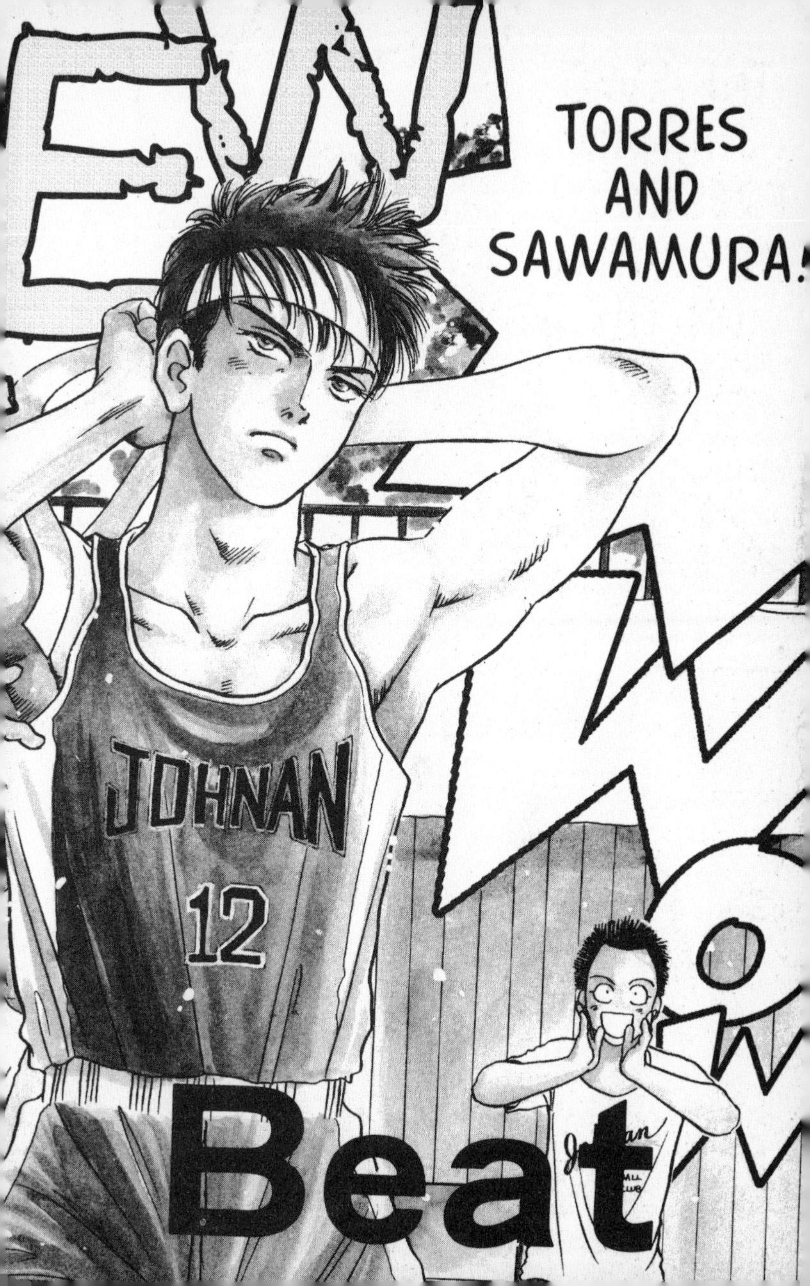
TORRES AND SAWAMURA!
JOHNAN
12
Beat

NARUCHO NO OKAIMONO
100 YEN
SALE
100 YEN
100 YEN
CHANGE!
KEKE

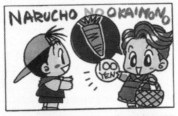

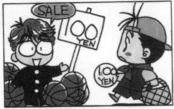

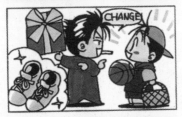

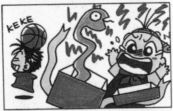

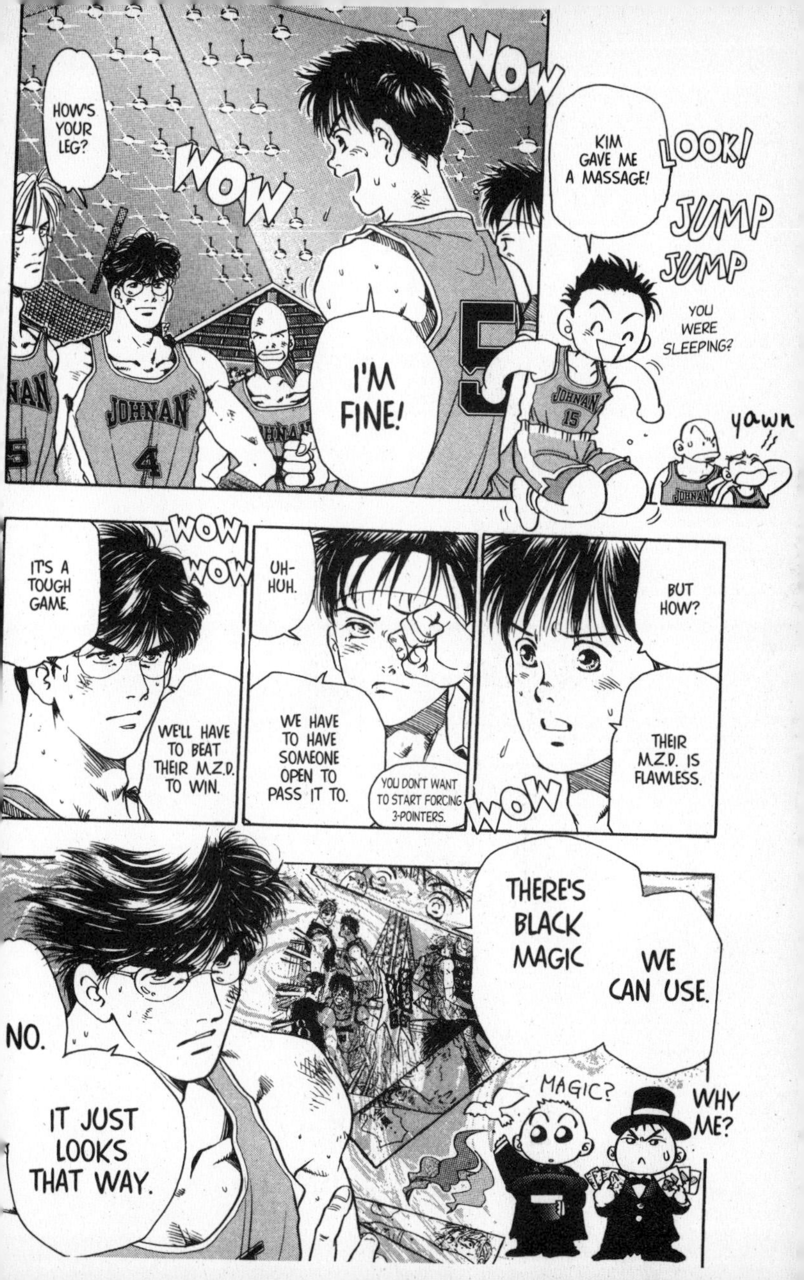
HOW'S YOUR LEG?
WOW
WOW
I'M FINE!
WOW
KIM GAVE ME A MASSAGE!
LOOK!
JUMP
JUMP
YOU WERE SLEEPING?
yawn
IT'S A TOUGH GAME.
WOW
WOW
WE'LL HAVE TO BEAT THEIR M.Z.D. TO WIN.
UH-HUH.
WE HAVE TO HAVE SOMEONE OPEN TO PASS IT TO.
YOU DON'T WANT TO START FORCING 3-POINTERS.
BUT HOW?
WOW
THEIR M.Z.D. IS FLAWLESS.
NO.
IT JUST LOOKS THAT WAY.
THERE'S BLACK MAGIC
WE CAN USE.
MAGIC?
WHY ME?

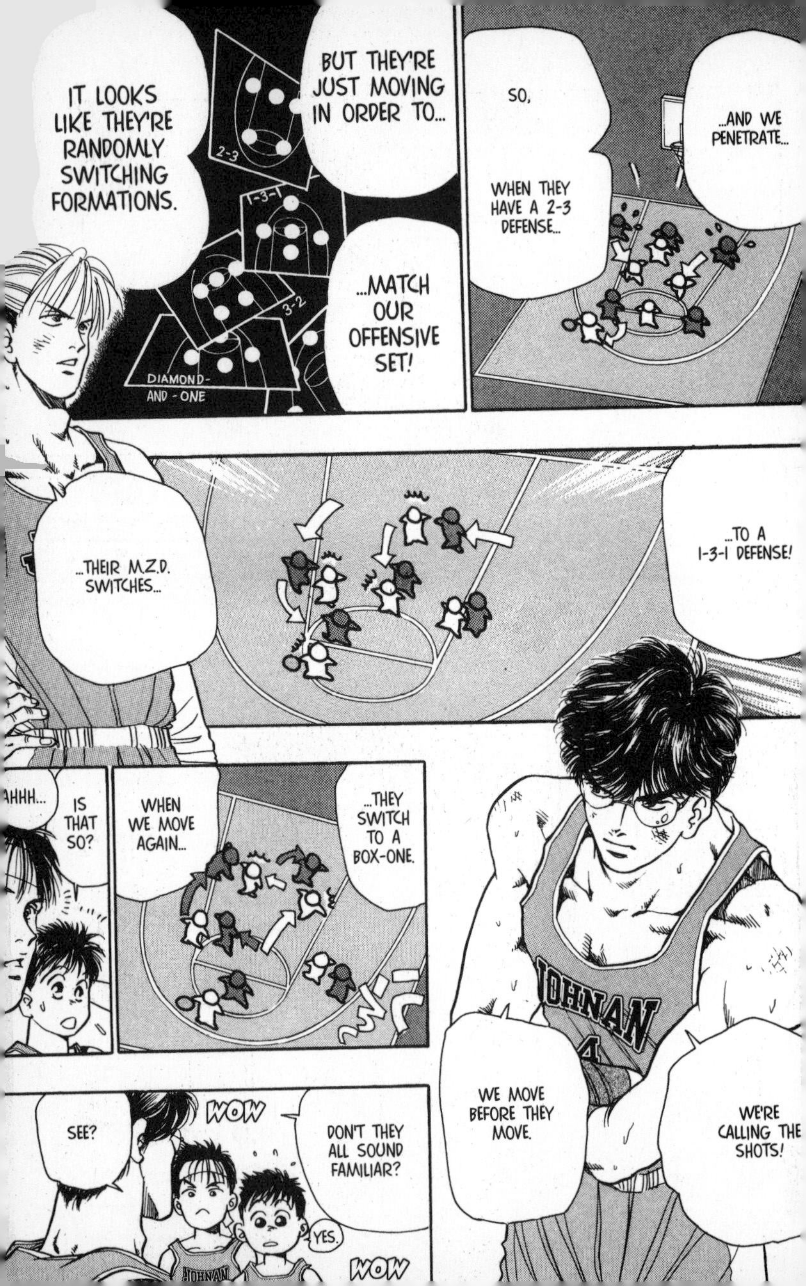
IT LOOKS LIKE THEY'RE RANDOMLY SWITCHING FORMATIONS.
2-3
1-3-1
3-2
DIAMOND-AND-ONE
BUT THEY'RE JUST MOVING IN ORDER TO...
...MATCH OUR OFFENSIVE SET!
SO,
WHEN THEY HAVE A 2-3 DEFENSE...
...AND WE PENETRATE...
...THEIR M.Z.D. SWITCHES...
...TO A 1-3-1 DEFENSE!
AHHH...
IS THAT SO?
WHEN WE MOVE AGAIN...
...THEY SWITCH TO A BOX-ONE.
SEE?
WOW
DON'T THEY ALL SOUND FAMILIAR?
YES.
WOW
WE MOVE BEFORE THEY MOVE.
WE'RE CALLING THE SHOTS!

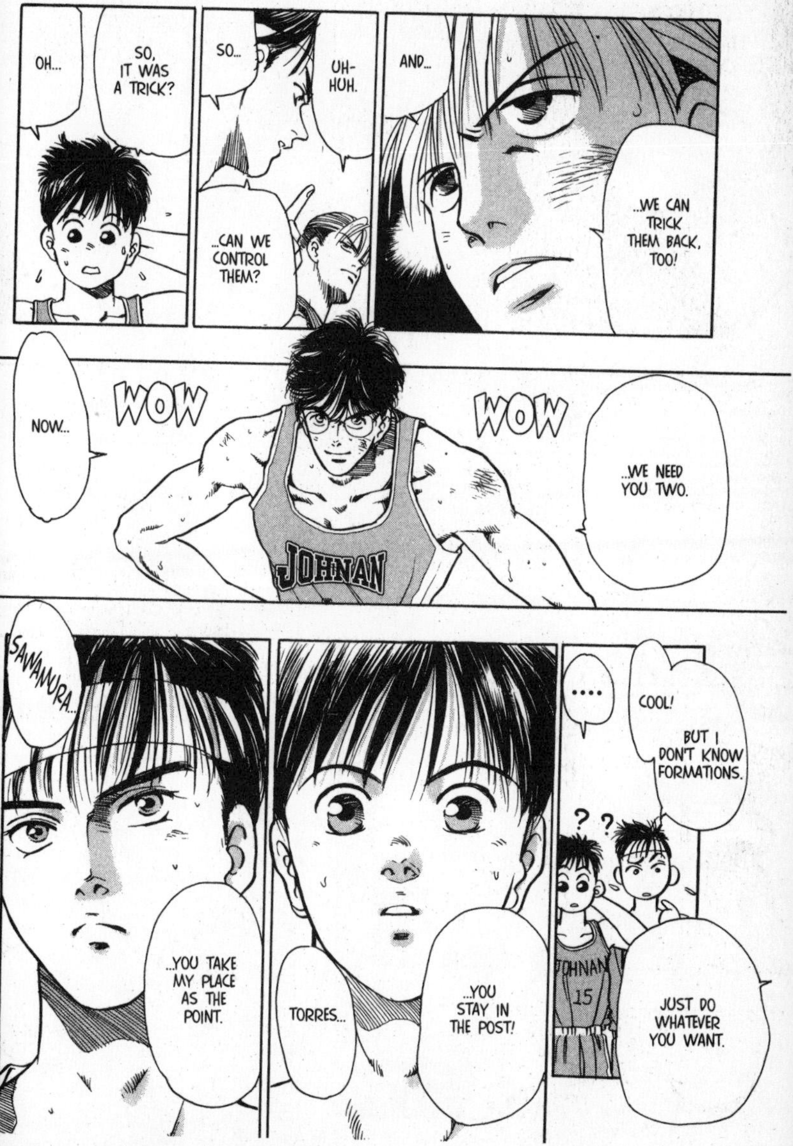
OH...
SO, IT WAS A TRICK?
SO...
UH-HUH.
...CAN WE CONTROL THEM?
AND...
...WE CAN TRICK THEM BACK, TOO!
NOW...
WOW
WOW
...WE NEED YOU TWO.
JOHNAN
SAWAMURA...
...YOU TAKE MY PLACE AS THE POINT.
TORRES...
...YOU STAY IN THE POST!
....
COOL!
BUT I DON'T KNOW FORMATIONS.
?
?
JOHNAN
15
JUST DO WHATEVER YOU WANT.

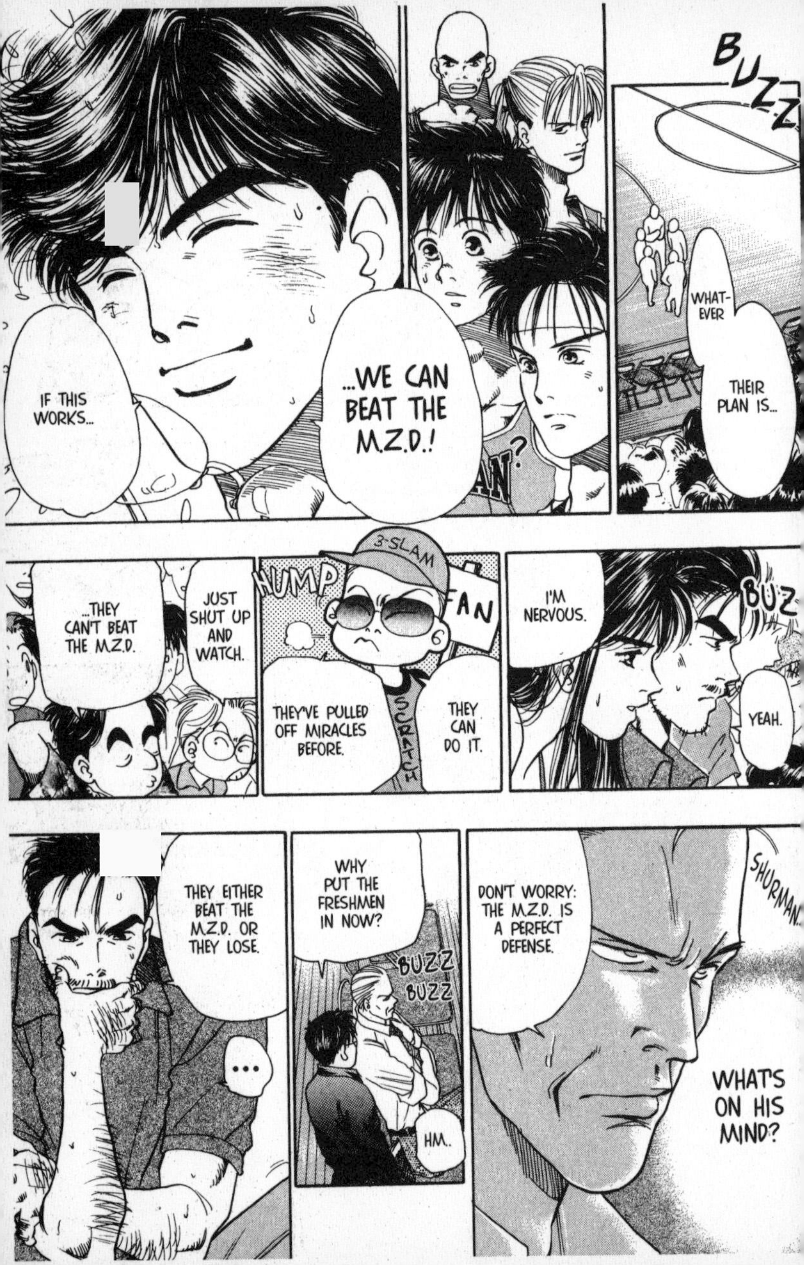
IF THIS WORKS...
...WE CAN BEAT THE M.Z.D.!
?
BUZZ
WHAT-EVER THEIR PLAN IS...
...THEY CAN'T BEAT THE M.Z.D.
JUST SHUT UP AND WATCH.
HUMP
3-SLAM
FAN
THEY'VE PULLED OFF MIRACLES BEFORE.
THEY CAN DO IT.
I'M NERVOUS.
BUZ
YEAH.
THEY EITHER BEAT THE M.Z.D. OR THEY LOSE.
...
WHY PUT THE FRESHMEN IN NOW?
BUZZ BUZZ
HM.
DON'T WORRY: THE M.Z.D. IS A PERFECT DEFENSE.
SHURMAN...
WHAT'S ON HIS MIND?

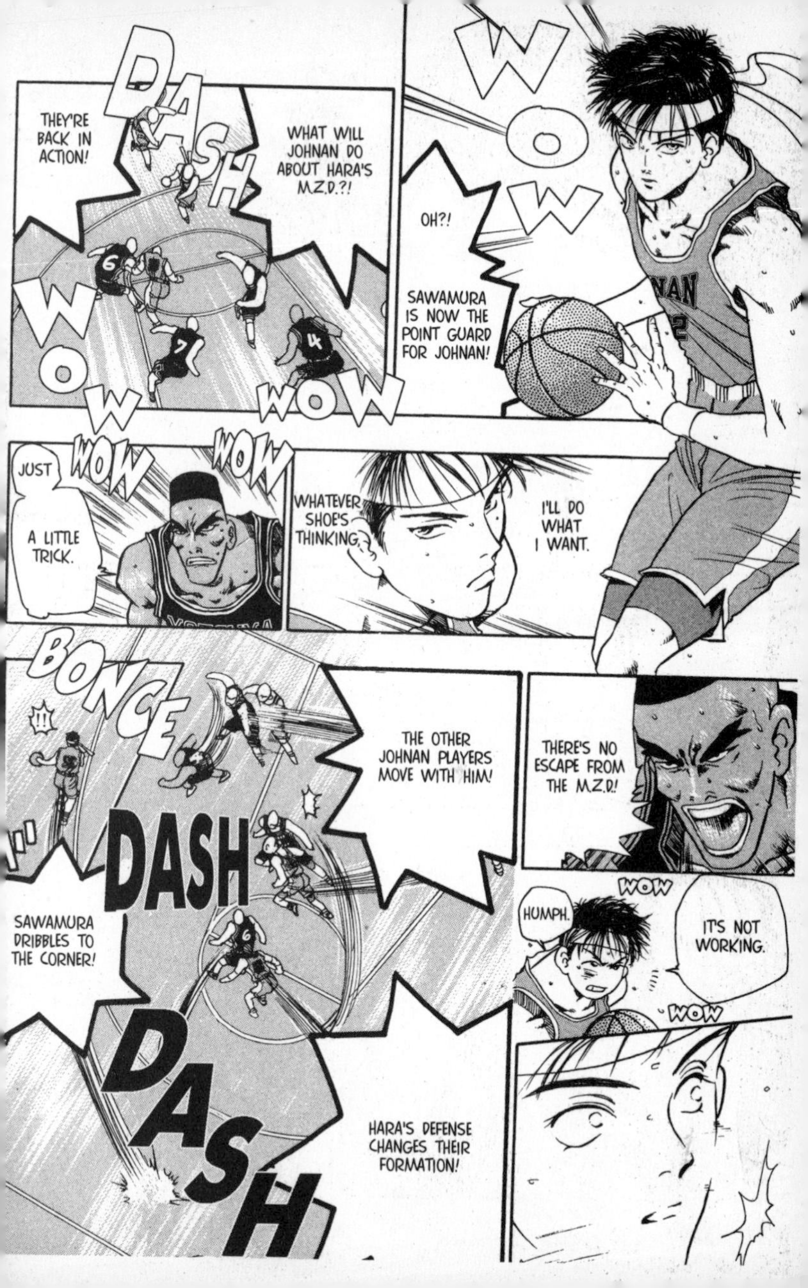
DASH
THEY'RE BACK IN ACTION!
WHAT WILL JOHNAN DO ABOUT HARA'S M.Z.D.?!
WOW
WOW
WOW
WOW
OH?!
SAWAMURA IS NOW THE POINT GUARD FOR JOHNAN!
WOW
WOW
JUST A LITTLE TRICK.
WHATEVER SHOE'S THINKING,
I'LL DO WHAT I WANT.
BONCE
!!!
DASH
SAWAMURA DRIBBLES TO THE CORNER!
THE OTHER JOHNAN PLAYERS MOVE WITH HIM!
DASH
HARA'S DEFENSE CHANGES THEIR FORMATION!
THERE'S NO ESCAPE FROM THE M.Z.D.!
WOW
HUMPH.
IT'S NOT WORKING.
WOW

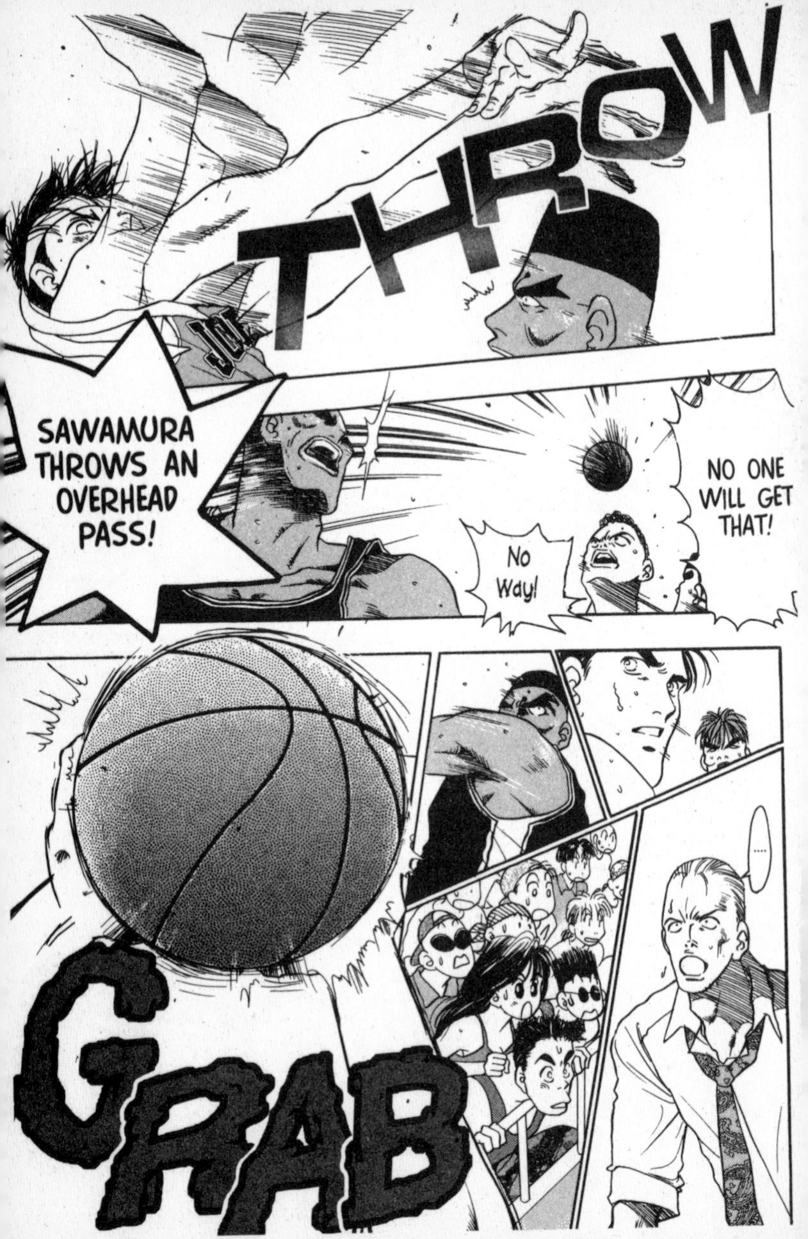
THROW
SAWAMURA THROWS AN OVERHEAD PASS!
NO ONE WILL GET THAT!
No Way!
....
GRAB

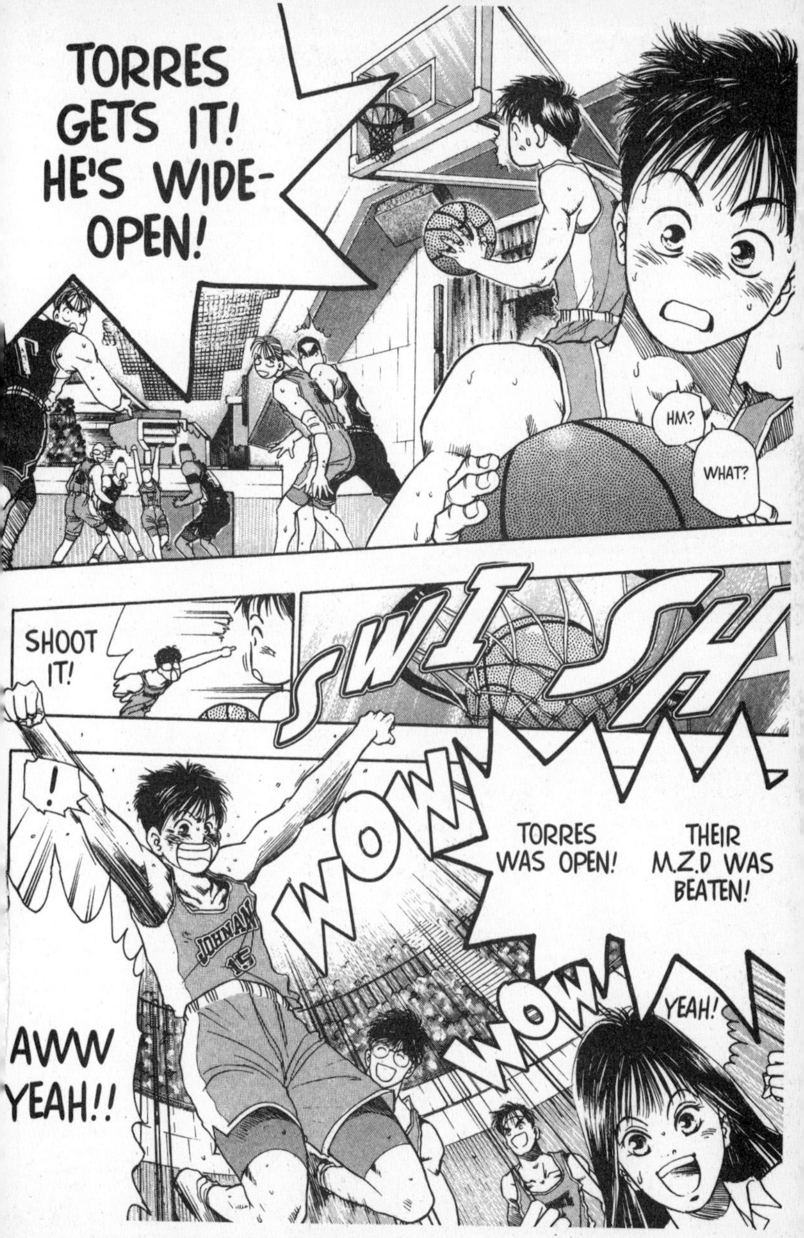
TORRES GETS IT! HE'S WIDE-OPEN!
HM?
WHAT?
SWISH
SHOOT IT!
WOW
THEIR M.Z.D WAS BEATEN!
TORRES WAS OPEN!
!
JOHNAN 15
YEAH!
WOW
AWW YEAH!!

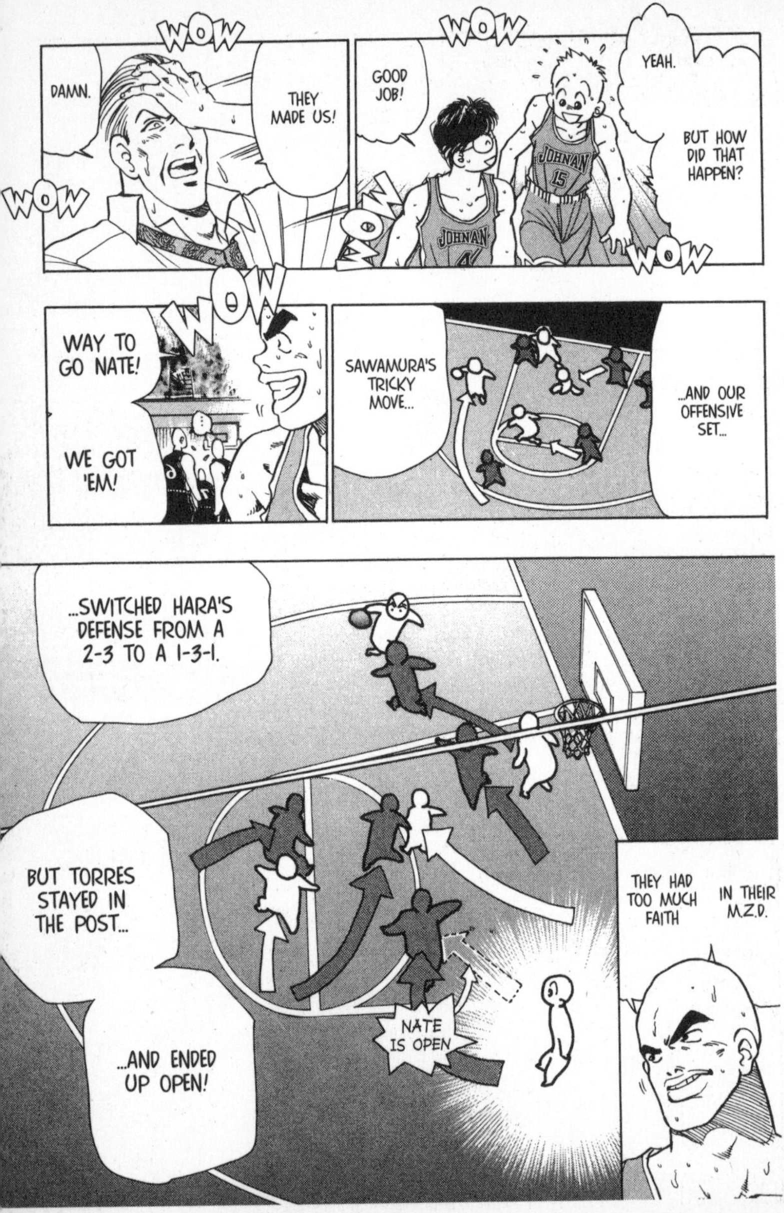
WOW
DAMN.
THEY MADE US!
WOW
WOW
GOOD JOB!
YEAH.
BUT HOW DID THAT HAPPEN?
WOW
WOW
WOW
WAY TO GO NATE!
WE GOT 'EM!
SAWAMURA'S TRICKY MOVE...
...AND OUR OFFENSIVE SET...
...SWITCHED HARA'S DEFENSE FROM A 2-3 TO A 1-3-1.
BUT TORRES STAYED IN THE POST...
...AND ENDED UP OPEN!
NATE IS OPEN
THEY HAD TOO MUCH FAITH
IN THEIR M.Z.D.

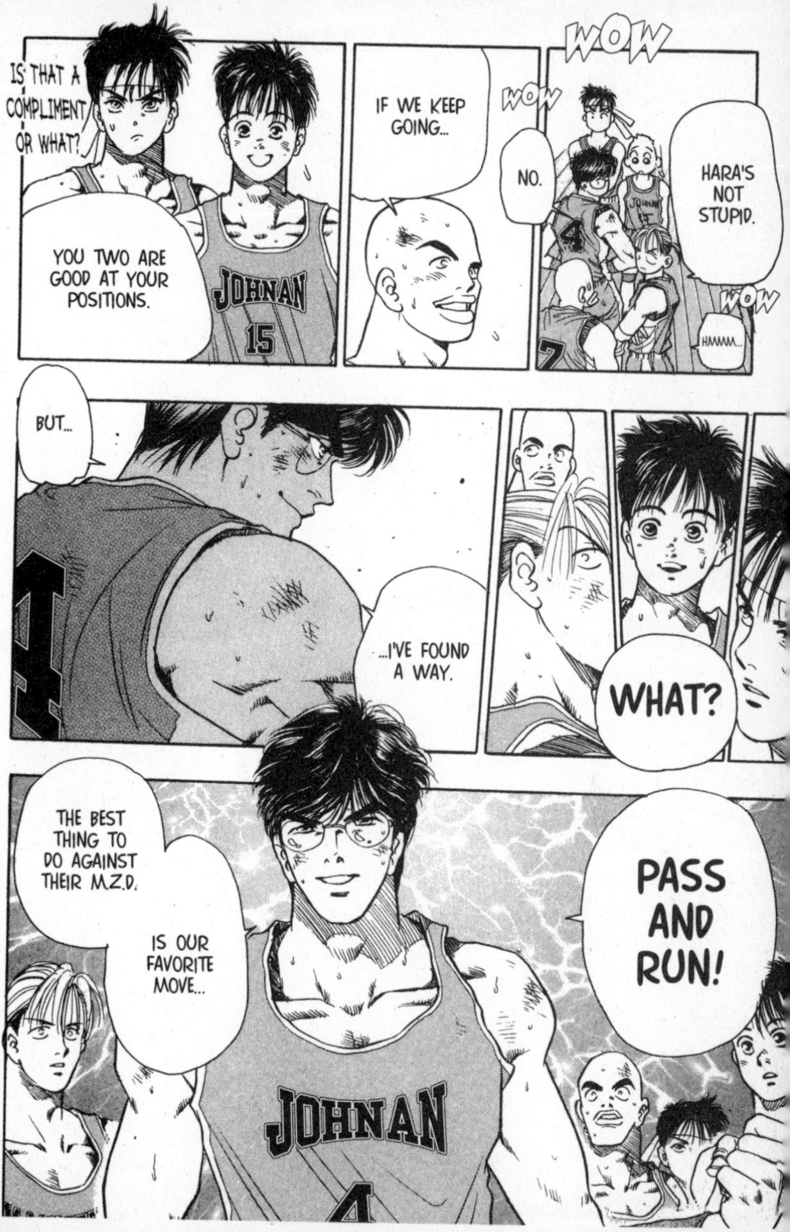
YOU TWO ARE GOOD AT YOUR POSITIONS.
IS THAT A COMPLIMENT OR WHAT?
IF WE KEEP GOING...
WOW
WOW
NO.
HARA'S NOT STUPID.
WOW
HMMMM...
BUT...
...I'VE FOUND A WAY.
WHAT?
THE BEST THING TO DO AGAINST THEIR M.Z.D.
IS OUR FAVORITE MOVE...
PASS AND RUN!

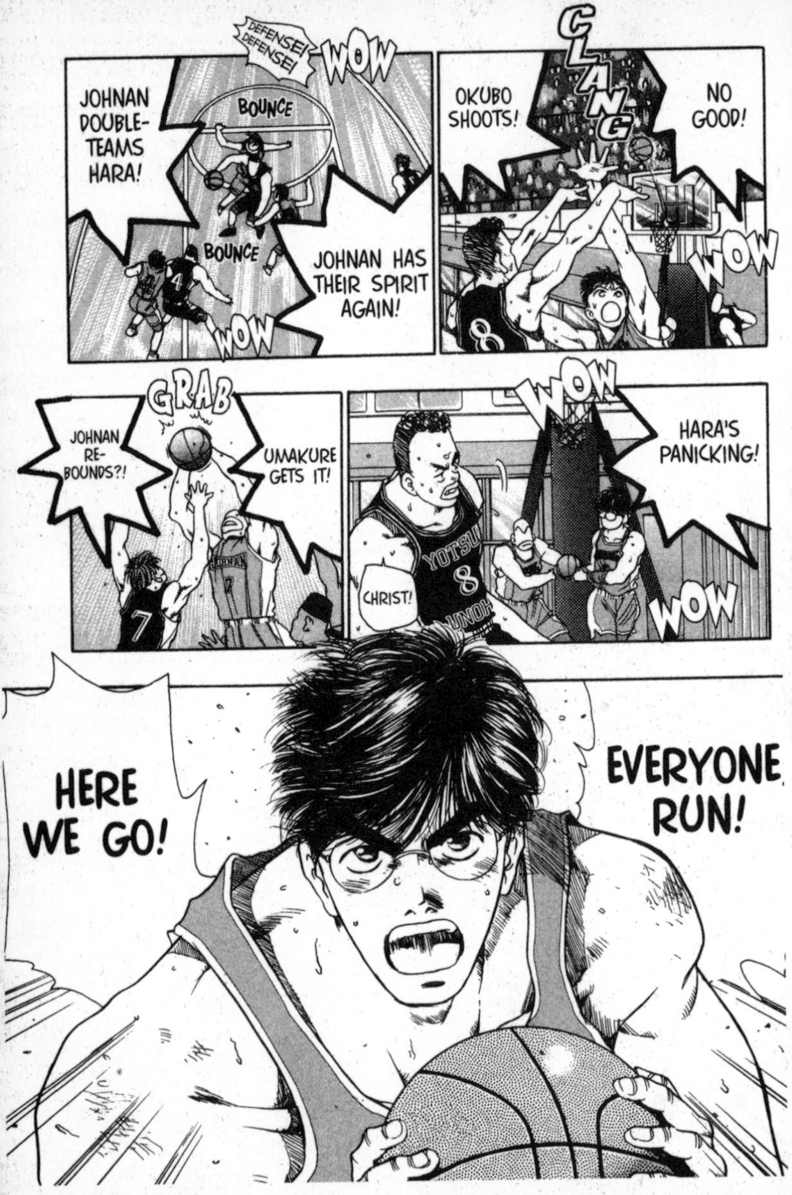
DEFENSE! DEFENSE!
WOW
JOHNAN DOUBLE-TEAMS HARA!
BOUNCE
BOUNCE
JOHNAN HAS THEIR SPIRIT AGAIN!
WOW
OKUBO SHOOTS!
CLANG
NO GOOD!
WOW
GRAB
JOHNAN REBOUNDS?!
UMAKURE GETS IT!
WOW
CHRIST!
HARA'S PANICKING!
WOW
HERE WE GO!
EVERYONE RUN!

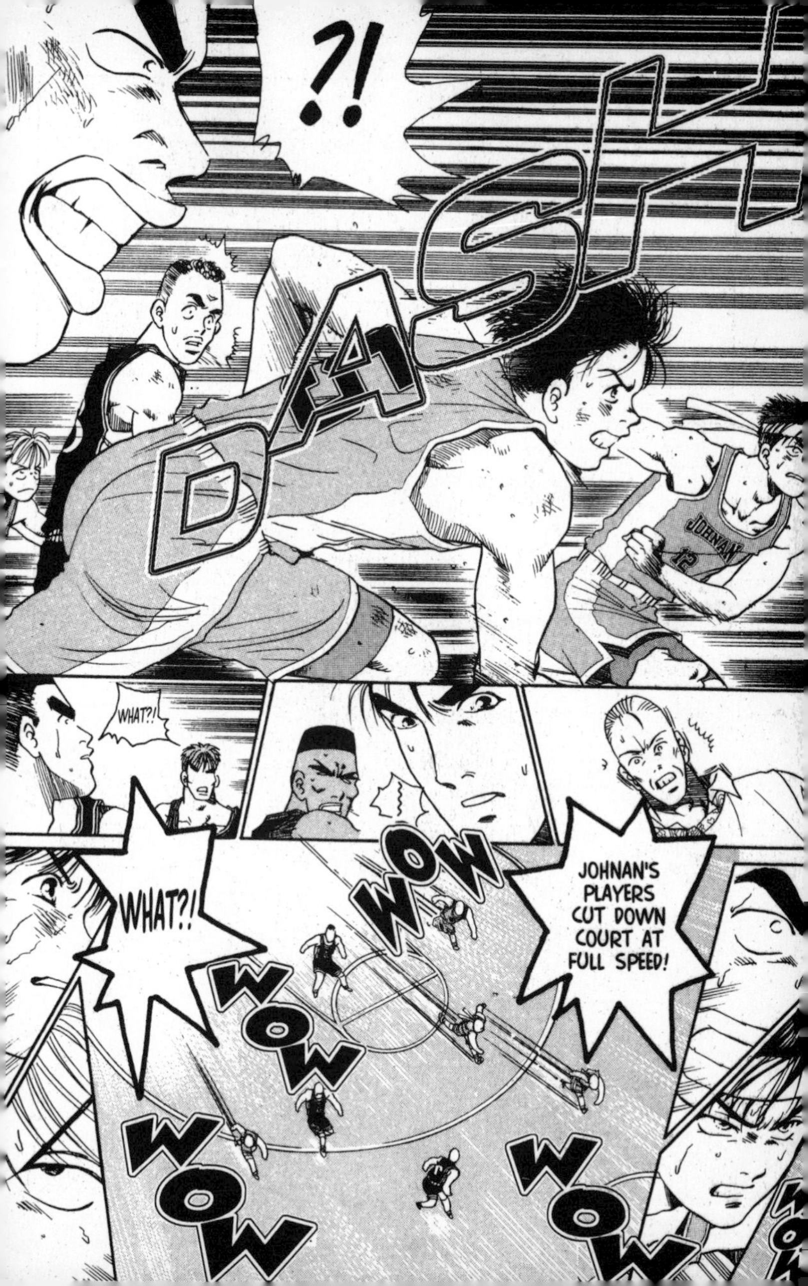
?!
DASH
JOHNAN
12
WHAT?!
JOHNAN'S PLAYERS CUT DOWN COURT AT FULL SPEED!
WOW WOW
WHAT?!
WOW WOW
WOW WOW
WOW WOW

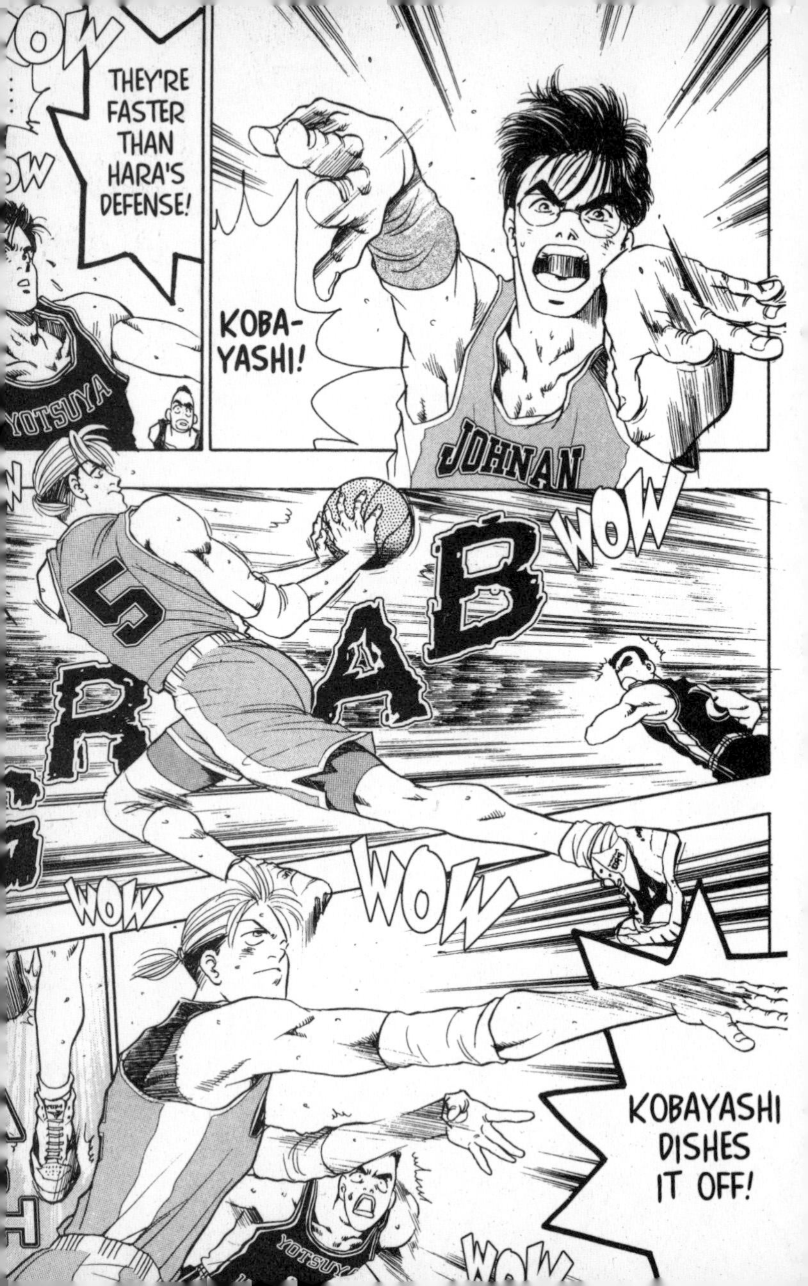
KOBA-
YASHI!
WOW
THEY'RE FASTER THAN HARA'S DEFENSE!
WOW
WOW
BAR
WOW
WOW
KOBAYASHI DISHES IT OFF!
WOW

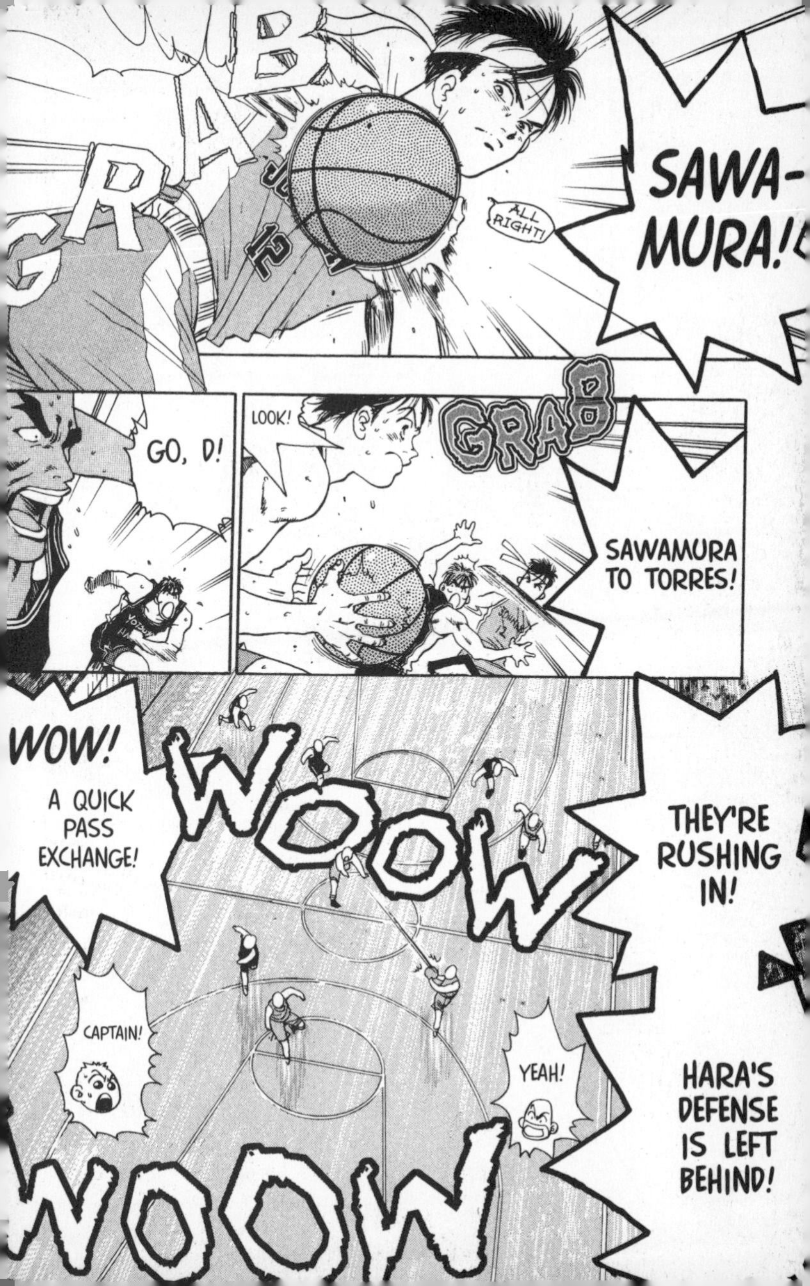
SAWA-MURA!
ALL RIGHT!
GRAB
GRAB
SAWAMURA TO TORRES!
LOOK!
GO, D!
THEY'RE RUSHING IN!
WOW!
WOOW
A QUICK PASS EXCHANGE!
HARA'S DEFENSE IS LEFT BEHIND!
YEAH!
CAPTAIN!
WOOW

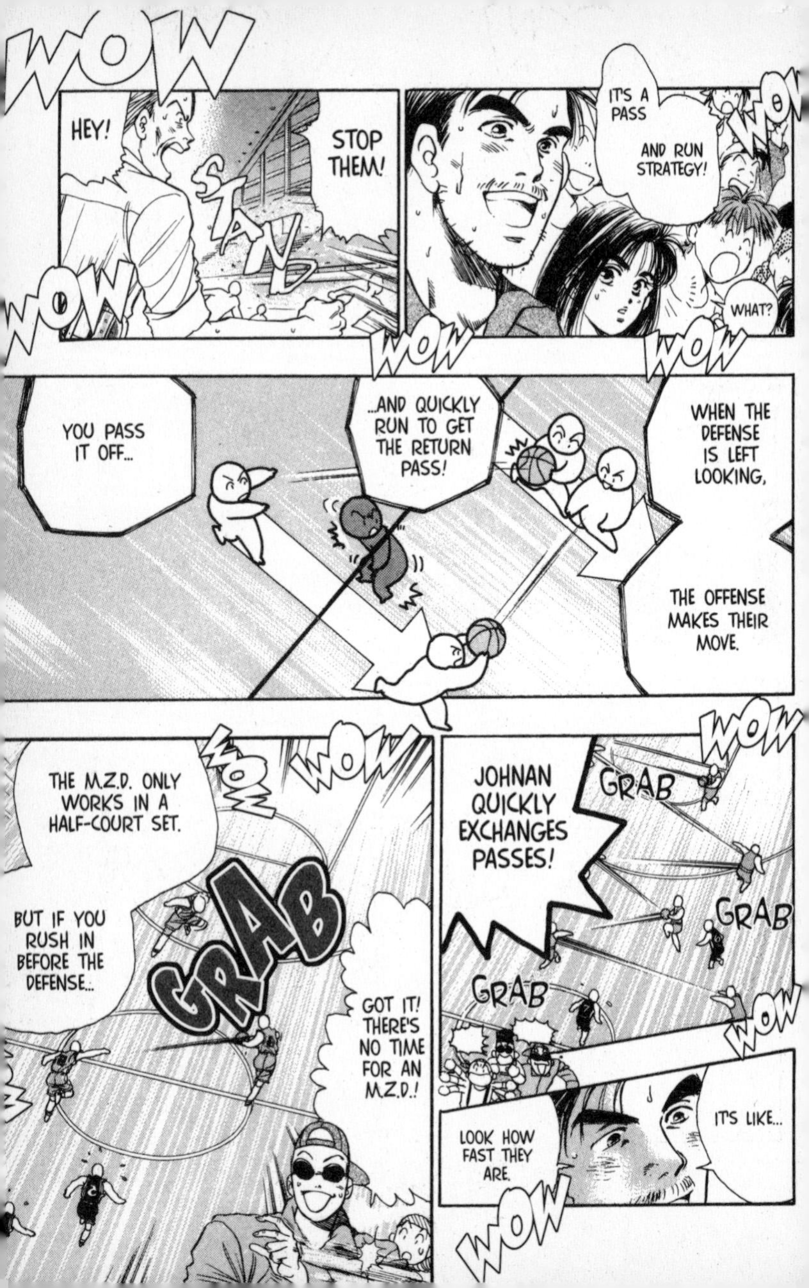
WOW
HEY!
STAND
STOP THEM!
WOW
IT'S A PASS AND RUN STRATEGY!
WOW
WHAT?
WOW
WOW
YOU PASS IT OFF...
...AND QUICKLY RUN TO GET THE RETURN PASS!
WHEN THE DEFENSE IS LEFT LOOKING,
THE OFFENSE MAKES THEIR MOVE.
WOW
WOW
THE M.Z.D. ONLY WORKS IN A HALF-COURT SET.
BUT IF YOU RUSH IN BEFORE THE DEFENSE...
GRAB
GOT IT! THERE'S NO TIME FOR AN M.Z.D.!
WOW
JOHNAN QUICKLY EXCHANGES PASSES!
GRAB
GRAB
GRAB
WOW
LOOK HOW FAST THEY ARE.
IT'S LIKE...
WOW

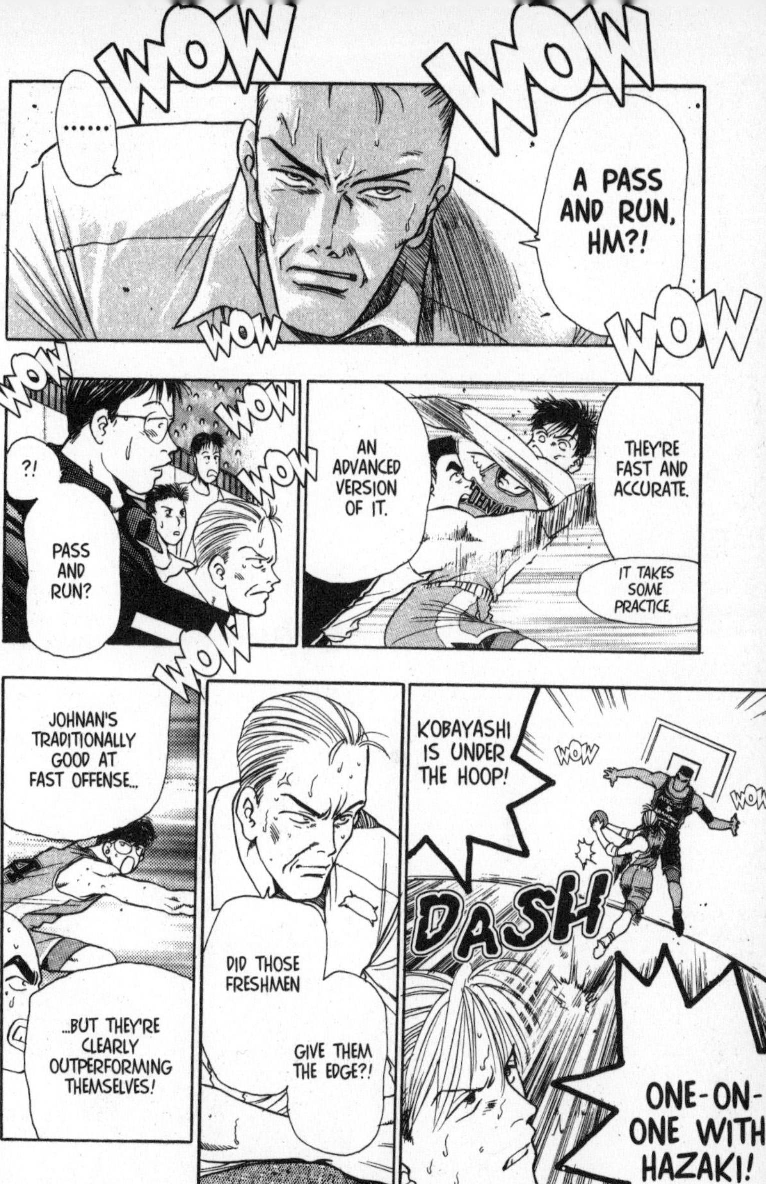
WOW
WOW
......
A PASS AND RUN, HM?!
WOW
WOW
WOW
WOW
WOW
?!
PASS AND RUN?
AN ADVANCED VERSION OF IT.
THEY'RE FAST AND ACCURATE.
IT TAKES SOME PRACTICE.
WOW
JOHNAN'S TRADITIONALLY GOOD AT FAST OFFENSE...
...BUT THEY'RE CLEARLY OUTPERFORMING THEMSELVES!
DID THOSE FRESHMEN
GIVE THEM THE EDGE?!
KOBAYASHI IS UNDER THE HOOP!
WOW
WOW
DASH
ONE-ON-ONE WITH HAZAKI!

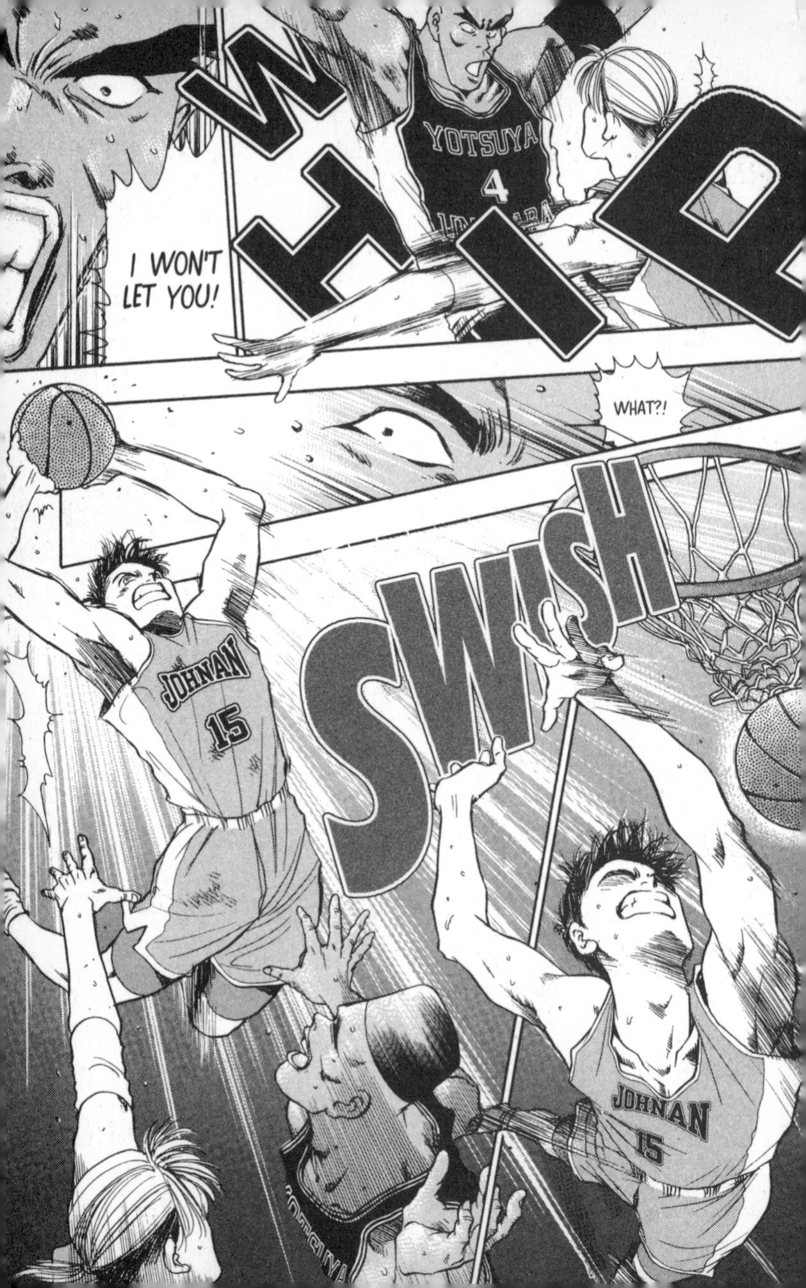
WHIP
I WON'T LET YOU!
WHAT?!
SWISH

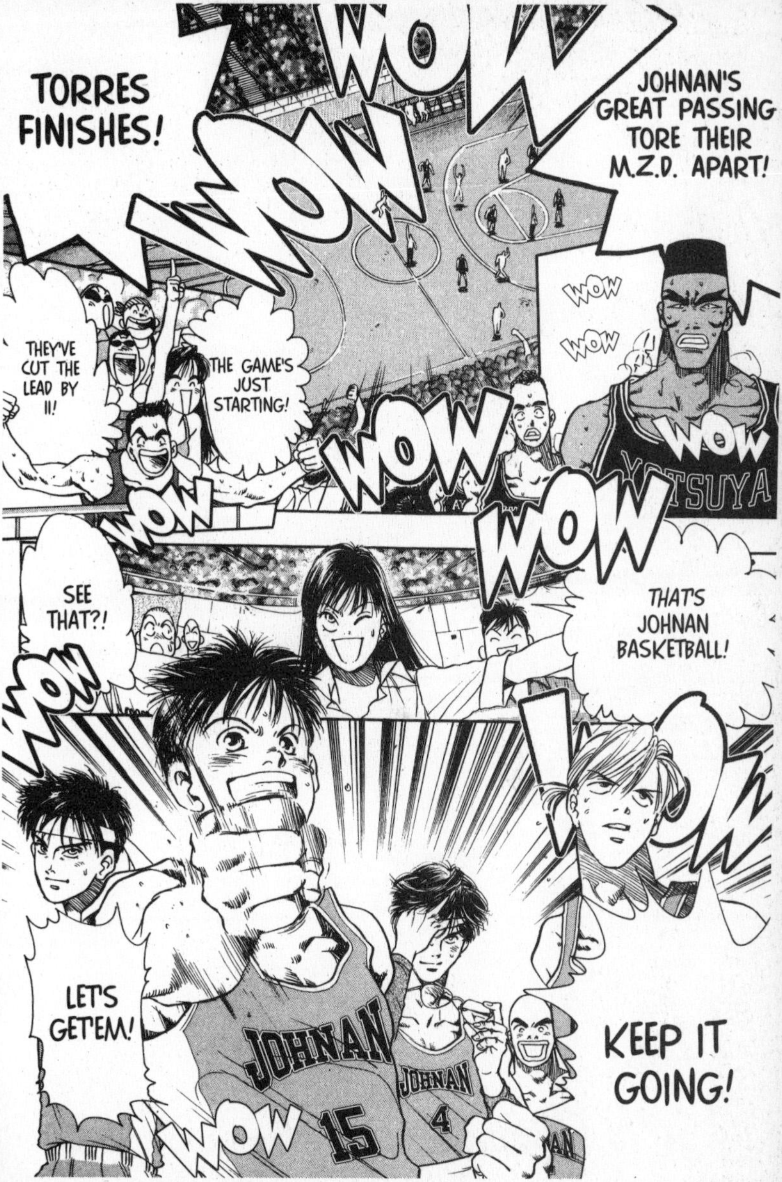
WOW
WOW
JOHNAN'S GREAT PASSING TORE THEIR M.Z.D. APART!
TORRES FINISHES!
WOW
WOW
WOW
WOW
THE GAME'S JUST STARTING!
THEY'VE CUT THE LEAD BY 11!
WOW
WOW
THAT'S JOHNAN BASKETBALL!
SEE THAT?!
WOW
WOW
KEEP IT GOING!
LET'S GET'EM!
WOW

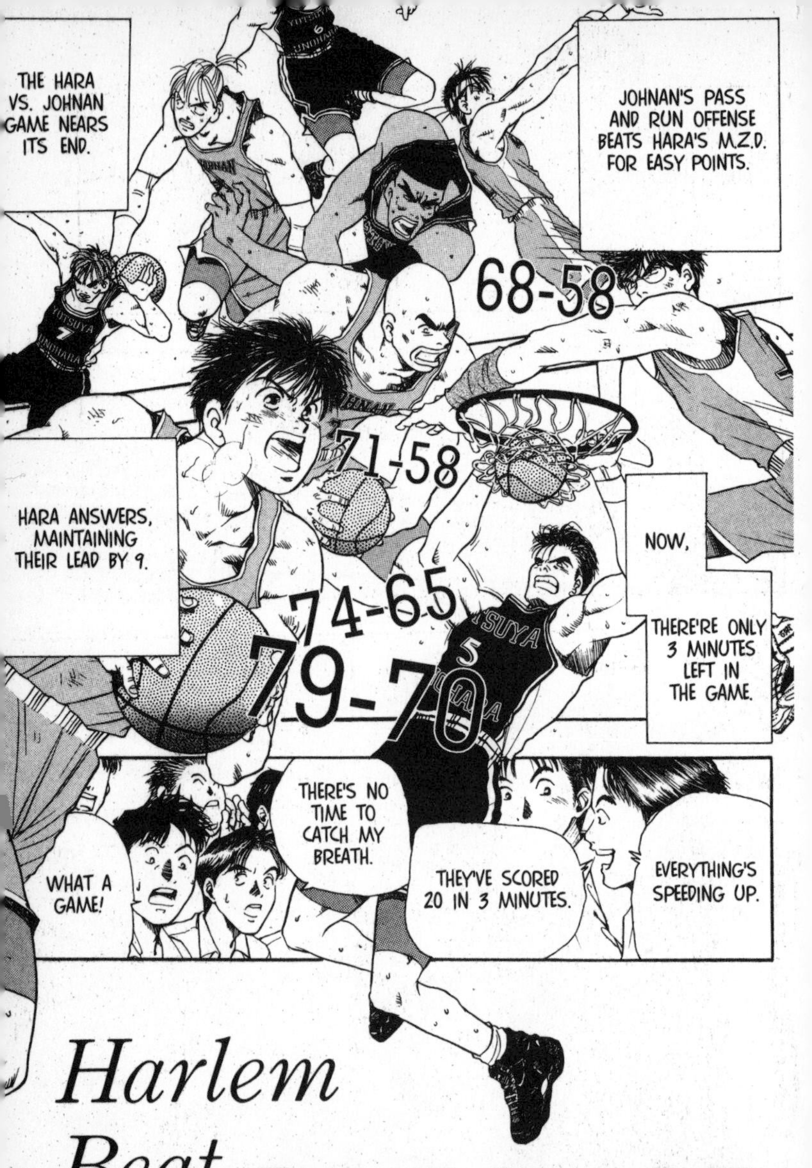
THE HARA VS. JOHNAN GAME NEARS ITS END.
JOHNAN'S PASS AND RUN OFFENSE BEATS HARA'S M.Z.D. FOR EASY POINTS.
68-58
HARA ANSWERS, MAINTAINING THEIR LEAD BY 9.
71-58
74-65
79-70
NOW,
THERE'RE ONLY 3 MINUTES LEFT IN THE GAME.
WHAT A GAME!
THERE'S NO TIME TO CATCH MY BREATH.
THEY'VE SCORED 20 IN 3 MINUTES.
EVERYTHING'S SPEEDING UP.

Harlem Beat

■Street 74 Tenacity To Win

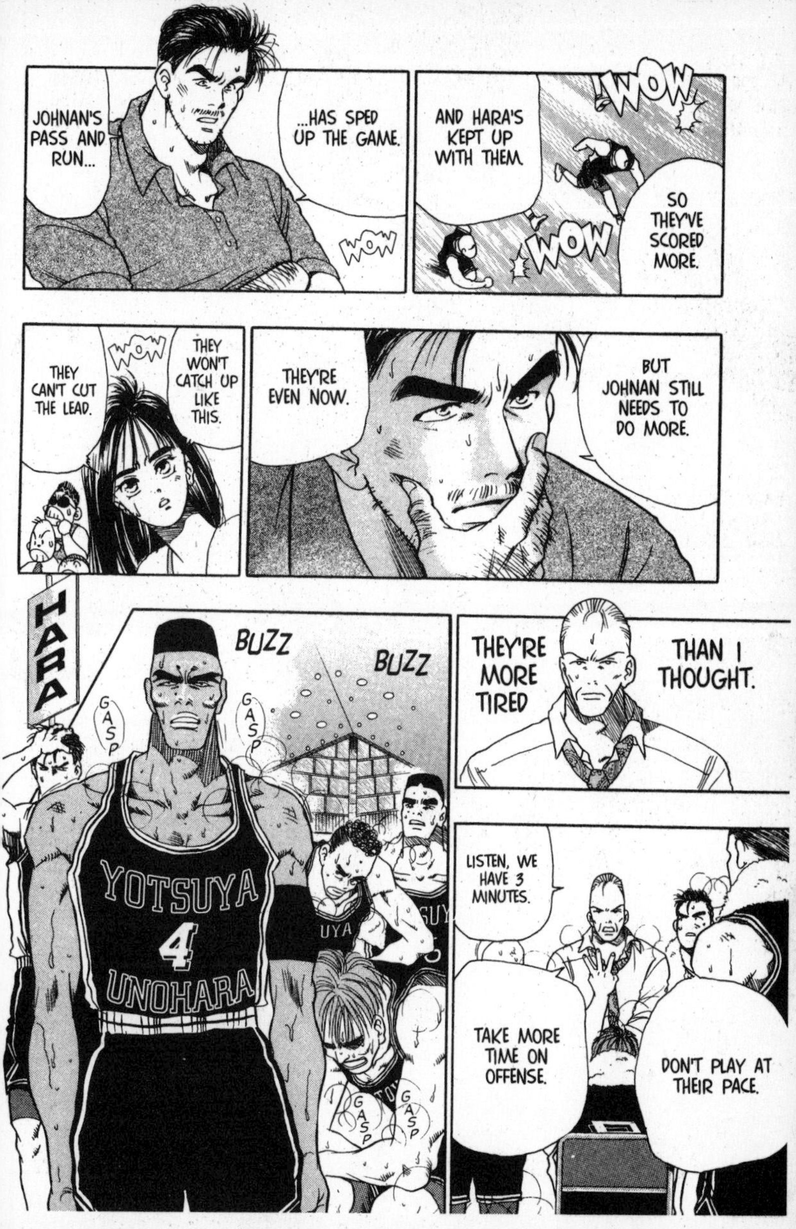
JOHNAN'S PASS AND RUN...
...HAS SPED UP THE GAME.
WOW
AND HARA'S KEPT UP WITH THEM
WOW
WOW
SO THEY'VE SCORED MORE.
THEY CAN'T CUT THE LEAD.
WOW
THEY WON'T CATCH UP LIKE THIS.
THEY'RE EVEN NOW.
BUT JOHNAN STILL NEEDS TO DO MORE.
HARA
BUZZ
BUZZ
GASP
GASP
YOTSUYA
4
UNOHARA
GASP
GASP
THEY'RE MORE TIRED
THAN I THOUGHT.
LISTEN, WE HAVE 3 MINUTES.
TAKE MORE TIME ON OFFENSE.
DON'T PLAY AT THEIR PACE.

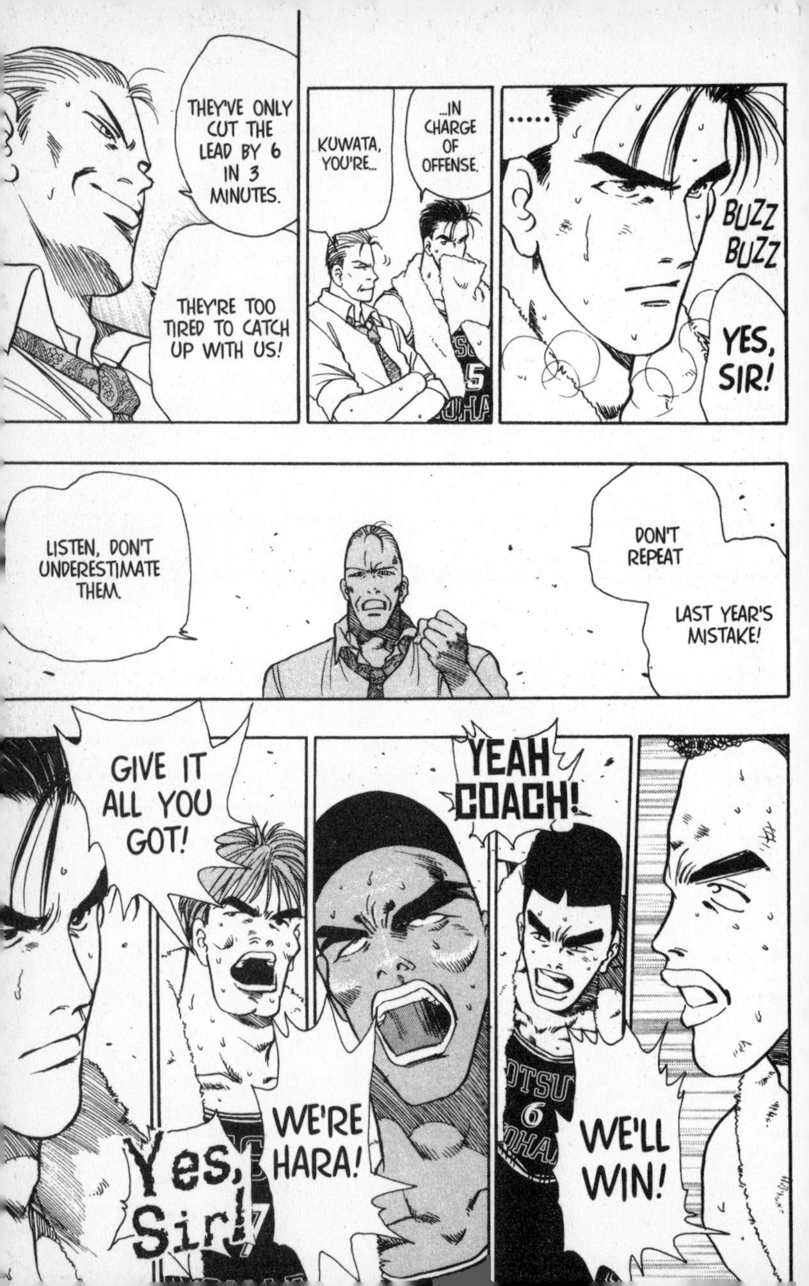
THEY'VE ONLY CUT THE LEAD BY 6 IN 3 MINUTES.
THEY'RE TOO TIRED TO CATCH UP WITH US!
KUWATA, YOU'RE...
...IN CHARGE OF OFFENSE.
......
BUZZ BUZZ
YES, SIR!
LISTEN, DON'T UNDERESTIMATE THEM.
DON'T REPEAT
LAST YEAR'S MISTAKE!
GIVE IT ALL YOU GOT!
Yes, Sir!
WE'RE HARA!
YEAH COACH!
WE'LL WIN!

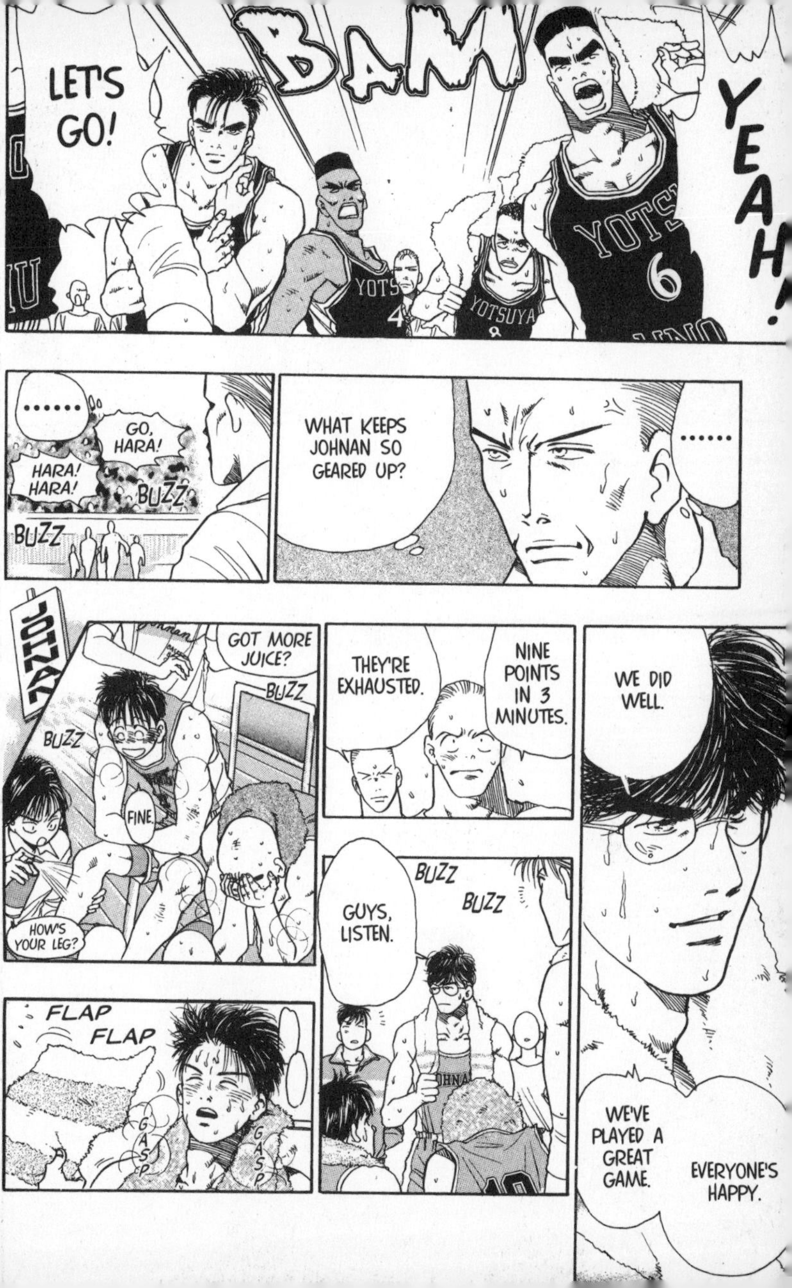
YEAH!
BAM
LET'S GO!
......
WHAT KEEPS JOHNAN SO GEARED UP?
......
GO, HARA!
HARA! HARA!
BUZZ
BUZZ
WE DID WELL.
WE'VE PLAYED A GREAT GAME.
EVERYONE'S HAPPY.
NINE POINTS IN 3 MINUTES.
THEY'RE EXHAUSTED.
GOT MORE JUICE?
BUZZ
BUZZ
FINE.
HOW'S YOUR LEG?
BUZZ
BUZZ
GUYS, LISTEN.
......
FLAP
FLAP
GASP
GASP

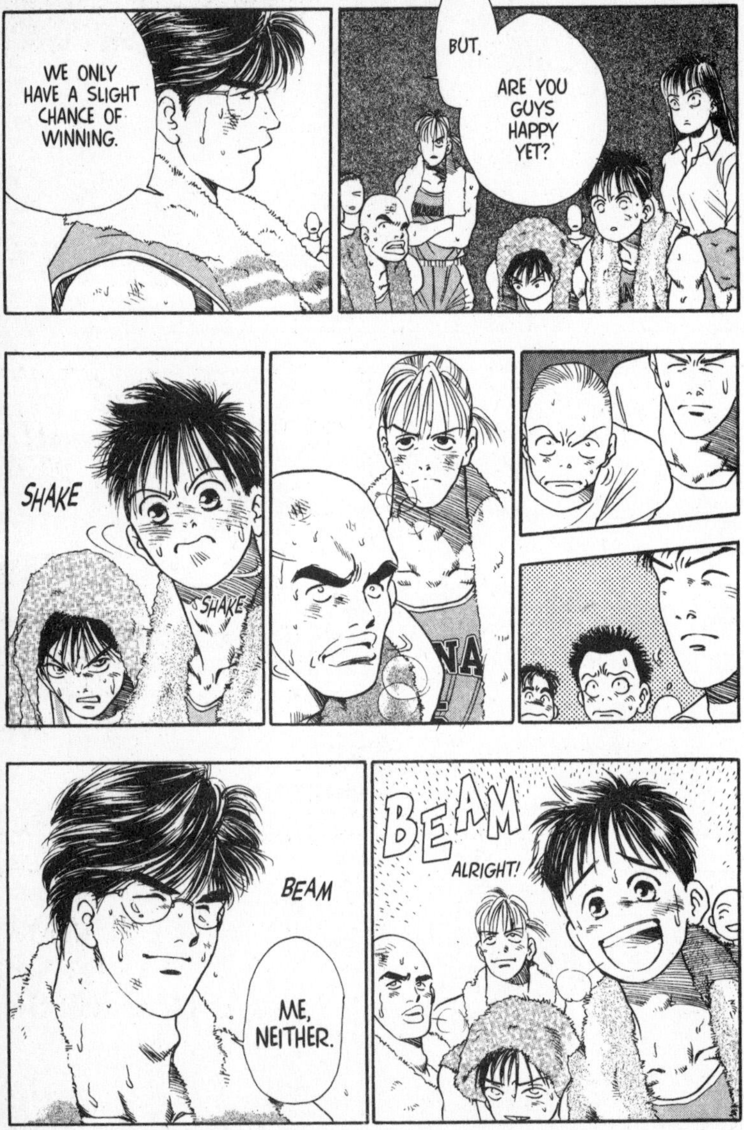
WE ONLY HAVE A SLIGHT CHANCE OF WINNING.
BUT,
ARE YOU GUYS HAPPY YET?
SHAKE
SHAKE
BEAM
ME, NEITHER.
BEAM
ALRIGHT!

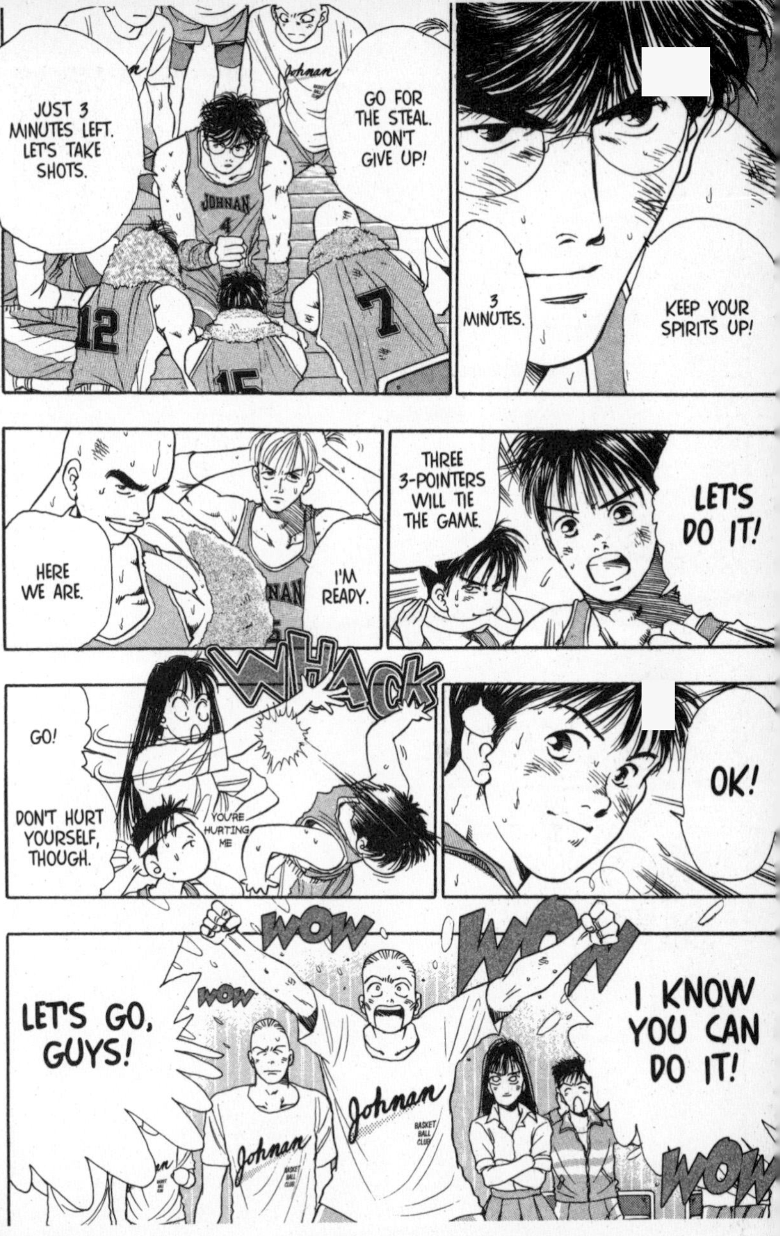
JUST 3 MINUTES LEFT. LET'S TAKE SHOTS.
GO FOR THE STEAL. DON'T GIVE UP!
3 MINUTES.
KEEP YOUR SPIRITS UP!
HERE WE ARE.
I'M READY.
THREE 3-POINTERS WILL TIE THE GAME.
LET'S DO IT!
WHACK
GO!
DON'T HURT YOURSELF, THOUGH.
YOU'RE HURTING ME
OK!
WOW
WOW
WOW
LET'S GO, GUYS!
I KNOW YOU CAN DO IT!
WOW

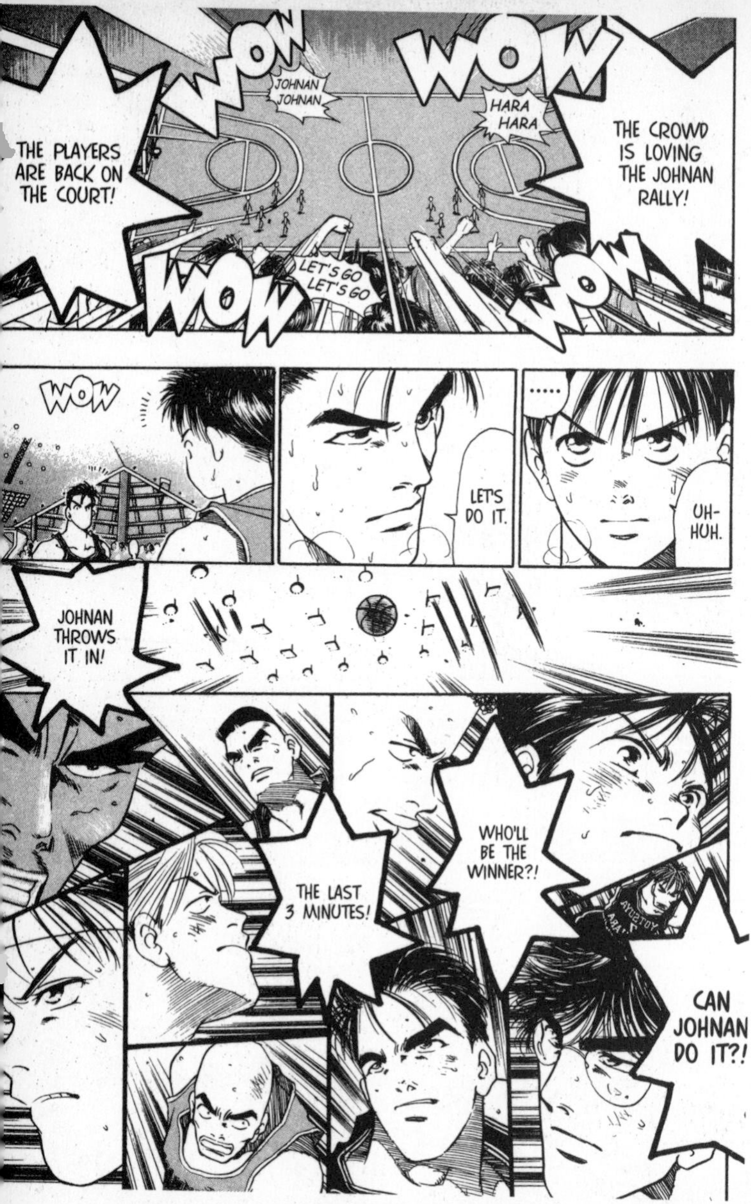
WOW
THE CROWD IS LOVING THE JOHNAN RALLY!
HARA HARA
JOHNAN JOHNAN
WOW
THE PLAYERS ARE BACK ON THE COURT!
WOW
LET'S GO LET'S GO
WOW
......
UH-HUH.
LET'S DO IT.
WOW
JOHNAN THROWS IT IN!
CAN JOHNAN DO IT?!
WHO'LL BE THE WINNER?!
THE LAST 3 MINUTES!

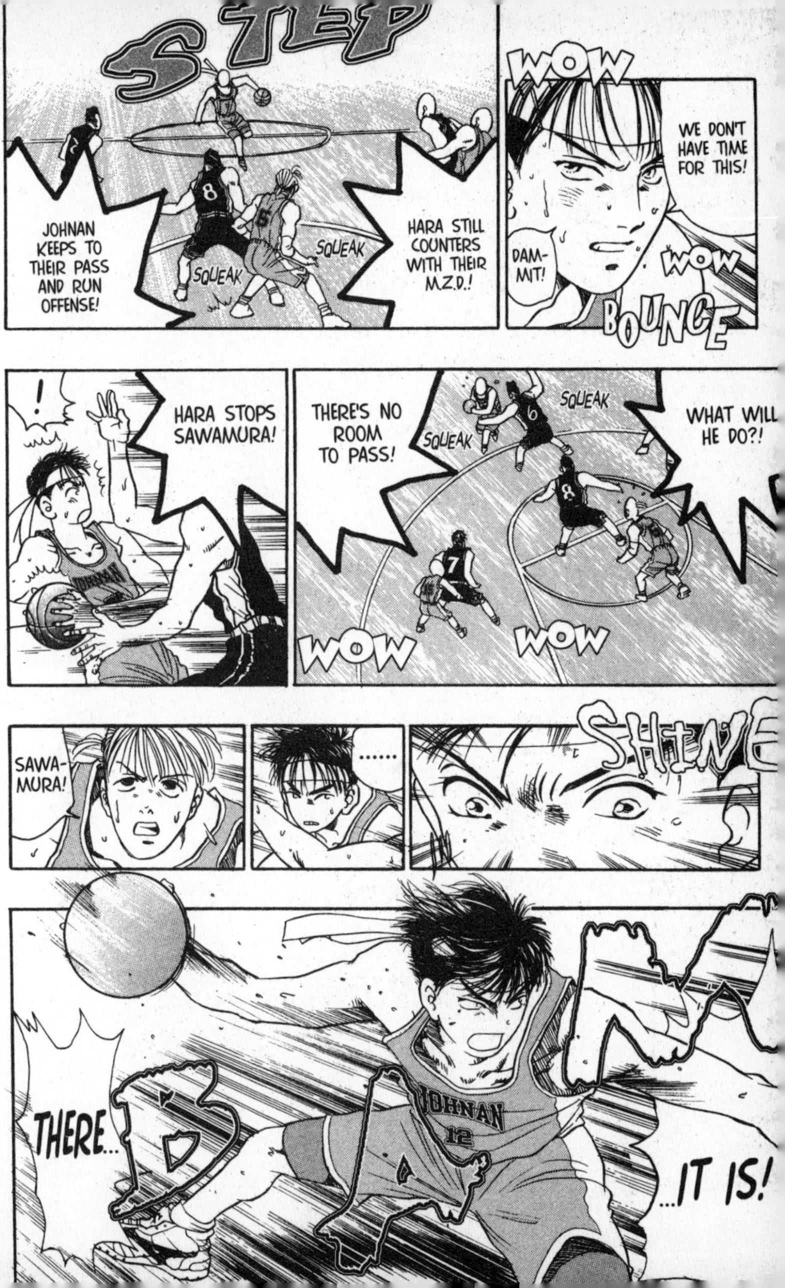
STEP
JOHNAN KEEPS TO THEIR PASS AND RUN OFFENSE!
SQUEAK
SQUEAK
HARA STILL COUNTERS WITH THEIR M.Z.D.!
WOW
WE DON'T HAVE TIME FOR THIS!
DAM-MIT!
WOW
BOUNCE
!
HARA STOPS SAWAMURA!
THERE'S NO ROOM TO PASS!
SQUEAK
SQUEAK
WHAT WILL HE DO?!
WOW
WOW
SAWA-MURA!
......
SHINE
JOHNAN
12
THERE...
...IT IS!

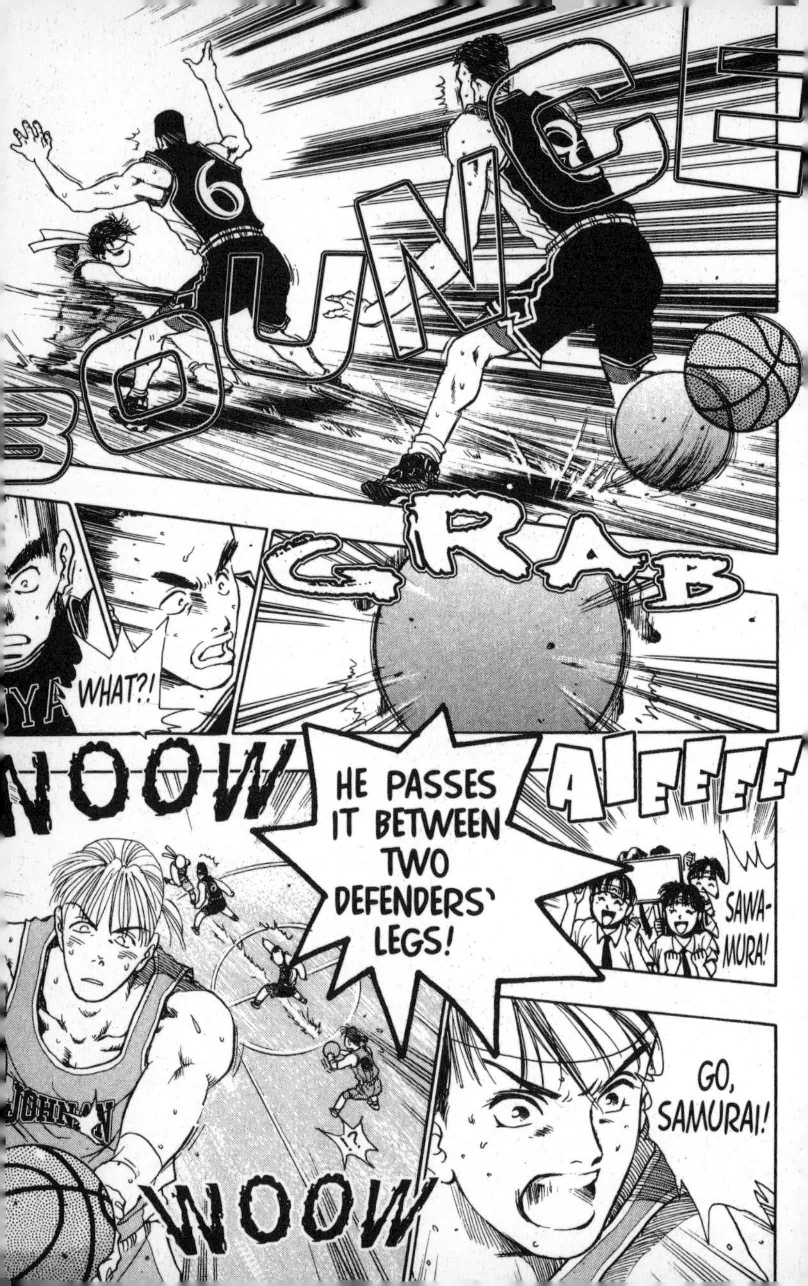
BOUNCE
GRAB
WHAT?!
AIEEEE
SAWA-MURA!
HE PASSES IT BETWEEN TWO DEFENDERS' LEGS!
NOOW
GO, SAMURAI!
!?
WOOW

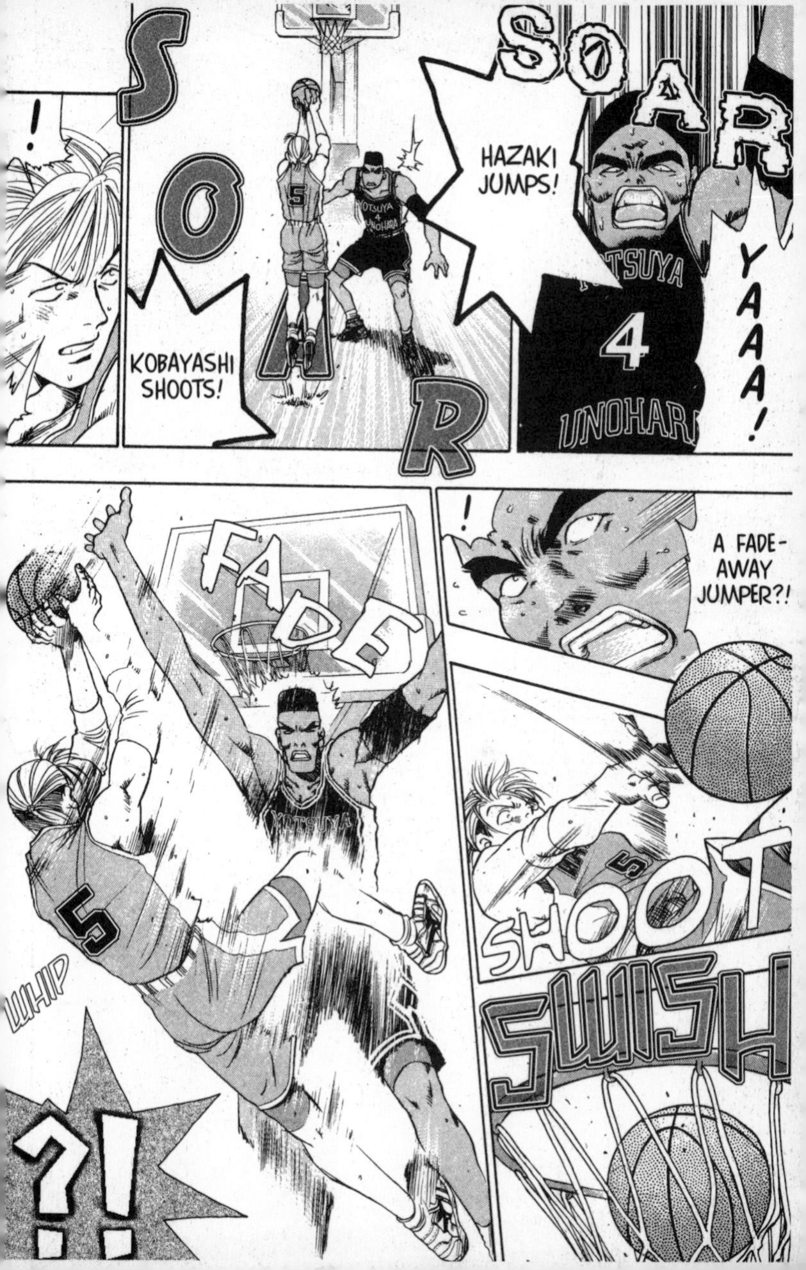
SOAR
YAAAA!
HAZAKI JUMPS!
YOTSUYA 4 UNOHARA
SOAR
KOBAYASHI SHOOTS!
!
!
A FADE-AWAY JUMPER?!
SHOOT
SWISH
FADE
WHIP
?!

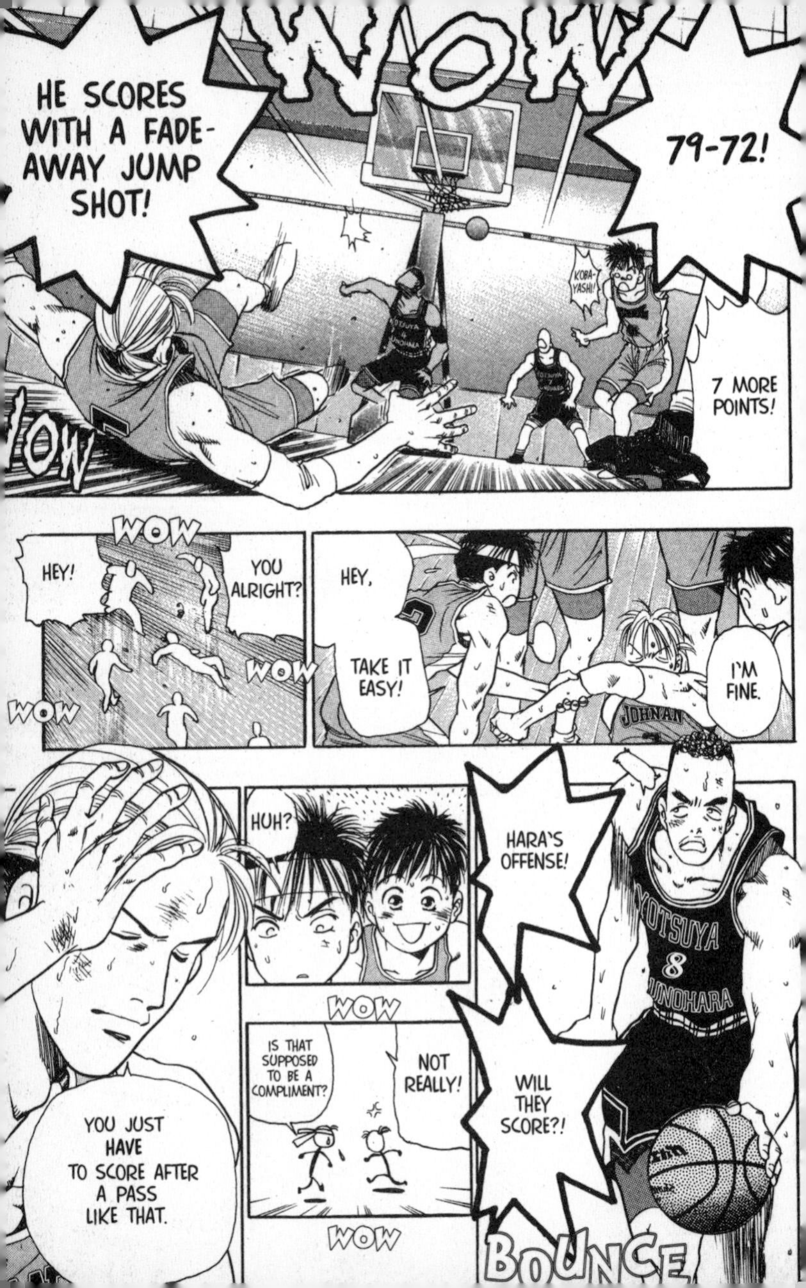
WOW
HE SCORES WITH A FADE-AWAY JUMP SHOT!
79-72!
KOBA-YASHI!
WOW
7 MORE POINTS!
WOW
HEY!
YOU ALRIGHT?
WOW
WOW
HEY,
TAKE IT EASY!
I'M FINE.
YOU JUST HAVE TO SCORE AFTER A PASS LIKE THAT.
HUH?
WOW
IS THAT SUPPOSED TO BE A COMPLIMENT?
NOT REALLY!
WOW
HARA'S OFFENSE!
WILL THEY SCORE?!
BOUNCE

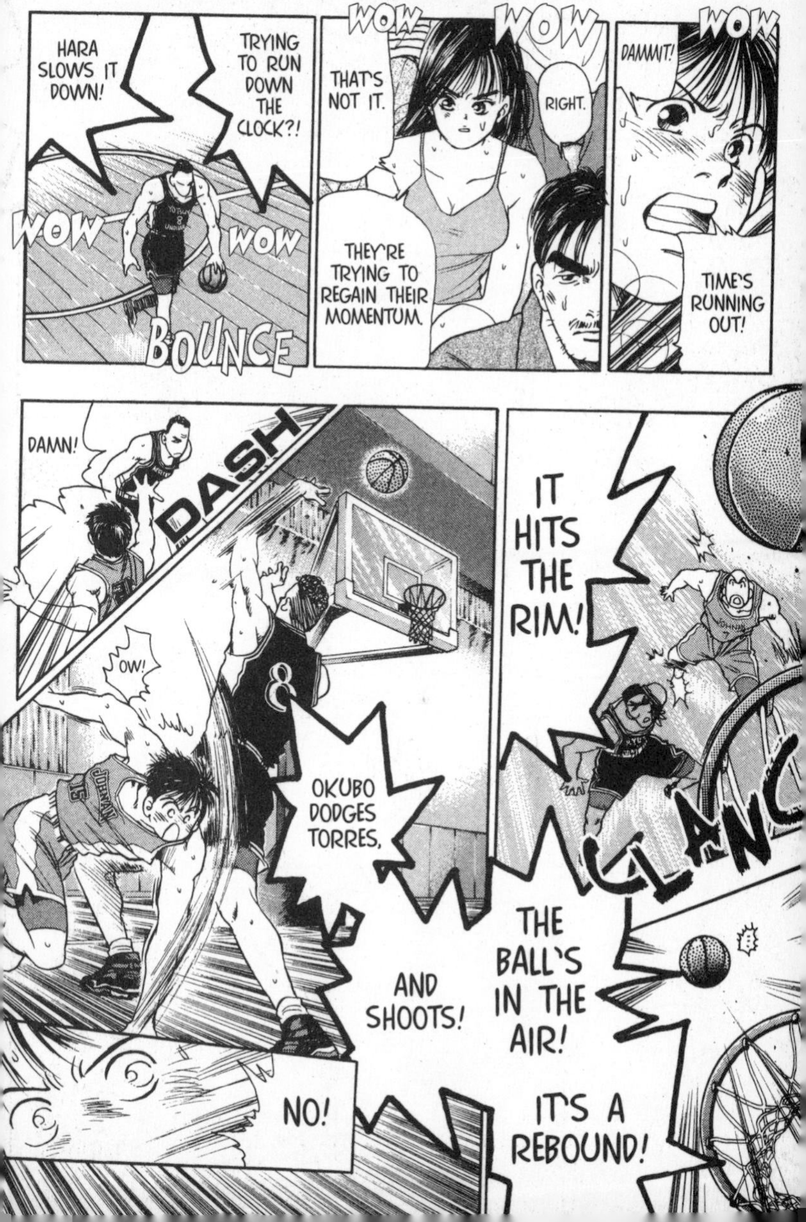
HARA SLOWS IT DOWN!
TRYING TO RUN DOWN THE CLOCK?!
WOW
WOW
BOUNCE
WOW
WOW
THAT'S NOT IT.
THEY'RE TRYING TO REGAIN THEIR MOMENTUM.
RIGHT.
WOW
DAMMIT!
TIME'S RUNNING OUT!
DAMN!
DASH
OW!
OKUBO DODGES TORRES,
AND SHOOTS!
NO!
IT HITS THE RIM!
CLANG
THE BALL'S IN THE AIR!
IT'S A REBOUND!

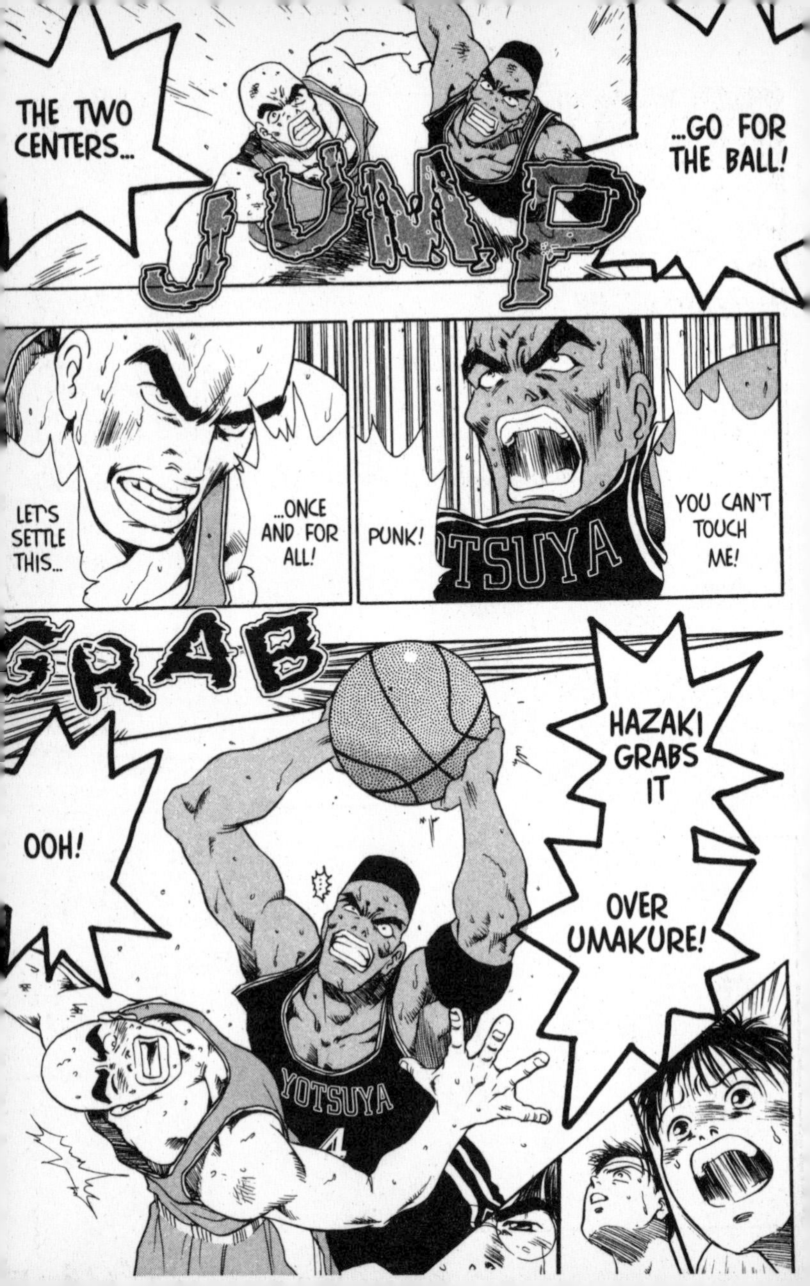
THE TWO CENTERS...
JUMP
...GO FOR THE BALL!
LET'S SETTLE THIS...
...ONCE AND FOR ALL!
PUNK!
YOTSUYA
YOU CAN'T TOUCH ME!
GRAB
OOH!
HAZAKI GRABS IT
OVER UMAKURE!
YOTSUYA
4

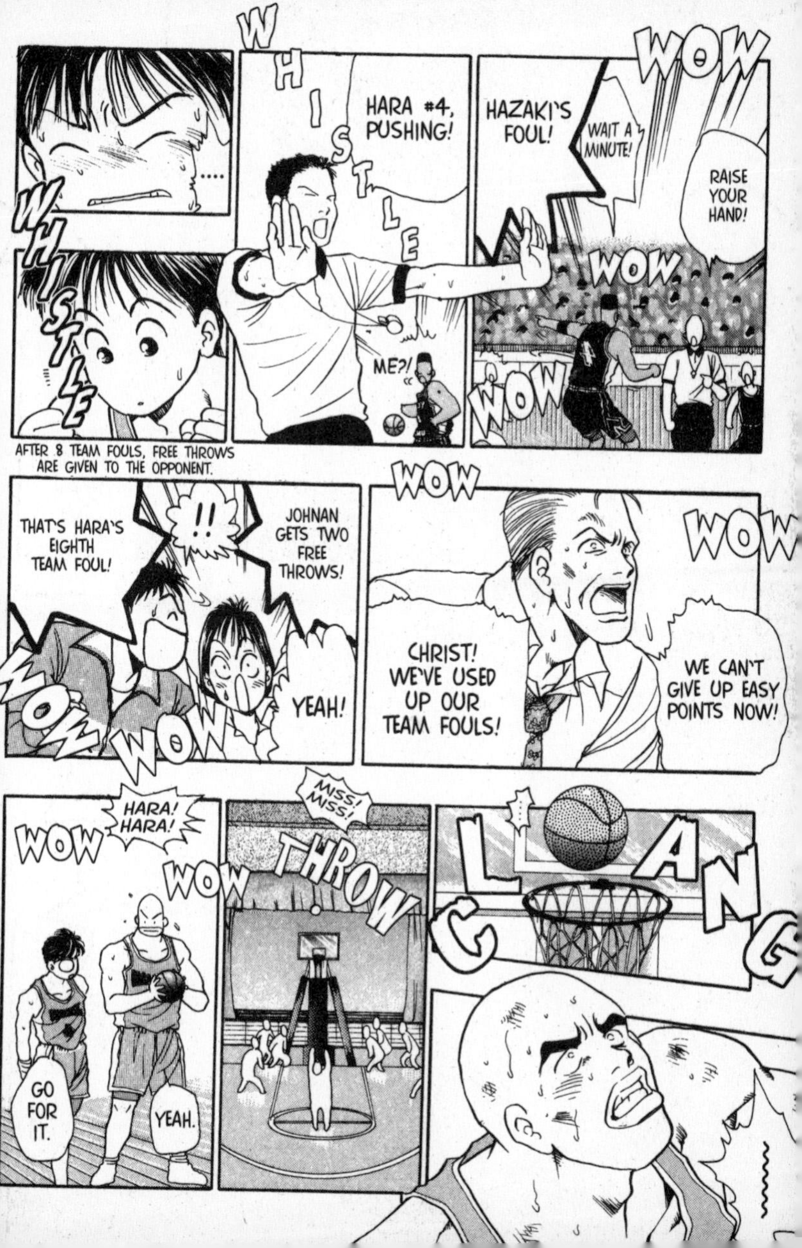
WHISTLE
....
WHISTLE
HARA #4, PUSHING!
ME?!
HAZAKI'S FOUL!
WAIT A MINUTE!
RAISE YOUR HAND!
WOW
WOW
WOW
AFTER 8 TEAM FOULS, FREE THROWS ARE GIVEN TO THE OPPONENT.
THAT'S HARA'S EIGHTH TEAM FOUL!
!!
JOHNAN GETS TWO FREE THROWS!
YEAH!
WOW
WOW
WOW
CHRIST! WE'VE USED UP OUR TEAM FOULS!
WE CAN'T GIVE UP EASY POINTS NOW!
WOW
WOW
HARA! HARA!
WOW
GO FOR IT.
YEAH.
MISS! MISS!
THROW
CLANG

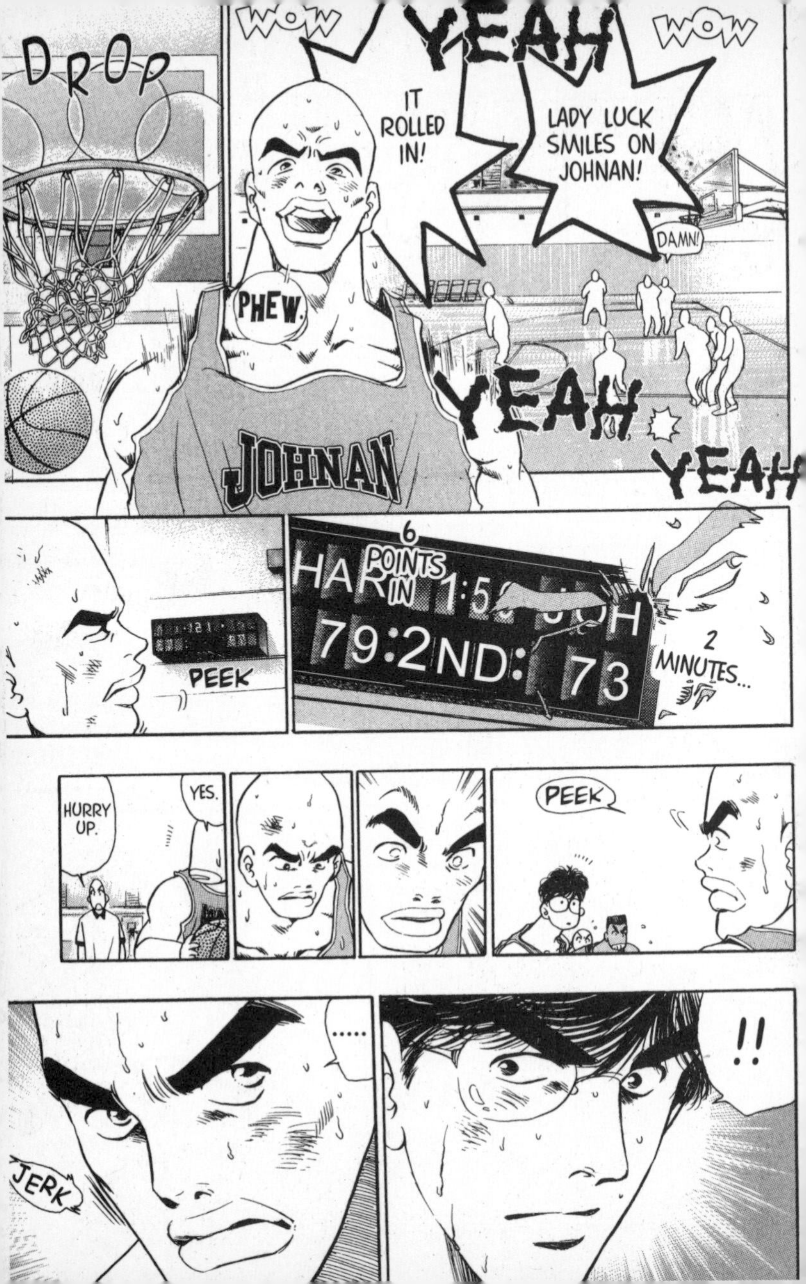
WOW
YEAH
WOW
LADY LUCK SMILES ON JOHNAN!
IT ROLLED IN!
DAMN!
PHEW.
YEAH
YEAH
DROP
6 POINTS IN
2 MINUTES...
PEEK
PEEK
YES.
HURRY UP.
!!
.....
JERK

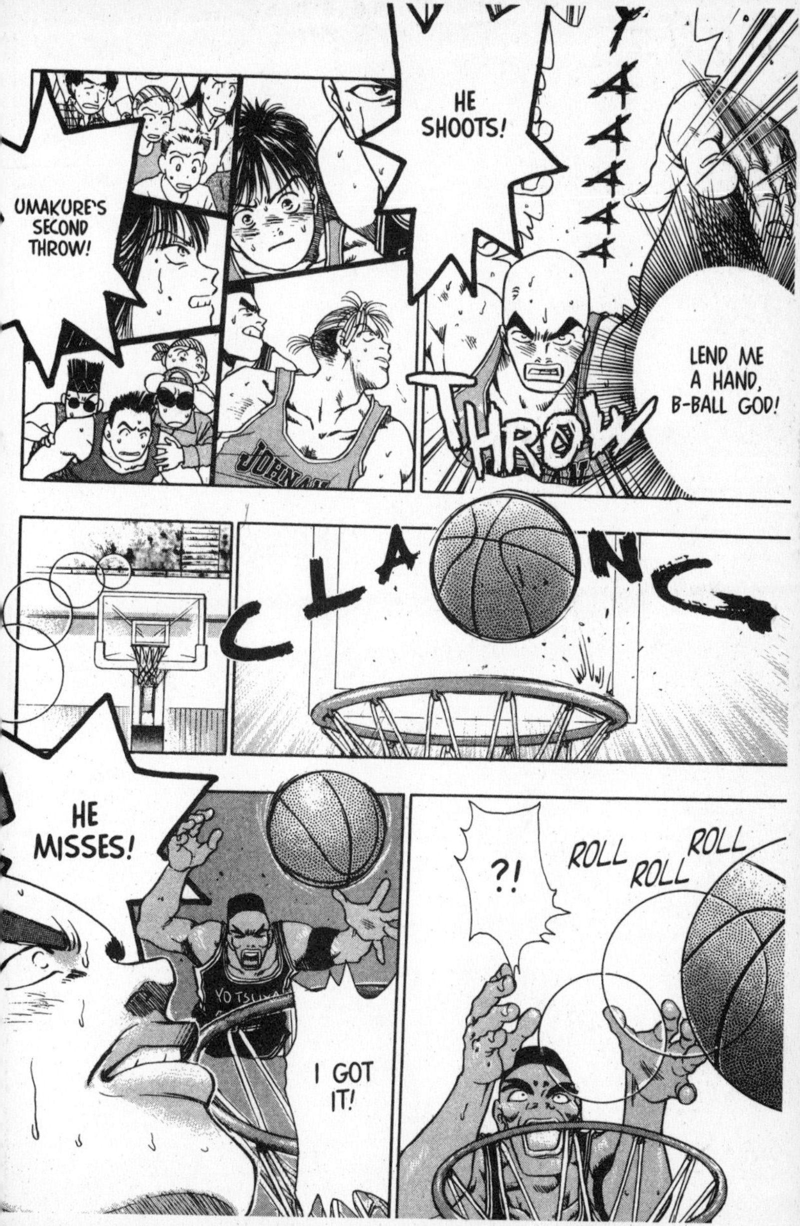
LEND ME A HAND, B-BALL GOD!
THROW
HE SHOOTS!
UMAKURE'S SECOND THROW!
CLANG
?!
ROLL
ROLL
ROLL
HE MISSES!
I GOT IT!

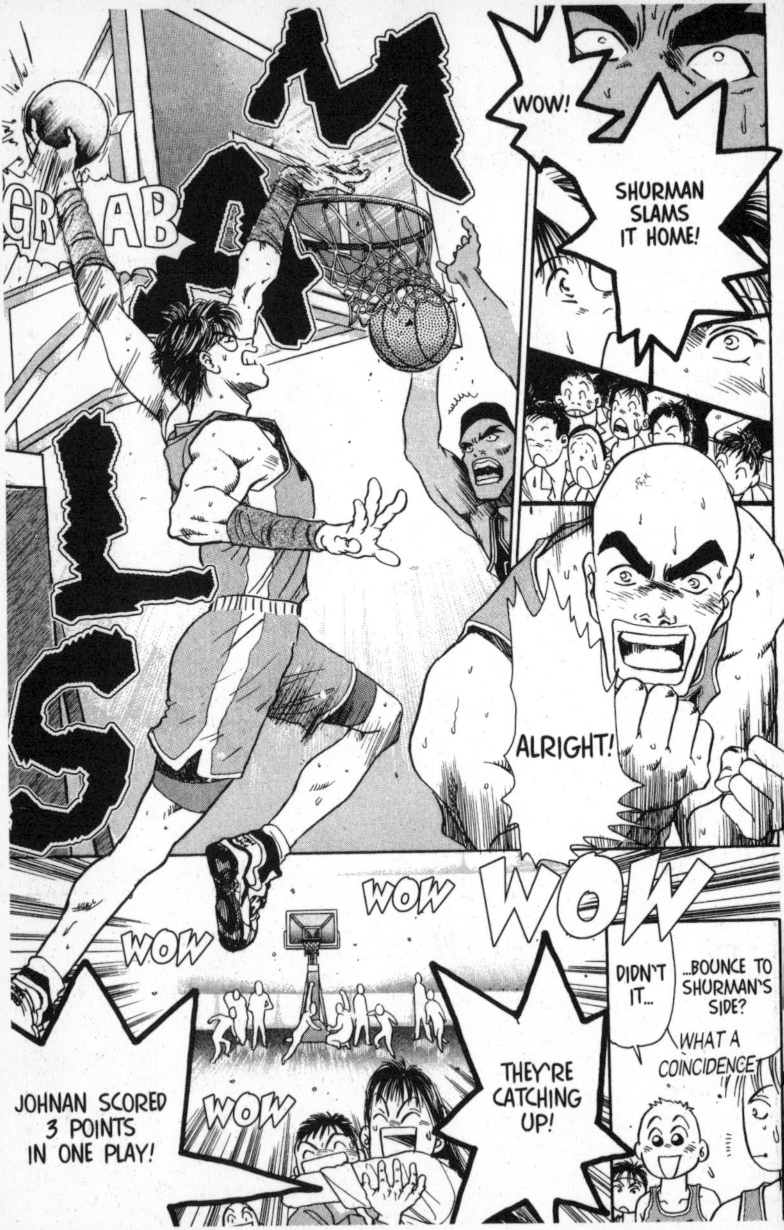
WOW!
SHURMAN SLAMS IT HOME!
ALRIGHT!
GRAB
SLAM
WOW
DIDN'T IT...
...BOUNCE TO SHURMAN'S SIDE?
WHAT A COINCIDENCE
WOW
THEY'RE CATCHING UP!
WOW
WOW
JOHNAN SCORED 3 POINTS IN ONE PLAY!

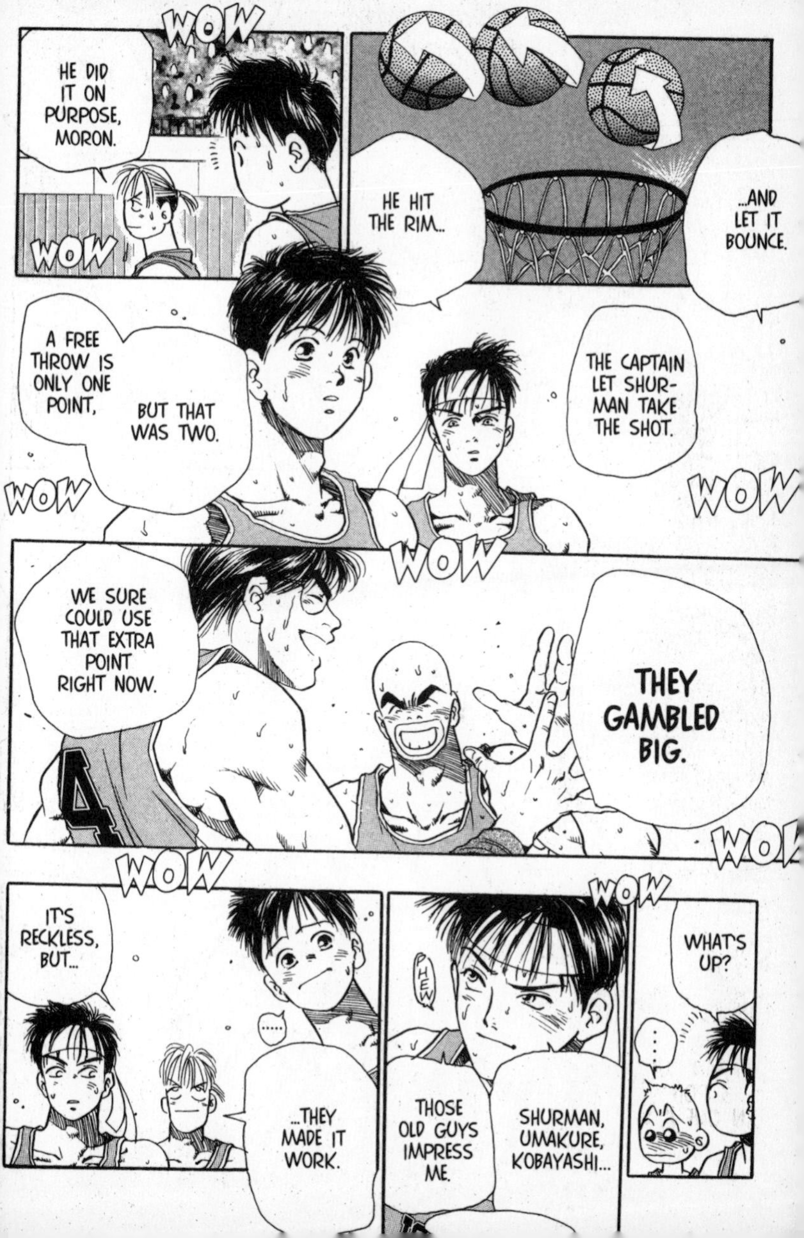
WOW
HE DID IT ON PURPOSE, MORON.
WOW
HE HIT THE RIM...
...AND LET IT BOUNCE.
A FREE THROW IS ONLY ONE POINT,
BUT THAT WAS TWO.
THE CAPTAIN LET SHURMAN TAKE THE SHOT.
WOW
WOW
WOW
WE SURE COULD USE THAT EXTRA POINT RIGHT NOW.
THEY GAMBLED BIG.
WOW
IT'S RECKLESS, BUT...
......
...THEY MADE IT WORK.
WOW
WHAT'S UP?
PHEW
...
SHURMAN, UMAKURE, KOBAYASHI...
THOSE OLD GUYS IMPRESS ME.

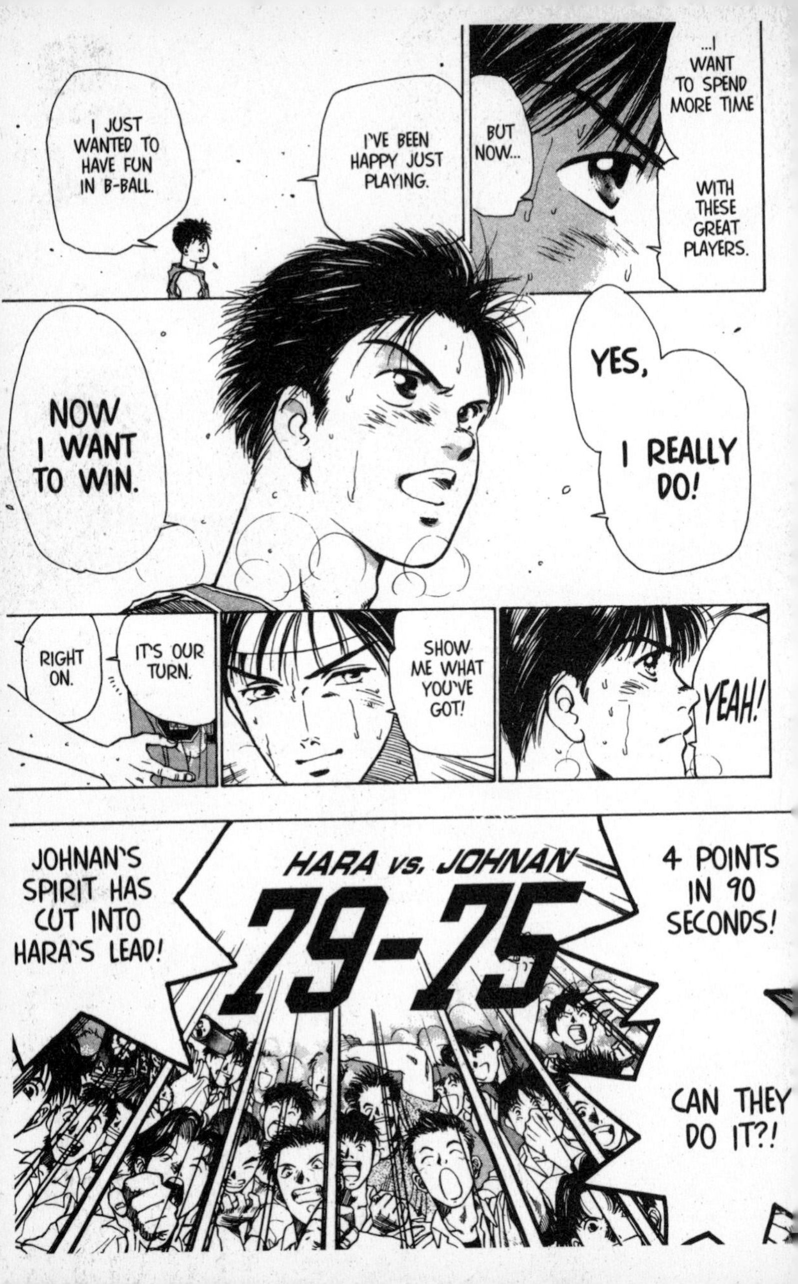
I JUST WANTED TO HAVE FUN IN B-BALL.
I'VE BEEN HAPPY JUST PLAYING.
BUT NOW...
...I WANT TO SPEND MORE TIME
WITH THESE GREAT PLAYERS.
NOW I WANT TO WIN.
YES,
I REALLY DO!
RIGHT ON.
IT'S OUR TURN.
SHOW ME WHAT YOU'VE GOT!
YEAH!
JOHNAN'S SPIRIT HAS CUT INTO HARA'S LEAD!
HARA vs. JOHNAN
79-75
4 POINTS IN 90 SECONDS!
CAN THEY DO IT?!

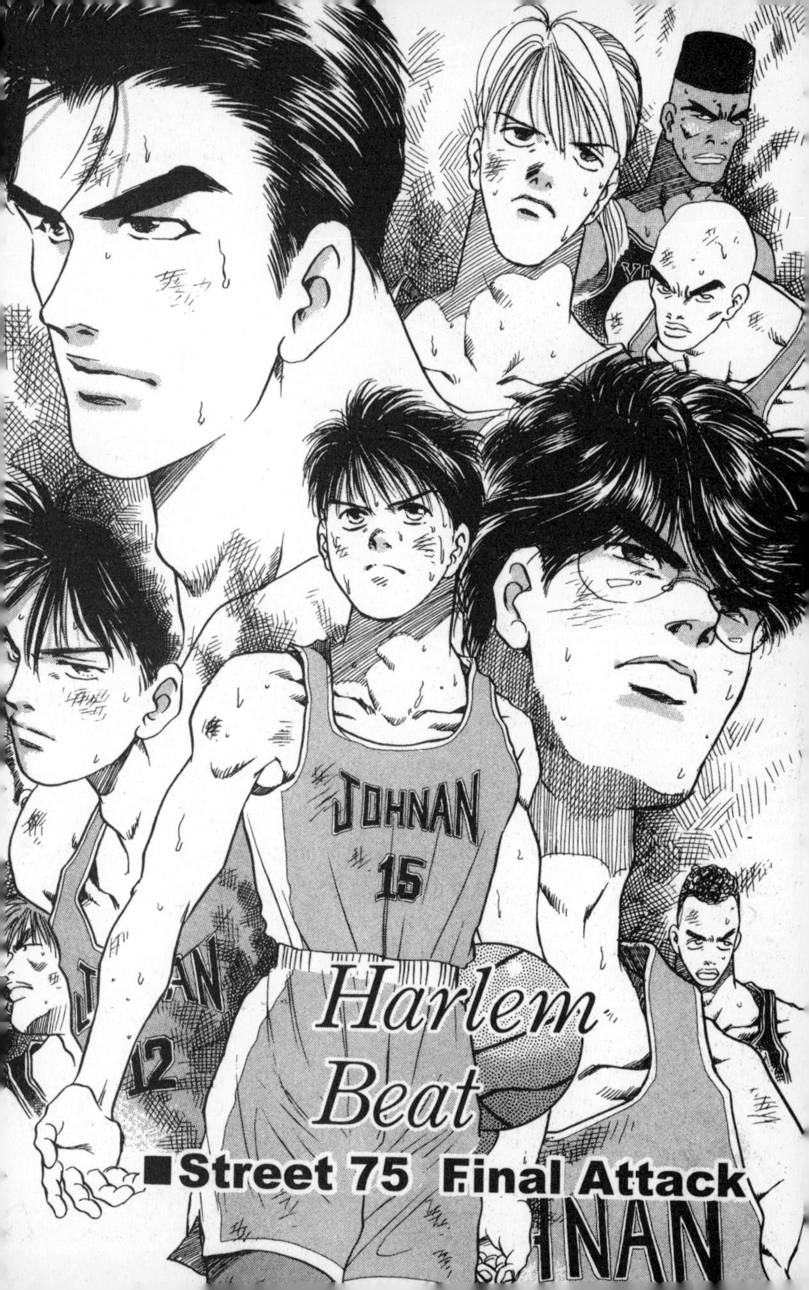
JOHNAN
15
Harlem Beat
■Street 75 Final Attack

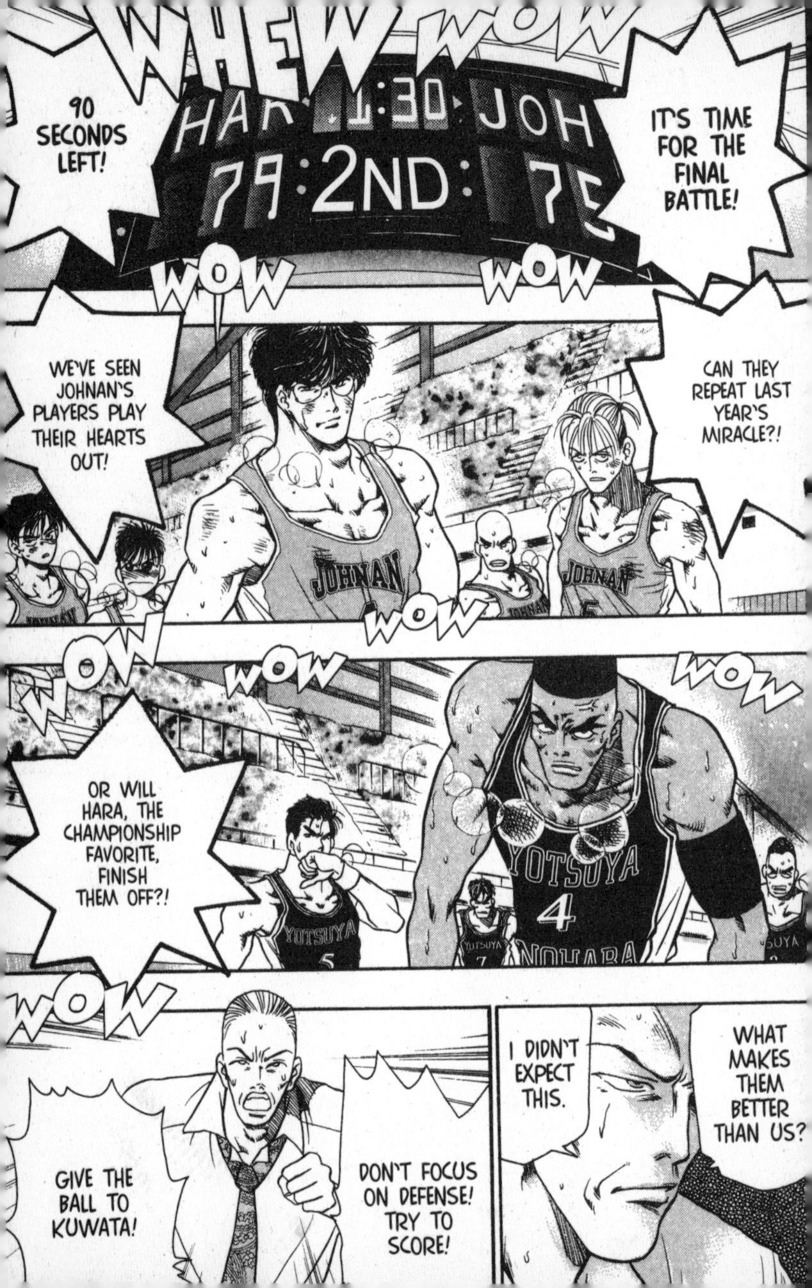
WHEW WOW
90 SECONDS LEFT!
HAR 1:30 JOH
79 2ND 75
IT'S TIME FOR THE FINAL BATTLE!
WOW WOW
WE'VE SEEN JOHNAN'S PLAYERS PLAY THEIR HEARTS OUT!
CAN THEY REPEAT LAST YEAR'S MIRACLE?!
JOHNAN
JOHNAN
WOW
WOW WOW WOW
OR WILL HARA, THE CHAMPIONSHIP FAVORITE, FINISH THEM OFF?!
YOTSUYA
4
YOTSUYA
5
WOW
GIVE THE BALL TO KUWATA!
DON'T FOCUS ON DEFENSE! TRY TO SCORE!
I DIDN'T EXPECT THIS.
WHAT MAKES THEM BETTER THAN US?

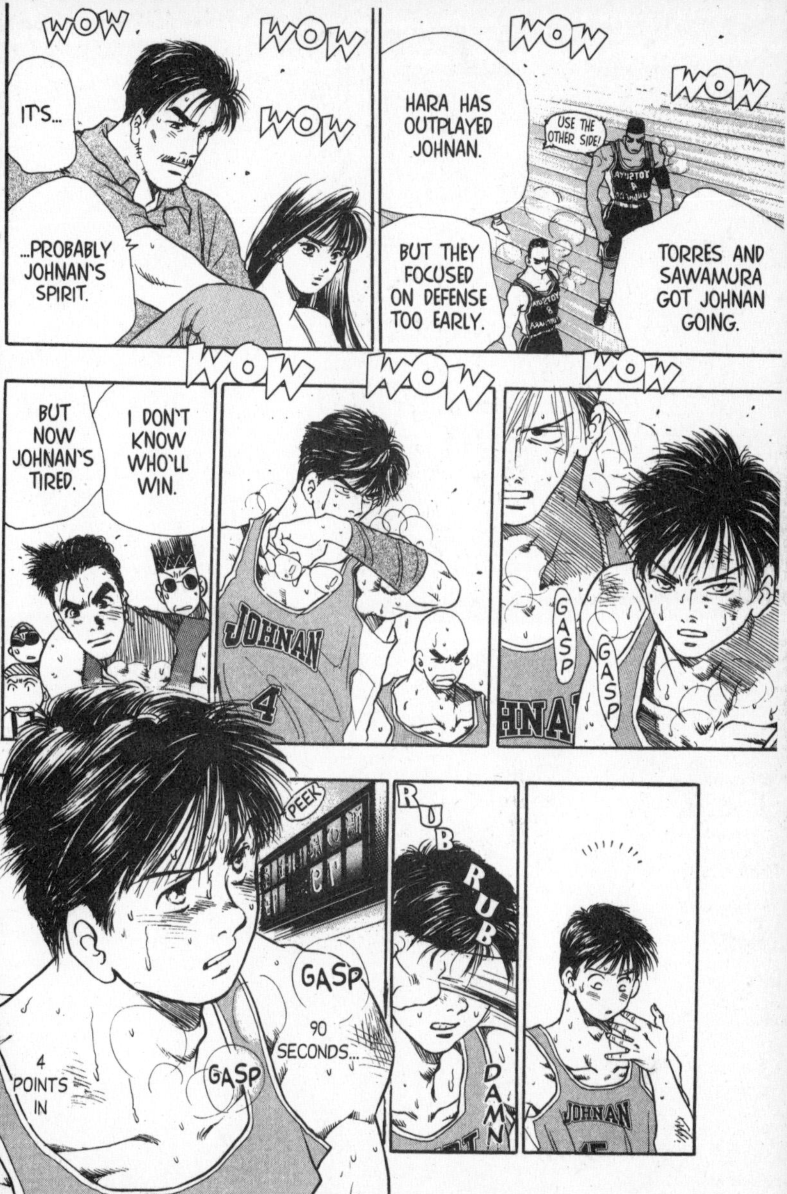
WOW
WOW
WOW
IT'S...
...PROBABLY JOHNAN'S SPIRIT.
WOW
WOW
HARA HAS OUTPLAYED JOHNAN.
BUT THEY FOCUSED ON DEFENSE TOO EARLY.
USE THE OTHER SIDE!
TORRES AND SAWAMURA GOT JOHNAN GOING.
WOW
WOW
WOW
BUT NOW JOHNAN'S TIRED.
I DON'T KNOW WHO'LL WIN.
JOHNAN
4
GASP
GASP
PEEK
GASP
90 SECONDS...
4 POINTS IN
GASP
RUB RUB
DAMN
JOHNAN

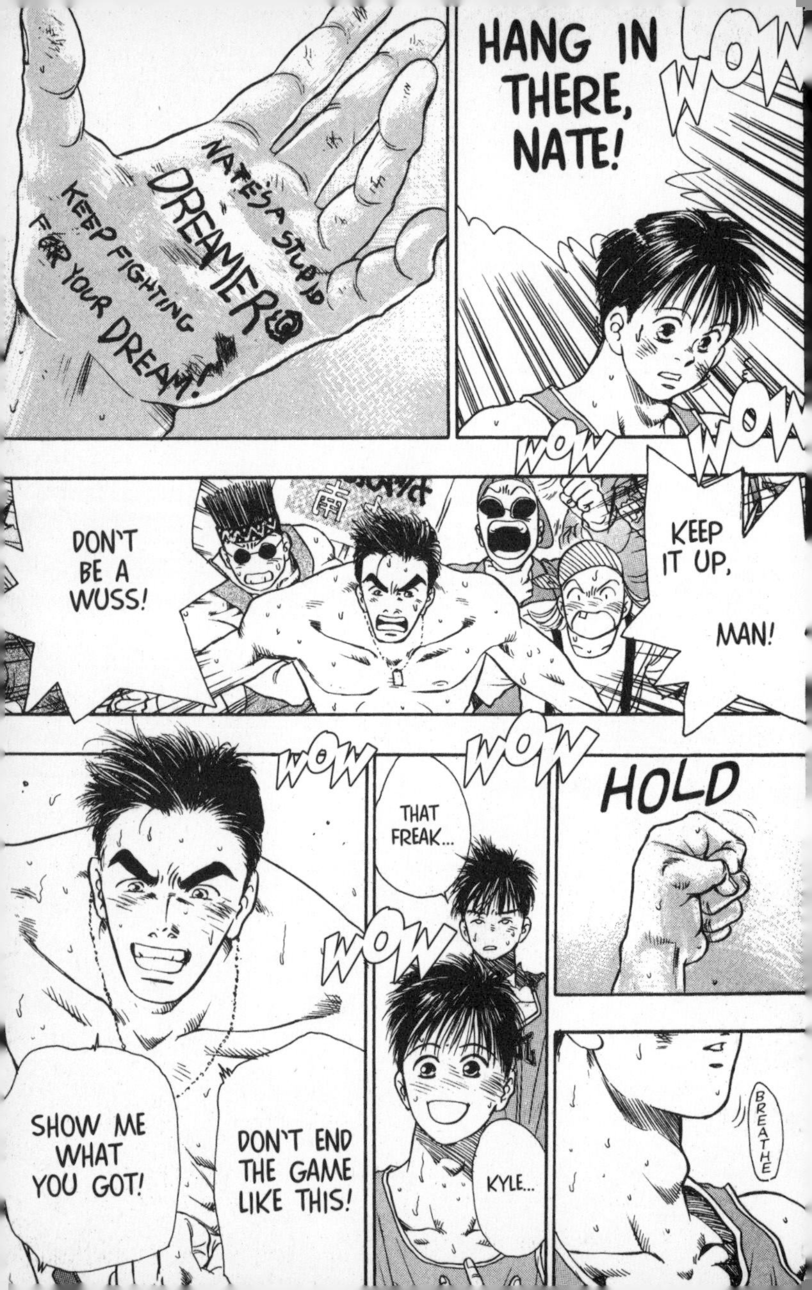
HANG IN THERE, NATE!
WOW
WOW
WOW
WOW
NATE'S A STUPID
DREAMER
KEEP FIGHTING
FOR YOUR DREAM!
KEEP IT UP, MAN!
DON'T BE A WUSS!
HOLD
BREATHE
WOW
WOW
THAT FREAK...
WOW
KYLE...
DON'T END THE GAME LIKE THIS!
SHOW ME WHAT YOU GOT!

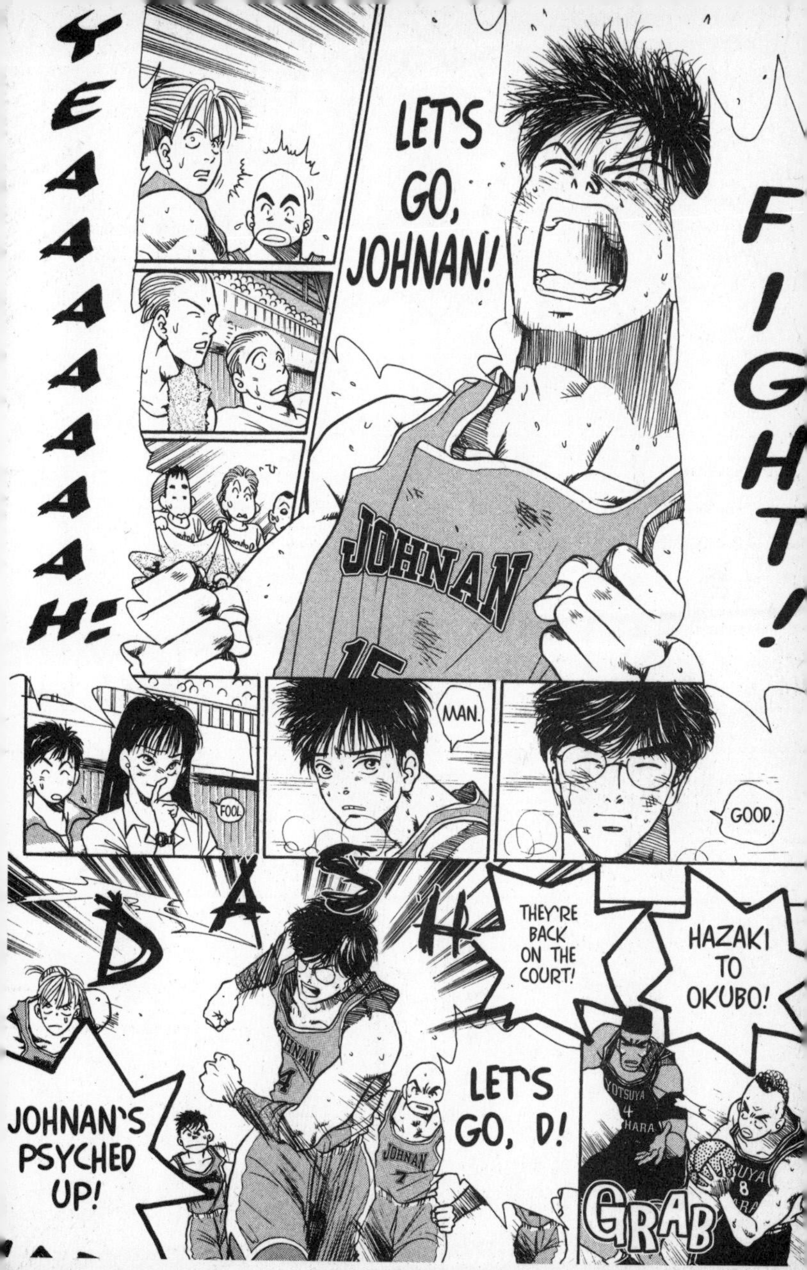
FIGHT!
LET'S GO, JOHNAN!
YEAAAAAAAH!
GOOD.
MAN.
FOOL
HAZAKI TO OKUBO!
THEY'RE BACK ON THE COURT!
DASH
GRAB
LET'S GO, D!
JOHNAN'S PSYCHED UP!

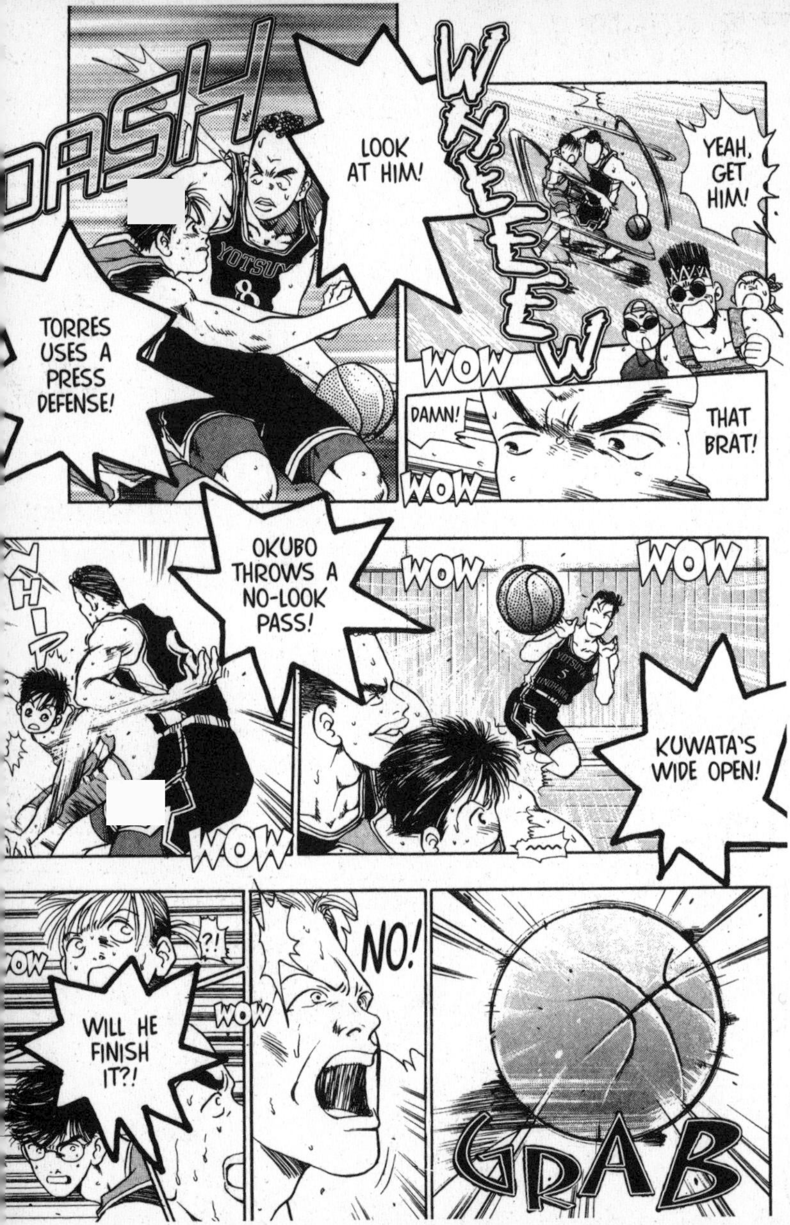
DASH
LOOK AT HIM!
TORRES USES A PRESS DEFENSE!
WHEEW
YEAH, GET HIM!
WOW
DAMN!
THAT BRAT!
WOW
WHIP
OKUBO THROWS A NO-LOOK PASS!
WOW
WOW
WOW
KUWATA'S WIDE OPEN!
?!
WILL HE FINISH IT?!
WOW
NO!
GRAB

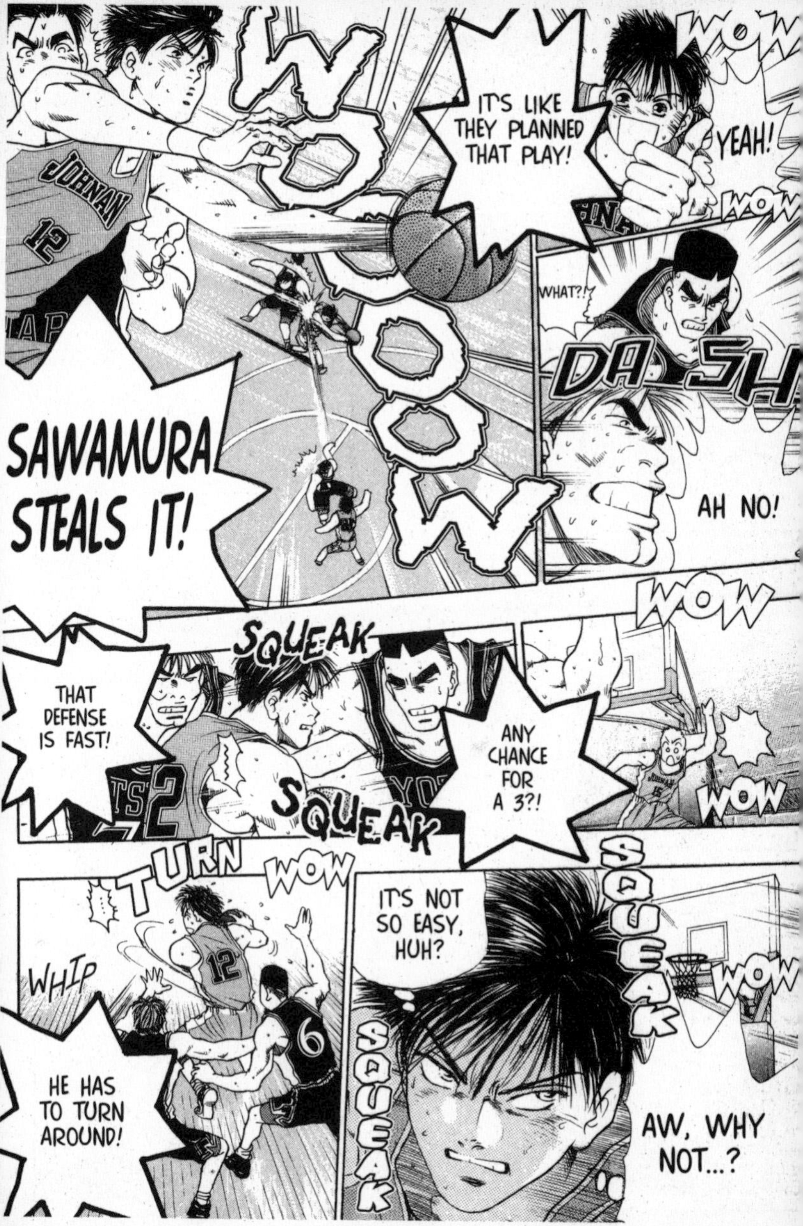
WOW
IT'S LIKE THEY PLANNED THAT PLAY!
YEAH!
WOW
WHAT?!
DASH
AH NO!
WOOOOW
SAWAMURA STEALS IT!
WOW
WOW
ANY CHANCE FOR A 3?!
SQUEAK
THAT DEFENSE IS FAST!
SQUEAK
SQUEAK
WOW
IT'S NOT SO EASY, HUH?
SQUEAK
AW, WHY NOT...?
TURN
WOW
WHIP
HE HAS TO TURN AROUND!

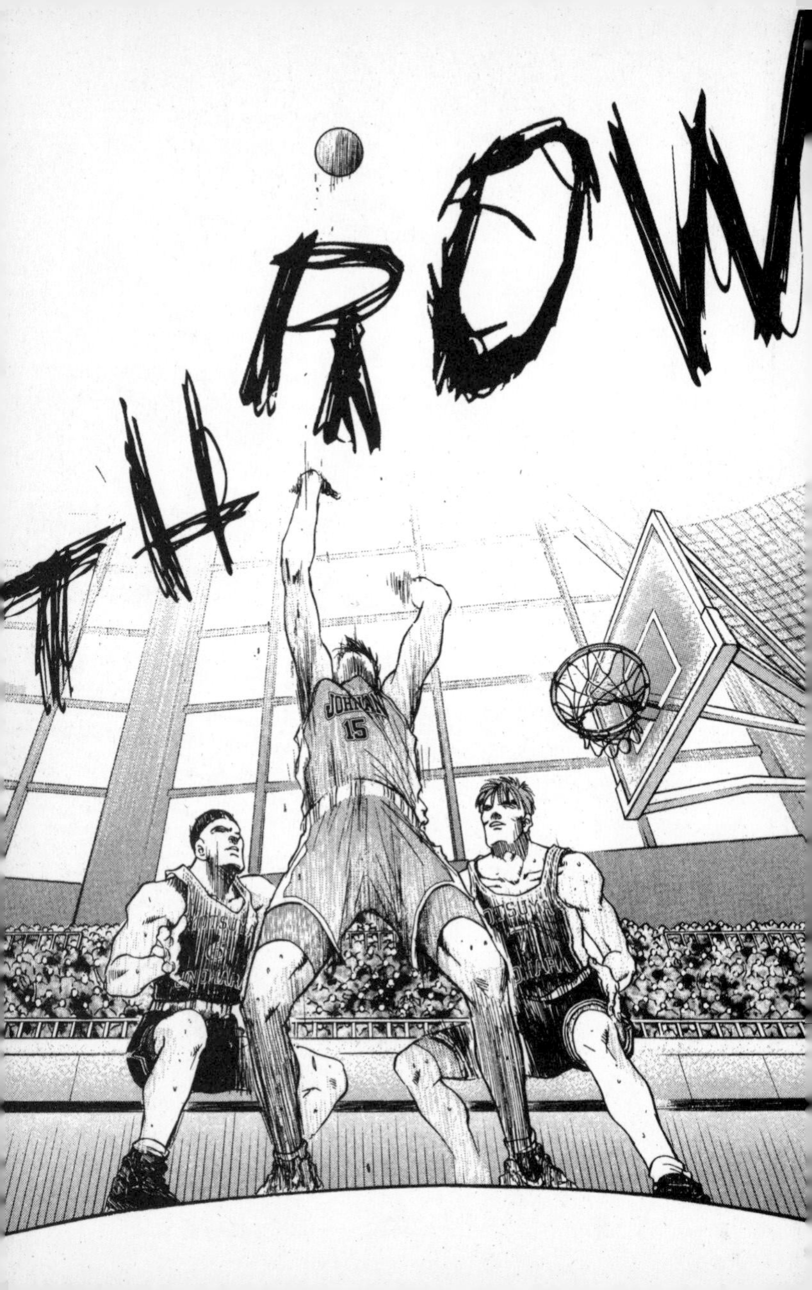
THROW
JOHNAN
15

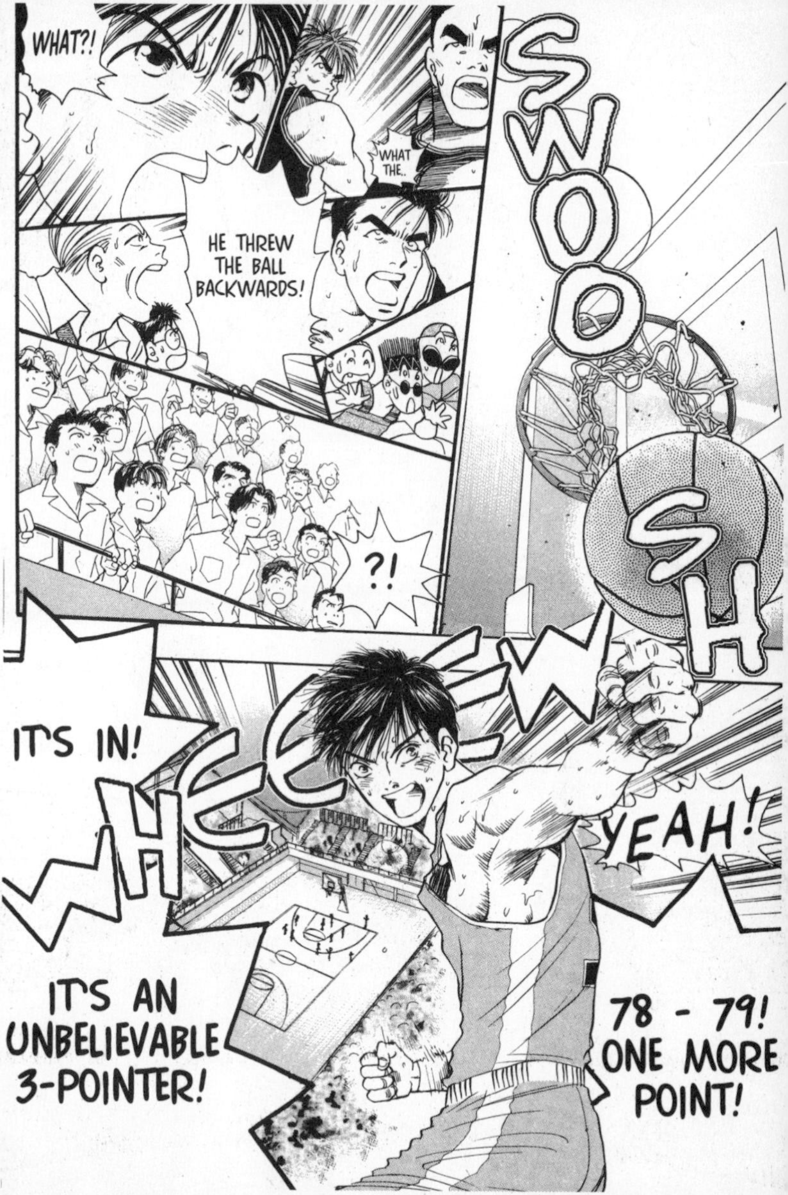
SWOOSH
WHAT THE..
WHAT?!
HE THREW THE BALL BACKWARDS!
?!
WHEEEW
YEAH!
IT'S IN!
78 - 79! ONE MORE POINT!
IT'S AN UNBELIEVABLE 3-POINTER!

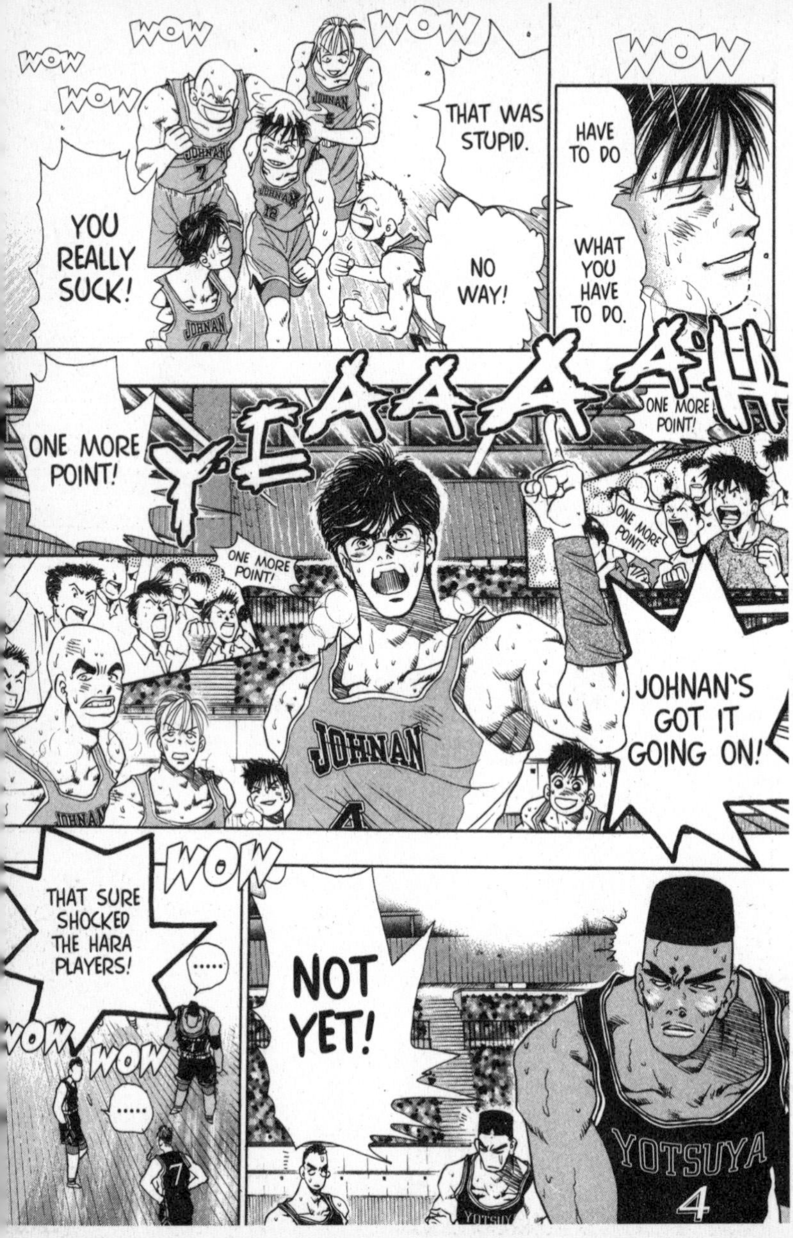
WOW
HAVE TO DO
WHAT YOU HAVE TO DO.
WOW
THAT WAS STUPID.
WOW
WOW
WOW
NO WAY!
YOU REALLY SUCK!
YEAAAAH
ONE MORE POINT!
ONE MORE POINT!
JOHNAN'S GOT IT GOING ON!
ONE MORE POINT!
ONE MORE POINT!
NOT YET!
WOW
THAT SURE SHOCKED THE HARA PLAYERS!
......
WOW
WOW
......

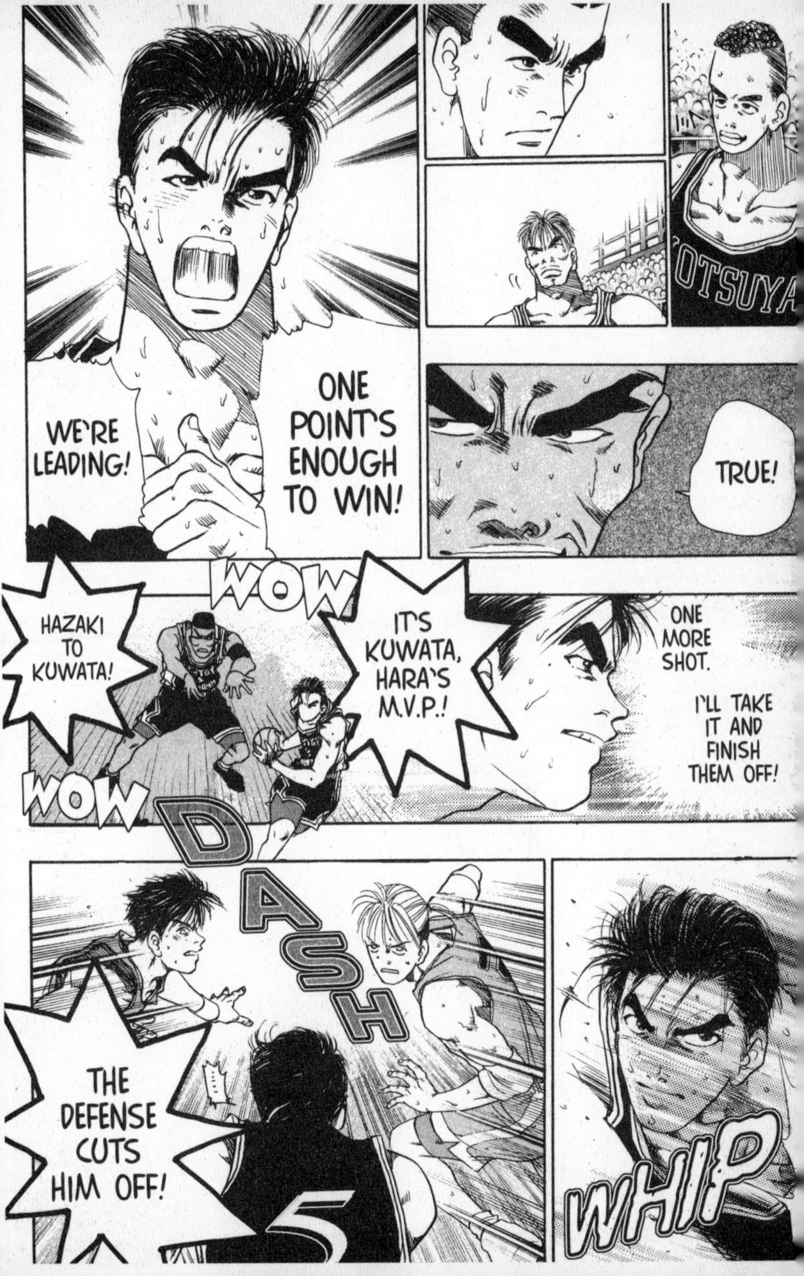
WE'RE LEADING!
ONE POINT'S ENOUGH TO WIN!
OTSUYA
TRUE!
WOW
HAZAKI TO KUWATA!
IT'S KUWATA, HARA'S M.V.P.!
ONE MORE SHOT.
I'LL TAKE IT AND FINISH THEM OFF!
WOW
DASH
THE DEFENSE CUTS HIM OFF!
WHIP

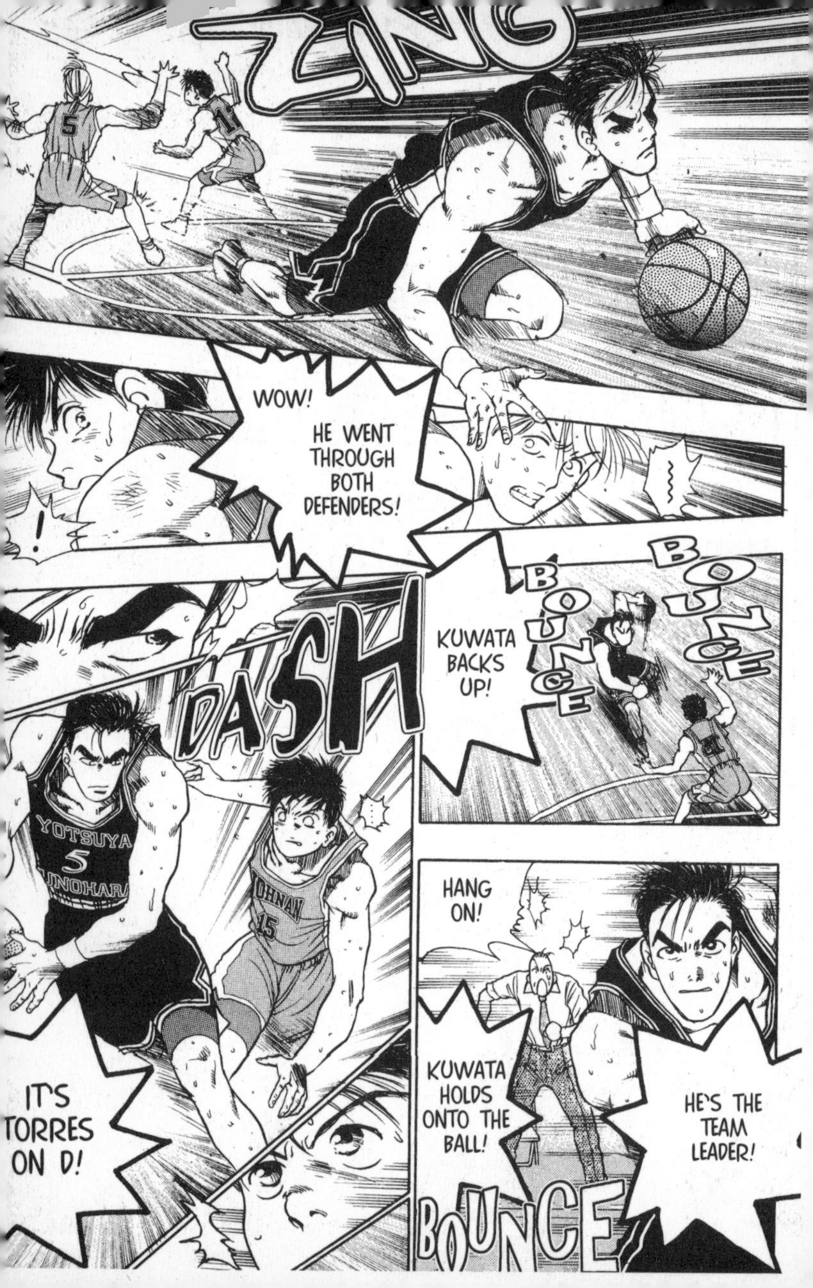
ZING
!
WOW!
HE WENT THROUGH BOTH DEFENDERS!
DASH
KUWATA BACKS UP!
BOUNCE
BOUNCE
YOTSUYA 5 UNOHARA
JOHNAN 15
IT'S TORRES ON D!
HANG ON!
KUWATA HOLDS ONTO THE BALL!
HE'S THE TEAM LEADER!
BOUNCE

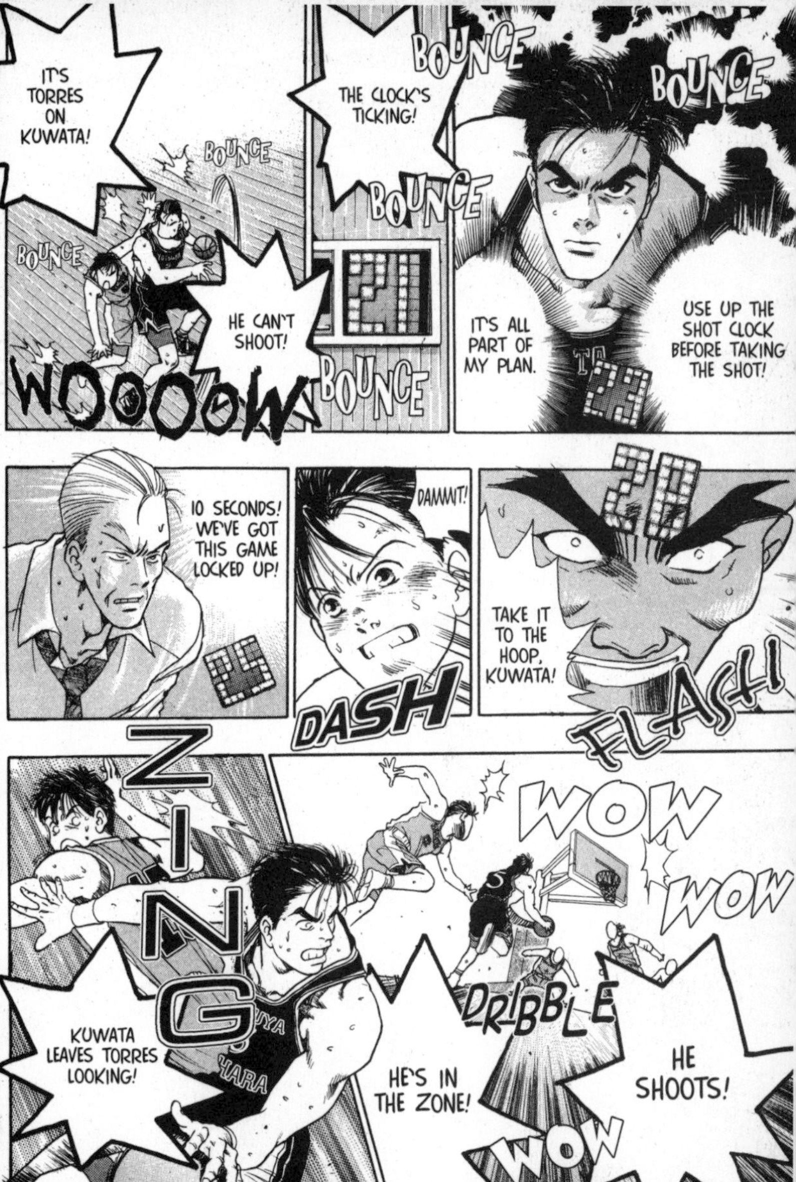
BOUNCE
BOUNCE
USE UP THE SHOT CLOCK BEFORE TAKING THE SHOT!
IT'S ALL PART OF MY PLAN.
BOUNCE
THE CLOCK'S TICKING!
BOUNCE
BOUNCE
IT'S TORRES ON KUWATA!
BOUNCE
BOUNCE
HE CAN'T SHOOT!
WOOOOW
TAKE IT TO THE HOOP, KUWATA!
FLASH
DAMMIT!
DASH
10 SECONDS! WE'VE GOT THIS GAME LOCKED UP!
WOW
WOW
HE SHOOTS!
DRIBBLE
HE'S IN THE ZONE!
WOW
ZING
KUWATA LEAVES TORRES LOOKING!

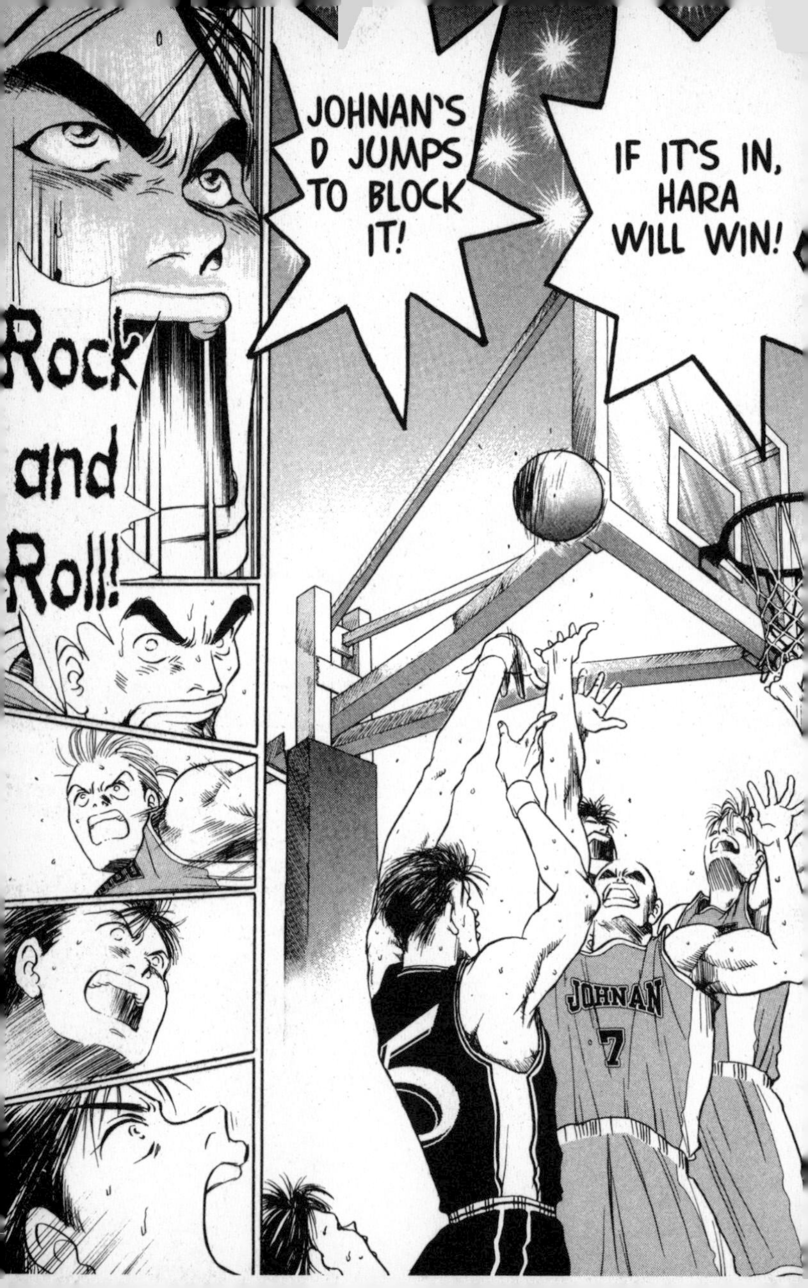
IF IT'S IN, HARA WILL WIN!
JOHNAN'S D JUMPS TO BLOCK IT!
Rock and Roll!

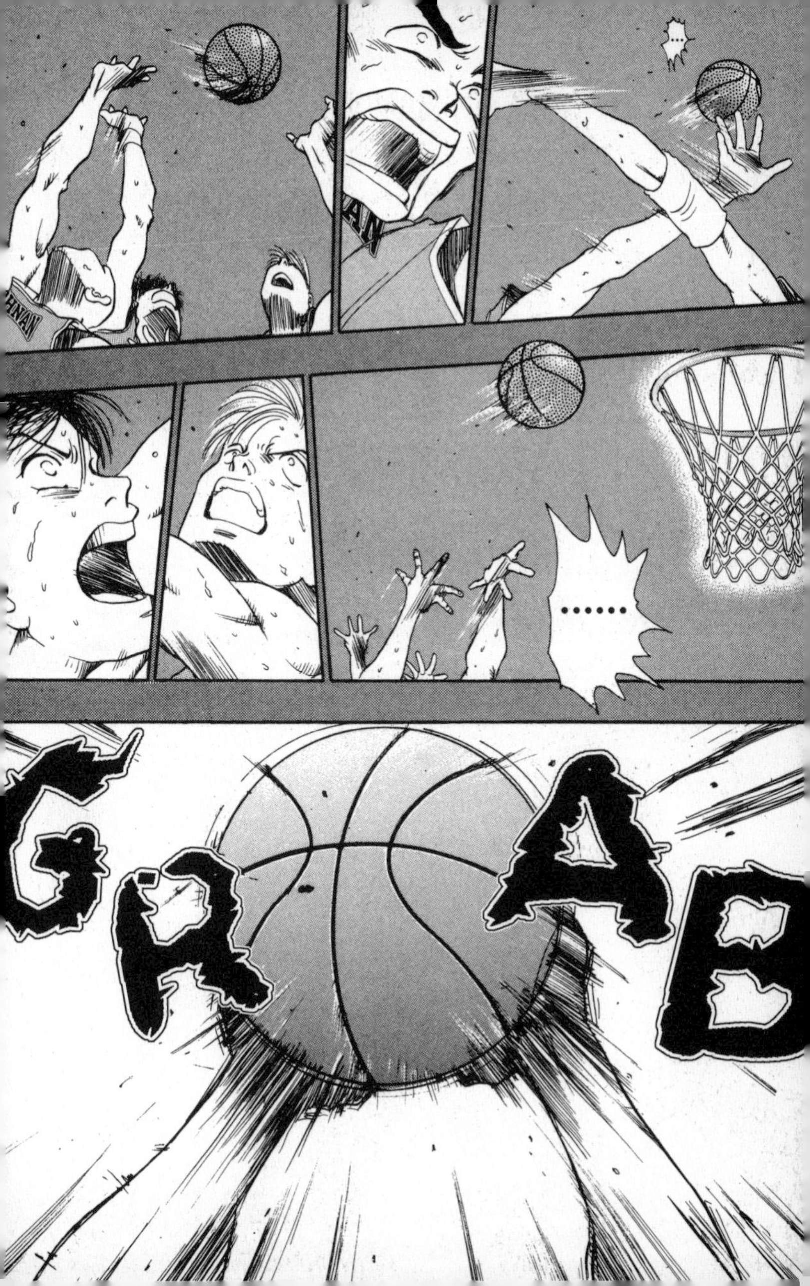
!
......
GRAB

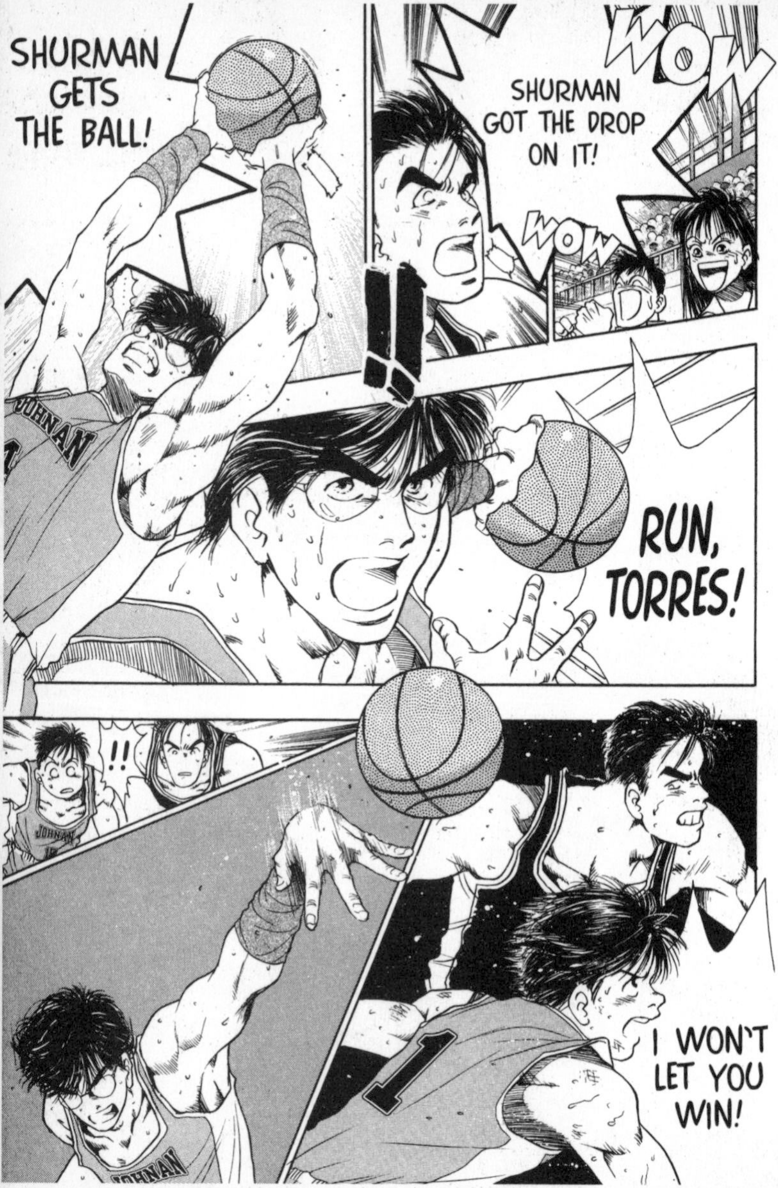
SHURMAN GETS THE BALL!
WOW
SHURMAN GOT THE DROP ON IT!
WOW
!!
RUN, TORRES!
!!
I WON'T LET YOU WIN!

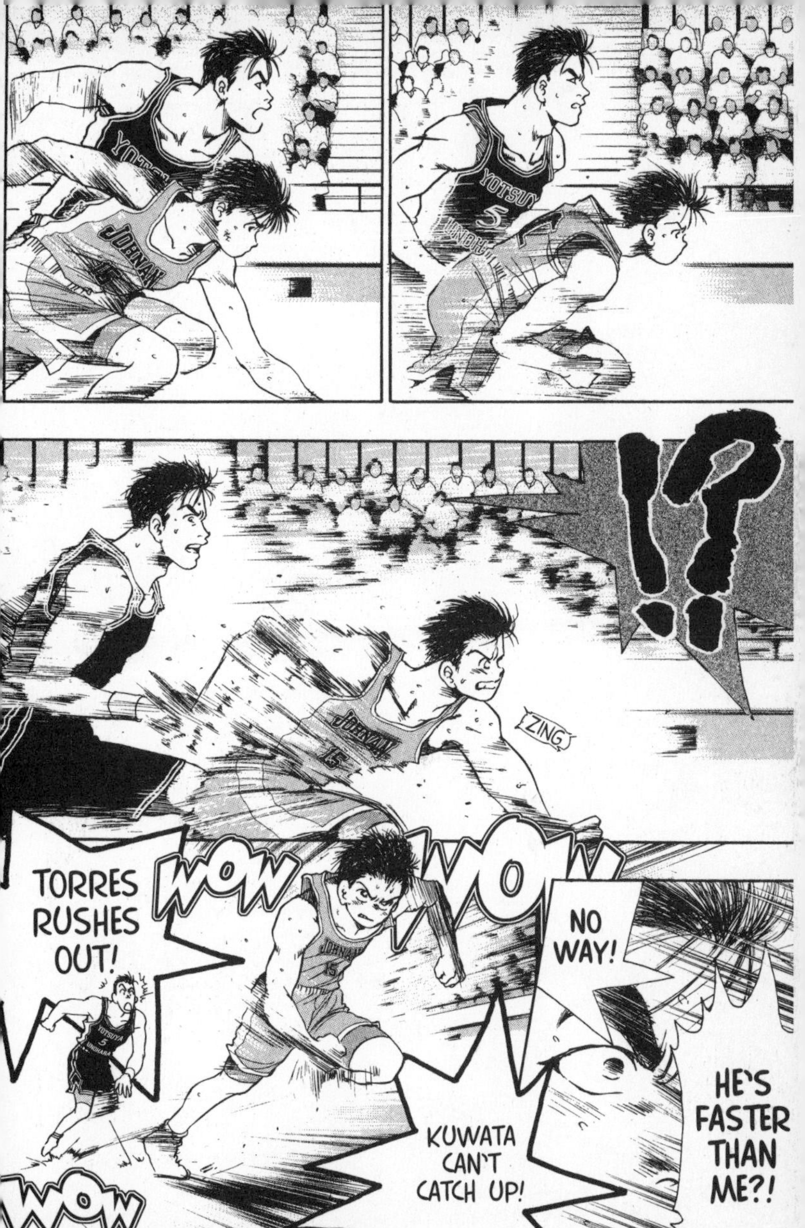
!?
ZING
HE'S FASTER THAN ME?!
NO WAY!
KUWATA CAN'T CATCH UP!
WOW WOW
TORRES RUSHES OUT!
WOW

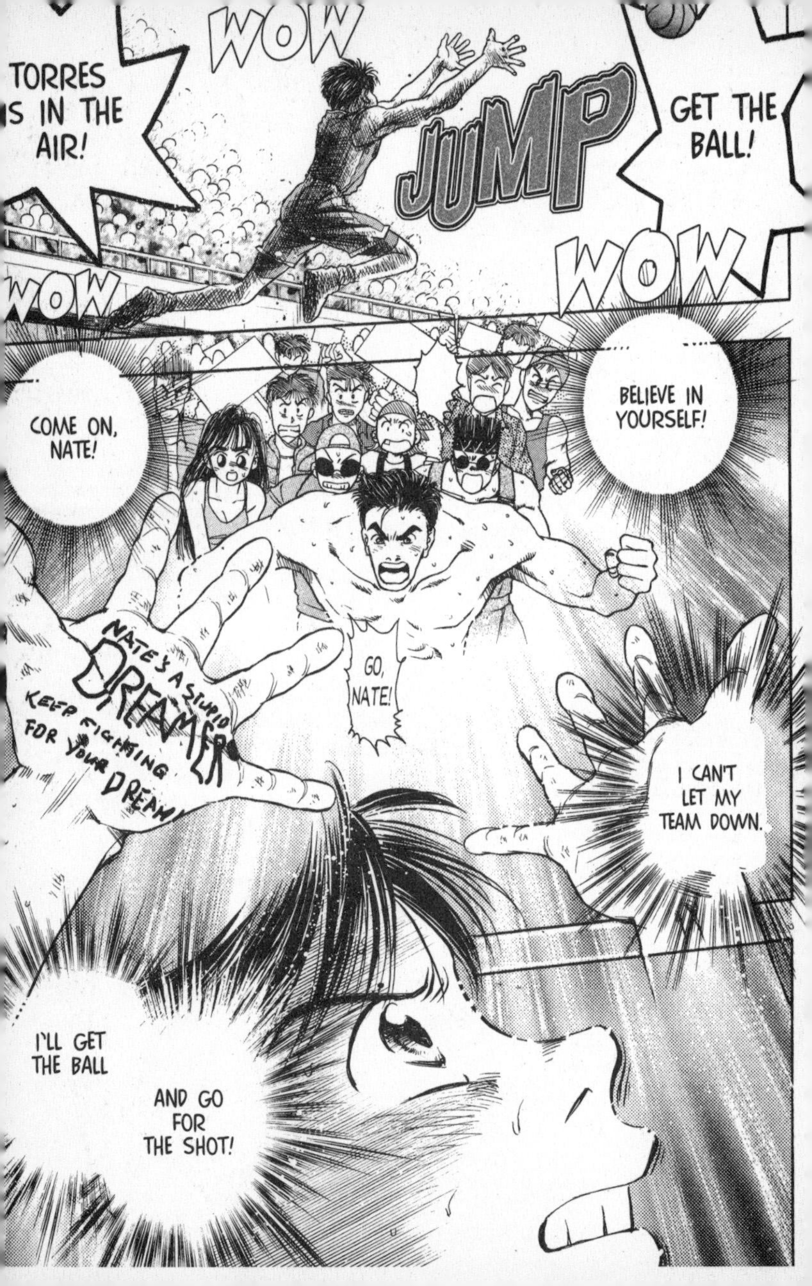
GET THE BALL!
WOW
JUMP
TORRES IS IN THE AIR!
WOW
WOW
BELIEVE IN YOURSELF!
COME ON, NATE!
GO, NATE!
NATE'S A STUPID DREAMER
KEEP FIGHTING FOR YOUR DREAM!
I CAN'T LET MY TEAM DOWN.
I'LL GET THE BALL
AND GO FOR THE SHOT!

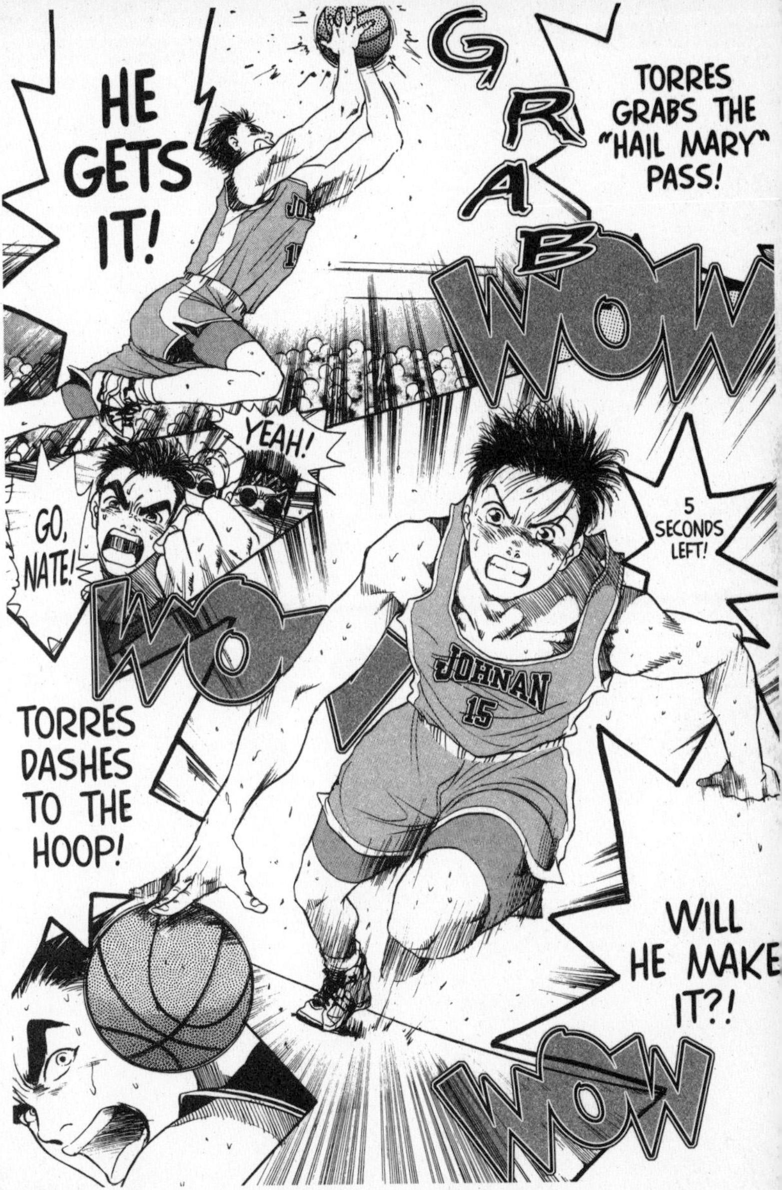
TORRES GRABS THE "HAIL MARY" PASS!
GRAB
HE GETS IT!
WOW
5 SECONDS LEFT!
YEAH!
GO, NATE!
WOW
TORRES DASHES TO THE HOOP!
WILL HE MAKE IT?!
WOW

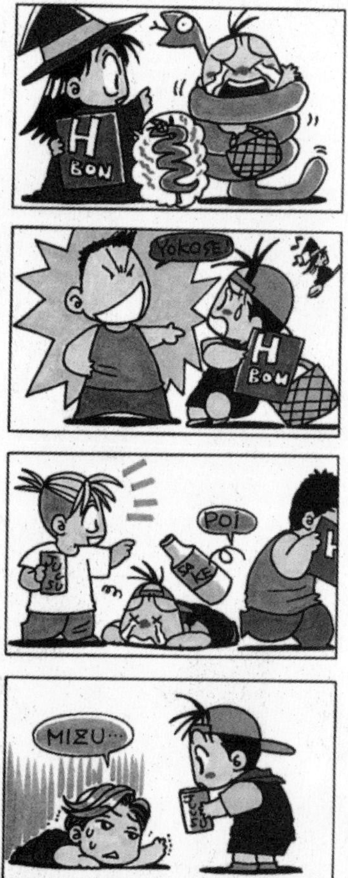
H
BON
YOKOSE!
H
BON
POI
SAKE
MIZU...

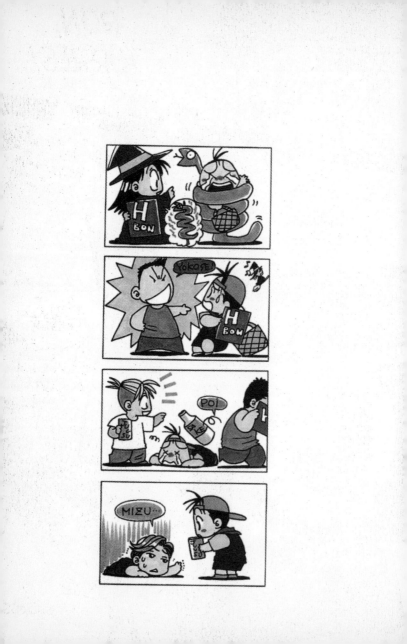

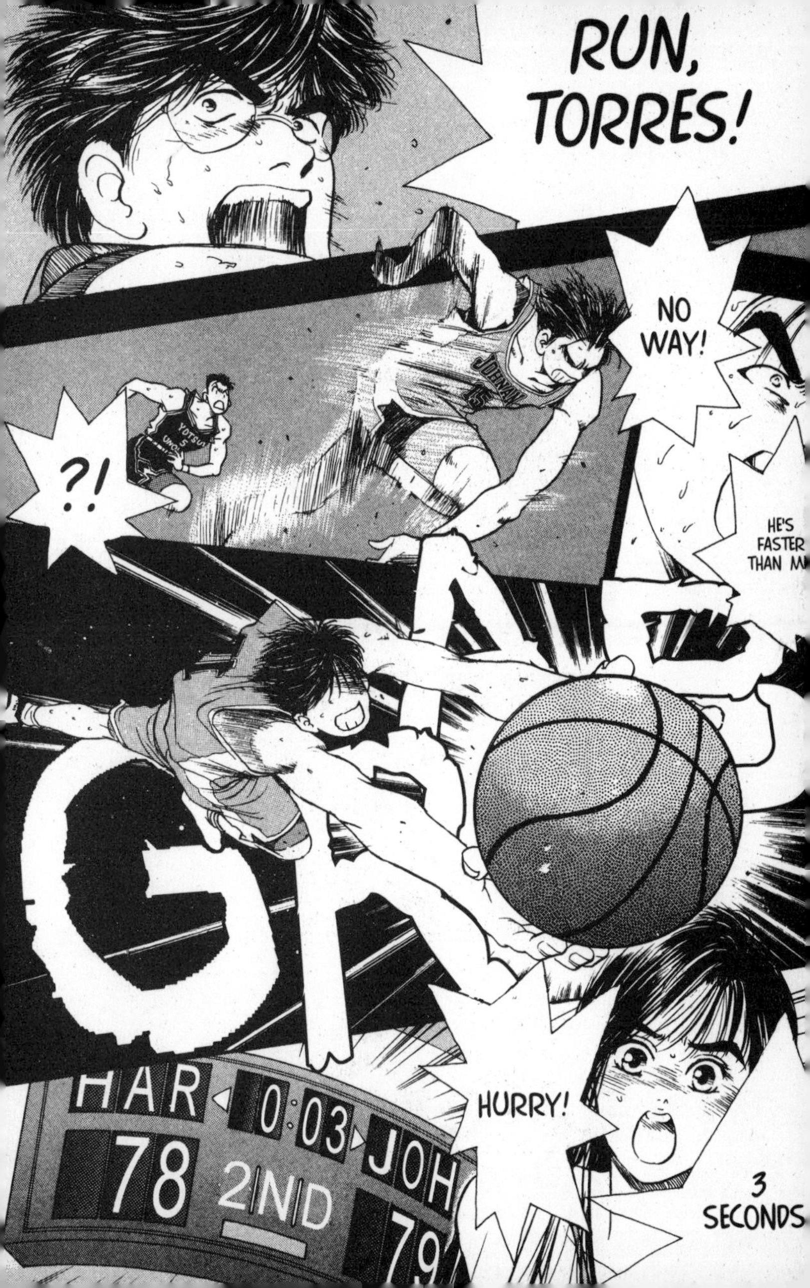
RUN, TORRES!
NO WAY!
HE'S FASTER THAN M
?!
HAR 0:03 JOH
78 2ND 79
HURRY!
3 SECONDS

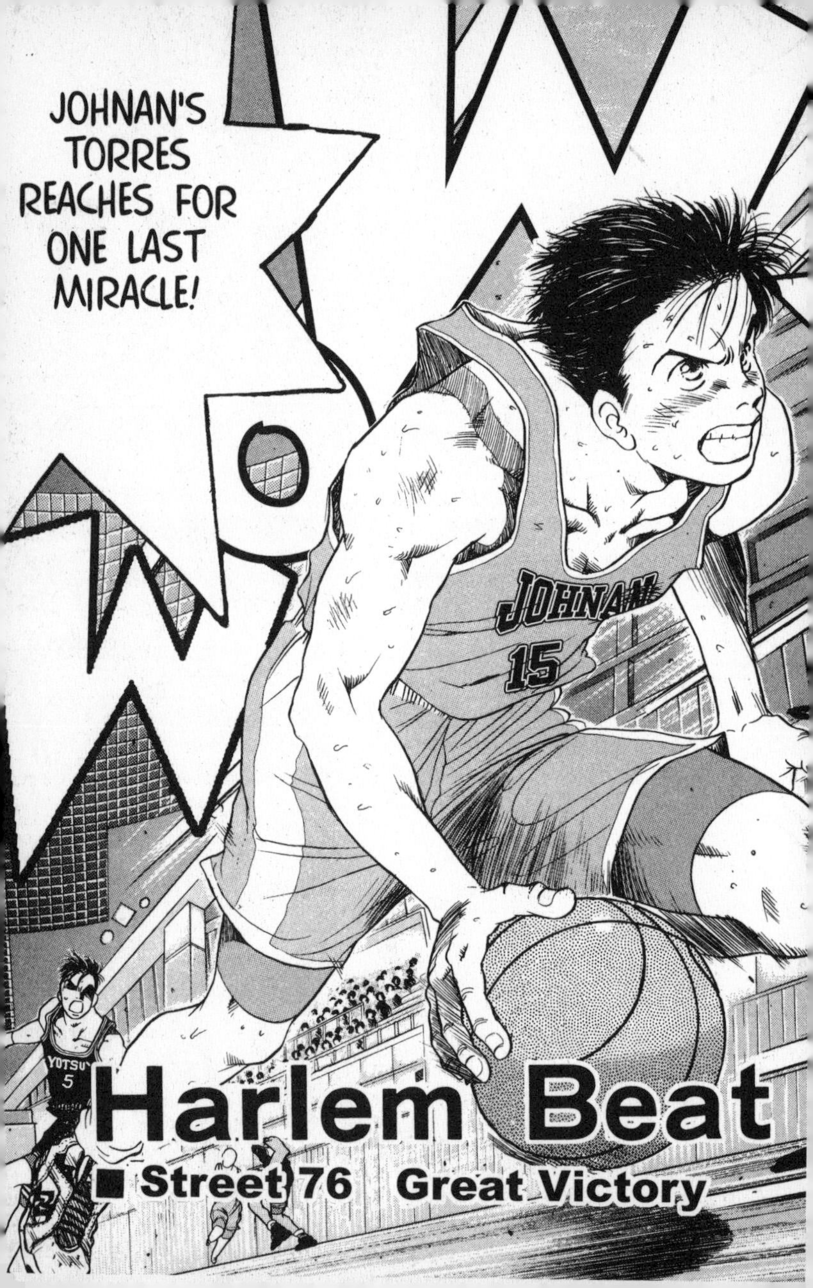
JOHNAN'S TORRES REACHES FOR ONE LAST MIRACLE!
WOW
JOHNAN
15
YOTSU
5
Harlem Beat
■ Street 76 Great Victory

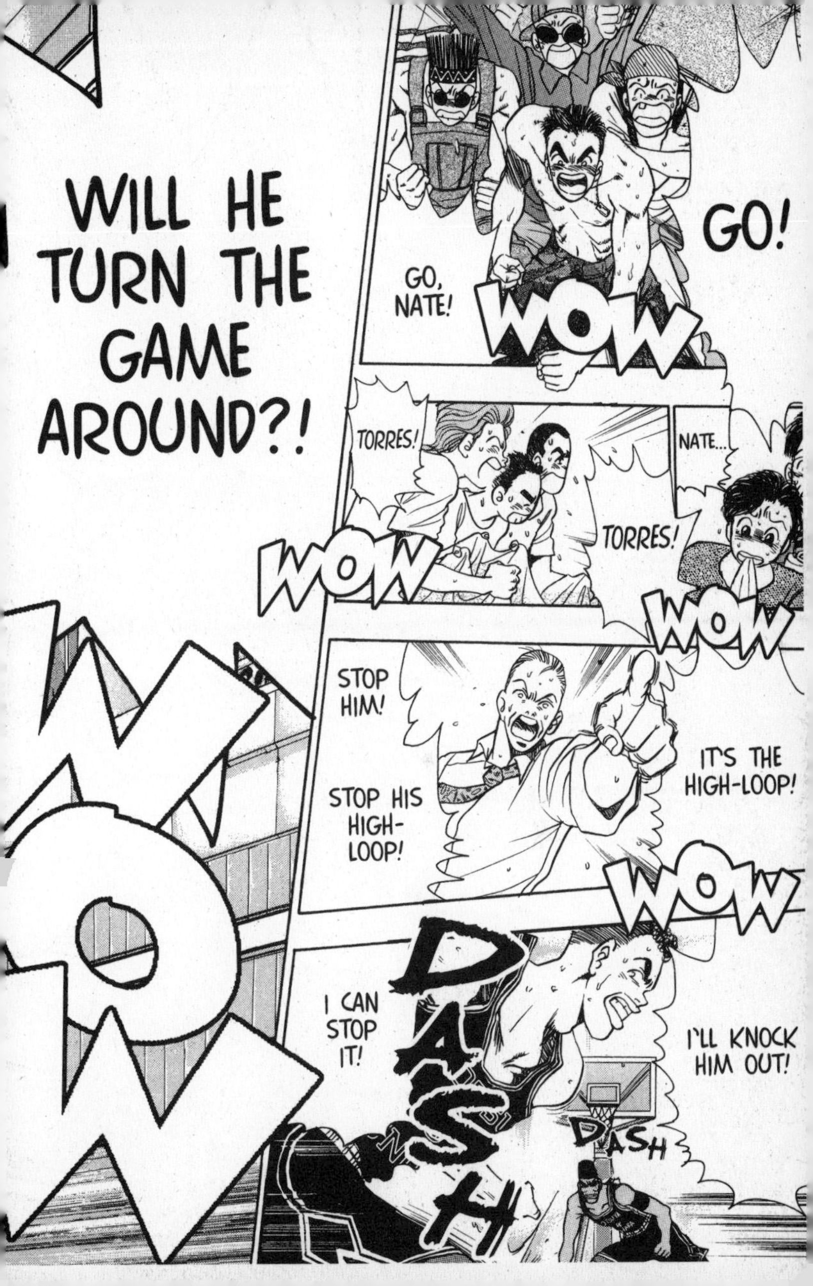
GO!
GO, NATE!
WOW
NATE...
WOW
TORRES!
TORRES!
WOW
IT'S THE HIGH-LOOP!
STOP HIM!
STOP HIS HIGH-LOOP!
WOW
I'LL KNOCK HIM OUT!
DASH
I CAN STOP IT!
DASH
WILL HE TURN THE GAME AROUND?!
WOW

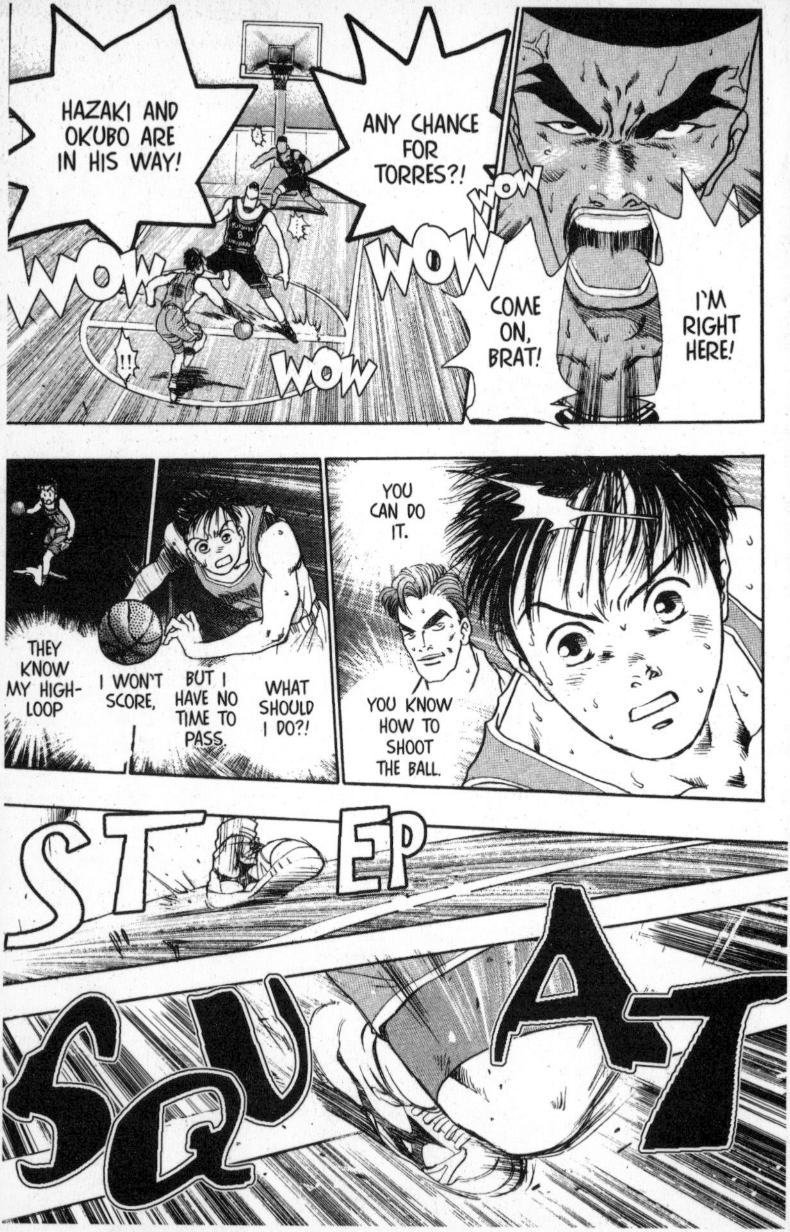

HAZAKI AND OKUBO ARE IN HIS WAY!
ANY CHANCE FOR TORRES?!
WOW
WOW
WOW
!!!
WOW
COME ON, BRAT!
I'M RIGHT HERE!
THEY KNOW MY HIGH-LOOP
I WON'T SCORE,
BUT I HAVE NO TIME TO PASS.
WHAT SHOULD I DO?!
YOU CAN DO IT.
YOU KNOW HOW TO SHOOT THE BALL.
STEP
SQUAT

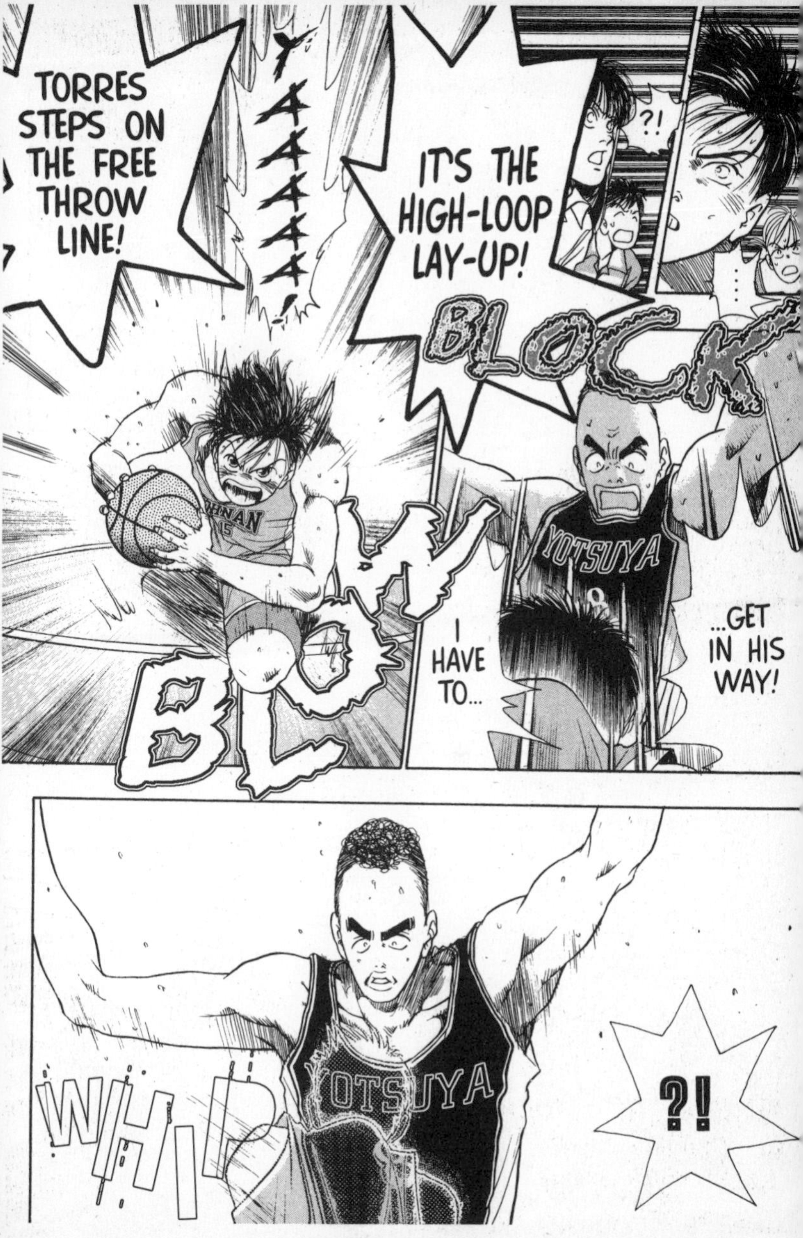
?!
...
IT'S THE HIGH-LOOP LAY-UP!
YAAAAA!
TORRES STEPS ON THE FREE THROW LINE!
BLOCK
I HAVE TO...
...GET IN HIS WAY!
BL
?!
WHIP

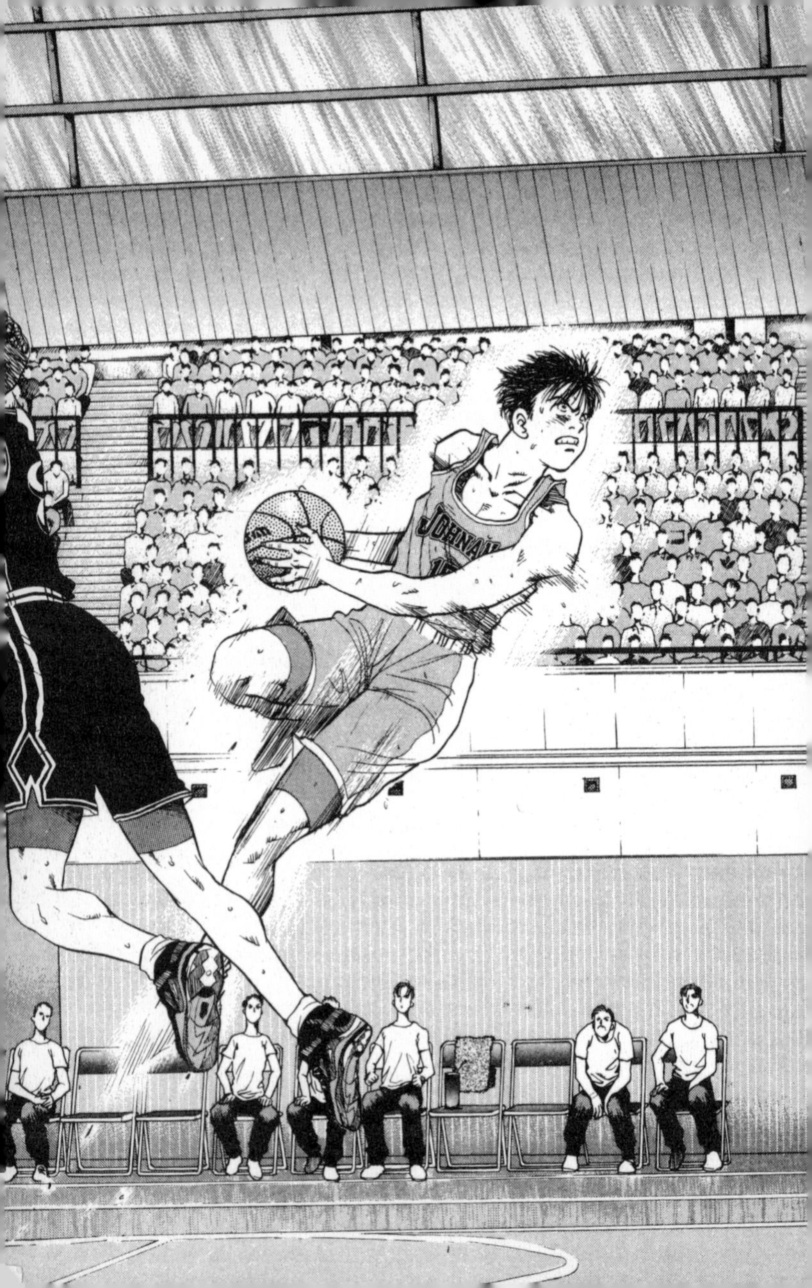
JOHNAN

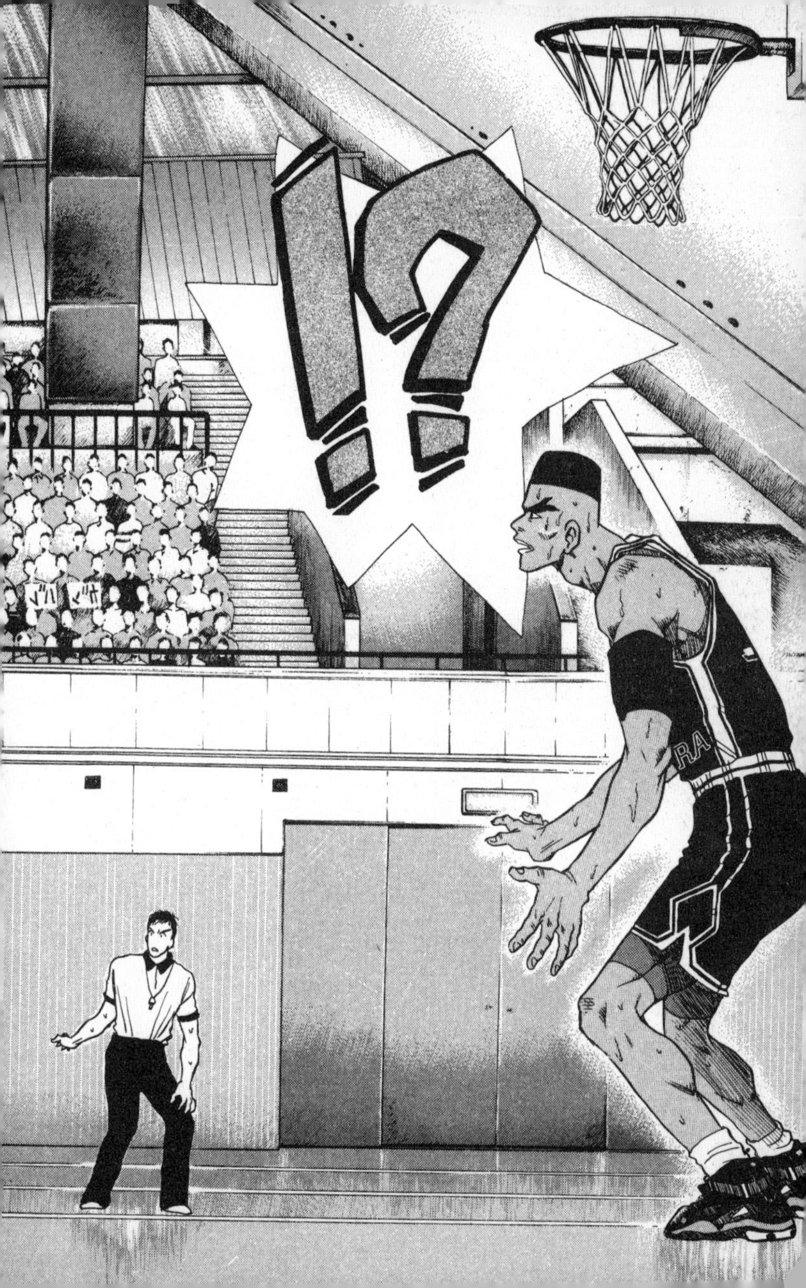
!?
RA

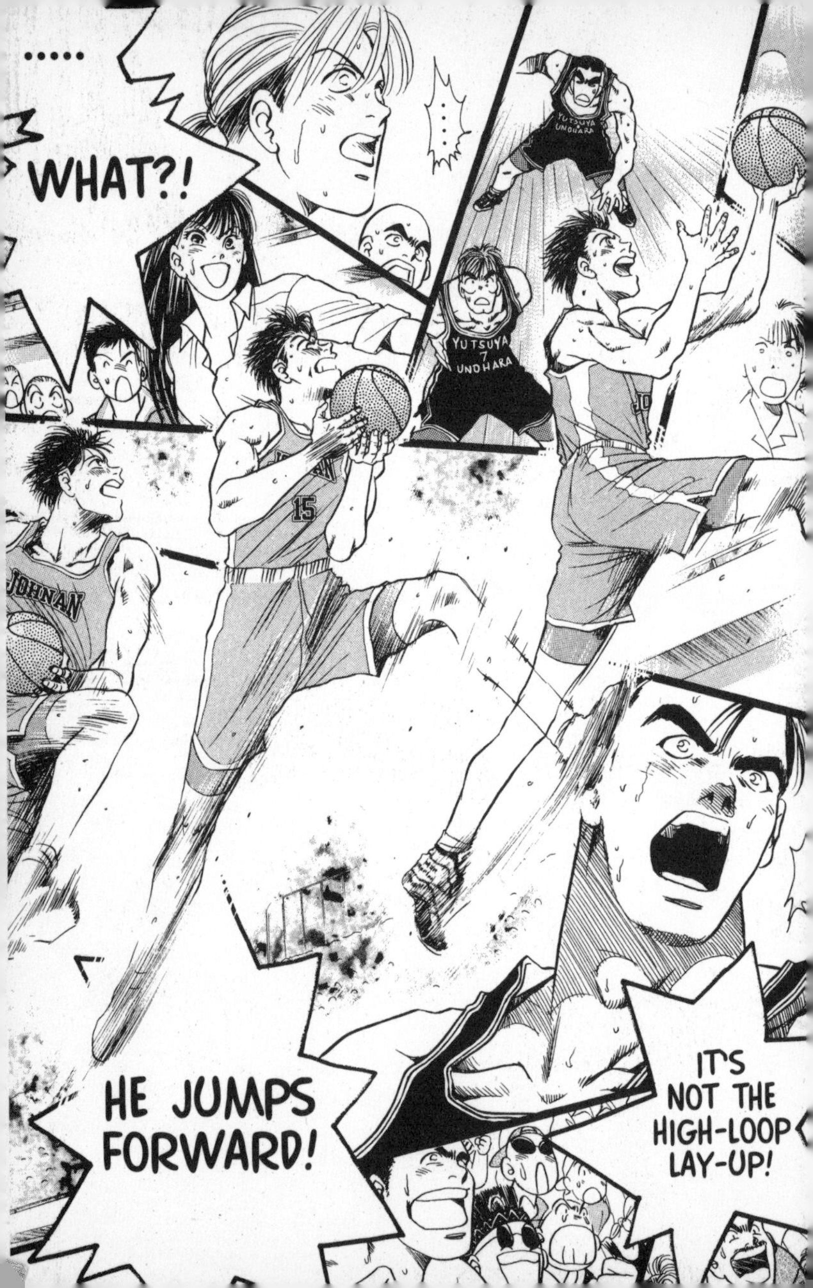

.....
WHAT?!
!
.....
YUTSUYA UNOHARA
YUTSUYA 7 UNOHARA
15
JOHNAN
IT'S NOT THE HIGH-LOOP LAY-UP!
HE JUMPS FORWARD!

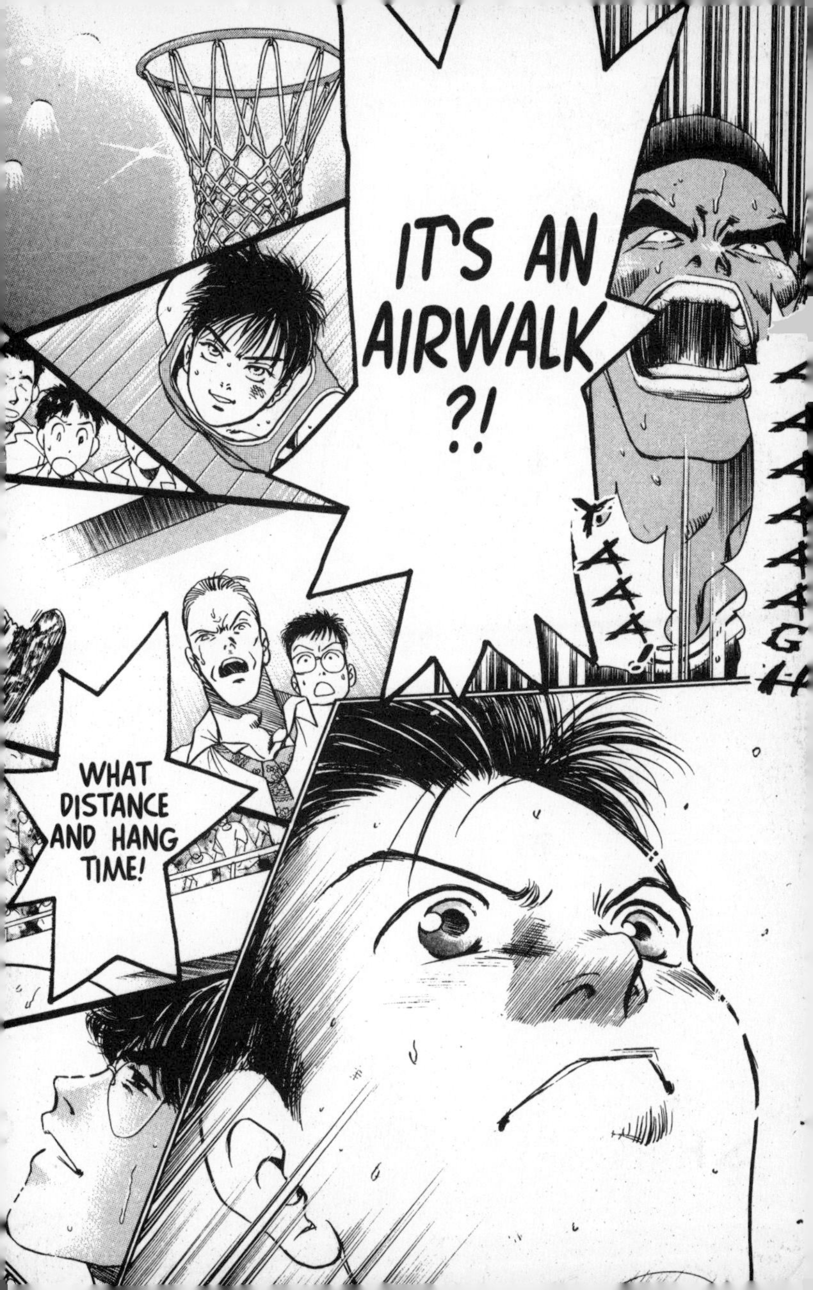
AAAAAAGH
YAAAA!
IT'S AN AIRWALK ?!
WHAT DISTANCE AND HANG TIME!

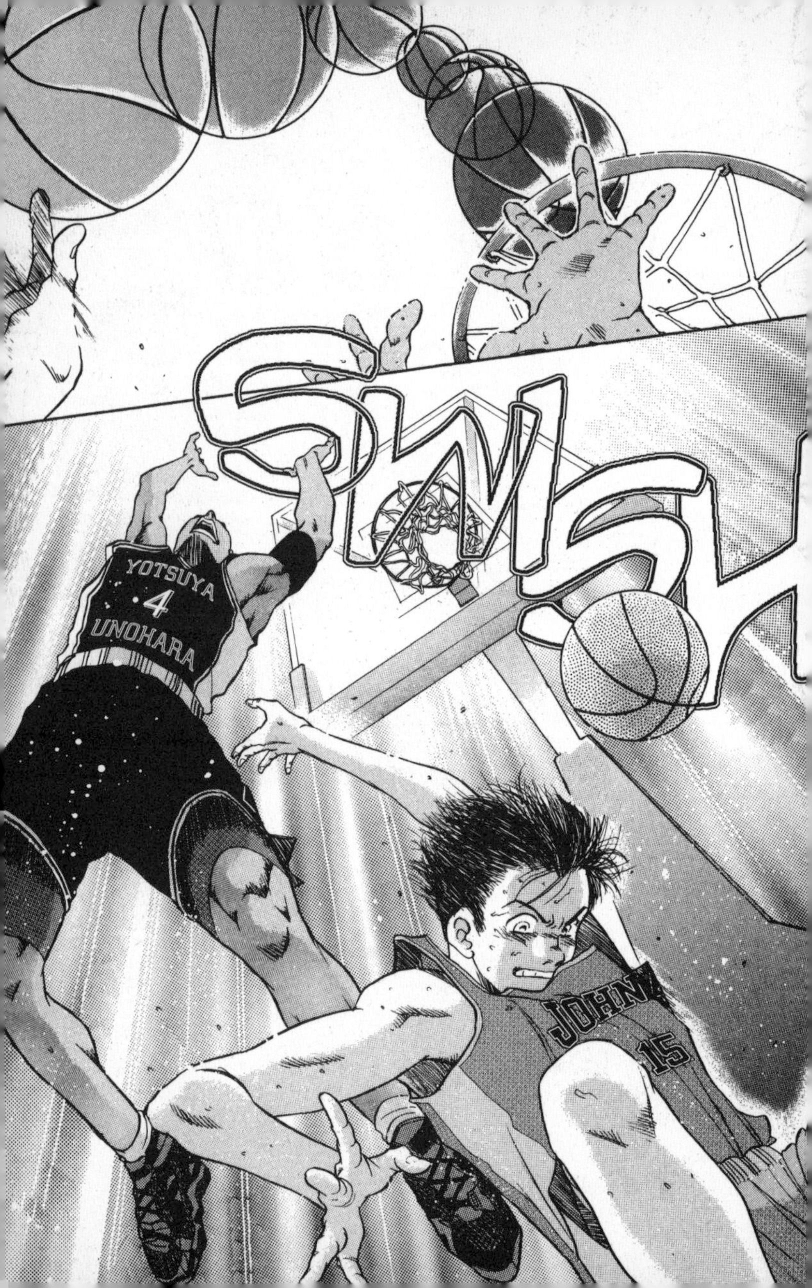
SWISH
YOTSUYA
4
UNOHARA
JOHN
15

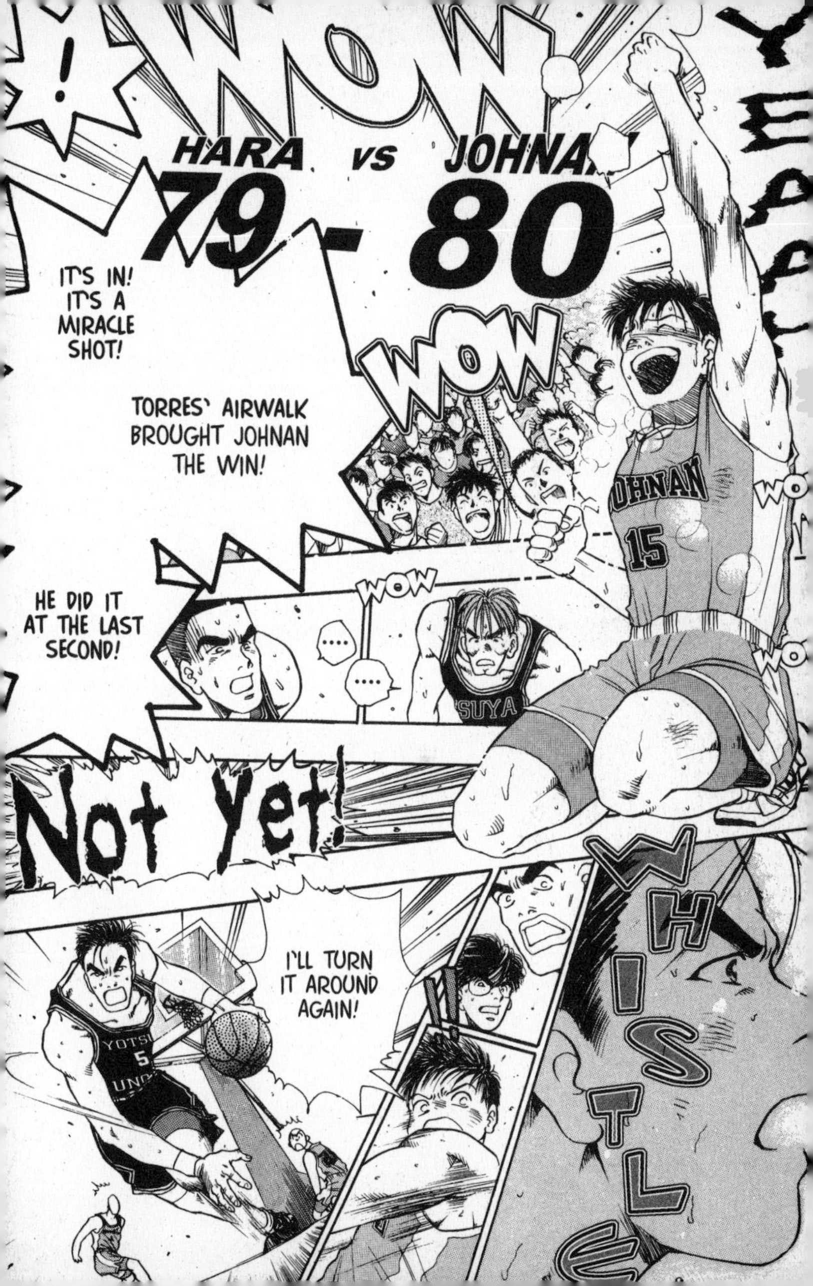
WOW!
YEAH
HARA VS JOHNAN
79 - 80
IT'S IN! IT'S A MIRACLE SHOT!
WOW
TORRES' AIRWALK BROUGHT JOHNAN THE WIN!
WO
HE DID IT AT THE LAST SECOND!
WOW
....
....
WO
Not Yet!
I'LL TURN IT AROUND AGAIN!
WHISTLE

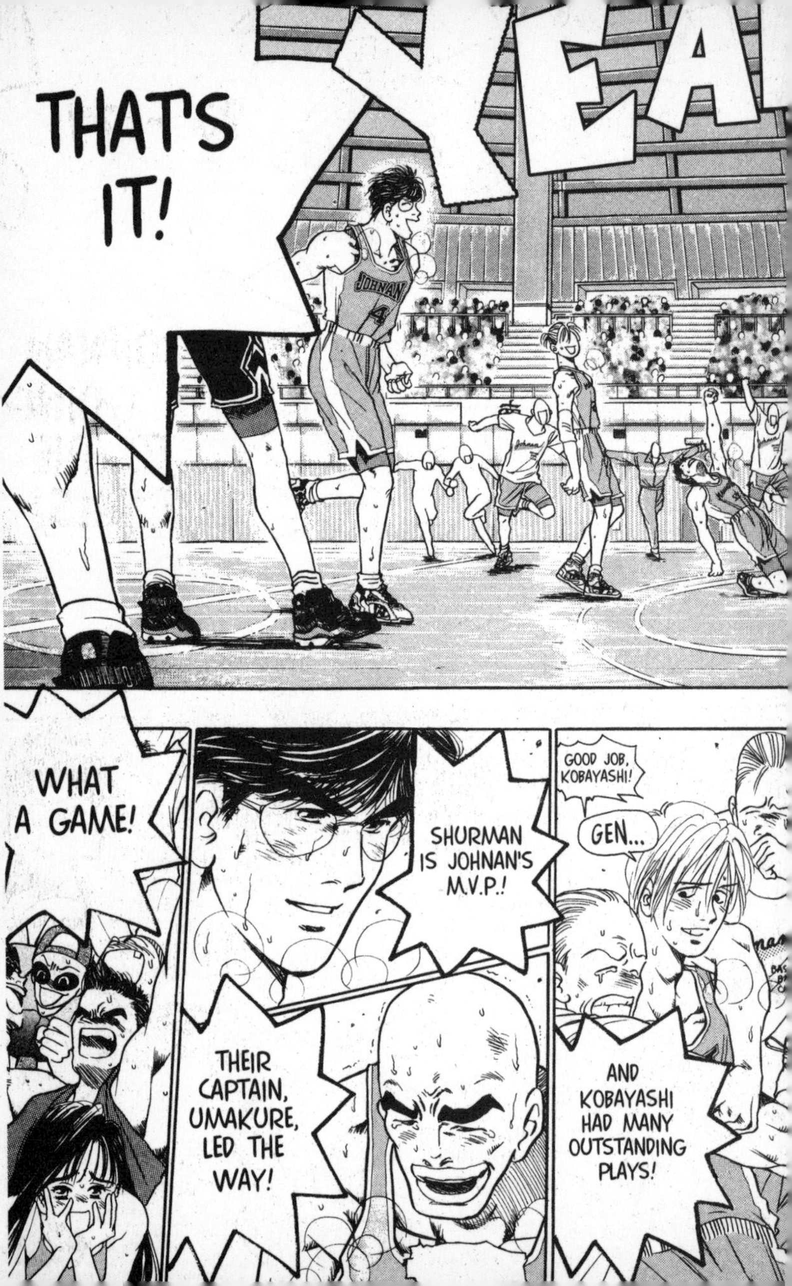
THAT'S IT!
YEA
WHAT A GAME!
SHURMAN IS JOHNAN'S M.V.P.!
THEIR CAPTAIN, UMAKURE, LED THE WAY!
AND KOBAYASHI HAD MANY OUTSTANDING PLAYS!
GOOD JOB, KOBAYASHI!
GEN...

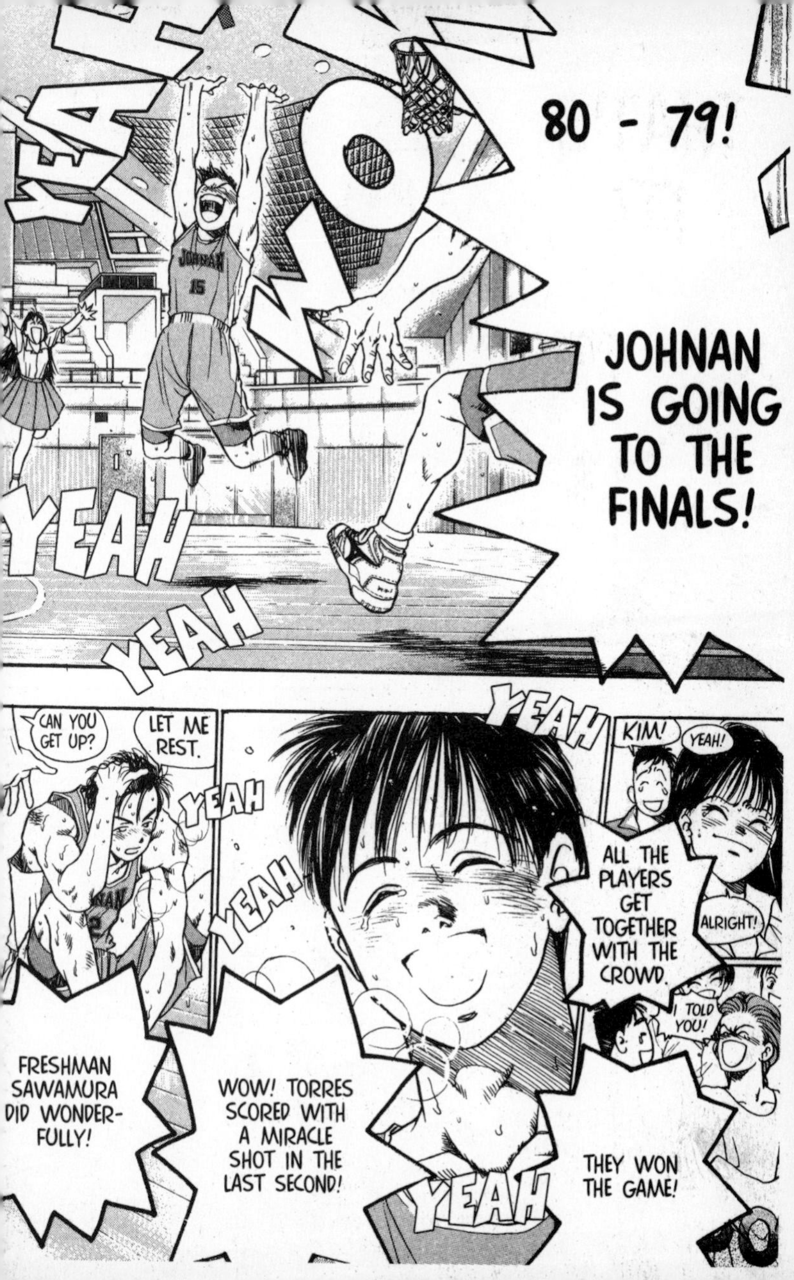
YEAH
WOW
80 - 79!
JOHNAN IS GOING TO THE FINALS!
YEAH
YEAH
CAN YOU GET UP?
LET ME REST.
YEAH
FRESHMAN SAWAMURA DID WONDERFULLY!
YEAH
WOW! TORRES SCORED WITH A MIRACLE SHOT IN THE LAST SECOND!
YEAH
YEAH
KIM!
YEAH!
ALL THE PLAYERS GET TOGETHER WITH THE CROWD.
ALRIGHT!
I TOLD YOU!
THEY WON THE GAME!

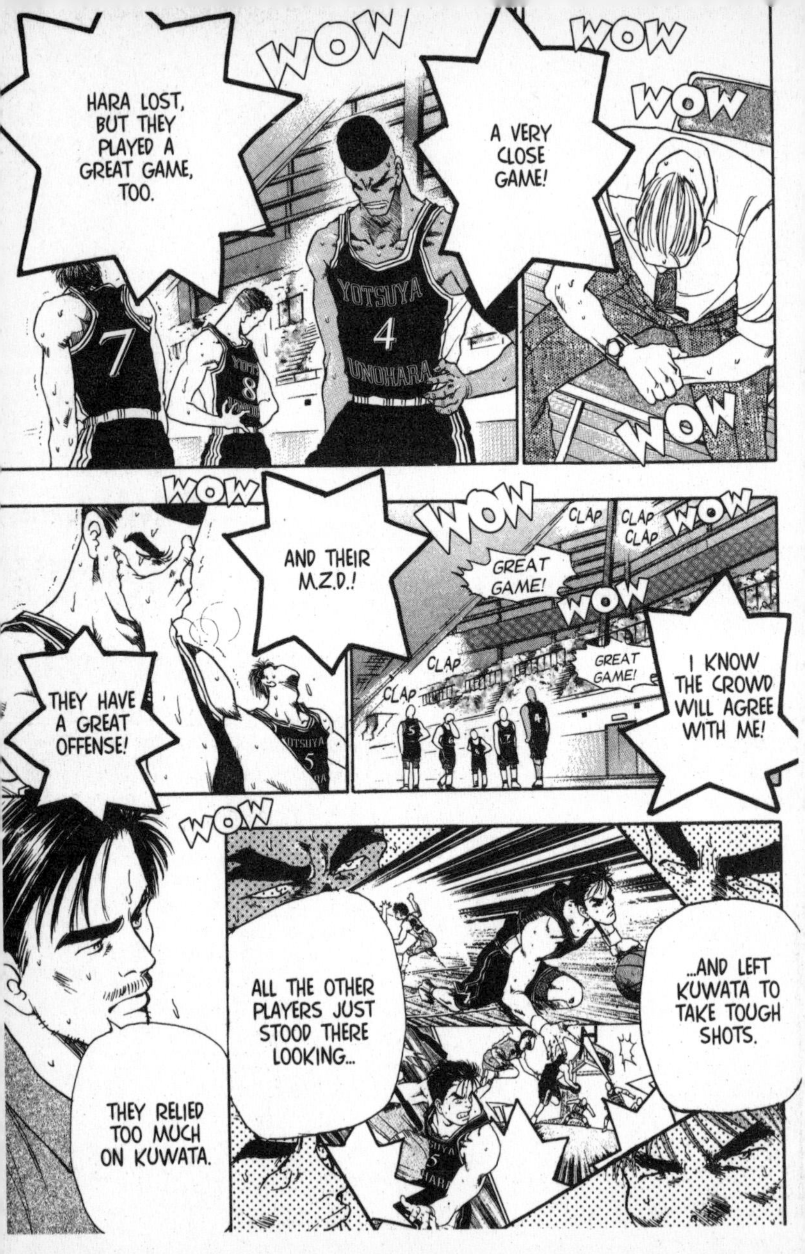
WOW
HARA LOST, BUT THEY PLAYED A GREAT GAME, TOO.
WOW
A VERY CLOSE GAME!
WOW
WOW
WOW
THEY HAVE A GREAT OFFENSE!
AND THEIR M.Z.D.!
WOW
CLAP
CLAP CLAP
WOW
GREAT GAME!
WOW
CLAP
CLAP
GREAT GAME!
I KNOW THE CROWD WILL AGREE WITH ME!
WOW
THEY RELIED TOO MUCH ON KUWATA.
ALL THE OTHER PLAYERS JUST STOOD THERE LOOKING...
...AND LEFT KUWATA TO TAKE TOUGH SHOTS.

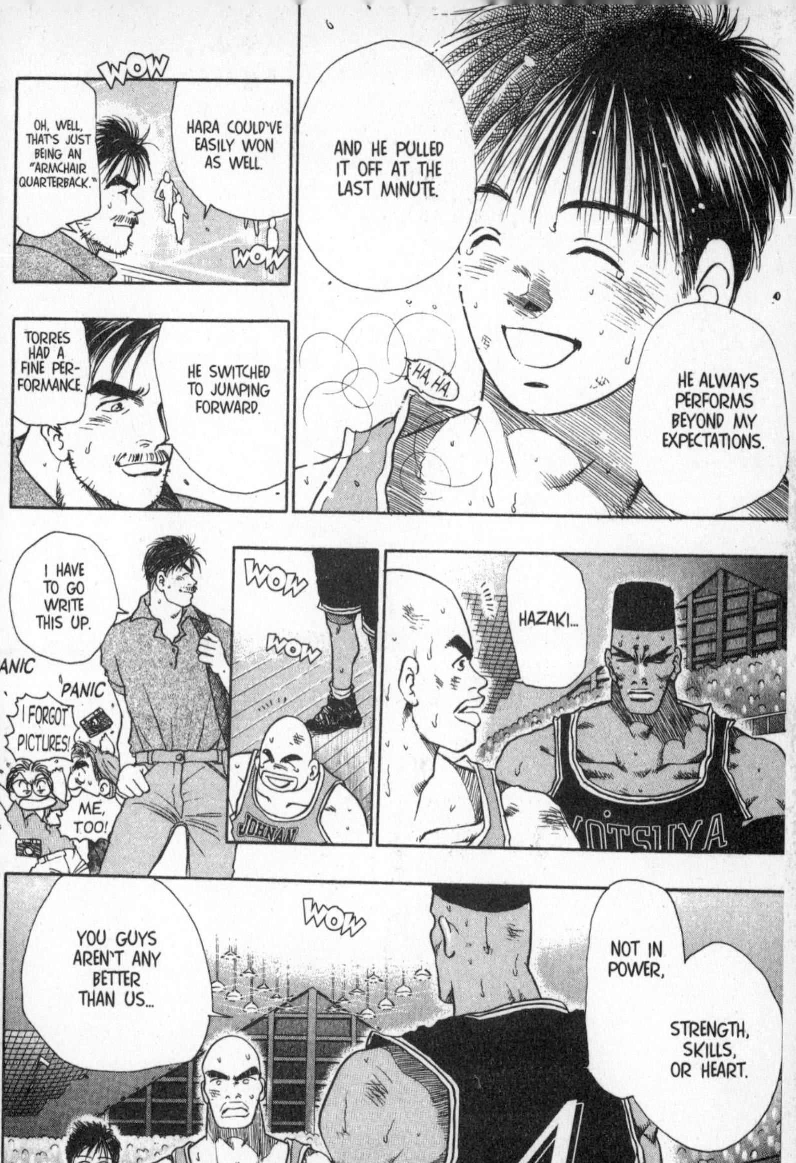
AND HE PULLED IT OFF AT THE LAST MINUTE.
HA, HA.
HE ALWAYS PERFORMS BEYOND MY EXPECTATIONS.
WOW
HARA COULD'VE EASILY WON AS WELL.
OH, WELL, THAT'S JUST BEING AN "ARMCHAIR QUARTERBACK."
WOW
HE SWITCHED TO JUMPING FORWARD.
TORRES HAD A FINE PERFORMANCE.
HAZAKI...
YOTSUYA
WOW
WOW
JOHNAN
I HAVE TO GO WRITE THIS UP.
PANIC
PANIC
I FORGOT PICTURES!
ME, TOO!
NOT IN POWER,
STRENGTH, SKILLS, OR HEART.
WOW
YOU GUYS AREN'T ANY BETTER THAN US...

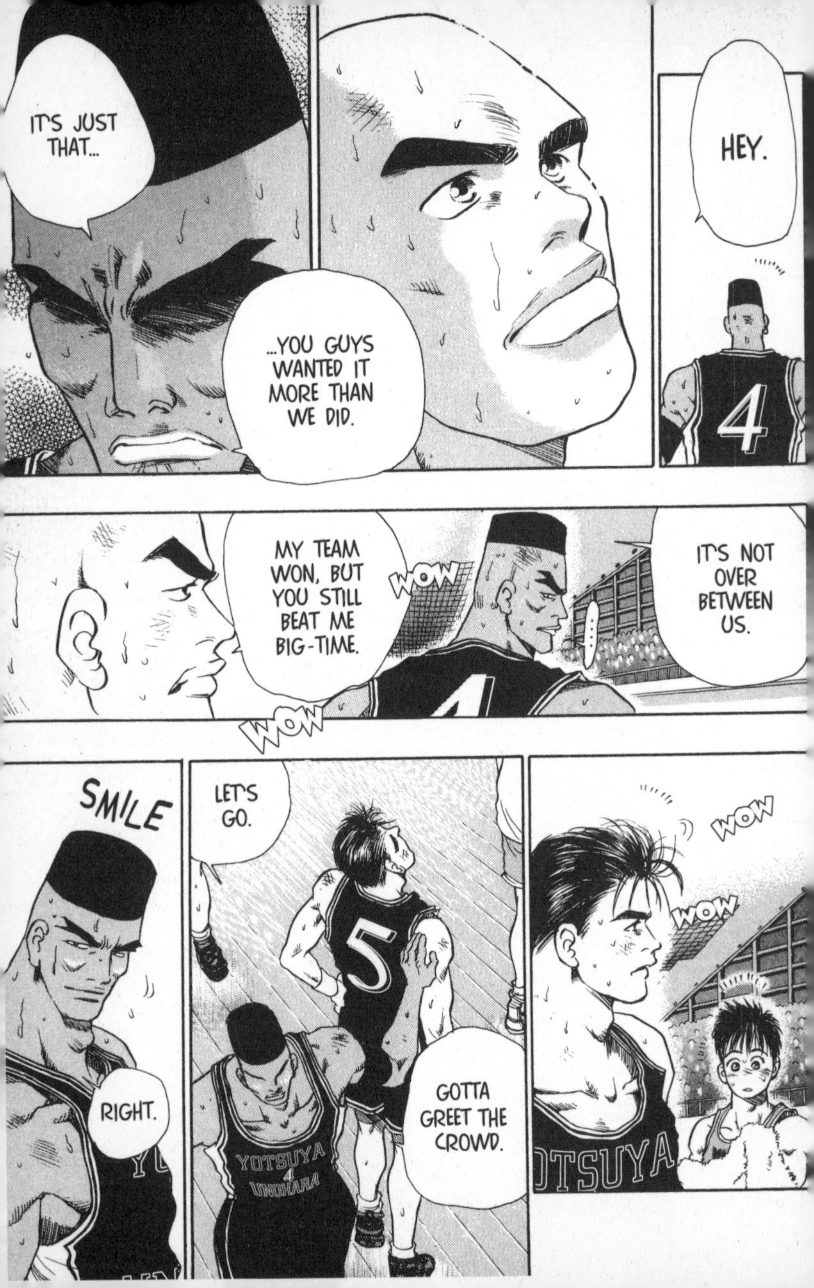
IT'S JUST THAT...
...YOU GUYS WANTED IT MORE THAN WE DID.
HEY.
MY TEAM WON, BUT YOU STILL BEAT ME BIG-TIME.
WOW
...
IT'S NOT OVER BETWEEN US.
WOW
SMILE
RIGHT.
LET'S GO.
YOTSUYA 4 UNOHARA
GOTTA GREET THE CROWD.
WOW
WOW
YOTSUYA

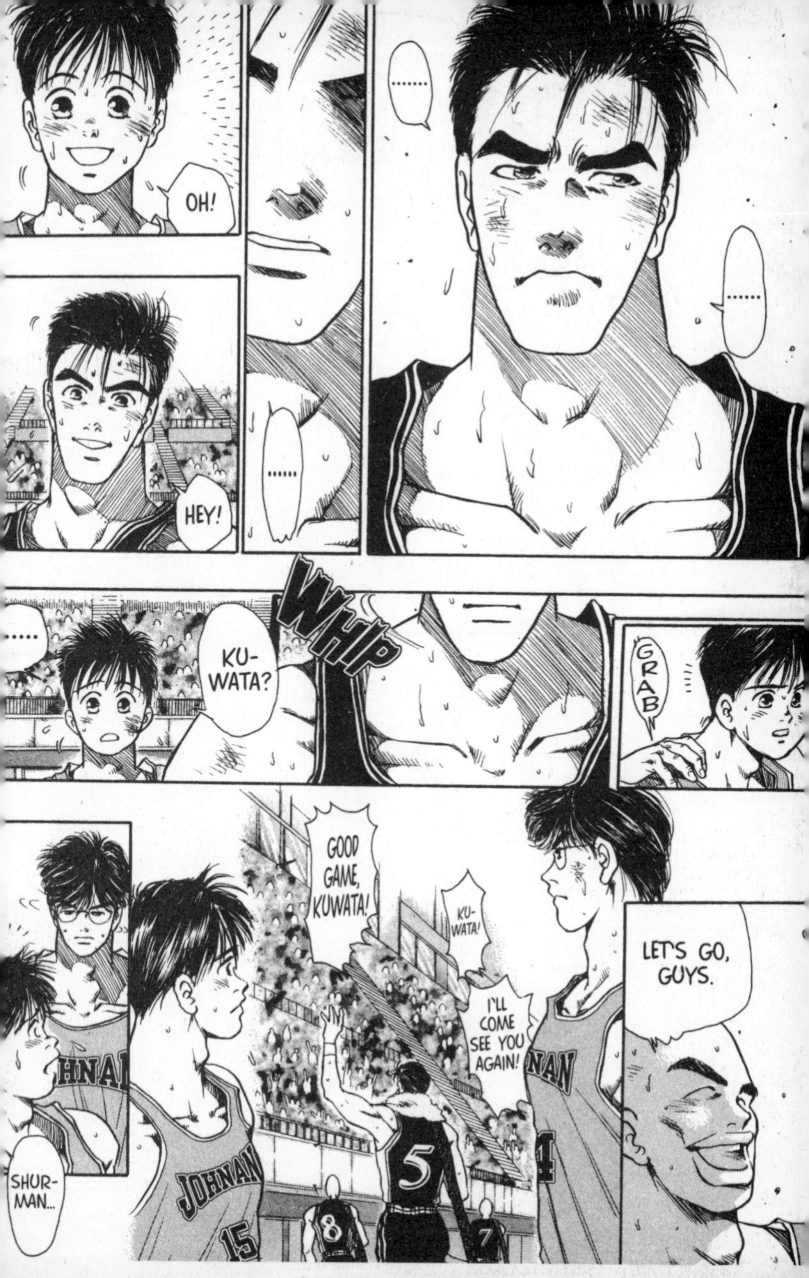
......
......
......
OH!
HEY!
GRAB
WHIP
KU-WATA?
......
LET'S GO, GUYS.
KU-WATA!
I'LL COME SEE YOU AGAIN!
GOOD GAME, KUWATA!
SHUR-MAN...

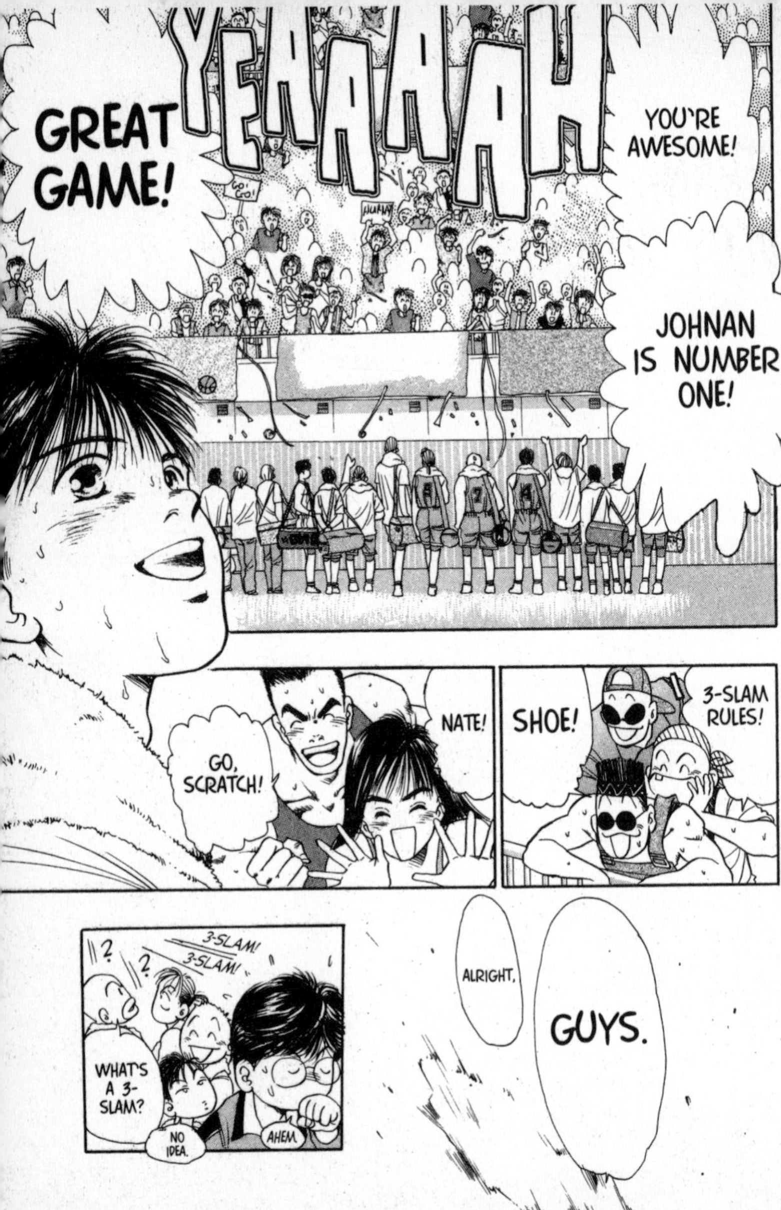
YEAAAAH
YOU'RE AWESOME!
GREAT GAME!
JOHNAN IS NUMBER ONE!
3-SLAM RULES!
SHOE!
NATE!
GO, SCRATCH!
ALRIGHT,
GUYS.
3-SLAM!
3-SLAM!
WHAT'S A 3-SLAM?
NO IDEA.
AHEM.

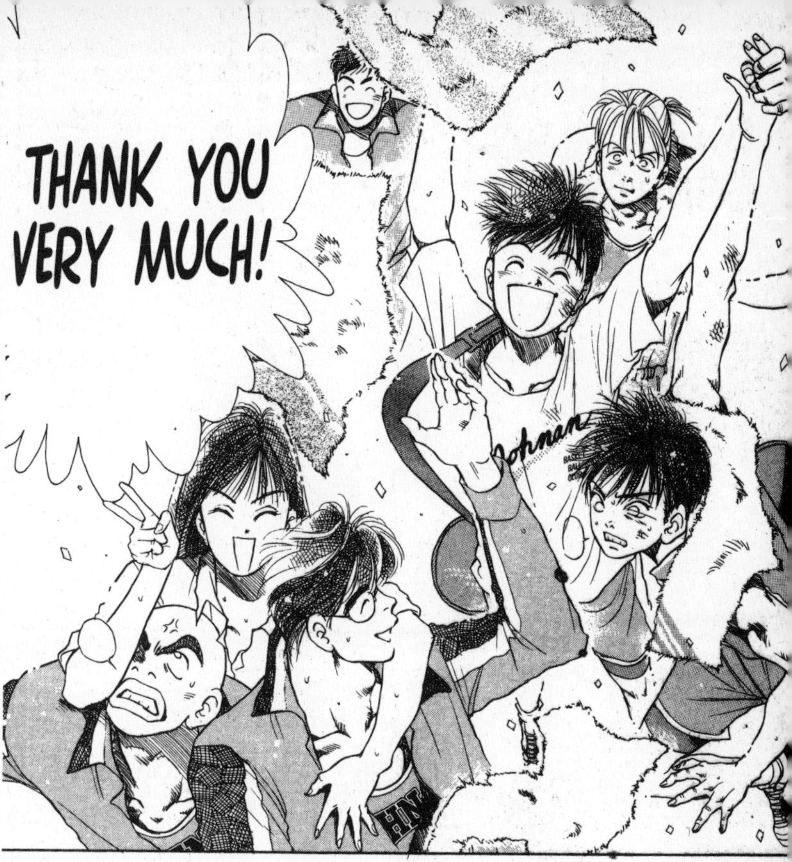
THANK YOU VERY MUCH!
Johnan

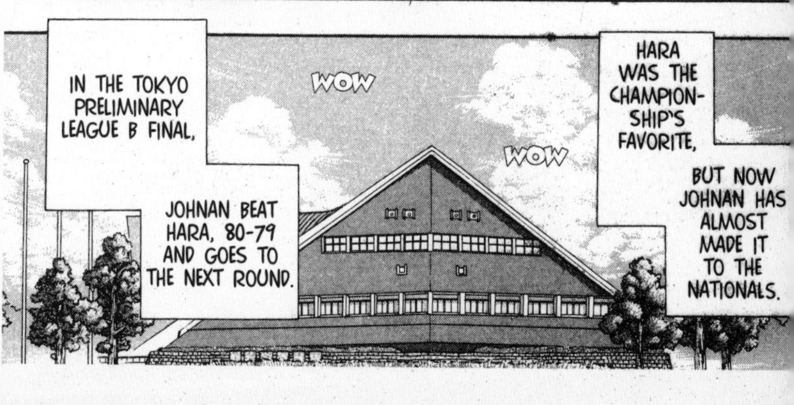
IN THE TOKYO PRELIMINARY LEAGUE B FINAL,
WOW
WOW
JOHNAN BEAT HARA, 80-79 AND GOES TO THE NEXT ROUND.
HARA WAS THE CHAMPION-SHIP'S FAVORITE,
BUT NOW JOHNAN HAS ALMOST MADE IT TO THE NATIONALS.

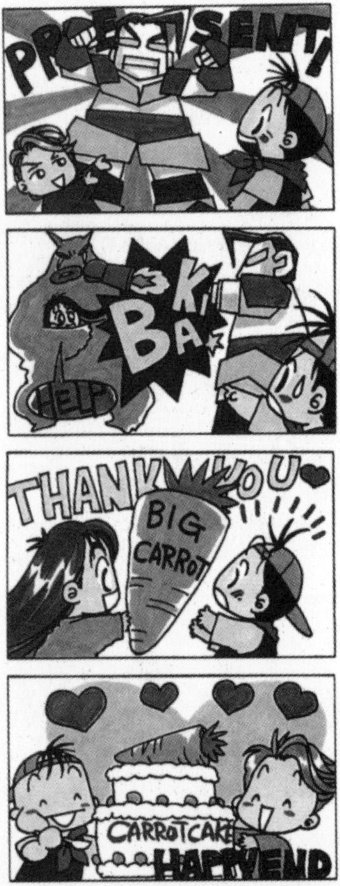
PRESENT!
BAKI
HELP
THANK YOU
BIG CARROT
CARROTCAKE
HAPPYEND

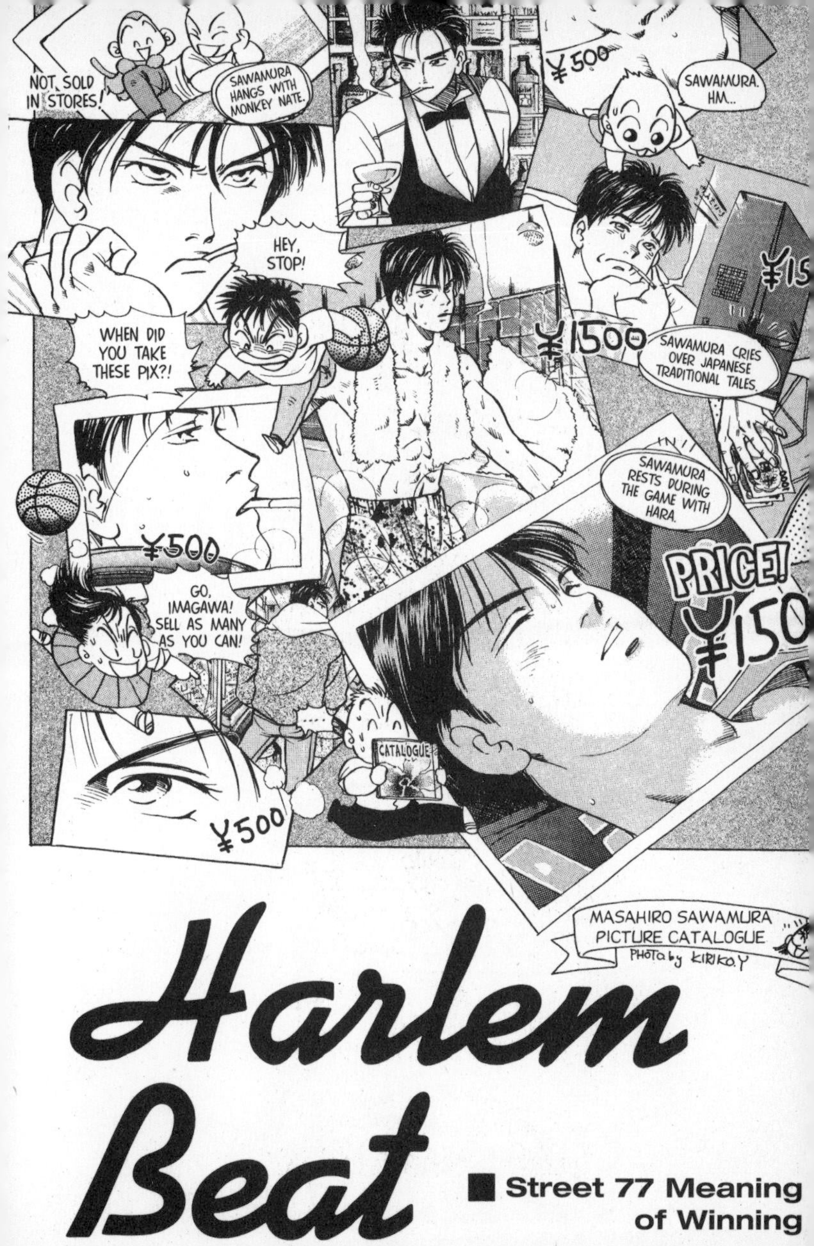
¥500
SAWAMURA. HM...
SAWAMURA HANGS WITH MONKEY NATE.
NOT SOLD IN STORES!
HEY, STOP!
¥15
¥1500
SAWAMURA CRIES OVER JAPANESE TRADITIONAL TALES.
WHEN DID YOU TAKE THESE PIX?!
SAWAMURA RESTS DURING THE GAME WITH HARA.
¥500
PRICE! ¥150
GO, IMAGAWA! SELL AS MANY AS YOU CAN!
CATALOGUE
¥500
MASAHIRO SAWAMURA PICTURE CATALOGUE
PHOTO by KIRIKO.Y

Harlem Beat

■ Street 77 Meaning of Winning

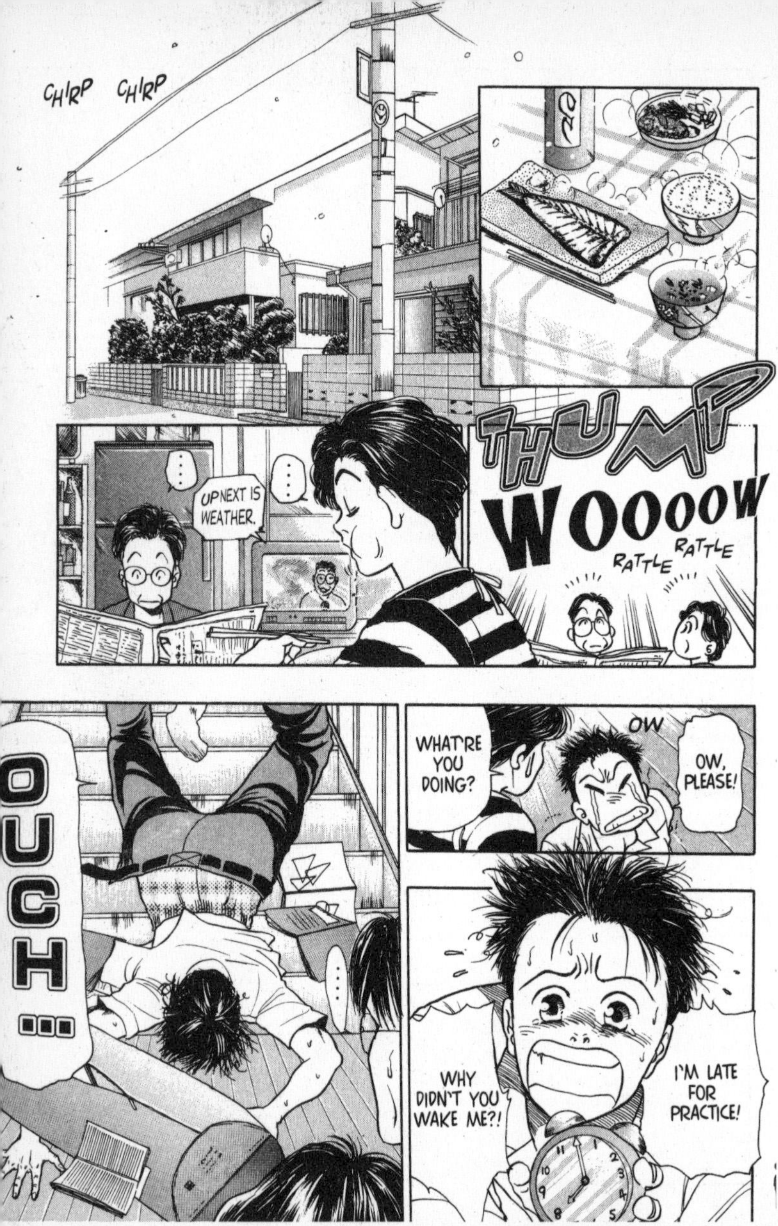
CHIRP CHIRP
THUMP
WOOOOW
RATTLE RATTLE
...
...
UP NEXT IS WEATHER.
OW
OW, PLEASE!
WHAT'RE YOU DOING?
I'M LATE FOR PRACTICE!
WHY DIDN'T YOU WAKE ME?!
OUCH...
....

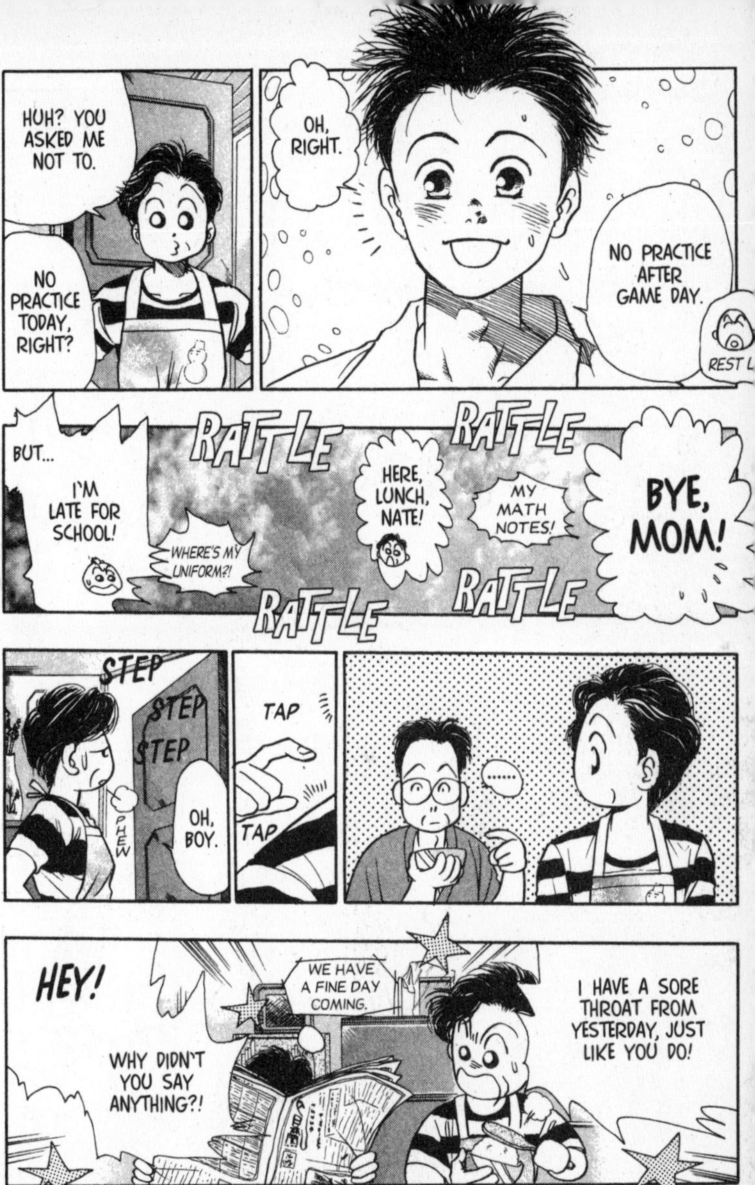
OH, RIGHT.
NO PRACTICE AFTER GAME DAY.
HUH? YOU ASKED ME NOT TO.
NO PRACTICE TODAY, RIGHT?
BYE, MOM!
RATTLE
MY MATH NOTES!
RATTLE
HERE, LUNCH, NATE!
RATTLE
WHERE'S MY UNIFORM?!
BUT...
I'M LATE FOR SCHOOL!
RATTLE
......
TAP
TAP
STEP
STEP
STEP
OH, BOY.
PHEW
I HAVE A SORE THROAT FROM YESTERDAY, JUST LIKE YOU DO!
WE HAVE A FINE DAY COMING.
HEY!
WHY DIDN'T YOU SAY ANYTHING?!

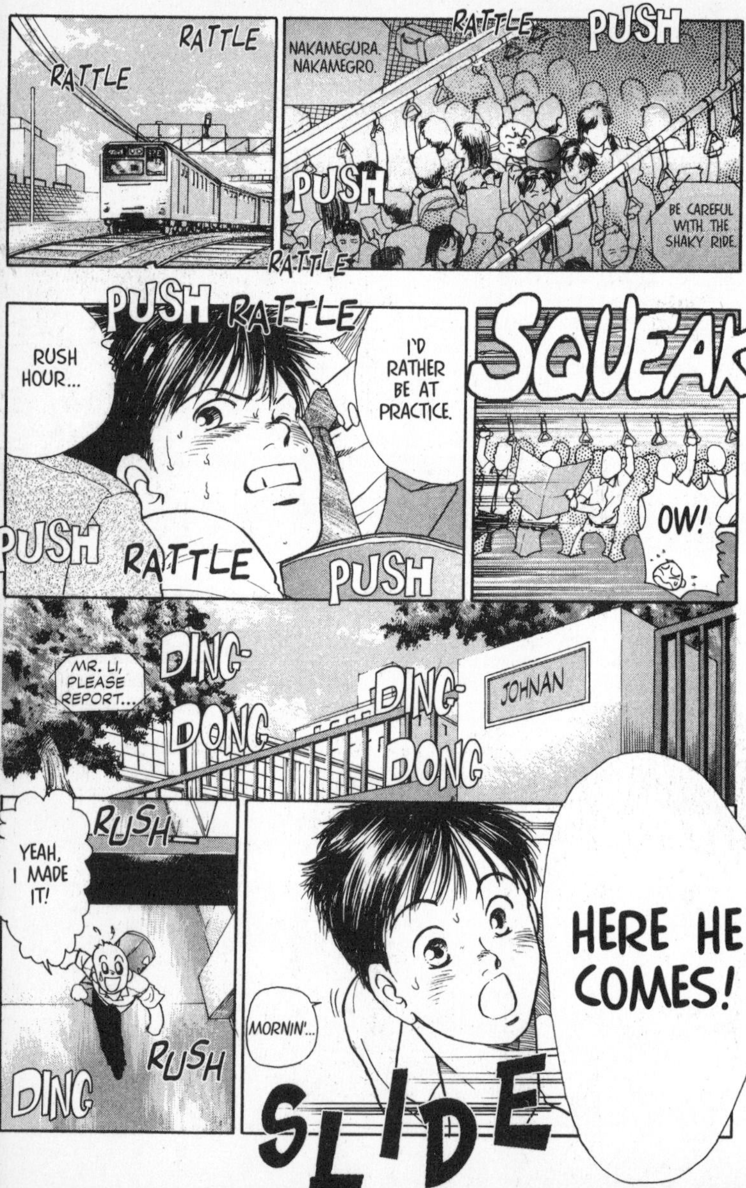
RATTLE
PUSH
NAKAMEGURA. NAKAMEGRO.
PUSH
BE CAREFUL WITH THE SHAKY RIDE
RATTLE
RATTLE
RATTLE
SQUEAK
OW!
PUSH RATTLE
I'D RATHER BE AT PRACTICE.
RUSH HOUR...
PUSH
RATTLE
PUSH
JOHNAN
DING-DONG
DING-DONG
DING-DONG
MR. LI, PLEASE REPORT...
HERE HE COMES!
MORNIN'...
SLIDE
RUSH
YEAH, I MADE IT!
RUSH
DING

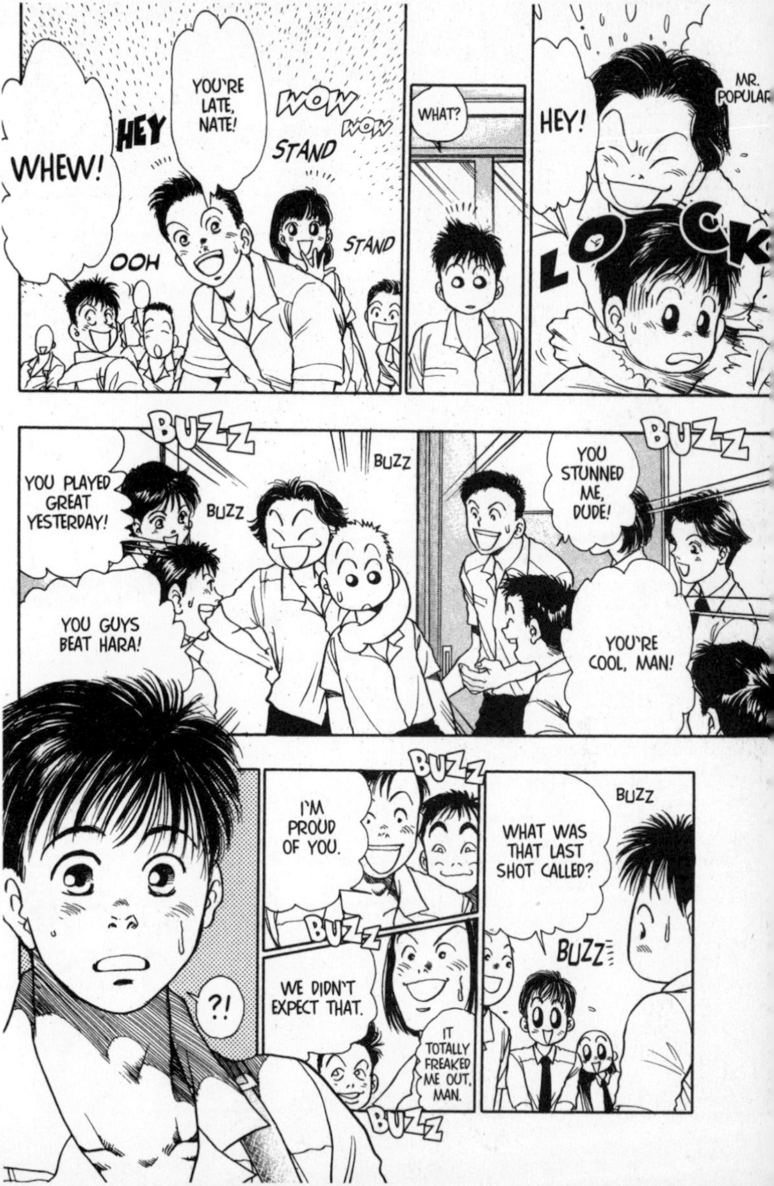
MR. POPULAR
HEY!
LOCK
WHAT?
WOW
WOW
YOU'RE LATE, NATE!
STAND
HEY
WHEW!
STAND
OOH
BUZZ
YOU STUNNED ME, DUDE!
YOU'RE COOL, MAN!
BUZZ
BUZZ
YOU PLAYED GREAT YESTERDAY!
BUZZ
YOU GUYS BEAT HARA!
BUZZ
WHAT WAS THAT LAST SHOT CALLED?
BUZZ
BUZZ
I'M PROUD OF YOU.
BUZZ
WE DIDN'T EXPECT THAT.
IT TOTALLY FREAKED ME OUT, MAN.
BUZZ
?!

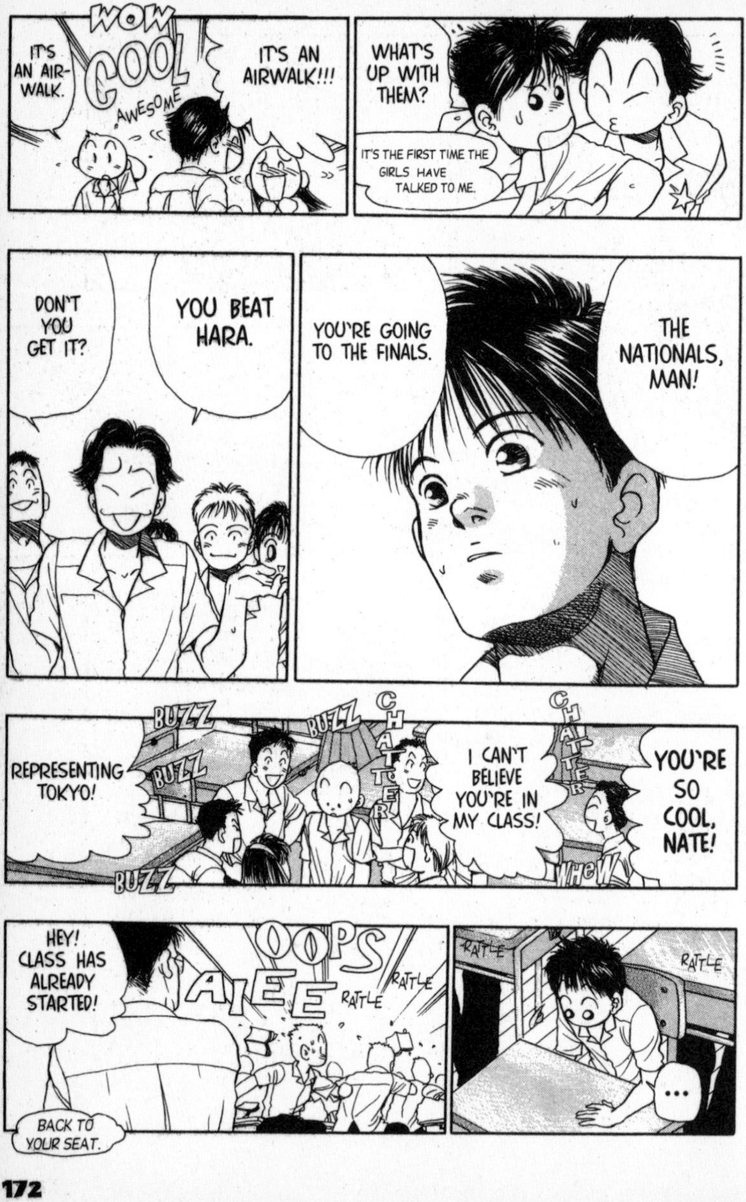
IT'S AN AIR-WALK.
WOW
COOL
AWESOME
IT'S AN AIRWALK!!!
WHAT'S UP WITH THEM?
IT'S THE FIRST TIME THE GIRLS HAVE TALKED TO ME.
DON'T YOU GET IT?
YOU BEAT HARA.
YOU'RE GOING TO THE FINALS.
THE NATIONALS, MAN!
REPRESENTING TOKYO!
BUZZ
BUZZ
BUZZ
BUZZ
CHATTER
I CAN'T BELIEVE YOU'RE IN MY CLASS!
CHATTER
YOU'RE SO COOL, NATE!
WHEW
HEY! CLASS HAS ALREADY STARTED!
BACK TO YOUR SEAT.
OOPS
AIEE
RATTLE
RATTLE
RATTLE
RATTLE
...

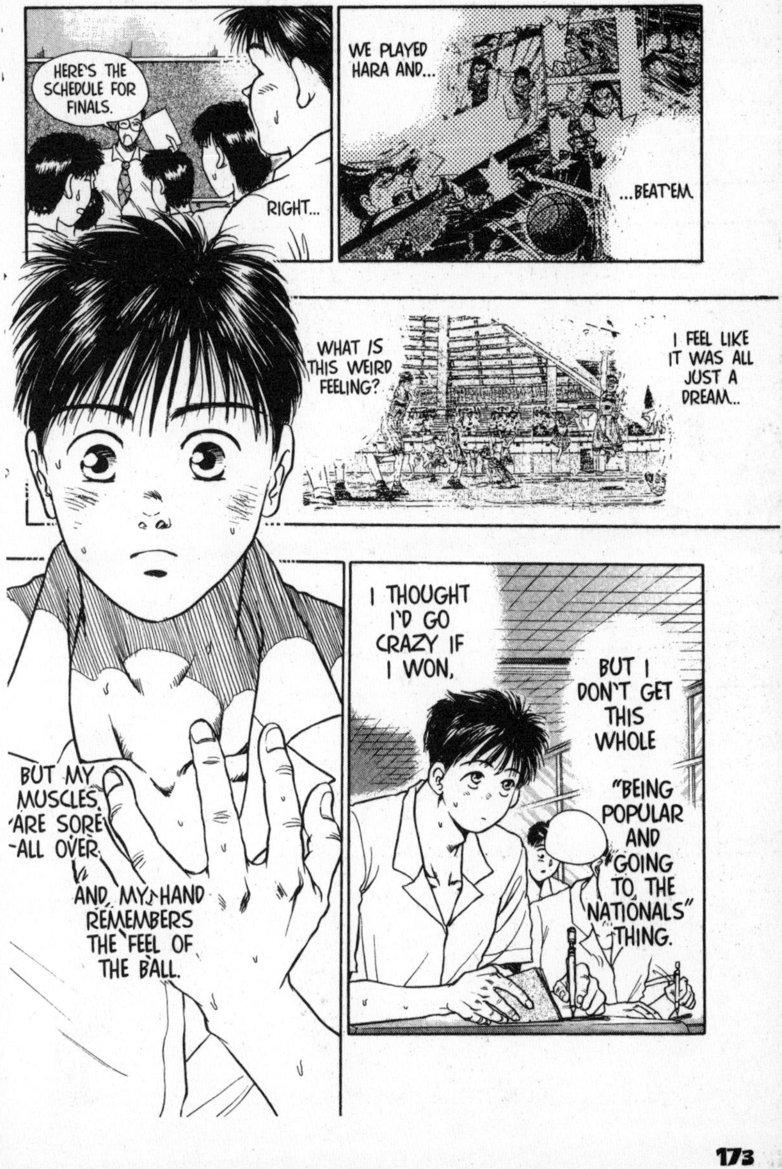
HERE'S THE SCHEDULE FOR FINALS.
RIGHT...
WE PLAYED HARA AND...
...BEAT'EM.
WHAT IS THIS WEIRD FEELING?
I FEEL LIKE IT WAS ALL JUST A DREAM...
BUT MY MUSCLES ARE SORE ALL OVER
AND MY HAND REMEMBERS THE FEEL OF THE BALL.
I THOUGHT I'D GO CRAZY IF I WON,
BUT I DON'T GET THIS WHOLE
"BEING POPULAR AND GOING TO THE NATIONALS" THING.

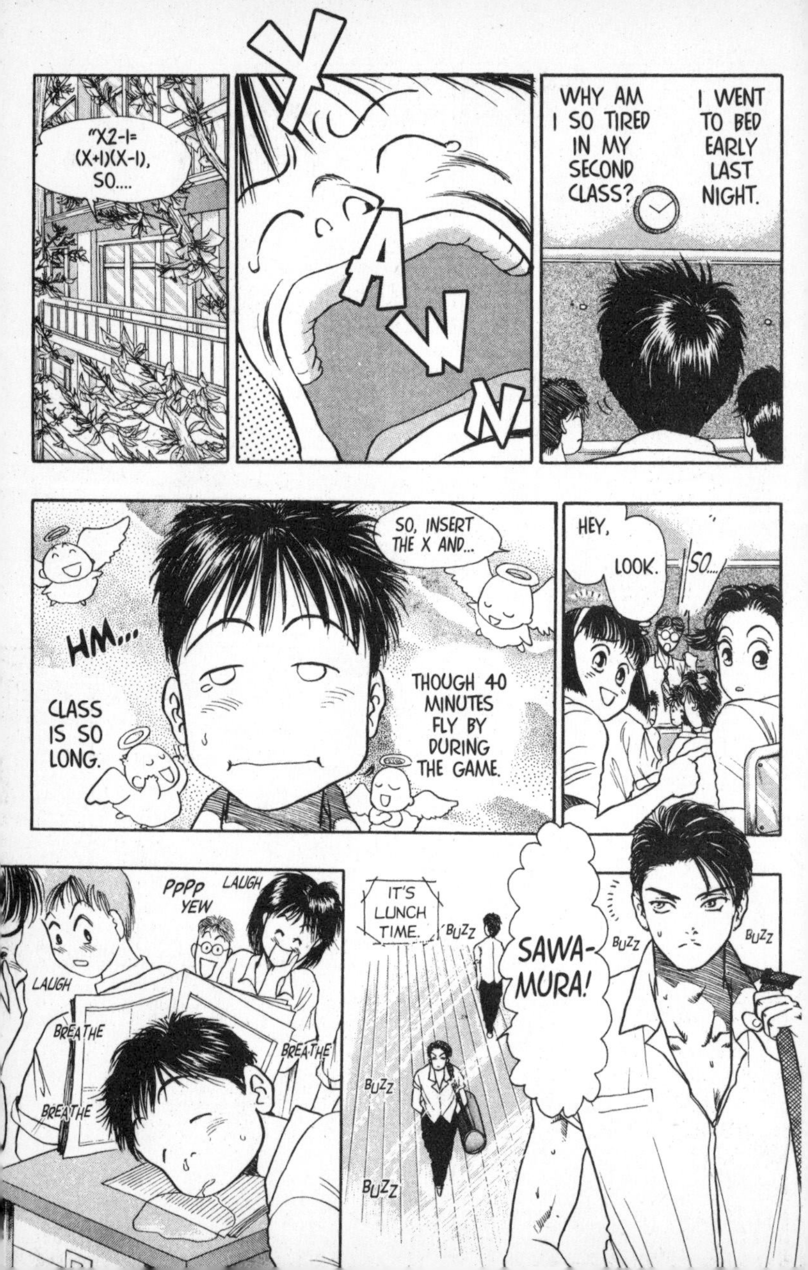
I WENT TO BED EARLY LAST NIGHT.
WHY AM I SO TIRED IN MY SECOND CLASS?
YAWN
"X2-1= (X+1)(X-1), SO....
HEY,
LOOK.
SO....
SO, INSERT THE X AND...
THOUGH 40 MINUTES FLY BY DURING THE GAME.
HM...
CLASS IS SO LONG.
BUZZ
BUZZ
SAWAMURA!
IT'S LUNCH TIME.
BUZZ
BUZZ
BUZZ
LAUGH
PPPP YEW
LAUGH
BREATHE
BREATHE
BREATHE

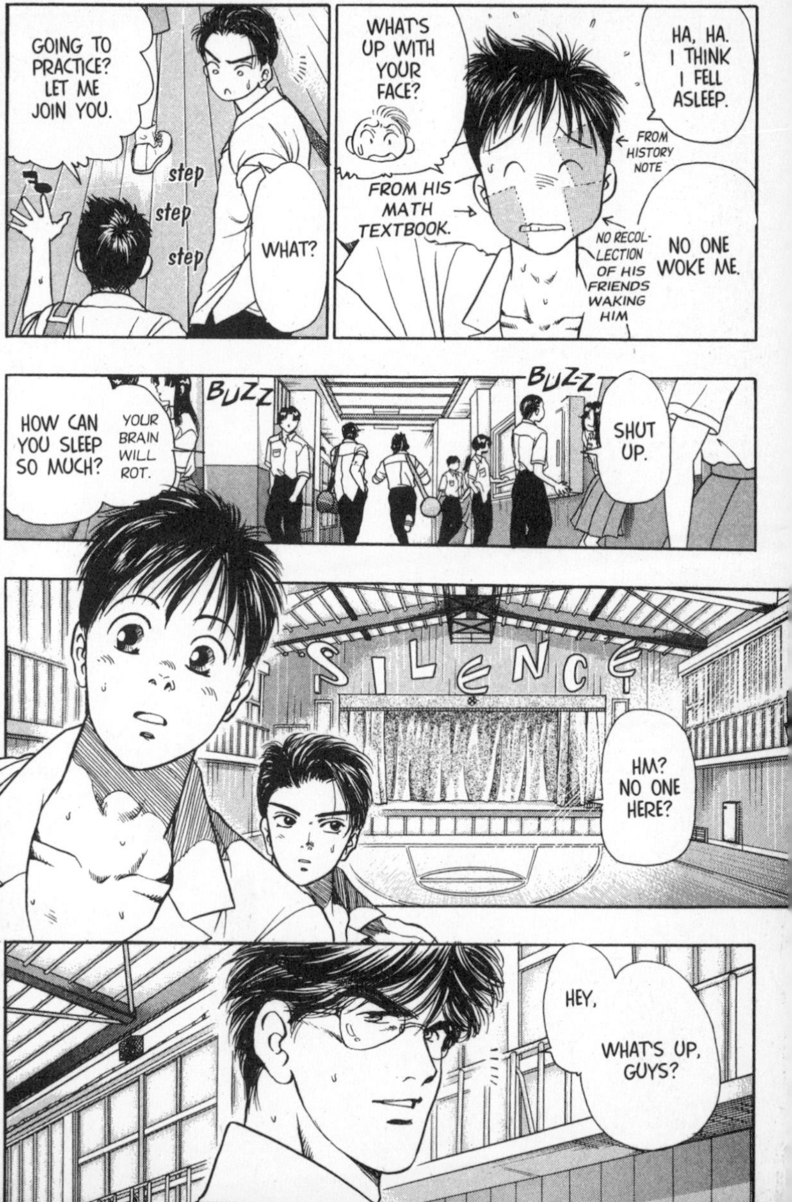
GOING TO PRACTICE? LET ME JOIN YOU.
step
step
step
WHAT?
WHAT'S UP WITH YOUR FACE?
HA, HA. I THINK I FELL ASLEEP.
FROM HISTORY NOTE
FROM HIS MATH TEXTBOOK.
NO RECOL-LECTION OF HIS FRIENDS WAKING HIM
NO ONE WOKE ME.
HOW CAN YOU SLEEP SO MUCH?
YOUR BRAIN WILL ROT.
BUZZ
BUZZ
SHUT UP.
SILENCE
HM? NO ONE HERE?
HEY,
WHAT'S UP, GUYS?

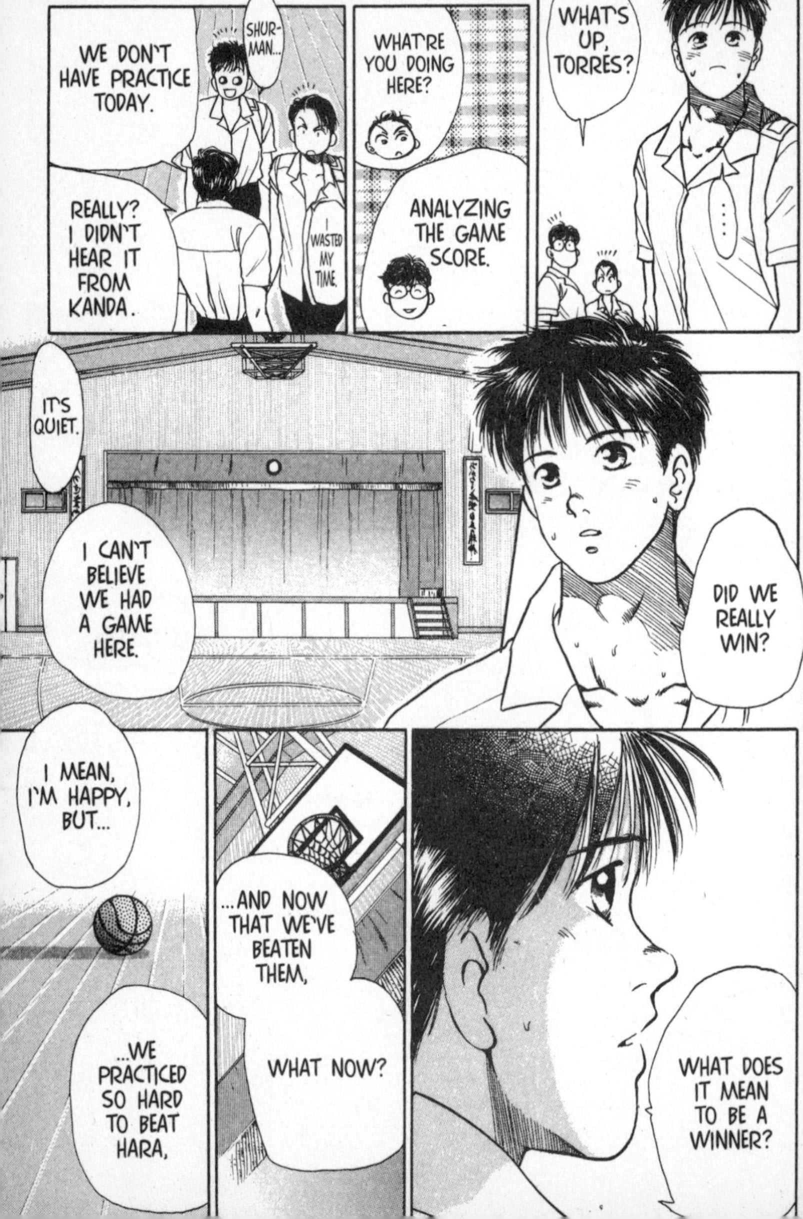
WE DON'T HAVE PRACTICE TODAY.
SHUR-MAN...
REALLY? I DIDN'T HEAR IT FROM KANDA.
I WASTED MY TIME.
WHAT'RE YOU DOING HERE?
ANALYZING THE GAME SCORE.
WHAT'S UP, TORRES?
....
IT'S QUIET.
I CAN'T BELIEVE WE HAD A GAME HERE.
DID WE REALLY WIN?
I MEAN, I'M HAPPY, BUT...
...WE PRACTICED SO HARD TO BEAT HARA,
...AND NOW THAT WE'VE BEATEN THEM,
WHAT NOW?
WHAT DOES IT MEAN TO BE A WINNER?

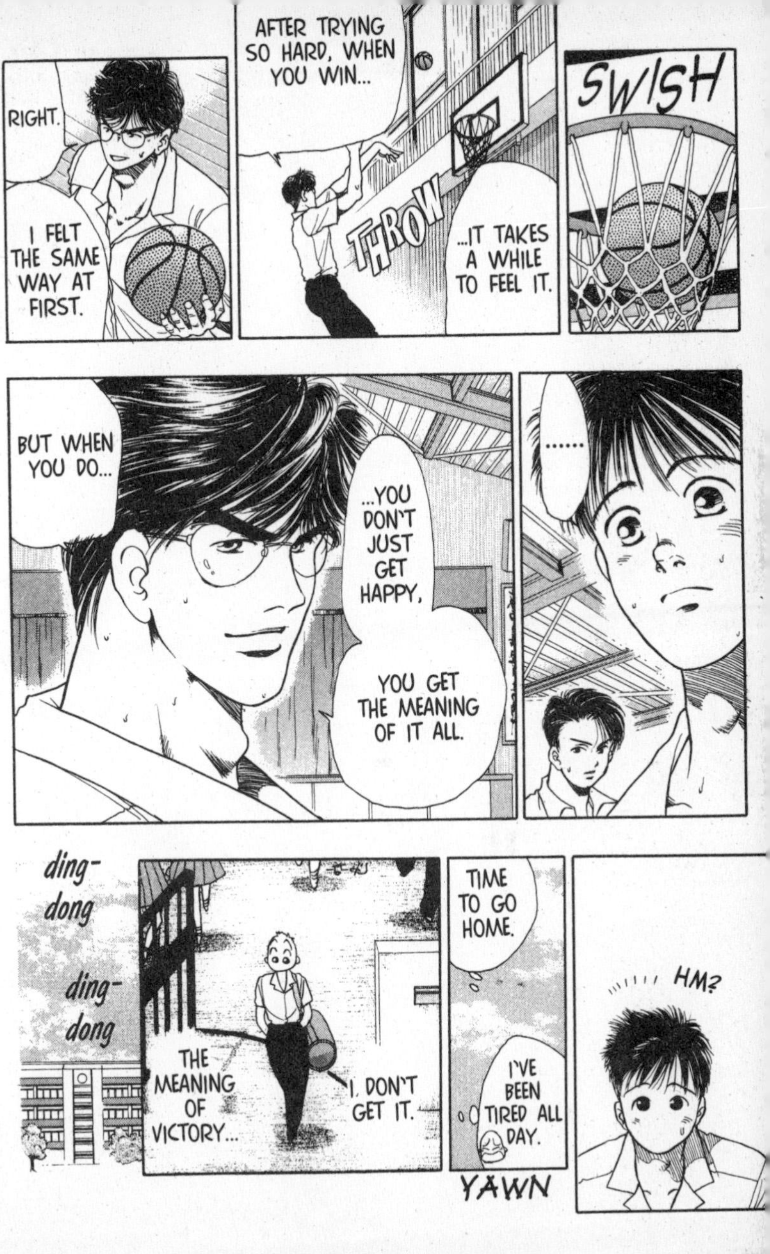
RIGHT.
I FELT THE SAME WAY AT FIRST.
AFTER TRYING SO HARD, WHEN YOU WIN...
THROW
...IT TAKES A WHILE TO FEEL IT.
SWISH
BUT WHEN YOU DO...
...YOU DON'T JUST GET HAPPY,
YOU GET THE MEANING OF IT ALL.
......
ding-dong
ding-dong
THE MEANING OF VICTORY...
I. DON'T GET IT.
TIME TO GO HOME.
I'VE BEEN TIRED ALL DAY.
YAWN
HM?

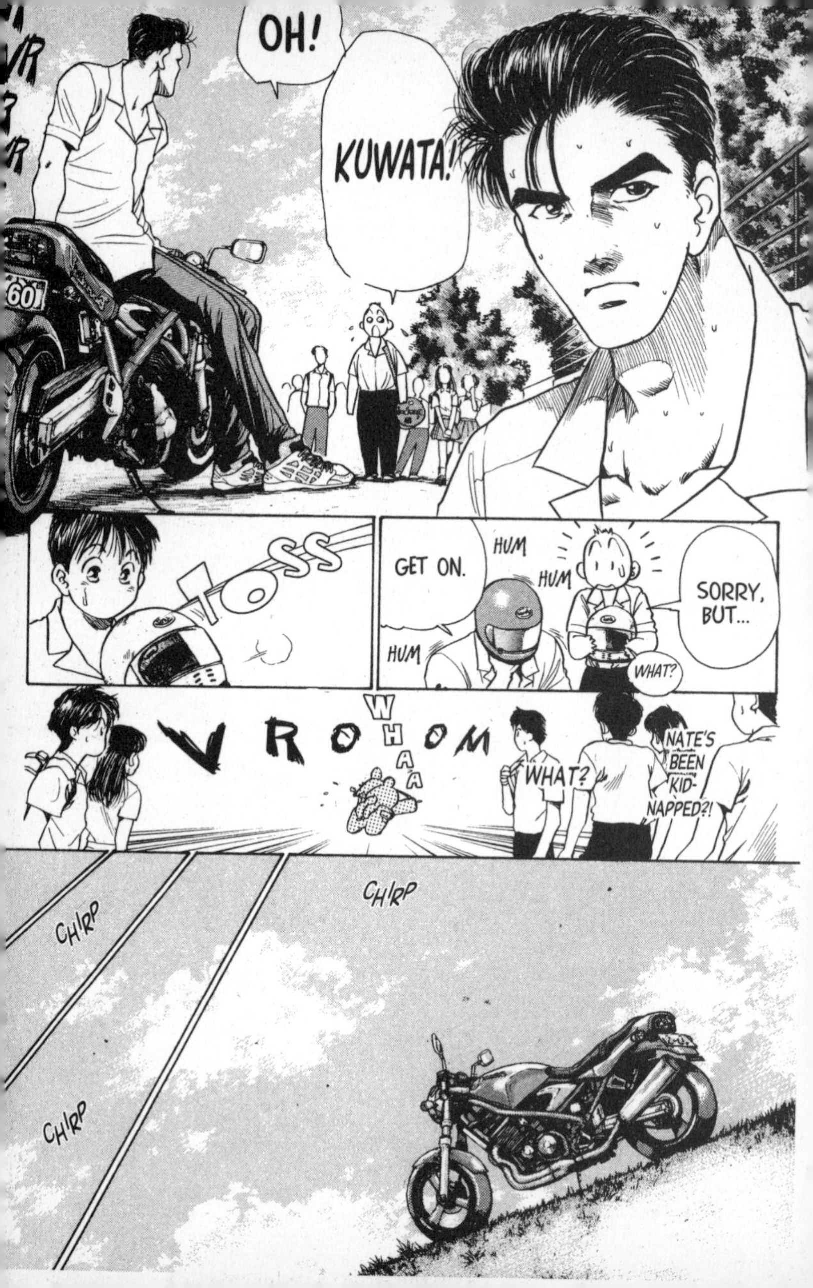
OH!
KUWATA!
SORRY, BUT...
WHAT?
HUM
HUM
GET ON.
HUM
TOSS
NATE'S BEEN KID-NAPPED?!
WHAT?
VROOM
WHAAA
CHIRP
CHIRP
CHIRP

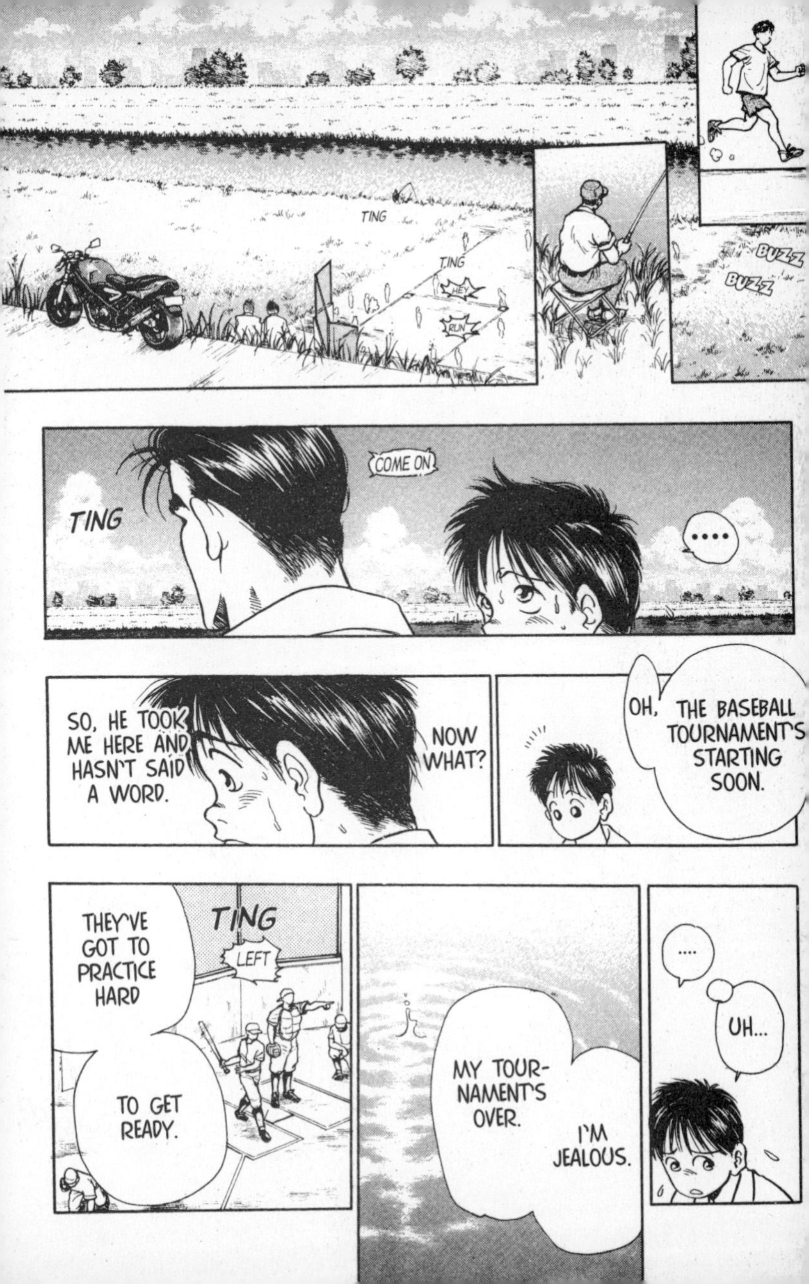
BUZZ
BUZZ
TING
TING
HEY
RUN
COME ON
TING
....
OH, THE BASEBALL TOURNAMENT'S STARTING SOON.
SO, HE TOOK ME HERE AND HASN'T SAID A WORD.
NOW WHAT?
....
UH...
MY TOUR-NAMENT'S OVER.
I'M JEALOUS.
THEY'VE GOT TO PRACTICE HARD
TING
LEFT
TO GET READY.

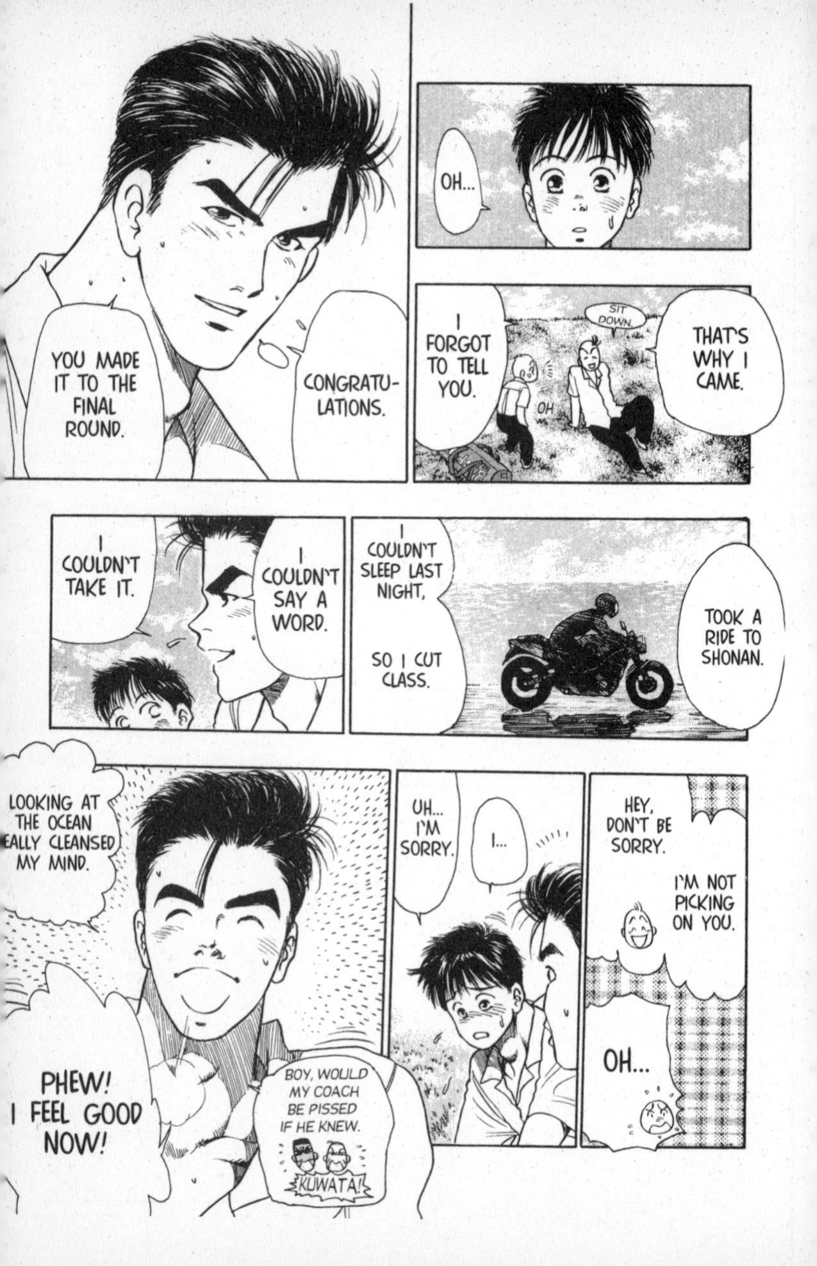
YOU MADE IT TO THE FINAL ROUND.
CONGRATU-LATIONS.
OH...
I FORGOT TO TELL YOU.
SIT DOWN.
OH
THAT'S WHY I CAME.
I COULDN'T TAKE IT.
I COULDN'T SAY A WORD.
I COULDN'T SLEEP LAST NIGHT,
SO I CUT CLASS.
TOOK A RIDE TO SHONAN.
LOOKING AT THE OCEAN EALLY CLEANSED MY MIND.
PHEW! I FEEL GOOD NOW!
BOY, WOULD MY COACH BE PISSED IF HE KNEW.
KUWATA!
UH... I'M SORRY.
I...
HEY, DON'T BE SORRY.
I'M NOT PICKING ON YOU.
OH...

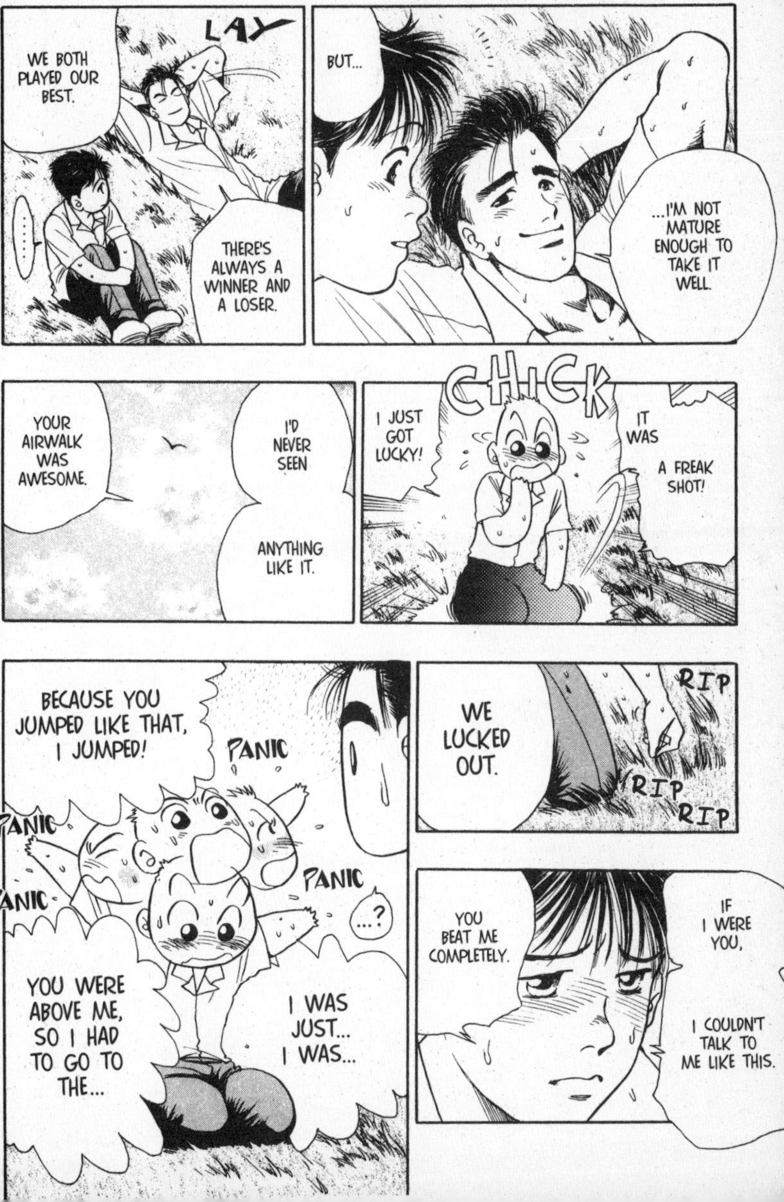
LAY
WE BOTH PLAYED OUR BEST.
...
THERE'S ALWAYS A WINNER AND A LOSER.
BUT...
...I'M NOT MATURE ENOUGH TO TAKE IT WELL.
YOUR AIRWALK WAS AWESOME.
I'D NEVER SEEN
ANYTHING LIKE IT.
CHICK
I JUST GOT LUCKY!
IT WAS
A FREAK SHOT!
BECAUSE YOU JUMPED LIKE THAT, I JUMPED!
PANIC
PANIC
PANIC
PANIC
...?
YOU WERE ABOVE ME, SO I HAD TO GO TO THE...
I WAS JUST... I WAS...
WE LUCKED OUT.
RIP
RIP
RIP
YOU BEAT ME COMPLETELY.
IF I WERE YOU,
I COULDN'T TALK TO ME LIKE THIS.

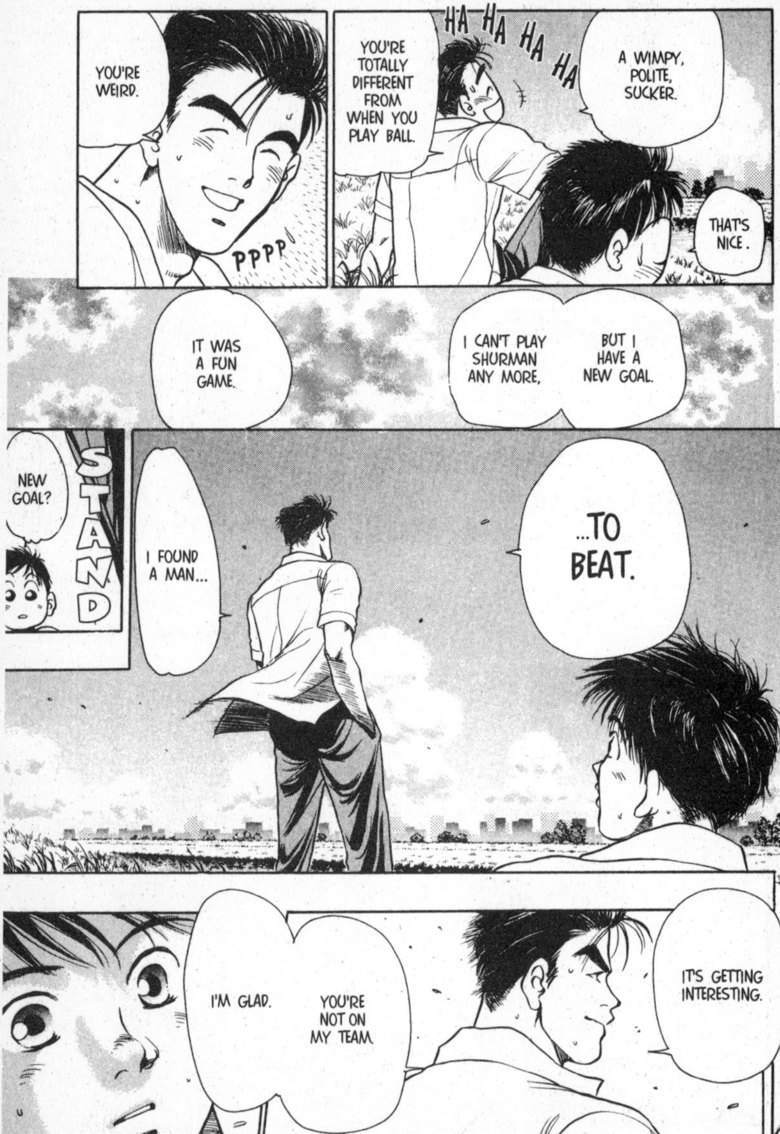
YOU'RE WEIRD.
PPPP
YOU'RE TOTALLY DIFFERENT FROM WHEN YOU PLAY BALL.
HA HA HA HA
A WIMPY, POLITE, SUCKER.
THAT'S NICE.
IT WAS A FUN GAME.
I CAN'T PLAY SHURMAN ANY MORE,
BUT I HAVE A NEW GOAL.
NEW GOAL?
STAND
I FOUND A MAN...
...TO BEAT.
I'M GLAD.
YOU'RE NOT ON MY TEAM.
IT'S GETTING INTERESTING.

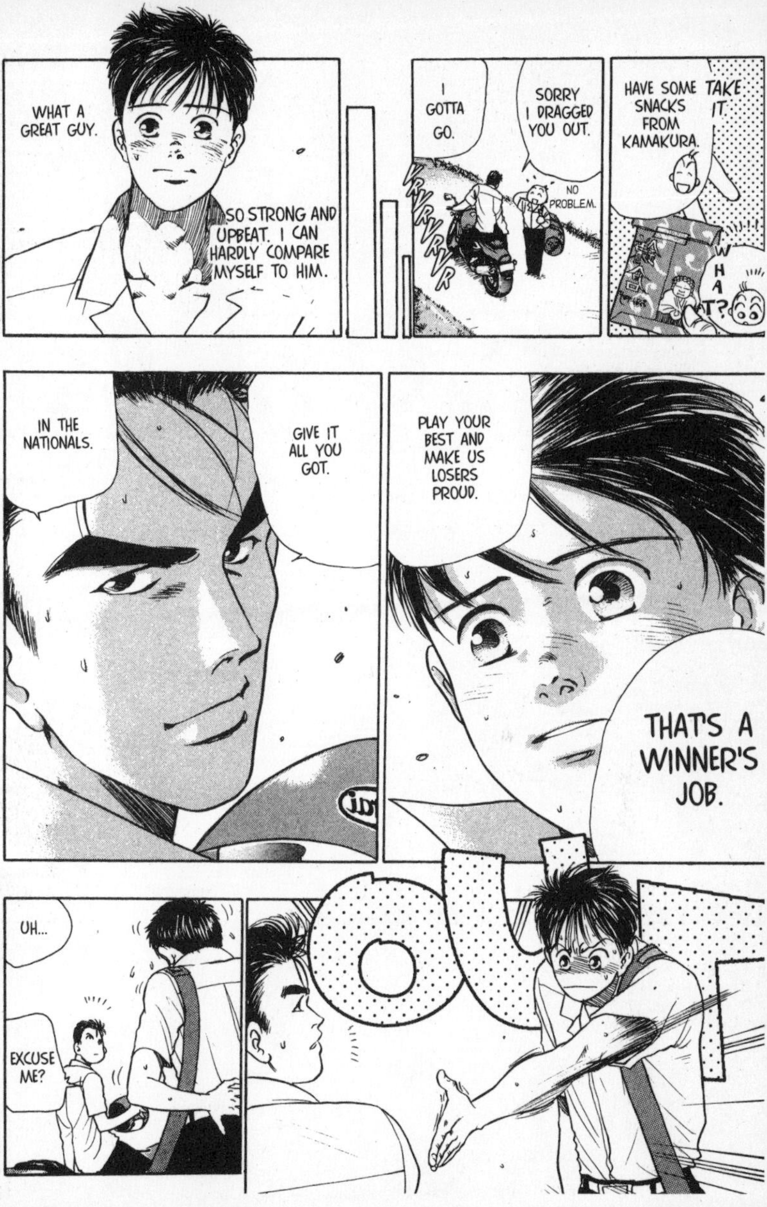
WHAT A GREAT GUY.
SO STRONG AND UPBEAT. I CAN HARDLY COMPARE MYSELF TO HIM.
I GOTTA GO.
SORRY I DRAGGED YOU OUT.
VRVRVRVRVR
NO PROBLEM.
HAVE SOME SNACKS FROM KAMAKURA.
TAKE IT.
WHAT?
IN THE NATIONALS.
GIVE IT ALL YOU GOT.
PLAY YOUR BEST AND MAKE US LOSERS PROUD.
THAT'S A WINNER'S JOB.
UH...
EXCUSE ME?
out

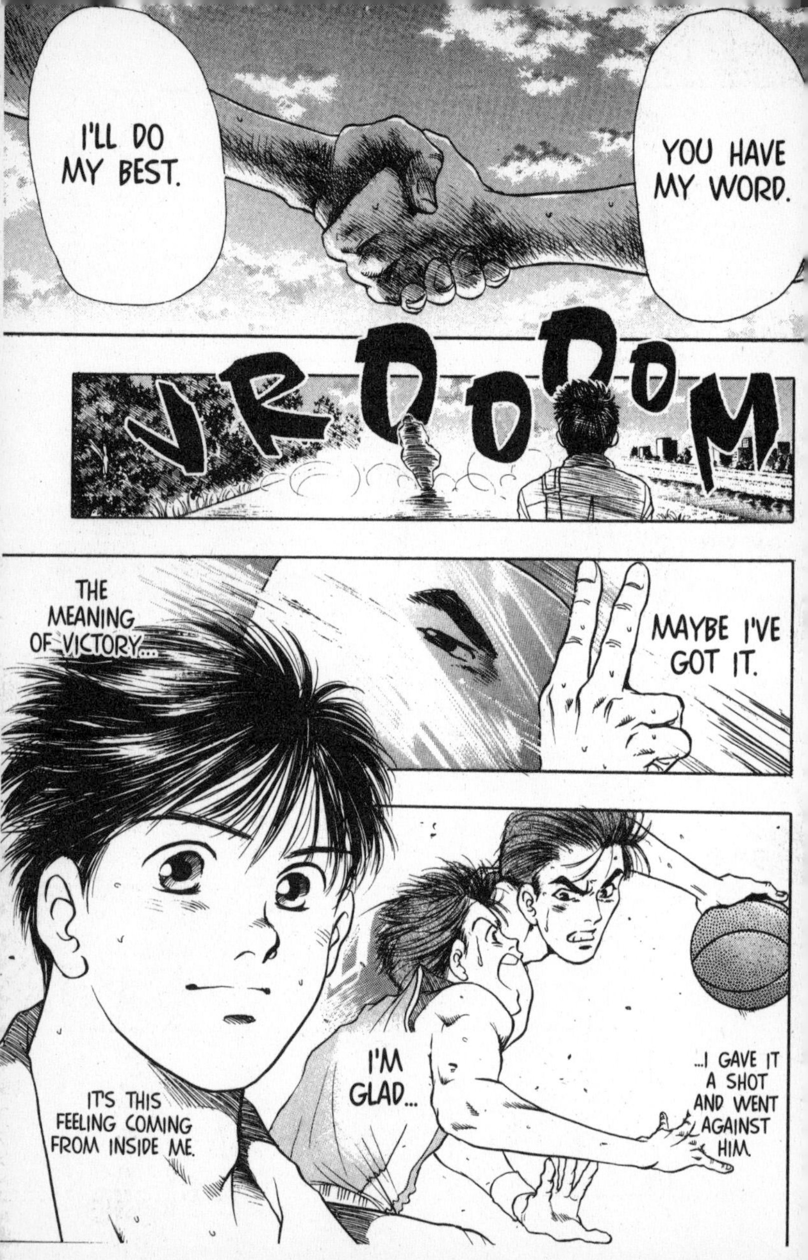
YOU HAVE MY WORD.
I'LL DO MY BEST.
VROOOOM
MAYBE I'VE GOT IT.
I'M GLAD...
...I GAVE IT A SHOT AND WENT AGAINST HIM.
THE MEANING OF VICTORY...
IT'S THIS FEELING COMING FROM INSIDE ME.

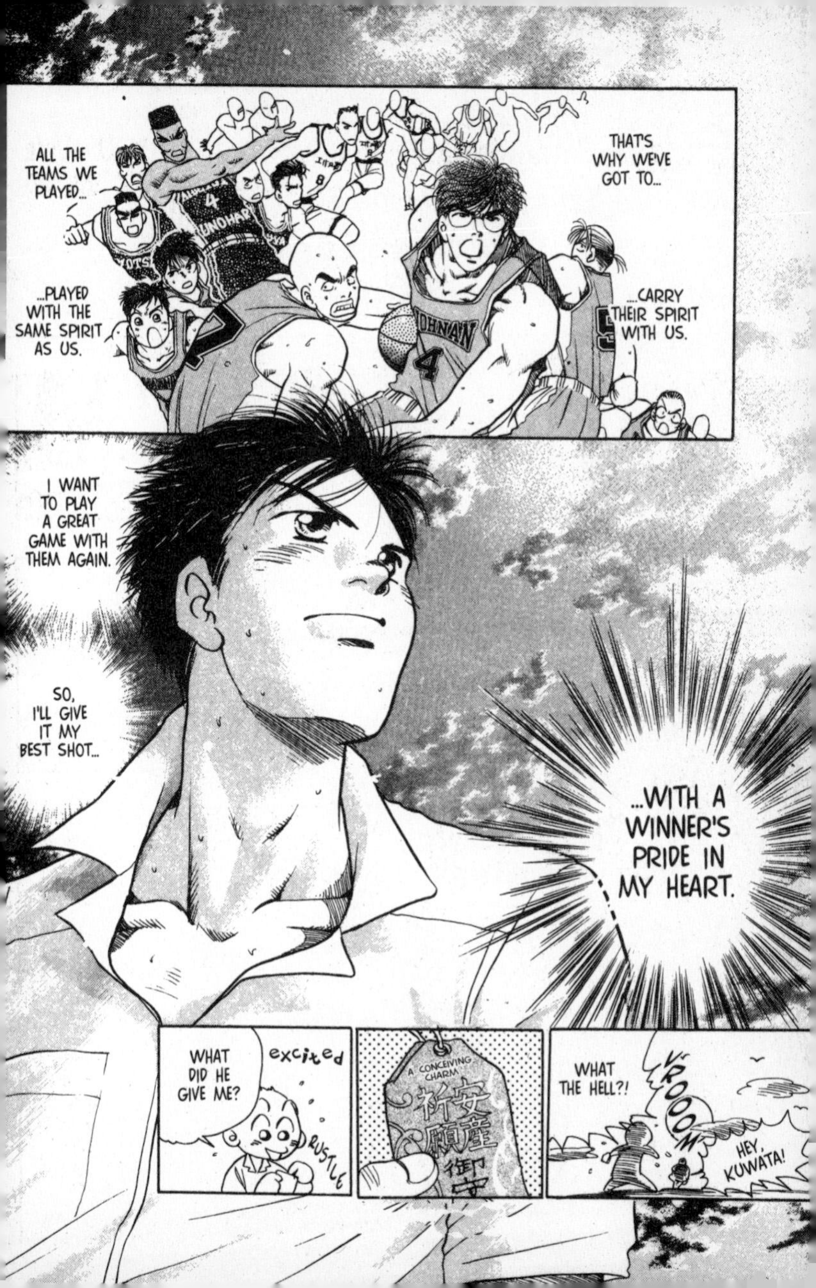
ALL THE TEAMS WE PLAYED...
...PLAYED WITH THE SAME SPIRIT AS US.
THAT'S WHY WE'VE GOT TO...
...CARRY THEIR SPIRIT WITH US.
SHOHNAN
4
I WANT TO PLAY A GREAT GAME WITH THEM AGAIN.
SO, I'LL GIVE IT MY BEST SHOT...
...WITH A WINNER'S PRIDE IN MY HEART.
WHAT DID HE GIVE ME?
excited
RUSTLE
A CONCEIVING CHARM
安産祈願
御守
WHAT THE HELL?!
VROOOOOM
HEY, KUWATA!

Epilogue:

With the end of the tournament looming, Nate, Sawamura, Shurman and the rest of Johnan High began gearing up for the big game, making frequent trips to the half-courts and back-alleys that had helped them build their skills.

When the big day arrived for the National Championship game, Johnan played their hearts out, once again facing insurmountable odds against Kyan High. Hiding Nate's new secret weapon, the Air Walk, Johnan scratched their way to a last-minute victory. When his shot was blocked, though, it seemed all was lost. But in a flash, with less than five seconds on the board, Shurman gave them their chance with a blind pass to Sawamura, who was sitting right in the middle of Kyan territory. And as the whole defense came down on him, Sawamura put up one of his notorious 3-pointers, miraculously nailing both the shot and the win for Johnan High.

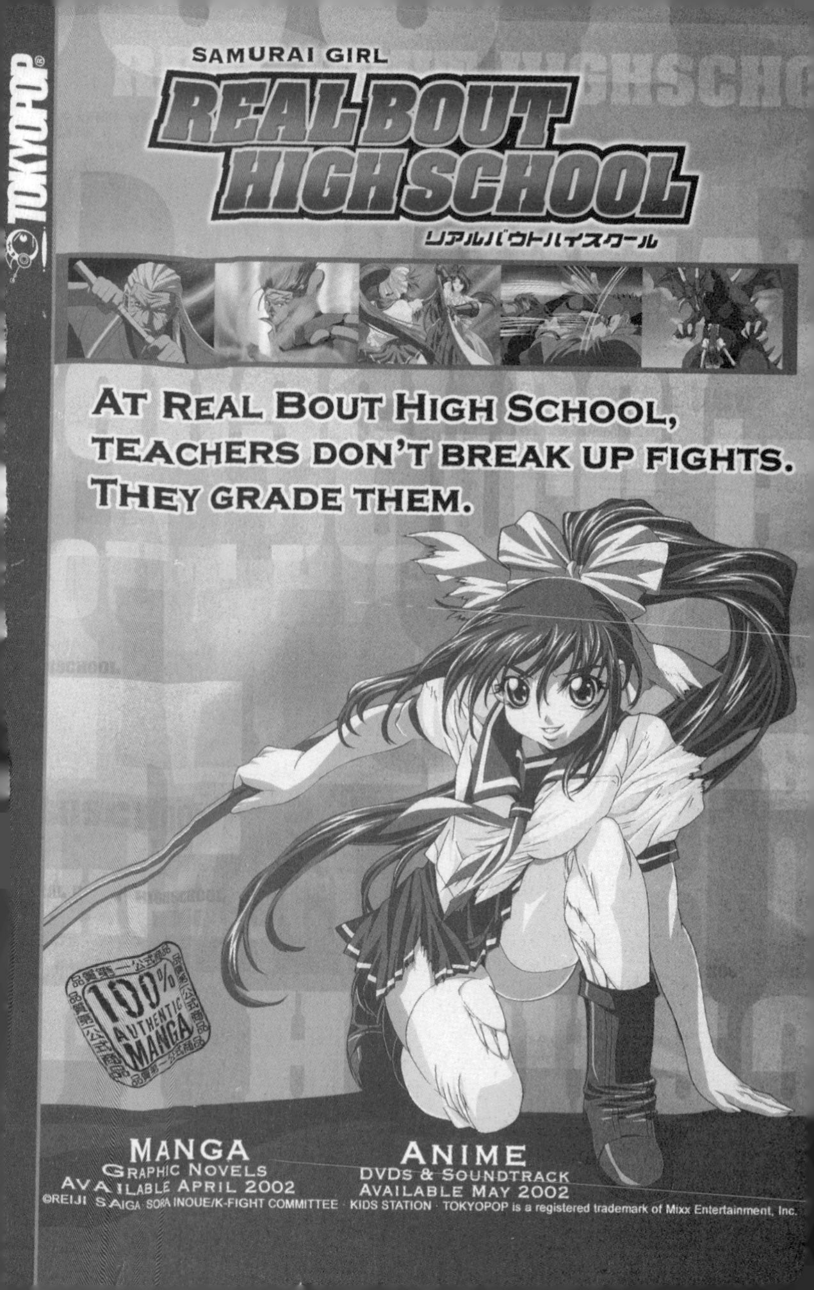
TOKYOPOP
SAMURAI GIRL
REAL BOUT HIGH SCHOOL
リアルバウトハイスクール
AT REAL BOUT HIGH SCHOOL, TEACHERS DON'T BREAK UP FIGHTS. THEY GRADE THEM.
100% AUTHENTIC MANGA
MANGA
GRAPHIC NOVELS
AVAILABLE APRIL 2002
ANIME
DVDS & SOUNDTRACK
AVAILABLE MAY 2002
©REIJI SAIGA · SORA INOUE/K-FIGHT COMMITTEE · KIDS STATION · TOKYOPOP is a registered trademark of Mixx Entertainment, Inc.

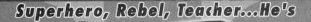

Unlike Any Videogame Soundtrack Ever Produced.

SOUNDS OF
ONIMUSHA
SAMURAGOCH'S BEST SELECTIONS

Time Magazine Says...

*"Just listen to the score for Capcom's Onimusha.....
the result is both haunting and inspirational,
reminiscent of majestic scores for films like Lawrence of Arabia."*

Time Magazine - Fall 2001 "Music Goes Global" edition

❖

SOUNDS OF ONIMUSHA
ORIGINAL SCORE BY MAMORU SAMURAGOCH
AVAILABLE IN STORES NOW

COWBOY BEBOP

WHAT'S MONEY BETWEEN FRIENDS... NOT A HECK OF A LOT!

Based on the smash hit anime series seen on CARTOON NETWORK

Spike, Jet, Faye, Ed and Ein are back and better than ever in the new tales of the bounty huntin'
Bebop crew. Graphic Novels in stores now. Also avalable from TOKYOPOP®, the *Cowboy
Bebop Anime Guides* give the low-down on the hit animated series - episode summaries,
character profiles, music lists...these six volumes have it all.

TOKYOPOP

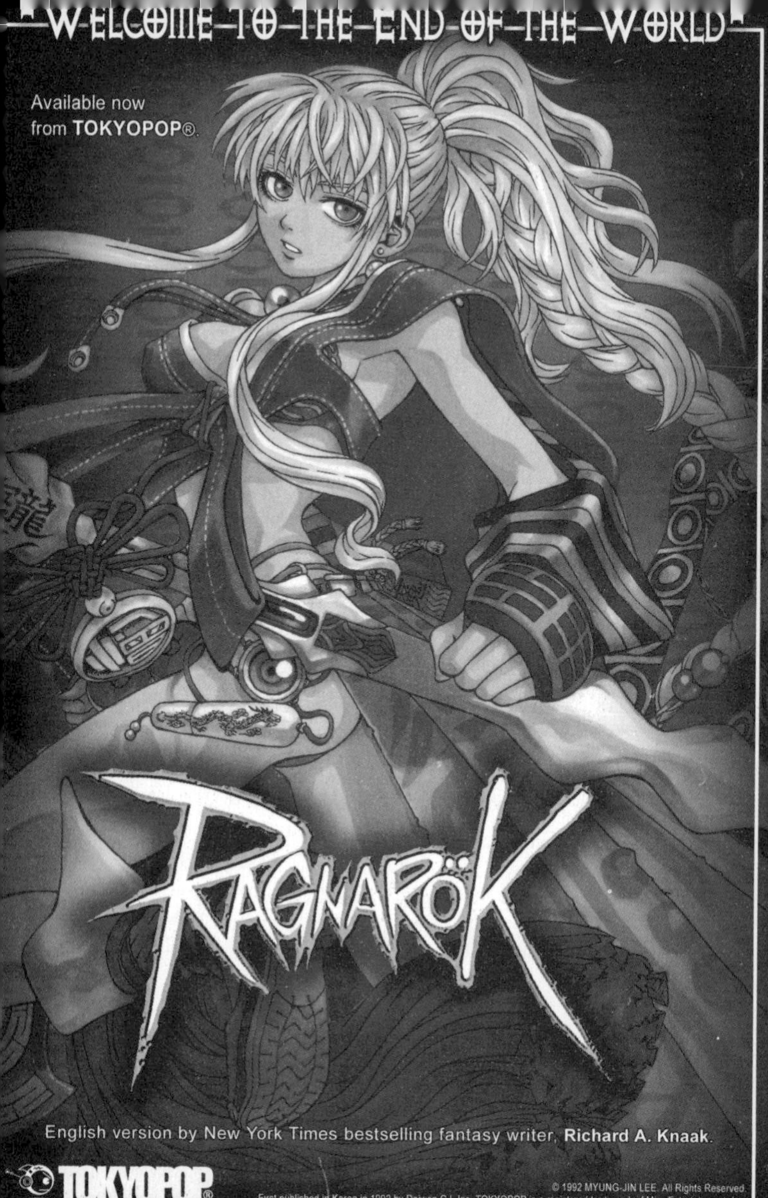
WELCOME TO THE END OF THE WORLD
Available now
from TOKYOPOP®.
RAGNARÖK
English version by New York Times bestselling fantasy writer, Richard A. Knaak.
TOKYOPOP®
© 1992 MYUNG-JIN LEE. All Rights Reserved.
First published in Korea in 1992 by Daiwon C.I. Inc. TOKYOPOP is a registered trademark of Mixx Entertainment, Inc.